Sustainable Tourism in the English Lake District

Edited by

D W G Hind
J P Mitchell

© D W G Hind and J P Mitchell

ISBN 1901888 29 0

First published 2004

Cover Design Tim Murphy Creative Solutions

Published in Great Britain by
Business Education Publishers Limited
The Teleport
Doxford International
Sunderland
SR3 3XD

Tel: 0191 5252410
Fax: 0191 5201815

British Cataloguing-in-Publications Data
A catalogue record for this book is available from the British Library

Printed in Great Britain by The Alden Group Oxford.

Contents

Chapter Four
The Lake District as a Tourist Destination in the 21st Century

Chapter Five
The Planning and Management of Tourism in the Lake District

Chapter Six
Accommodation Providers: Towards Sustainability

Chapter Seven
Sustainable Transport Management and Cycle Tourism

Chapter Eight
The Impacts of Tourism in the Lake District

Chapter Nine
The Future of Tourism in the Lake District

Index

Contributors

The Editors

David Hind

David Hind has worked in the tourism industry for over 20 years. He started his career as the Commercial Manager of Venture East, a specialist tour operator to South East Asia. He was appointed to Newcastle-upon-Tyne Polytechnic in 1985 (Northumbria Univeristy) as a founder member of the team responsible for developing the UK's first degree in Travel & Tourism. In the 1990s he transferred to the University's Carlisle Campus, from where his interest in tourism in Cumbria and the Lake District developed. He was appointed Head of the Centre for Tourism Management at Leeds Metropolitan University in 2001. Leeds Metropolitan University is one of the most successful providers of tourism education in Europe.

John Mitchell

John Mitchell is a Senior Lecturer in Leisure Management at University College Chester. A native of the 'auld grey town' of Kendal, and educated at Kendal Grammar School, he completed teacher training at St. Peter's College, Birmingham and the University of Birmingham. He taught Physical Education at Woodlands School, Coventry and gained the Master of Education degree at the University of Liverpool.

Members of his extended family are accommodation providers in Cumbria and he is a committed environmentalist. Other interests include cycling, skiing and wildlife. He has spent many days walking the fells of the Lake District, which he knows intimately. He particularly enjoys ending a hike in a local hostelry with a pint of hand-pulled beer.

The Contributors

Chapter One
Sustainable Tourism: An Introduction

D W G Hind BA (Hons), MBA, Cert Ed, FTS, FITT, Head, Centre for Tourism Management, Leeds Metropolitan University.

Chapter Two
Tourism and the Lake District: Social and Cultural Histories

C O'Neill BA, MA, PhD, Senior Lecturer in History, St Martin's College of Higher Education, Lancaster.

J K Walton BA, PhD, Professor of Social History, University of Central Lancashire.

Chapter Three
The Context of Tourism in the Lake District

D W G Hind BA (Hons), MBA, Cert Ed, FTS, FITT, Head, Centre for Tourism Management, Leeds Metropolitan University.

Chapter 4
The Lake District as a Tourist Destination in the 21st Century

P A Blakey BA (Hons), MA, Cert Ed Lecturer in Leisure Management, University College, Chester.

D W G Hind BA (Hons), MBA, Cert Ed, FTS, FITT, Head, Centre for Tourism Management, Leeds Metropolitan University.

C K Rawding BA, MA, DPhil, PGCE, Senior Lecturer in Geographical Education, Edge Hill College of Higher Education.

Chapter Five
The Planning and Management of Tourism in the Lake District

J Darrall BSc (Hons), PhD, Policy Officer, Friends of the Lake District.

D W G Hind BA (Hons), MBA, Cert Ed, FTS, FITT, Head, Centre for Tourism Management, Leeds Metropolitan University.

O C Maurice MRICS, Director of the National Trust North West Region (retired), The National Trust.

K E Royce Partnership Manager, The Lake District Tourism and Conservation Partnership.

P H Tiplady BA (Hons), MA, MSc, MRTPI, MLI, National Park Officer, Lake District National Park Authority.

Chapter Six
Accommodation Providers: Towards Sustainability

J P Mitchell Cert Ed, BEd, MEd, University College Chester.

Chapter Seven
Sustainable Transport Management and Cycle Tourism

D Holding BA (Hons), MSc, MCIT, MILT, Chair of Traffic and Transport Working Group, Lake District National Park Authority.

N D Morpeth BA (Hons), MSc, PhD, Senior Lecturer in Tourism, Leeds Metropolitan University.

D H Robinson BA (Hons), PhD, Trails Adviser, Lake District National Park Authority.

Chapter Eight
The Impacts of Tourism in the Lake District

R Sharpley BA (Hons), MSc, PhD, Reader, Travel & Tourism Management, Northumbria University.

Chapter Nine
The Future of Tourism in the Lake District

D W G Hind BA (Hons), MBA, Cert Ed, FTS, FITT, Head, Centre for Tourism Management, Leeds Metropolitan University.

Preface

The English Lake District can be considered an international shrine of tourism. For over 200 years tourists have been visiting this region in the north west of England to enjoy the natural beauty of the lakes, fells, and mountains. Writers and artists first promoted tourism to the region in the 19th century through their work, attracting scholars, fellow writers and artists to wonder at the special characteristics of the Lake District's relatively inhospitable landscape. In the 20th century the Lake District emerged as a mass market tourist destination attracting tourists in their millions. In the 21st century, it is still the natural beauty of the landscape and the opportunities provided for leisure and recreation that are the key factors motivating tourist visits to the Lake District. Indeed, the Lake District landscape and its rural communities have changed very little over the last 200 years, despite the region being a significant tourist destination.

In the 19th century sustainable tourism management was not part of the vocabulary of William Wordsworth and his peers. However, the concept of safeguarding the natural environment from the ravages of hordes of tourists became a very important element in the activities and work of Wordsworth and his contemporaries such as John Ruskin, and towards the end of the 19th century the work of Beatrix Potter and Canon Rawnsley. One hundred years ago there was a very clear understanding that increasing numbers of visitors would have a detrimental impact on the natural beauty of the Lakeland landscape. Wordsworth, Ruskin, Potter, Rawnsley and others were strong advocates for controls to be put in place to restrict the development of the tourism superstructure and infrastructure. Major successes were achieved through their lobbying. At a time of railway expansion, objections to the extension of the railway into the heart of the Lake District proved successful.

National institutions that are now taken for granted as key players in sustainable tourism management had their roots in the Lake District. Founding members of the National Trust were Beatrix Potter and Canon Rawnsley. The Friends of the Lake District advocated strongly for National Parks to be created and designated by central government. The Lake District Tourism Conservation Partnership is a current example of best practice in the establishment of a framework for public, private, not-for-profit organisations to work together with tourists to conserve and preserve the essential ingredients of the Lake District landscape.

But over the last 200 years, the Lake District has experienced many of the adverse impacts of mass tourism. At certain times of the year the narrow country roads are congested. Townscapes have changed to reflect the needs of modern tourism – car parks have been created, souvenir shops have replaced more general retailers, neon signs adorn shop fronts, and litter and pollution have increased. Footpaths on the fells have been eroded, and lakes have become congested with water borne tourists. However, the multitude of agencies responsible for the management and development of tourism in the region have worked to counter these negative impacts of mass tourism, to ensure that the special characteristics of the Lake District that attracted tourists 200 years ago, are still the key attractants today.

The work of the Lake District National Park Authority, the National Trust, Friends of the Lake District, Cumbria Tourist Board, Cumbria County Council, and the local district councils of Cumbria has resulted in the principles of sustainable tourism being implemented within the Lake District. These organisations work in partnership to ensure that the very special features of the lakes, mountains, fells, valleys and communities of the region are preserved for the benefit of future generations.

It is for the above reasons that the idea for this book emerged. The Lake District is an internationally known tourist destination, and one that is recognised as being managed on the principles of sustainable tourism – indeed it is the first region in the world to be accredited as a sustainable tourist destination by Green Globe 21. As the literature on sustainable tourism has burgeoned and as the challenges and practicalities of implementing sustainable tourism strategies have been widely debated it was felt that the time was right to produce a detailed case study of one tourist destination. The purpose being to highlight some of the issues arising from mass tourism, and how these issues are managed in a practical way. It is hoped that through reading this book, the reader understands more thoroughly how tourism has evolved and is managed sustainably in the English Lake District.

The chapters of this book have been written by tourism experts. The authors are drawn from either the academic world, or from public or not-for-profit organisations that are heavily engaged in planning, managing and developing tourism in the Lake District. Without their studious and invaluable contributions this book would not exist and the Editors express their thanks to all contributors. Thanks are also offered to the Department of Leisure and Sport, and library staff, both of University College Chester, and Helen Tate of the Cumbria Tourist Board, for their cooperation and assistance, and to Moira Page and Andrea Murphy at Business Education Publishers for their support and help in taking the raw manuscript into the final published form.

Sustainable Tourism in the English Lake District

Chapter One

Sustainable Tourism: An Introduction

"As tourism has burgeoned in the latter half of the twentieth century it has been accused of many things: a despoiler of pristine natural environments, a destroyer of valued lifestyles and age-old cultures, and an exploiter of poor nations. Tourism, it is claimed, ultimately degrades the attractive natural and cultural features of a place and thus can neither sustain the basic resources on which it relies, nor rely on itself as an industry in the long term."

Griffin (2002:24)

One of the implications of the above quotation is that if tourism is not restrained it will ultimately destroy the very features that attract tourists to the destination in the first place. This is one perspective on the development and growth of tourism. An alternative perspective is that if tourism is managed and developed in a responsible way, then it should be possible to safeguard the features of the destination that are so important for attracting tourists. This should ensure the long term future of tourism and the environments and communities to which tourists are attracted.

This book uses a case study of the English Lake District to contribute to the discussion of sustainable tourism management. For over 200 years tourists have been visiting the Lake District in north west England to enjoy the beauty and splendour of the mountains, lakes, and valleys. The Lake District was designated as a National Park on the 9th May 1951 under the National Parks and Access to the Countryside Act 1949. It was home then to some 42,000 people and still is. These residents normally welcome around 15 million visitors each year (Locum Destination Consulting, 2003). Around a third of the resident population derives a direct income from tourism, which rises to a half in the Windermere area (LDNPA, 1998). The Lake District National Park is the largest of England's National Parks, covering some 2292 square kilometres. The area includes England's highest mountain (Scafell Pike 977m), her deepest body of water (Wastwater 70m) and her longest body of water (Windermere 20 kilometres). Geological activity has shaped these features but the Lakeland landscape has many special characteristics that have been nurtured more recently by the actions of man, in particular farmers and foresters. The settlement patterns, the built features and the local traditions all grow from the relationship between man and the environment. The National Park is very important to north west England, and indeed the United Kingdom. The Lake District has earned an international reputation as a tourist destination and as a result, tourism is a key contributor to the local economy. Thus, as a tourist destination, much of the Lake District's success is based on the beauty of the landscape and natural environment, and the opportunities these provide for leisure and recreation. A survey undertaken in 2002 indicated that the most popular tourist experience was "admiring" what the National Park has to offer, whether by car or on foot (Creative Research, 2002). The most important of the National Park's special qualities, as perceived by residents and visitors alike, was the quiet enjoyment of the area and the second was the freedom to use the fells for recreation (Countryside Commission, 1995). The Lake District needs the planning and management of tourism if it is to prosper. Checks and balances have to be put in place to ensure that tourism, and the development of the necessary superstructure and infrastructure to support a vibrant tourism industry, does not result in adverse impacts on the local communities, economy, and landscapes. The Lake District National Park Authority is charged with being the lead body in this respect. To achieve this goal, the Authority has to seek or establish effective partnerships and relations with a number of bodies and agencies that also have an interest in the good management of this special area.

Since the 1950s a variety of different tourism management and development strategies have been implemented to conserve and preserve the landscape, local communities and the built environment for the benefit of future generations. As a result, the Lake District is not just one of England's iconic tourist destinations, but it is also a region that is home to a distinct local culture, with tourism being the dominant sector of the local economy. For the future, policies and strategies are in place to ensure that the natural and cultural features of the Lake District will not be degraded, but will in fact be conserved and preserved so that these essential resources for tourism can be sustained. Thus, the evolution and development of tourism in the Lake District warrants studying, to identify some of the reasons why this region appears to be relatively free from the ravages of mass tourism as suggested by Griffin (2002).

The purpose of this book is to provide a case study that demonstrates how the English Lake District, an internationally significant tourist destination, is managed on the principles of sustainable tourism. Much has been written about the theoretical and conceptual aspects of sustainable tourism, see Butler (1991), Clarke (1997), Hunter (1997), Stabler (1997), and Wahab (1997). This book, whilst utilising academic concepts to provide frameworks for understanding the complex aspects of sustainable tourism management, is primarily an opportunity to demonstrate the realities of trying to achieve sustainable tourism management principles in a diverse and complex geographic region. The aim is not to use the Lake District as an example of 'best practice' in sustainable tourism management, but to use it as a case study to draw out lessons that might be of relevance to tourist destination managers in other regions. Students of tourism will find the content of the following chapters a valuable contribution to the body of knowledge on sustainable tourism management in a mass market tourist destination.

Conceptualising Sustainable Tourism

This book will not enter into, or contribute to, the theoretical debate on what sustainable tourism is, and the different means by which it can be achieved. This will be left to other writers, for example Hunter (1997, 2002), Collins (1999), Holden (1999), Bramwell and Lane (2000). As stated above, the purpose of this book is to provide a detailed case study of how one tourist destination has remained relatively unchanged for over 200 years, as a result of the implementation of sustainable tourism management policies and practices. However, there is a need to provide an introduction to the concept of sustainable tourism, and to briefly consider the key stages in the evolution of the concept.

Over the last three decades there has been considerable debate and discussion in academic and professional circles on the meaning of sustainable tourism. "Since its introduction in the late 1980s, the concept of 'sustainable tourism' has become one of the most frequently addressed issues among tourism researchers and practitioners" (Weaver, 2000:300). The importance of planning and managing tourism so that it contributes positively to the sustainable development of the communities and landscapes within which tourism activities take place is not contested (Robinson, 2000:295). What is more uncertain is the actual process and practice of managing tourism sustainably (Weaver, 2000:301). As demonstrated in Chapter Two, concern for the impacts of tourism in the Lake District were first highlighted by William Wordsworth and John Ruskin in the 19th century. However, the academic debate and concern for tourism's impact on the environment emerged in the 1970s, with the publication of a number of studies that highlighted the nature of the relationship between tourism and the environment (Budowski 1976, Bosselman 1978, and Cohen 1978 in Knowles *et al*, 2001). In the 1980s the environmental impacts of business strategies in general became the focus of concern and in 1982 the World Bank established an Environmental Department (ibid). The initial discussions and debate on sustainable development, and subsequently sustainable tourism, can be traced to the publication of *Our Common Future* by the World Commission on Environment and Development in 1987, more commonly referred to as the Brundtland Report (WCED, 1987). The Brundtland Report proposed that economic growth and environmental conservation are not only compatible, but they are necessary partners. By the end of the 1980s there was an acceptance of the "three states of the tourism-environment relationship, that of co-existence, conflict and symbiosis" (ibid:102). In the late 1980s sustainable tourism was viewed as an alternative form of tourism leading to the introduction of the term eco-tourism, indicating that the tourism product was environmentally responsible, normally being implemented on a small-scale. Mass tourism was upheld as being environmentally irresponsible with the potential negative aspects arising from such forms of tourism needing to be controlled.

The concept of sustainable tourism was further considered at the 1992 United Nations Conference on Environment and Development – the Rio Earth Summit (United Nations,

1993) from which Local Agenda 21 (LA21) emerged. This represented another "...significant indication of the growing commitment of decision-makers to meaningful public consultation in the formulation of policies affecting the environment and tourism" (Brent Ritchie, 2000:44). Throughout the 1990s the academic literature on the many facets of sustainable tourism expanded dramatically, and as Robinson (2000:295) suggests there is a "lion's den of semantics" when the concepts of sustainable development and sustainable tourism are now considered. In the 1990s, there was a move away from mass tourism being seen as only harmful on the environment (Weaver, 2000). Mass tourism did not have to result in negative impacts on the environment if managed effectively. The concept of sustainability was "extended right across the entire spectrum of tourism activity, and not just confined to the small-scale end of that continuum" (Clarke,1997 in Weaver, 2000:301).

There was much debate in the 1990s on how to define sustainable tourism, see Muller (1994), Butler (1999) and Hunter (2002), leading to a certain degree of ambiguity in the use of the term, and a lack of precision in its definition (Robinson, 2000). "Everybody is calling for sustainable or 'environmentally and socially compatible' tourism, but whenever these demands crop up, it becomes apparent that everybody interprets the concepts differently" (Muller, 1994:131). For some writers sustainable tourism was used to refer to the sustainability of products, while to other writers it was either a process of development, or a principle to be adopted by all, (Knowles *et al.* 2001). If a private sector tourism operator embraced the concept of sustainable tourism it was seen as a tool to be used to enhance the financial performance of the business. From a destination perspective, sustainable tourism was seen as a means of maintaining the resource base of the destination. Thus, the debate and discussion on sustainable tourism can fragment into different schools of thought, see Knowles (2001:111-118).

Muller defines sustainable tourism development as a pentagon with the following angles, where no one angle predominates, resulting in balanced tourism development being achieved:

➢ economic health;

➢ subjective well-being of the locals;

➢ unspoilt nature, protection of resources;

➢ healthy culture;

➢ optimum satisfaction of guest requirements.

Source: Muller (1994:132)

Although there is discussion and debate on how to define sustainable tourism, there is agreement that it is a "forward-looking form of tourism development and planning that promotes the long-term health of natural and cultural resources, so that they will be maintained as durable, permanent landscapes for generations to come. The concept also accepts that tourism development needs to be economically viable in the long term and must not contribute to the degradation of the sociocultural and natural environments" (Timothy, 2000:21). Ham and Weiler (2002:36) concur with Timothy, by stating that sustainable tourism is "developed and maintained in a manner, and at such a scale, that it remains economically viable over an indefinite period and does not undermine the physical and human environment that sustains and nurtures it."

In trying to attain sustainable tourism development, Muller suggests there are "any number of principles, theories, and suggestions as to how the desired situation can be achieved" (Muller, 1994:132). The basic principles of sustainable tourism were identified in the early 1990s by Bramwell and Lane (1993:2):

> ➢ holistic planning and strategy-making is necessary;
>
> ➢ the process will preserve essential ecological processes;
>
> ➢ it will protect both human heritage and biodiversity;
>
> ➢ productivity will be sustained for future generations.

Weaver (2000:302) suggests that there are six steps involved in the implementation of sustainable tourism, "though the stages do not necessarily always follow one another in a neat linear fashion":

Step 1 – Define goals and objectives in terms of what is to be sustained in relation to socio-cultural, economic and environmental factors.

Step 2 – Establish the planning and management parameters so that a framework can be developed to take account of the "spatial, sectoral, political and temporal parameters of the implementation process" (ibid:303).

Step 3 – Select appropriate and feasible indicators – the measurement criteria, benchmarks and standards that will provide data that can be used to judge whether the goals and objectives in Step 1 have been met.

Step 4 – Measure and monitor the indicators in Step 3.

Step 5 – Determine whether the goals are being achieved by "assessing cumulative performance of the selected indicators, and determine what progress is being made in the direction of sustainable tourism" (ibid:309).

Step 6 – Implement remedial actions where necessary in order to ensure that sustainable tourism practices are maintained.

In presenting and discussing the above six steps (drawn from Consulting and Auditing Canada, 1995, and Maclaren, 1996) Weaver (2000) acknowledges that the process as presented above is simplistic and that in applying the process in practice there are many challenges and difficulties at each step. For example, in relation to step 1 which element of sustainable tourism should be the focus of attention, and should the objective be to maintain, or further develop, tourism? Clearly different strategies will be required dependent on which perspective is adopted. At the same time, Weaver (2000) raises the question of whether the strategy should be product or market led. Should it be the destination (the product) that is sustained, or should the emphasis be on sustaining market demand? The geographic area in which the tourism management strategies are to be implemented have also to be defined and agreed amongst the various stakeholders – this also could be problematic in reaching a consensus of agreement. Problems and challenges will also occur in establishing the planning and management parameters. At which level should the strategies for sustainable tourism be designed, for example the region as a whole, sub-regional level or at the resort level? Which sectors of the economy should be included in the strategy? Tourism clearly operates alongside other industries within an economy and the sustainable tourism strategy cannot be planned in a vacuum. It needs to be designed in collaboration with sustainable strategies being designed for other sectors of the local economy. The political structure of the geographic area will also have to be taken into account when devising and implementing the sustainable tourism strategy, as a diverse range of governmental and non-governmental stakeholders will be responsible for the governance and administration of the area. The time frame for implementing the strategies and the funding needed to support implementation will also have to be determined. When it comes to setting and measuring sustainability indicators (steps 3 and 4) controversy and difficulties are also apparent as there is "an array of indicators that should be considered" (Weaver, 2000:308). However, the choice and selection of indicators should be realistic and manageable – setting too many indicators will prove to be problematic when it comes to their measurement. What should the balance be between socio-cultural, environmental, and economic indicators – where does the priority lie? From what basis should measurements be made – are baseline data available? In terms of monitoring performance against the indicators, how frequently should monitoring occur and who will undertake the task? Finally, when it comes to determining whether the goals and objectives set in step 1 have been achieved, Weaver (2000:309) feels that it is "questionable whether any reliable conclusions can be drawn as to the status of sustainability in the destination". This is because of the problems that are inherent in the six steps. Determining what remedial action might be needed is also problematic given this scenario.

Setting clearly defined objectives and targets for sustainable tourism is possible, reaching them is much more difficult in the dynamic and turbulent world in which tourism currently operates. In terms of the academic debate on sustainable tourism, it is now widely accepted that the philosophy of sustainable tourism is valid. What is more contentious, and open to different interpretations is the means by which sustainable tourism is to be achieved – its practice and implementation. Weaver (2000) acknowledges that his critique of the six steps results in a very pessimistic assessment of the processes involved in designing and implementing strategies for sustainable tourism. He concludes though by arguing that there are three key reasons why the challenges and difficulties discussed above should not deter the move towards sustainable tourism. Firstly, to do nothing and to ignore the principles of sustainable tourism will inevitably lead to the negative impacts of tourism proliferating. Even some modest progress in designing and implementing sustainable tourism strategies will be better than doing nothing at all. Secondly, the problems of setting indicators and the challenges inherent in their measurement can be addressed if a flexible approach is adopted. The view that should be taken is that the indicators are only indicators and should be used to demonstrate that the destination is moving forwards in terms of sustainability rather than backwards. The third reason he gives to support sustainable tourism is his reflection on the fact that the concept is still relatively new and that considerable progress has actually been made in understanding all the diverse facets and elements of it. In the early years of the 21st century Weaver believes that rapid progress will also be made in developing further the understanding of the many aspects of sustainable practice.

However, actually achieving the position where the claim can be made that sustainable tourism development has been attained is problematic, as implementing sustainable tourism principles and practices is a long and difficult process. There are many uncontrollable influences and forces that affect the implementation of sustainable tourism principles. These, when combined with the special characteristics of each tourist destination, with its own form of administration and governance, and a variety of stakeholders who are influenced by, and have influence over tourism, add to the complexity of implementing sustainable tourism principles. In addition, the needs of each tourist destination in terms of the preservation and conservation of the physical and cultural elements of the destination, aligned with the local economic development aspirations, contribute to the challenge of managing the destination sustainably.

The Role of Partnerships in Sustainable Tourism Management

In trying to attain the principles of sustainable tourism within the context of a tourist destination it is clear that the political process for the governance and administration of tourism will have to bring together the diverse range of stakeholders involved with or influenced by the tourism sector. These stakeholders will include representatives of the local community, tourism operators, agencies involved in the management and development of tourism, and organisations involved with the management of the environment. Co-ordinated collaborative strategic planning will be needed to ensure that all stakeholders have the same vision for the attainment of sustainable tourism principles.

Tourism management in the Lake District is a prime example of the need for a diverse set of independent agencies to work together in order to develop and manage tourism sustainably. Chapter Five identifies and explains the role of the key agencies involved with tourism management in the Lake District.

When a diverse set of stakeholders is involved with tourist destination management, sustainable tourism can only be achieved through these stakeholders collaborating and working in partnership (Bramwell and Lane, 2000). Collaboration and partnership are the keys to achieving sustainable tourism because in tourism, no single organisation is responsible for all components that comprise the tourist product, or tourism experience.

Many different organisations are involved in providing the tourist product – private sector operators and a diverse range of public sector, and not-for-profit, agencies. These stakeholders need to work together through formal mechanisms in order to devise and implement strategies that will result in the tourist destination attaining the principles of sustainable tourism. How can partnership and collaboration be defined? Bramwell and Lane (2000:1) define partnership as: "regular, cross-sectoral interactions between parties based on at least some agreed rules or norms, intended to address a common issue or to achieve a specific policy goal or goals." Such partnerships should be able to take a holistic perspective of all the issues that will influence sustainable tourism in the tourist destination. Collaboration involves bringing together

> "…a range of interests in order to develop and sometimes also implement tourism policies…involving face-to-face interactions between stakeholders who may be in the public, semi-public, private or voluntary sectors, including pressure and interest groups" (ibid:1).

When stakeholders collaborate, a number of different terms can be used to formally identify the new entity: "…coalitions, forums, alliances, task forces, and public-private sector partnerships" (Bramwell and Lane, 2000:2). In practice the terms collaboration and partnership tend to be used interchangeably. Partnerships and collaborations can have a variety of different administrative structures and organisation, with a range of diverse time frames in order to attain their objectives. Irrespective of the form of the partnership or collaboration it is felt that they do offer benefits for decision-making. The benefits of partnership and collaboration are that communication will arise between the stakeholders, discussions will take place, and normally consensus is reached on the form and scope of the tourism plan that is to be developed for the destination. By working together, the resources and expertise of each partner can be drawn upon, for the good of the partnership as a whole (Bramwell and Lane, 2000).

The United Kingdom government firmly endorses the use of partnerships for tourism development, see *Tomorrow's Tourism* (DCMS, (1999) and within the UK partnerships and collaboration are increasingly being recognised as the means by which to develop and implement sustainable tourism strategies. In north west England a significant change is currently being implemented in the administration and management of tourism. The North West Development Agency (the Regional Development Agency) published in 2003 a new strategy for tourism which will reorganise the Regional Tourist Boards into new Destination Management Organisations. The tourism strategy for north west England, and the establishment of a new Destination Management Organisation for Cumbria (the county within which the Lake District lies) will rely heavily on partnerships and collaboration for its successful implementation. Chapter Nine will discuss in greater detail the future administration and management of tourism in the Lake District. Weaver (2000:309), though, identifies significant problems with the process of collaboration and partnership indicating the tendency of stakeholders to "…cling stubbornly to their own agendas and ideologies, and their further tendency to harness the political process as much as possible to further these agendas". These challenges will also be discussed in Chapter Nine.

The Challenges of Developing and Implementing the Principles of Sustainable Tourism

It is evident from the discussion so far in this chapter that the challenges and difficulties of implementing sustainable tourism management policies and strategies are well documented, see Bramwell and Lane (2000) and Harris *et al.* (2002). From a policy perspective one of these challenges is establishing a framework by which the government and non-government agencies involved with the management and development of tourism can work in partnership to co-ordinate and manage sustainable tourism practices at the destination. In developed nations of the world there is a comprehensive system of laws and regulations to manage the physical development of rural and urban environments. In the United Kingdom there is a trend for government and non-governmental agencies to work together on the design and implementation of policies to benefit the communities they serve. Each nation, however, will have its own set of legislation and modus operandi, that will be a reflection of the governance and public administration systems and laws in place. Such administrative structures are an accepted part of the means by which nations are able to control and influence the development of tourism in a sustainable way. In the United Kingdom, national parks have been created to conserve and preserve distinctive natural environments so that they can be enjoyed by future generations. In north west England, the Lake District National Park Authority has been charged with the task of conserving and preserving this special landscape, and as such plays a central role in the development and implementation of sustainable management strategies. The work of the Lake District National Park Authority will be explained in detail in Chapter Five.

In the early years of the 21st century there is strong pressure, supported by the United Nations, for businesses to broaden their objectives to include social and environmental objectives of business success, as well as financial measures of performance – this is known as the triple bottom line. However, encouraging and motivating private sector enterprises to adopt and implement sustainable tourism management strategies in their operations is also challenging. This is especially the case when the tourism enterprises are small, independent operators achieving modest or marginal levels of profitability. Tourism enterprises are prone to many uncontrollable forces such as economic cycles, the after effects of war and terrorist atrocities, and unforeseen events such as the 2001 Foot and Mouth epidemic that devastated the rural economy of many parts of England. Responding to these uncontrollable forces is challenging enough and contributes to the financial fragility of running a tourism business. At times of such turbulence, encouraging business managers to devise and implement environmentally and socially responsible business strategies is extremely difficult, when the business's prime objective is to attract a sufficient number of tourists to stay solvent. Irrespective of these challenges the development of sustainable tourism management policies and strategies is seen as a priority by a number of private sector stakeholders who see this as not only contributing to the successful financial performance of the business, but also to the long term viability of the destination. Examples of private sector enterprises embracing the concept and principles of sustainable tourism in the Lake District will be provided in subsequent chapters, see for example Chapters Four and Seven.

From the above discussion it is apparent that designing and implementing sustainable tourism management strategies for a destination is extremely challenging. The process will involve considerable co-operation and collaboration between all stakeholders over a prolonged period of time, and with uncertain resources available to support the implementation process. At times there will be conflict because each stakeholder will have its own perspective on the issues being discussed. It is evident, though, that no single agency or organisation can take sole responsibility for sustainable tourism management. For the principles of sustainable tourism to be achieved there has to be a shared acceptance of what constitutes sustainable tourism for that particular destination, with a shared vision on how the principles of sustainable tourism are to be achieved. Considerable time may be taken in actually arriving at this stage of consensus before progress can be made in implementing sustainable strategies. Indeed, what is more likely to be the case is that an evolutionary approach is adopted to the design of sustainable tourism management policies, with such policies being modified and amended over time to react to new influences on, and developments at, the destination.

Sustainable Tourism in the Lake District

There is strong evidence that a wide range of organisations and a small number of tourist destinations are adopting and implementing the principles of sustainable tourism management. Green Globe 21, established in 1994 by the World Travel and Tourism Council to formally accredit travel and tourism organisations and destinations meeting defined standards of environmental management had 651 members by the end of 2001 in all regions of the world (Griffin and Delacey, 2002). Cumbria and the Lake District was the first tourist destination in the world to achieve full accreditation by Green Globe 21 as a destination able to demonstrate its full commitment to the principles of sustainable tourism management.

Green Globe 21 was established by the World Travel and Tourism Council (WTTC) in 1994, as a response to the 1992 Rio Earth Summit (Griffin and DeLacey, 2002). The Rio Earth Summit identified that the travel and tourism industry, including resorts and destinations, needed to develop in sustainable ways. The requirement was for the industry not to harm the environments that attract tourists, and for local people to benefit economically and socially from tourism. Green Globe accreditation recognises Cumbria and the Lake District's awareness of Agenda 21, and all the issues involved with Agenda 21. Green Globe 21 is an independent company limited by guarantee, with a steering committee comprising "...representatives from the tourism industry, non-government organisations and environmental consultancies around the world" (ibid:59). The organisation's main role is to operate a formal accreditation scheme that recognises achievement by tourism organisations and tourist destinations in meeting certain specified standards in sustainable tourism management. One example of this in the Lake District, is that the region can demonstrate an "integrated public transport system, that utilises a variety of means of transport – buses, trains, boats, bicycles and heritage transport (steam railways and lake steamers)" (Windermere Lake Cruises 2003:1). This example will be developed further in Chapter Four. In this way it is hoped that improvements in sustainable tourism management will occur throughout the world. Upon successful achievement of Green Globe's standards, the GREEN GLOBE logo can be used to promote the successful organisation or destination.

The certification process provides an independent verification that the organisation or tourist destination is meeting the specified standard for sustainable tourism, incorporating the "…triple bottom line principles of economic, socio-cultural and ecological sustainability" (Griffin and DeLacey, 2002:68). Verification and certification are carried out by independent companies. Certification is open to all forms of tourism organisation and tourist destination. For a tourist destination to be accredited, the destination has to "…demonstrate environmental performance according to the principles of Agenda 21. Subsequent to certification, it must demonstrate continuous improvement" (ibid: 76). In addition, the destination must encourage co-operation between various stakeholders in taking forward sustainable tourism management at the destination, which recognises the special local political, cultural and social characteristics. The stakeholders include the tourism industry, central and local government, non-government agencies and local communities. The tourist destination that is seeking accreditation has to undertake research to develop clear indicators, benchmarks and targets to demonstrate that it is meeting the required standards for sustainable tourism compliance. As a result of Green Globe accreditation of the destination it is hoped that private sector companies commit themselves to implementing sustainable tourism principles and policies – as is the case with Windermere Lake Cruises – see Chapter Four.

It is clear that the Green Globe 21 accreditation scheme is complex and one that requires considerable investment of resource in order to achieve certification. Cumbria Tourist Board was the lead organisation in securing Green Globe 21 accreditation for the Lake District.

The recognition of the Lake District as a tourist destination that implements the principles of sustainable tourism is seen as critical to the future development and success of tourism not just in Cumbria, but in the north west of England as a whole. The North West Development Agency sees the Lake District as becoming Europe's premier national park in the years ahead, and will use the Lake District as an 'attack brand' to draw tourists to north west England. With further investment in the tourism superstructure and infrastructure of the Lake District, it is intended that the region will become a world class 21st century tourist destination, but one that continues to be managed by the implementation of the principles of sustainable tourism. The following chapters of this book illustrate how tourism has developed and is managed in the Lake District in a sustainable way, so that the criticisms levied against tourism in the quotation presented at the beginning of this chapter by Griffin (2002), do not hold true. It will be shown that with effective management of the landscape and the built environment that tourism has not:

> ➢ despoiled a pristine natural environment;

> ➤ despoiled a valued lifestyle;

> ➤ despoiled age-old cultures.

This book will illustrate how the special characteristics and features of the Lake District have remained relatively unchanged since the early years of tourism in the 19th century. The distinctive landscape is still characterised by high fells, tarns, and valleys with lakes. Traditional farming and forestry practices are still used resulting in the pattern of fields and dry stone walls that have typified the Lakeland landscape for centuries. Strict planning regulations have preserved the built landscape and traditional architectural styles of the hamlets, villages, and towns. The crafts and traditions of the local population can still be found in the distinctive sports and country fairs that are held not only for the enjoyment of tourists but locals alike. Tourism as already mentioned in this chapter is a key element of the local economy and has been since the arrival of the first tourists in the 19th century.

These features of sustainable tourism have not occurred by accident but by the implementation of policies and practices from a variety of different stakeholders over a long period of time. William Wordsworth was probably the first proponent of the need to control the development of tourism in the Lake District, lobbying against the extension of the railway beyond the railhead at Windermere. His vociferous actions were successful and prevented the railway line from being extended into the heart of the Lake District. The National Trust, founded in the late 19th century has had a major influence over the preservation of the natural landscape and traditional farming and forestry practices by being a significant owner of land and properties in the Lake District. The Friends of the Lake District, a charitable organisation founded in the 1930s, campaigned for the establishment of a National Park Authority, and ever since has been a well-respected special interest group ensuring that thorough debate is held on developmental issues that might have detrimental effects on the Lakeland landscape, its communities and residents. In terms of organisations with a statutory role to devise and implement strategies and policies to influence tourism in the Lake District, the picture is complex. The Lake District National Park Authority is the local planning authority for all developments proposed within the national park. Cumbria County Council and the local district councils provide services for residents and tourists. Cumbria Tourist Board and the North West Development Agency are key organisations in the development and marketing of the Lake District as a tourist destination. The totality of the work of all of the aforementioned agencies and organisations, plus the activities of private sector tourism operators, contributes to the preservation and conservation of a distinctive landscape and socio-cultural environment that has remained little changed for centuries. It is this distinctive landscape that will continue to attract tourists to the north west of England throughout the 21st century.

Figure 1.0 *Contributors to sustainable tourism in the Lake District*

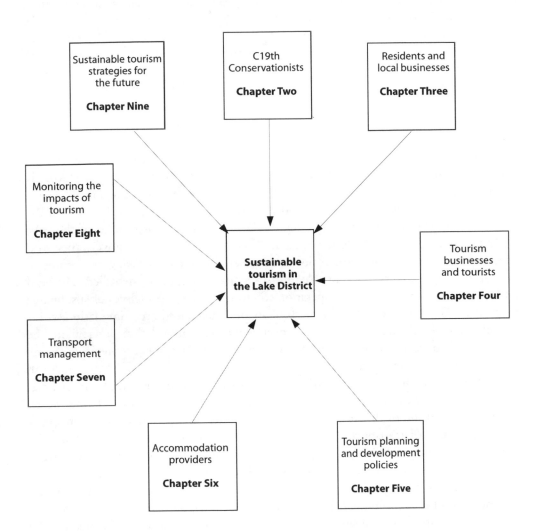

The chapters of this book provide a detailed case study of the history, development, planning, management and impacts of tourism in the Lake District. Through the following chapters it is hoped that the reader will be able to appreciate the challenges and complexities of managing tourism on the principles of sustainable development. Clearly, though, the contents of this book are destination specific, referring to a well-established tourist destination in a developed nation. It is hoped, however, that some of the issues raised in this book have relevance to tourist destinations in other parts of the world. Following this introduction, Chapter Two provides an account of the history and evolution of tourism in the Lake District from the early years of tourism when the writers and artists first publicised the region as an area of outstanding natural beauty. No study of sustainable tourism would be complete without a consideration of the social, cultural, economic, and political characteristics of the destination. Chapter Three presents an overview of these special characteristics of the Lake District demonstrating how challenging it actually is to manage and develop tourism in a complex and diverse geographic region. The Lake District as a tourist destination is assessed in Chapter Four with an explanation of the main attractions of the region, reiterating the fact that the core attractants of the Lake District have remained little changed for over 200 years. The governance and administration of tourism in the region is considered in Chapter Five with the role of each of the major players in sustainable tourism management being identified. The need for these agencies to work in co-operation to ensure that the principles of sustainable tourism are attained is clearly evident. Tourists obviously need accommodation whilst on holiday and Chapter Six provides an overview of accommodation providers in the region with a focus on how environmentally responsible management strategies are being implemented by some operators to contribute to sustainable tourism. A key element of tourism management and development is that of transport management. The policies implemented to manage transport in the Lake District are discussed in Chapter Seven with a consideration of the measures used to encourage and facilitate environmentally sensitive means of transport. Chapter Eight progresses to evaluate the economic, environmental and socio-cultural impacts of tourism demonstrating how these impacts are both positive and negative, but with a balance being achieved through the implementation of the principles of sustainable tourism management. The future development of tourism in the Lake District is assessed in Chapter Nine. The early years of the 21st century see considerable forces having an impact and influence on the development and evolution of tourism, and this chapter uses expert opinion to indicate the likely shape of tourism in the Lake District in the years ahead. Through the chapters of this book important lessons can be learned about the challenges of developing sustainable tourism in a mass market tourist destination such as the English Lake District.

References

Bramwell, B. and Lane, B. (Eds) (2000) *Tourism Collaboration and Partnerships: Politics, Practice and Sustainability*. Clevedon: Channel View Publications.

Brent Ritchie, J. R. (2000) Interest Based Formulation of Tourism Policy for Environmentally Sensitive Destinations. In Bramwell, B. and Lane, B. *Tourism Collaboration and Partnership: Politics, Practice and Sustainability*. Clevedon: Channel View Publications.

Bosselman, F. (1978) *In the Wake of the Tourist*. Washington DC: The Conservation Foundation.

Budowski, G. (1976) Tourism and conservation: conflict, coexistnce or symbiosis? *Environmental Conservation* 3(1), 27-31.

Butler, R. W. (1991) Tourism, environment and sustainable development. *Environmental Conservation* 18(3), 201-9.

Butler, R. W. (1999) Sustainable tourism: a state-of-the-art review. *Tourism Geographies* 1 (1), 7-25.

Clarke, J. (1997) A framework of approaches to sustainable tourism. *Journal of Sustainable Tourism* 5(3), 224-33.

Cohen, E. (1978) The impact of tourism on the physical environment. *Annals of Tourism Research* 5(2), 179-202.

Collins, A. (1999) Tourism development and natural capital. *Annals of Tourism Research* 26(1), 98-109.

Consulting and Auditing Canada (1995) *What Tourism Managers Need to Know: A practical Guide to the Development and Use of Indicators of Sustainable Tourism*. Ottawa, Canada: Consulting and Auditing Canada.

Countryside Commission (1995) *1994 All Parks Visitor Survey*. Cheltenham: Centre for Leisure Research and JMP Consultants Ltd.

Creative Research (2002) *Cumbria Tourism Survey 2002 Report of Findings*. London: Creative Research.

Department for Culture, Media and Sport (1999) *Tomorrow's Tourism. A Growth Industry for the new Millennium*. London: DCMS.

Griffin, T. (2002) An optimistic perspective on tourism's sustainability. In Harris, R., Griffin, T. and Williams, P. *Sustainable Tourism: a Global Perspective*. Oxford: Butterworth Heincmann.

Griffin, T. and Delacey, T. (2002) Green Globe: sustainability accreditation for tourism. In Harris, R., Griffin, T. and Williams, P. *Sustainable Tourism: a Global Perspective*. Oxford: Butterworth Heinemann.

Ham, S. H. and Weiler, B. (2002) Interpretation as the centrepiece of sustainable wildlife tourism. In Harris, R., Griffin, T., and Williams, P. *Sustainable Tourism: a Global Perspective.* Oxford: Butterworth Heinemann.

Harris, R., Griffin, T. and Williams, P. (2002) *Sustainable Tourism: a Global Perspective.* Oxford: Butterworth Heinemann.

Holden, A. (1999) High Impact tourism: a suitable component of sustainable policy? The case of downhill skiing development at Cairngorm, Scotland. *Journal of Sustainable Tourism* 7(2), 97-107.

Hunter, C. (1997) Sustainable tourism as an adaptive paradigm. *Annals of Tourism Research* 24(4), 850-67.

Hunter, C. (2002) Aspects of the sustainable tourism debate from a natural resources perspective. In Harris, R. Griffin, T. and Williams, P. *Sustainable Tourism: a Global Perspective.* Oxford: Butterwoth Heinemann.

Knowles, T., Diamantis, D. and El Mourhabi, J. B. (2001) *The Globalisation of Tourism and Hospitality: A Strategic Perspective.* London: Continuum.

Locum Destination Consulting (2003) *Cumbria Strategic Tourism Market and Development Forecasts: Market Trends Report – Final.* Haywards Heath: Locum Destination Consulting.

Maclaren, V. (1996) Urban sustainability reporting. *Journal of the American Planning Association,* 62(2), 184-206.

Muller, H. (1994), The Thorny Path to Sustainable Development. *Journal of Sustainable Tourism* 2(3), 131-136.

Robinson, M. (2000) Collaboration and Cultural Consent: Refocusing Sustainable Tourism. In Bramwell, B. and Lane, B. (eds) *Tourism Collaboration and Partnerships: Politics, Practice and Sustainability.* Clevedon: Channel View Publications.

Stabler, M. J. (1997) An overview of the sustainable tourism debate and the scope and content of the book in Stabler, M. J. (ed.) *Tourism and Sustainability: From Principles to Practice.* Wallingford: CAB International.

Timothy, D. J. (2000) Cross-Border Partnership in Tourism Resource Management: International Parks along the US-Canada Border. In Bramwell, B. and Lane, B. *Tourism Collaboration and Partnerships Politics, Practice and Sustainability.* Clevedon: Channel View Publications.

United Nations (1993) *Report of the United Conference on Environment and Development,* Rio de Janeiro, (Vol 1). New York: United Nations.

Wahab, S. (1997) Sustainable tourism in the developing world. In Wahab, S. and Pigram, J. J. (eds) *Tourism Development and Growth: The Challenge of Sustainability.* London: Routledge.

Weaver, D. (2000) Sustainable Tourism: Is it Sustainable? In Faulkner, B. *et al* (authors)(eds). *Tourism in the 21st Century Lessons from Experience*. London: Continuum.

Windermere Lake Cruises (2003) *Sustainable Tourism Policy Statement. Summary*. Ambleside: Windermere Lake Cruises.

World Commission on Environment and Development (1987) *Our Common Future*. Oxford: Oxford University Press.

The Political Boundaries of Cumbria and the Lake District National Park

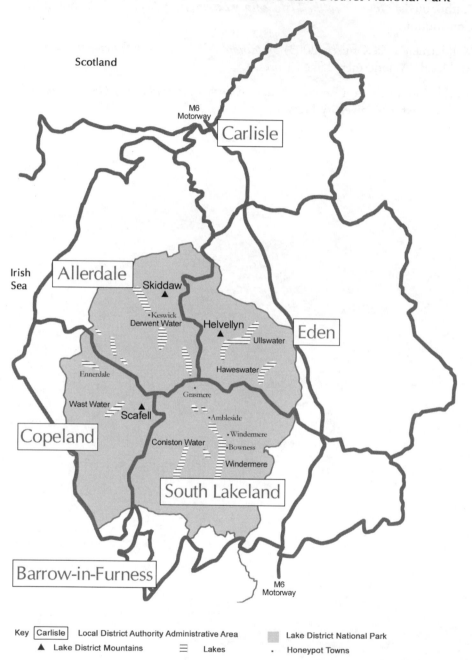

Scotland

M6
Motorway

Carlisle

Irish
Sea

Allerdale

Skiddaw ▲

• Keswick
Derwent Water

Helvellyn ▲

Ullswater

Eden

Haveswater

Ennerdale

Grasmere

Wast Water ▲
Scafell

• Ambleside

• Windermere

Copeland

Coniston Water
• Bowness

Windermere

South Lakeland

Barrow-in-Furness

M6
Motorway

Key | Carlisle | Local District Authority Administrative Area   Lake District National Park
    ▲   Lake District Mountains   ☰ Lakes   •   Honeypot Towns

Chapter Two

Tourism and the Lake District: Social and Cultural Histories

This chapter provides an essential introductory perspective on the English Lake District and 'sustainable tourism' by charting its history of well over two centuries as a magnet for visitors from Britain and, increasingly, Europe and the wider world, taking the story up to around 1980 to provide a platform and context for current analysis. The chapter begins by examining the nature of the region's attractions, asking what has made them so outstandingly distinctive, and offering an extended commentary on the nature of the Lake District's distinctiveness as a tourist icon: the features that distinguish it from other areas with claims to special landscape value, or traditions, or literary associations, or a combination of these things. Why, for example, does the Lake District have a higher international profile than the Peak District, or the Wye Valley, or Snowdonia, or even Dartmoor? If this profile is measured in terms of visitor numbers, then there is no question as to the greater popularity of Lakeland. Its total figure of 13,925,000 visitor days in 1994, was more than 1.5 million ahead of the number for the Peak District and more than double that of Snowdonia, for instance. The comparatively small land area of the Lake District, and its fragility and vulnerability to over-exploitation is then considered. But it is the Lake District's iconic core area, which makes the continuity of its tourist identity, in terms of landscape values, literary associations, outdoor activities and access to solitude and spiritual uplift, all the more remarkable. For over two centuries of increasing accessibility and popularity, and of changing values and expectations in the mainstream visiting public, the iconic core of the Lake District is still the key attractant of tourists to the region. The chapter then provides a substantial analysis of continuity, change and conflict in Lakeland tourism, set in the broader context of the region's economy and society, from the age of the post-chaise in the eighteenth century to that of the stagecoach, the railway and the automobile. Building on these discussions, the robust persistence of the Lake District's tourist identity is then explained, and the economic and social arrangements in which it has been embedded, by looking at successive threats to the sustainability of such an identity, and the ways in which they have been muted, neutralised or averted. In concluding, questions are asked about the viability of the Lake District's historical identity as an international tourism icon in the new millennium, which will provide a direct introduction to the themes that will be pursued in the rest of the book.

The Attractions, Importance and Iconic Status of the Lake District

The Lake District's status as a regional, national and international tourist magnet is of long standing, as the following commentary will demonstrate. Its landscape is its dominant attractive feature; but what matters is not so much the geology or vegetation in themselves, as the ways in which the results of these characteristics have been represented, verbally (especially) and pictorially, in ways that communicate a sense of something especially alluring and enthralling, capable of conferring mental and spiritual as well as physical benefits upon the discerning visitor. The 'place-myth' of the Lake District was firmly grounded, from the beginning of tourism in the area, in 'scenic beauty and... associations with the Romantic poets' (O'Neill, 2000:10-12; Shields, 1991:6-10; Urry, 1995: 25-27). It appealed to the fashionable canons of the 'picturesque', emerging in the mid-eighteenth century and inviting the observer to correlate landscape qualities with the templates provided by Italian landscape painters, ordering the prescribed mix of woodland, fields, rocks and water according to prescribed criteria. From the mid-eighteenth century onwards a market developed for prints of Lake District scenery, and from the 1760s picturesque tours of rural Britain became fashionable. Travel journals and guide-books began to proliferate in remarkable numbers, the latter not only defining the 'best' viewpoints but also prescribing the emotions they should evoke in the cultivated observer. Hitherto, it should be emphasised, mountains (like seashores) had provoked aversion and even horror among travellers whose preferred landscapes were controlled, cultivated and fertile; and early picturesque travellers had preferred to emphasise the softer, low-lying beauties of lakes and woodland (Bicknell, 1990; Gilpin, 1996; Roberts, 2001; Ousby, 1990; Corbin, 1994). But within a few years the Lake District also proved capable of providing the stronger stimulus of the 'sublime', harrowing the observer with fear and wonder at the sight of profound crevasses, beetling crags, teetering rocks and threatening precipices, which lent themselves to descriptions couched in a conventional language of hyperbole which was already falling victim to observant parodists in the early nineteenth century (Nicholson, 1955; Chard, in Berghoff *et al.*, 2002). These perceptions did not come naturally: they arose from a set of learned conventions that became part of the cultural capital of the self-consciously civilised observer, enjoying the contemplation of a deliciously dangerous 'other' from a safe distance (Buzard, 1983). These attributes did not, in themselves, make the Lake District outstanding even within Britain: those like Rev. William Gilpin, Prebendary of Salisbury Cathedral, who wrote the early manuals of picturesque tourism, were 'discovering' other areas with equal enthusiasm. Gilpin himself toured North Wales and the Wye Valley before visiting the Lakes, and his published picturesque itineraries came to cover most of Britain, including East Anglia and the south coast (Gilpin, 1996). It took the conversion of parts of the Lake District into a 'literary landscape', which entailed the idealisation of a society and an imagined way of life, to elevate it to the special and unique status it came to enjoy in British culture.

The crucial moment of transition in this respect can be identified with the rise of the 'Lake Poets', William Wordsworth and his associates, especially his sister Dorothy, Samuel Taylor, Coleridge, Robert Southey and Thomas De Quincey. Their collective association with the Lake District spanned the period from the 1790s to the mid-nineteenth century, although they were never all resident at any given time. William Wordsworth became by far the most visible figure outside literary and academic circles in the long run. As Hanley points out, some of Wordsworth's most 'memorable poetry' has its topographical foundations in Wales, the West Country, North Yorkshire and indeed Switzerland; but he became indelibly associated in the public mind with the landscapes of the Lake District, especially the southern half of the area, between Black Combe in the south-west and Ullswater near the centre (Hanley and Milbank, 1992).

Even within the Lake District, however, Wordsworth's role as a magnet for subsequent tourists (an ironical development) was concentrated mainly into the area around his homes in Grasmere and Rydal. His influence on tourist topography has been significantly selective. Wordsworth's birthplace at Cockermouth and his schooldays at Hawkshead have been far less prominent on the tourist landscape, while the Duddon sonnets and the early poems that described Esthwaite Water and Black Combe did not precipitate tourist invasions of locations that remained difficult to access. This is a reminder that there were limits to the combined power of poetry and celebrity to channel tourist flows in precise directions, and that more prosaic factors like transport and convenience came into play. Nevertheless, Wordsworth's ability to relate descriptions of landscape and idealised social arrangements to the development of a sense of tranquillity and of the meaning of existence in the individual self did strike an enduring chord, even in those whose direct contact with Romantic poetry came at second- or third-hand, or through little more than classroom contact with the famous 'Daffodils' poem. William Wordsworth became an inspiration to those who sought to preserve or conserve the Lake District as a 'traditional' society, as far as possible an imagined 'republic of shepherds' or at least of virtuous, abstemious, independent yeoman farmers, while excluding manifestations of the urban, the modern and especially the industrial from making an impact on landscape or society. The continuing publication in the late twentieth century of both 'academic' and 'popular' books providing, to take one example, 'a guide to the poems and their places', is evidence of Wordsworth's lasting importance to the tourist identity of the Lake District (McCracken, 1984; Mitchell, 1984). So is the continuing availability of Wordsworth's own guide-book to Lakeland scenery and society, first published in 1810 and reissued in serially amplified editions, culminating with that of 1835 (Bicknell, 1991). This gave the poet's imprimatur to the cultural value of a Lake District visit, while articulating his holistic sense of the intimate relationship between geology, agriculture, landscape and society, and indeed of the transient nature, on a geological timescale, of what he was celebrating. A perception that did not inhibit him from attacking the alien incursions of villa builders and the planters of alien trees, while enthusing about the imagined virtues of the rustic inhabitants (Whyte, 1998; Winchester, 1998; Marshall, 1972). His celebration of 'pedestrianism' as the proper way to realise the 'peaceful self' in communion with the Lake District landscape also had a lasting influence, as did his intimation that in the solitude of the fells the attentive visitor could encounter not only 'Nature', but 'Nature's

God' (Hanley, 1992; Buzard, 1983). All these Wordsworthian influences fed into the creation of a distinctive kind of place-myth and a matching set of tourism practices.

As can be seen later, Wordsworth's values were very far from being the only influences on the rise of the Lake District as tourist destination and, importantly, playground. This was true in his own time, and the alternative perceptions of the region and how to enjoy it became stronger and more intrusive with the passing years. Many of the tourists who besieged his home at Rydal Mount in the 1840s, especially after the railway to Windermere (whose continuation further into the Lakes he had fiercely opposed) opened in 1847, were literary lion-hunters rather than disciples of a creed with which they were unfamiliar (Martineau, 1855). But Wordsworth's ideas were central to the Lake District's development of a distinctive, iconic status as, in effect, a holy place whose special attributes called forth impassioned defence against transgressive interference in pursuit of frivolity and profit.

Further literary influences built on this, although Harriet Martineau's celebration, in 1855, of the civilising mission of railways and tourists offers a reminder that much appreciation of Lakeland landscape looked to prettiness rather than sublimity or philosophical uplift: for Martineau it existed to be sketched rather than to inspire awe in the beholder, and her delight in the diffusion of hotel bathrooms and other modern comforts was accompanied by a perception of local society that emphasised hard drinking and sottish ignorance, and looked forward to the spread of enlightenment through schooling as well as the importation of role models. Her's was a universalising discourse of 'progress' and 'improvement', with little interest in romanticising or sustaining older ways of life (Martineau, 1855; Walton, 1998). It was undoubtedly closer to much of the mainstream visiting public than the doctrines of preservation and conservation that were advocated by those who self-consciously picked up Wordsworth's mantle in the later nineteenth century.

From the 1870s, particularly, the Lake District also became identified with John Ruskin, who commented with increasing bitterness and dismay on the pollution of industrial England by philistine manufacturers of 'illth', whose clouds of industrial smoke and steam were extending their corrupting fingers even into his lakeside fastness of Brantwood, on Coniston Water. Ruskin was an economic heretic (an opponent of unchecked industrial growth and the competitive consumption of mass-produced articles), but his advocacy of fulfilment through art, craftsmanship and appreciation of the natural world attracted many sympathetic readers among potential Lake District visitors in the late nineteenth century and beyond. Just as Wordsworth had opposed the incursions of railways and steamers into the heart of the Lake District in the 1840s, so Ruskin lent his cultural authority to campaigns against renewed 'rash assaults' by interwoven railway, mine, quarry and tourist interests, and by urban governments who wanted reservoirs to tap into the abundant rainfall of the fells. This discussion will return to these conflicts of the 1870s onwards: the point here is that Ruskin's impassioned defence of the Lake District against (among other things) what he saw as the threatened encroachment of a 'mass tourism' of railborne trippers, who would damage the landscape and destroy the tranquillity without appreciating either, reinforced the special, almost sacred image of the region as somewhere unique and worthy of protection. Close to the surface here is the important distinction between the 'traveller' and the 'tourist', which Buzard adapted from Bourdieu (Buzard, 1983). Ruskin, like Wordsworth before him, wanted an 'unspoiled' Lake District to be open to those who could appreciate its peaceful landscapes and established customs for their own sake in the spirit of appreciative and enquiring travellers, a category that embraced those serious-minded working men (this was a gendered concept) who were willing to make the necessary sacrifices in time and effort; but mere frivolous 'tourists', who would want changes and development to meet their standardised ideas about entertainment and comfort, were anathema. Here can be seen some roots of what became the opposition to what Ritzer has labelled, in a later but not unrelated context, McDonaldization (Ritzer, 1998). These values can also be identified with the 'romantic' as opposed to the 'collective' gaze identified by Urry, as the 'good traveller' through the Lake District sought silent individual communion with 'Nature and Nature's God', although where the context of such communion was shaped by the itinerary and prescribed viewpoints of the guide-book some important complications ensued (Urry, 1990, 1995). Interestingly, however, the association of the Picturesque with painterly ways of looking at the landscape, and the enduring popularity of image-making among visitors, did not generate a strong association between the Lake District and landscape painting as high art, despite productive visits by such artists as Constable and Turner. Popular representational paintings by such as Heaton Cooper came to be a different matter. It was a literary, indeed a poetic, rather than a painterly or indeed a musical landscape: it became 'Wordsworth country', and 'Constable country' lay elsewhere.

Ruskin's writings went quickly out of fashion in the early twentieth century, but as regards the Lake District his influence lingered on, at one and more removes, not least through the role of Ruskin disciples such as Octavia Hill and Canon Hardwicke Rawnsley in the founding and early development of the National Trust (Wheeler, 1995; Murphy, 1987; Ranlett, 1983). Rawnsley, in particular, developed a distinctive personal voice as a ferocious 'guardian (or watchdog) of the Lakes' on the national stage, building on earlier campaigns against railway and reservoir proposals to become a key proponent of the Lake District Defence Society, founded in 1883. This organisation, which (significantly) recruited strongly from members of the Wordsworth Society and from the public schools (especially Charterhouse) and universities, articulated resistance to threats of 'despoliation' through development of the national elite media. The National Trust, whose concern to buy up threatened monuments and treasured tracts of countryside and preserve them in perpetuity drew it into extensive Lake District activity, was another perpetuator of Ruskinian and Wordsworthian values (though in contested and complicated ways). It grew slowly from its initial foundation in 1895, and it was not until well after the Second World War that it became a really important national institution with a mass membership; but it both grew out of and perpetuated a shared sense among a cultural elite of the Lake District's special and even sacred nature (Walton in Wheeler, 1995; Walton, 1998).

Rawnsley was also an important figure in the movement to sustain and revive 'traditional' Lakeland crafts, and in the broader construction of Lake District histories and traditions that contributed to the sense that here was a distinctive and valuable place. His promotion of the Keswick School for Industrial Arts from 1884, which was effectively run by his wife Edith, was one of several attempts at the turn of the century, claiming inspiration from Ruskin, to revive traditional craft work: it stands alongside (for example) the Langdale Linen Industry and Annie Garnett's Spinnery at Bowness-on-Windermere (Brunton, 2001). There were many other such initiatives across Britain in these years, but the association created between the Lake District and 'traditional' crafts proved enduring. The sense that revival here derived from recent experience, in association with the rustic virtues of a Quaker yeomanry, rather than being reinvented after a long gap at the behest of romantic outsiders, helped to engender a sense of authenticity. So did recourse to the Scandinavian and Germanic motifs, which were written up in W. G. Collingwood's histories of the Lake District and identified enthusiastically in surviving craft work of the seventeenth and eighteenth century. Something approximating to a Romantic myth of quasi-nationhood was here being manufactured, again accentuating the special nature of the Lake District (Chapman, 1998; Brunton, 2001). It was reinforced by Rawnsley's own prolific literary output; and all these developments, while repudiating the corrosive influence of mainstream (if not 'mass') tourism on regional character, also provided grist to the mill of the proliferating guide-books (including Rawnsley's own, especially his contributions to the popular Baddeley series). The anti-tourist pursuit or re-creation of 'authenticity' had results that were themselves, in what has become a familiar paradox, attractive to the discerning and well-read, but irreducibly commercial, Lake District visitor market (Walton, 1998).

Overlapping with these representations and perceptions, but with a vitality of their own, were developing visions of the Lake District as a national playground, offering unparalleled opportunities for exploration and the testing of strength, skill and stamina. The development of rock-climbing was the outstanding early example of this. Here again, this was not unique to the Lake District: it developed in parallel ways in Snowdonia and Scotland, to say nothing of the British in the Alps, and of contemporary developments in other European countries. The origins of rock climbing can be dated to the 1870s and 1880s, although Coleridge's descent of Broad Stand from the summit of Scafell in 1802, which formed part of the sort of solitary, contemplative walking tour that itself made a significant contribution to the Lake District place-myth, was followed by a steady flow of ascents of Pillar Rock during the middle decades of the nineteenth century. The Wasdale Head area, visited by hardy middle-class walkers (often in mixed parties) in their dozens rather than the hundreds of Coniston or the thousands of Windermere, became the nursery of rock-climbing as a sport, dominated in the first instance by professional men and students from the universities and public schools. People of lower social status, with shorter holidays and limited resources, followed slowly and belatedly. This was another aspect of the Lake District's distinctiveness to be associated with the well-connected and articulate, with access to the sort of elite media that could confirm and amplify a reputation, and duly did so. The climbers might enjoy the view and the solitude, but they were also preoccupied with the technicalities of their emergent craft and, above all, their personal struggle with the rock and the elements. This was more than just romantic contemplation: it involved dominating the landscape, and imposing the grids of detailed mapping and classification on it, as well as mere gazing (Hankinson, 1988; Griffin, 2000).

As the vogue for rock climbing developed in the twentieth century, so it became more an end in itself: climbers regarded long walks up fellsides as a waste of time and energy, and convenient spots like Shepherd's Crag ('discovered' in 1922) gained in popularity, becoming 'no place to seek solitude' (Hankinson, 1988:1-3) This significant change marched in step with less demanding associations between the Lake District and outdoor sports and games, which also made it distinctive in national terms. Windermere became indelibly associated with yachting, the preserve of the comfortable middle classes of industrial and commercial Lancashire (Westall, 1991). The Arthur Ransome *Swallows and Amazons* stories, more concerned with messing about in boats and enjoying adventures in the rough country around Windermere and Coniston Water, gained a lasting vogue among middle-class children and their parents, which generated a demand for books that searched for the 'real Swallows and Amazons country' in the late twentieth century (Wardale, 1986; Welberry, 2000). But 'messing about in boats' also extended to steamers, and later motor-boats and even power-boats, generating conflict between Wordsworthian contemplatives and the more overtly materialistic enjoyment of speed, noise and technology. Sir Malcolm Campbell and his son Donald's pursuit of water speed records on Coniston Water lent an air of heroic martyrdom to this aspect of the Lakes in the middle decades of the twentieth century (Knowle and Beech, 2001). The Lake District as adventure playground was to be highly productive of conflict in the motor age, especially with the advent of off-road motorcycles; and these aspects of its distinctive national profile were to become increasingly pronounced as the twentieth century proceeded. The National Park, when established in 1951 (as perhaps the most prominent of these important post-war initiatives), had the unenviable task of negotiating the tensions between the contemplative and the expressive, the 'simple life' and the technologically adventurous wings of middle-class culture, both of which wanted to enjoy the Lake District, but for different and sometimes incompatible purposes. The tremendous success from the mid-1980s of Alfred Wainwright's guides for fell-walkers, with their impeccable script and detailed drawings, demonstrated the enduring attractions of the high fells and their scenery, but even here the almost obsessive need in some users to collect routes and follow them to the letter, the air of prescription about the chosen viewpoints, and the rapid appearance of 'how-to' manuals to accompany the original books, conjured up the collective and directed rather than the romantic gaze (Allen and Linney, 1995). It might be added that Wainwright, too, did not confine his attentions to the Lakes: early works covered Scotland, Wales and other parts of Northern England, and his eventual success probably depended on the high demand for Lake District works of this kind, which had not been replicated elsewhere. He was elaborating, amplifying, codifying and benefiting from a place-myth, rather than creating one.

In spite of all this, and of the rapid development of the Lake District (especially since the opening of the M6 motorway and its associated link roads) as an excursion and picnic goal for car-borne visitors who are more interested in shopping and sightseeing than contemplating romantic scenery, what makes the Lake District special is still the Wordsworthian legacy, however mutated over the generations. The Lake District is no-one else's 'country', and unlike (for example) the North York Moors it has not become attached to a long-running television series: there is no Lake District equivalent of Heartbeat. The ideas surrounding the region's Romantic origins as a tourist destination still affect the policies that can be adopted, ruling activities out of court that would be acceptable elsewhere, and making others controversial. Aspirations towards the celebration of the 'romantic gaze' persist into what might otherwise be defined as an age of 'mass tourism', although this latter label poses an infinity of problems when examined critically (Berghoff *et al.*, 2002). The Lake District has become internationally famous for a tourism that celebrates idealised landscapes and an idealised past. It therefore depends on sustainability; but it does so in a limited compass and a fragile environment.

The Vulnerability and Fragility of the Lake District

The Lake District's recurrent failure to achieve UNESCO World Heritage Site status is due in part to its perceived vulnerability. The recently-created 'cultural landscape' category under which it had been encouraged to reapply at the Budapest meeting in June 2002 did not, in practice, provide a way into the charmed circle, although (for example) the Ferto/Neusiedlersee area of Hungary and Austria met the criteria. The epidemic of Foot and Mouth disease in the previous year underlined the precarious nature of a claim based on a cultural landscape crafted by a thousand years of farming traditions, as well as the way in which the landscape inspired great literary works. Paul Tiplady, Chief Executive of the Lake District National Park Authority warned that without the distinctive local breeds of sheep and the farming practices that went with them, the essential continuity that underlay the 'cultural landscape' would be lost, and the hillsides would revert to scrub (Herbert, 2001).

But the threat to 'traditional' upland farming, of which the reaction to Foot and Mouth disease was a particularly emotive aspect, was one symptom among many of the Lake District's increasing vulnerability to its own accessibility. Its proximity to conurbations in south Lancashire and the Midlands, expressed in terms of travelling time, was increased by the opening of the M6 motorway to access gateways to (most significantly) the south-east and east of the area in 1970, and the displacement of rail by road as the dominant mode of access shifted 'honeypots' away from the urban railheads to a variety of points along the spinal road system defined by the A591 and A592, with less popular but still intrusive offshoots to 'beauty spots' like the Langdale valley. Car parking needs also compromised landscape values, while a growing interest in upland walking, albeit often for short distances from car parks, created erosion problems on favoured paths that scarred the pristine greenery of the hillsides in ways that were visible over long distances. The new accessibility provided by road access improvements gave day-trippers by car more time to drive around the Lake District, while staying visitors and day-trippers with shorter journeys were able to penetrate the northern and western parts of the area in greater numbers, spreading the pressure into valleys that had still been relatively quiet in the mid-1960s. Road transport posed particular problems, setting expectations of democratic access against established amenity values in more pervasive and intrusive ways than earlier forms of transport innovation. This was already an issue in the inter-war years, as shown later, but the expansion of car ownership from the 1950s exacerbated the problems. During the 1960s the National Park Planning Board itself recognised the need for road improvements to cope with the growing traffic, despite their impact on the scenery. But attempts to reduce this mobility through demand management, by encouraging honeypot development along the central axis, including the National Park centre at Brockhole itself, created pressures of their own. By the late twentieth century the Lake District had become a prisoner of its own popularity, and the continuing incompatibility of noisy technological pleasures with enjoyment of the landscape and ambience, in the eyes of significant numbers of visitors (and those who catered for them), was illustrated by the renewed battles over attempts to reduce motorboat speed and noise on Windermere towards the turn of the millennium. The visual and aural evidence of external human intervention in the 'cultural landscape' of the Lake District was more than sufficient to compromise its bid for World Heritage Site status. These pressures and conflicts had antecedents that dated back to the earliest days of the Lake District as a tourist centre. But first there is a need to chart the growth and changing nature of the industry itself (Marshall and Walton, 1981; Countryside Commission, 1969).

The Development of the Lake District Tourist Industry

The point at which a tourist 'industry' in the Lake District can be identified is itself debatable. Developments in the late eighteenth and early nineteenth century, encouraged by the easier access afforded by turnpike road improvements to, and then through, the area and the subsequent establishment of stage-coach services, were on a very limited scale, largely making use of existing farmhouse accommodation. A few inns catered for tourists as well as local travellers, but standards were very variable, and contemporary comments suggest that a preference for rustic innocence already sat uneasily alongside a desire for appetising food and creature comforts (Marshall, 1971). The small scale and elitist nature of tourism in the late eighteenth century is illustrated by the tale of Mary Robinson, the Maid of Buttermere. Robinson became famous for her innocence and beauty among the readership circle of Joseph Palmer's notes of a Lakeland tour in 1792, and attracted interested visitors to her father's small inn by the side of the lake, without bringing about any significant growth in local tourist activity, even when the sad tale of her marriage to a bigamist and impostor in 1802 was publicised more widely when he was exposed, tried and executed. Her story has been used as a metaphor for the compromising of innocence and authenticity by tourism's importation of a commercial and emulative spirit (Bragg, 1991), and in the same way the entertainments and simulacra provided on Pocklington's Island on Derwentwater, involving artificial ruins and the firing of cannon to arouse the echoes, or the development of Crosthwaite's museum of curiosities in Keswick, aroused conflicting feelings, dividing visitor sentiments between those who enjoyed the commercial frivolity and those who deplored it, without generating much employment or economic development (Nicholson, 1955). The adverse comments on the transforming power of tourism in Wordsworth's *Guide* expressed such unease, but the scale of innovation remained minuscule, despite the spread of gentlemen's houses and their gardens on the eastern side of Windermere. The pace of development was accelerating by the 1830s: the three main urban centres catering for tourist demand (Keswick, Ambleside and Bowness-on-Windermere) experienced population growth at between two and three times the rate for Cumbria as a whole between 1831 and 1841. In this decade up to a thousand people per season might sign the visitors' book at Crosthwaite's Museum in Keswick, where university reading-parties and other élite visitors were already creating a demand for prostitutes from the industrial towns of West Cumberland. But beyond these nuclei the economic impact of tourism was, and long remained, negligible: an inn here, a carriage or boat there, a scattering of mountain guides. It took the arrival of the railways in the mid-nineteenth century to stimulate a level of economic activity that brought visitors in their thousands rather than their hundreds and really began to make a wider impact on the landscape (Marshall and Walton, 1981; Walton and McGloin, 1981).

The first railway to penetrate the Lake District, the Kendal and Windermere line from Oxenholme, on the newly-opened line from London to Scotland over Shap, to a terminus at Birthwaite on the hill above the lake, was opened in 1847. This made an immediate difference to visitor numbers and population growth in the immediate area, attracting new development (including a railway hotel) to the vicinity of the station, and stimulating new housing along the road from the existing lakeside settlement. During 1843-4 12,000 people passed through the Plumgarths toll bar on the Kendal-Windermere turnpike road, perhaps half of whom were tourists. The railway carried 120,000 passengers in its first year of operation, and the seasonal pattern suggests that at least 27,000 were tourists: so the immediate impact of the railway probably multiplied the tourist traffic by four or five, although its convenience would also have diverted travellers from other routes. This cheaper and faster form of travel also opened the Windermere area out to a broader spectrum of middle-class demand, enabling longer stays, and to working-class day-trippers at special cheap fares, although distance from population centres and lack of popular amusements ensured that such visitors were rare birds until at least the 1870s. The railway also made second-home ownership more convenient for the wealthy, and even long-distance commuting to Liverpool and Manchester for those who kept short office hours. All this enabled Bowness and Windermere to overtake the older-established market towns of Ambleside and Keswick in population terms. Between 1841 and 1861 Bowness grew from 1479 to 2987, while Ambleside (which was within easy reach of the railhead by horse-drawn carriage) expanded more modestly from 1281 to 1603, and Keswick, whose railway did not arrive until 1862, moved only from 2442 to 2610. The convenience of train travel had tilted the economic balance towards the south-eastern Lakes. Keswick caught up considerably in the late nineteenth century, reaching 4500 in 1901 compared to Bowness's 5061 and Ambleside's 2536; but the latter resort developed the most specialised tourist economy, benefiting from becoming a hotel and coaching centre for the better-off visitors with more time at their disposal, and enjoyed modest prosperity throughout the period, in spite of being one of the three largest English towns without a railway at the 1911 census (Walton and McGloin, 1981; Simmons, 1986).

This was not spectacular urban growth by the standards of the time, as the rapid development of contemporary seaside resorts on favoured shorelines demonstrated (Walton, 1983). The three main towns put together would have been almost invisible in industrial Lancashire. Nor was it associated with remarkable expansion in visitor accommodation: lodging-houses listed in trade directories for the three towns more than doubled between the late 1840s and the late 1860s, but only to figures in the thirties and forties, although hotels were also being built and inns refurbished, while cheaper accommodation during the short summer season (basically confined to July and August) was provided by private residents. In the early 1870s one house in thirteen in Bowness and Windermere provided tourist accommodation, while the Ambleside and Keswick figures were one in seven and one in eleven respectively. By 1891 the figures were one in six, one in seven and one in ten, respectively, as the tourist trade in late Victorian Bowness underwent renewed expansion (Walton and McGloin, 1981). This reflected the growth of more down-market tourism from the lower middle and upper working classes, alongside a considerable increase in week-end excursion traffic from (especially) industrial Lancashire, which expanded from the 1870s on a larger scale than the similar trainloads from Carlisle, West Cumberland and Durham that visited Keswick. But the lifeblood of these resorts was the industrial and professional middle classes, with a leavening of well-known writers, high-ranking military officers and aristocrats. This was even truer of the quieter places to the west and north, although the Lakeside and Coniston branch railways brought circular tours to link up with the lake steamers. The visitors to Wasdale who appeared in the visitors' books from the 1870s onwards, and included the pioneers of rock climbing, were overwhelmingly drawn from the public schools, universities and learned professions (Jackson and Jackson, 1980; Hankinson, 1988). Even in the urban resorts, visitor numbers were far from overwhelming: perhaps 1250 visitors at the seasonal peak in Bowness and Windermere in the late 1870s, and 2000 in 1900, a figure to which Ambleside laid claim in 1876, while Keswick stood at around 1500 in the late 1870s. This was much less impressive than the figures for seaside resorts of similarly modest size (Walton and McGloin, 1981). What mattered much more than the ephemeral patronage of day excursionists, who might number 10,000 at most in the Windermere of the late nineteenth century, and half that number in Keswick, was the lucrative patronage of the reliable, regular upper- and middle-class visitors who stayed for weeks at a time, and the wealthy residents who came to form the core of the Windermere Yacht Club, whose house parties expanded the local visiting public, and who employed most of the 'agricultural workers' listed in the Windermere census to look after their extensive gardens (Westall, 1991). Visitors to the main resorts were drawn from industrial Lancashire (around 40 per cent in the late nineteenth century), London and the Home Counties (around 10 per cent, and more than twice that level in Keswick), and the North-East (up to ten per cent), with limited representation from Yorkshire, which had its own upland playgrounds nearer home. As early as the mid-1870s, however, up to one-eighth of Windermere's listed visitors came from overseas, especially the United States. The Lake District's core visiting public came from the middle classes of industrial and commercial Lancashire, but grafted on to this was a highly significant and relatively numerous metropolitan and cosmopolitan element that set it apart from other tourist areas in the north of England, with the possible exception of quaint and picturesque Whitby (Walton and McGloin, 1981).

This visitor profile ensured that there was little demand for large-scale commercial entertainment, and any attempt to cater for working-class visitors was liable to founder on the antipathy of local government, which was dominated by comfortably-off residents and tradesmen catering for the mainstream market. The hotels accounted for a high proportion of the visiting public, and they provided their own exclusive entertainment: dances, card parties, dinners. Very little, beyond bands and public open spaces, was provided otherwise. Boating was the dominant amusement, and wet days drove the trippers straight into the pubs and beerhouses, thereby strengthening existing adverse stereotypes about them. The Lake District was, after all, a place of outdoor attractions, despite its unreliable weather, and it was important to safeguard values identified with landscape, contemplation and tranquillity. As an Ambleside hotelier remarked in 1887, '…the lower class we see less of… unless they have a taste for the beauties of our district, and receive culture therefrom, they do not come twice' (Marshall and Walton, 1981:185). A few serious-minded working men did tackle the fells in Wordsworthian spirit, such as the Liverpool bookbinder Hugh Shimmin as early as the 1850s, and the numbers (of both sexes) were growing with the first stirrings of a popular 'outdoor movement' from the 1890s; but this remained a small minority (Walton and Wilcox, 1991; Taylor, 1997).

This continued to be the dominant pattern throughout the first half of the twentieth century: a predominantly regional tourist trade, often practised in conjunction with other sources of income and even more resistant to convincing quantification than most (there is no hope of calculating a convincing multiplier effect operating through what is anyway an unknown number of visitors), with a top-dressing of elite cultural tourism from further afield and an irregular and sometimes indigestible admixture of working-class day-trippers and week-enders, and a supply side dominated by the provision of accommodation, mainly in family businesses run by local people, and including a very limited entertainment sector. That is not to suggest that the system remained entirely stable over this long period, however, as will be evident (O'Neill, 2001).

The big changes in the tourist trade itself during the first half of the twentieth century were most marked in the inter-war years, and involved the growing impact of road transport and the internal combustion engine, the effects of the trade depression of the early 1930s, and the rising importance of farmhouse accommodation and of camping and youth hostelling. The two World Wars put most developments on hold for the duration. But visitor numbers certainly grew: the June census of 1921 found nearly 1300 visitors in Windermere and Keswick, though only 600 in Ambleside, well before the start of the high season, and, as will be seen, motor traffic increased significantly through the 1920s and 1930s without arrivals by rail showing any apparent decline. The cycling craze of the beginning of the century was not sustained, although bicycles accounted for between 15 and 40 per cent of most August traffic surveys undertaken in the Westmorland part of the Lake District in 1926 and 1929. Cyclists probably tended to avoid the main roads, and they accounted for higher proportions of traffic on quieter highways elsewhere in the county, so this evidence probably understates their importance. But much more impressive was the growth of motor transport, with the key transition from horse to car and charabanc taking place within four years after the First World War. August traffic censuses showed further increases in motor vehicle numbers of the order of 60 to 70 per cent between 1928 and 1938, whether we look at the approaches to Windermere, at checkpoints in Grasmere or between Windermere and Keswick, or at the Ullswater area; and tourist journeys would take their full share of this growth. The charabanc or motor bus excursion increased the potential multiplier per vehicle; and all this growth took place alongside sustained rail traffic, some of which was coming from longer distances, especially from Scotland (O'Neill, 2001).

The greater flexibility of road transport affected the tourist trade by decentralising demand, as more farmhouses offered genuinely rural holidays and a taste of the 'simple life' to city dwellers, although some also upgraded their accommodation for more sophisticated tastes. Touring holidays with short stays in individual places developed alongside the earlier pattern of a settled week or fortnight in a hotel or boarding-house. The boarding-house keepers suffered from these changes, and their numbers seem to have declined, although a 'backwash' from the countryside into fallback accommodation in the towns was noted at busy times. The hiking craze of the 1930s made a significant impact, and camping offered cheap and informal accommodation alternatives (for women as well as men), while generating opposition from the established accommodation interests, who complained of unfair competition, environmental damage and unseemly behaviour. From the early 1930s the Youth Hostel Association's incursions into the Lake District were similarly controversial, but the number of bednights spent in Lake District hostels increased sixfold between 1932 and 1938, from 12,000 to just over 72,000. There were also straightforwardly commercial ventures like the conversion of the old Elterwater gunpowder works into a holiday chalet camp in the early 1930s. (See Langdale Estate case study, Chapter Six.) Growth was temporarily interrupted by the depression of the early 1930s, which damaged the hotel trade and left some summer residences standing empty as well as causing problems lower down the scale; but the deflationary trend of the inter-war years ensured that most people's spending power remained resilient. The overall trend was to growth according to an existing model and set of expectations, with a more down-market element whose priorities were nevertheless directed towards the enjoyment of landscape and outdoor pursuits. Commercial entertainment remained at a premium, although local authorities did make efforts to provide outdoor sports facilities and to safeguard and expand public open spaces and footpath provision (O'Neill, 2001).

Thus far, tourism in the Lake District might still be regarded as a collection of trades rather than an industry. It was grafted on alongside agriculture and mining. Many of its seasonal activities were part of mixed family economies. Businesses were generally small and locally run, although some outside investment and management was coming into the larger hotels by the 1930s. Permanent environmental impacts were almost entirely confined to a few substantial houses, some relatively modest extensions of the built-up areas of old market towns, and the presence of railways which had mostly been established primarily with mining and heavy industry, mainly beyond the Lake District itself, in mind. Camping might make an impact on the landscape during July and August, but this was local and temporary. For all its national and international fame, the Lake District remained locked into an early stage of the tourism product cycle. Developments in the second half of the twentieth century began to challenge that cosy situation, and to make a genuine issue out of the sustainability of Lake District tourism (Walton, 2000).

The fiercest pressures were driven by further transport innovations, as the explosion of car ownership from the 1950s onwards made its impact felt. By the mid-1960s, when most of the Lake District's passenger railways had already closed and the Windermere branch line was being downgraded, 70 per cent of Lakeland's staying visitors travelled by car. By 1972 the accepted figure was over 80 per cent. Once in the Lake District, people used their cars to get around, and around 40 per cent of the numerous day and half-day trippers had no specific destination in mind, devoting their outings to driving around the area. Estimates for the mid-1960s had around 23,000 car-borne visitors staying in the Lake District over a mid-August week-end, supplemented by 4,500 week-end visitors, 13,000 day-trippers using cars, and 9,000 half-day excursionists (Countryside Commission, 1969; English Tourist Board, 1973). Numbers of vehicles per day travelling over Dunmail Raise, between Ambleside and Keswick, during the summer months almost doubled between 1935 and 1974 (Marshall and Walton, 1981). Although drivers tended to follow familiar routes on a Windermere-Ambleside-Grasmere-Keswick circuit, with the Langdales as a popular side-trip, improving road and motorway access from outside the area reduced journey times and increased opportunities for exploration beyond this beaten track (Countryside Commission, 1969). All this generated pressure on narrow roads and car parking capacity on an unprecedented scale, and road-widening and straightening activities began to make an impact on landscape character, which had been presaged on a much smaller scale between the wars.

On one estimate the counties of Cumberland and Westmorland (more than just the Lake District, but omitting the part that then lay in Lancashire) could accommodate 66,000 overnight visitors in about 1960, and 668,000 people spent holidays there (Marshall and Walton, 1981). This is probably a generous estimate, but it is far ahead of any conceivable calculation for the 1930s. The profile of the visitors themselves had probably shifted downwards. A survey of 1972 found only 25 per cent from the affluent and firmly middle-class AB groups, 35 per cent from the white-collar C1 level, 29 per cent from 'skilled manual' C2 and 10 per cent from the least-affluent classes D and E. Adults dominated, especially in the 25-44 age-group. And the North of England still supplied most of the visitors, with 62 per cent of this large sample (10,547 people) coming from the North and Scotland, while London and the South-East supplied 14 per cent, and 8 per cent were from overseas (English Tourist Board, 1973). Where there was long-term continuity in the profiles, however, the key point was the considerable increase both in numbers and in environmental impact.

What attracted the visitors was still the 'beautiful scenery' of the region, its 'national and indeed international reputation as a scenic area'. But visitors now took in the panorama through car windscreens and windows, or through activities that kept them close to their vehicles: picnicking, taking short walks, looking at the lakes. According to the 1966 survey of motorists' preferences (Countryside Commission, 1966), 'The demand for these types of landscape-oriented leisure far exceeded any demand for specific forms of recreation such as sailing or swimming.' Here was another long-run continuity, and one that was calculated to ensure that a degree of landscape protection remained high on the agenda of the post-war National Park and tourist authorities. But this was qualified by the list of visitor priorities recorded in 1972. Driving around appealed to 70 per cent, sightseeing in towns and villages 58 per cent, shopping for presents and souvenirs 52 per cent, and visiting a pub 47 per cent. These were the leading preferences (English Tourist Board, 1973; Countryside Commission, 1969). Here was tourism on a more 'industrial' scale, and this evidence put the search for Wordsworthian solitude and solemn contemplation in its place: the landscape was a pretty accompaniment to more conventional holiday activities, rather than, for most people, an awe-inspiring end in itself. The Lake District had become more playground than literary landscape or place in which to communicate with Nature and Nature's God; and acceptance of this was itself an inducement to give convenience and comfort as high a priority as preservation and protection. These tensions will be developed further in the sections that follow.

The Challenges to Sustainability

The reader has seen that the cultural formulation of the Lake District as a place of natural wonder and delight originated in the new appreciation of mountain scenery created by the Picturesque movement of the eighteenth century. The region was thus transformed in public perceptions into a place of great physical beauty, rural simplicity and tranquillity, and these features have largely formed the basis of the Lakeland holiday trade to this day. The Lakeland tourist industry rests, however, on a fundamental paradox. As in all areas of natural beauty, the problems associated with the continued development of tourism – the increased crowds, the need for improved communications, the resultant noise and pollution – can compromise the natural attractions and serenity on which it depends. Over the years, this pressure has been compounded in the Lake District by the demands of other industries to exploit its natural resources and, in the twentieth century, by the efforts of government agencies to 'modernise' the region. From the very beginning, therefore, there has been a variety of challenges to the sustainability of tourism, as economic and commercial imperatives, some intrinsic to the industry itself, others extrinsic, have threatened the fragile landscape and atmosphere of the district, although ruling definitions of the intolerable have also been steadily relaxed over the years. Not surprisingly, in an area that increasingly came to be viewed as a hallowed landscape, these pressures have generated a preservationist movement that has maintained complex and at times uneasy relations with members of the tourist industry.

The Picturesque period, the earliest period of tourism, exhibited some of these tensions. Many books that extolled the pleasures of the Lake District at the time also contained worries about some of the consequences of its 'discovery'. Writers such as Hutchinson, Gilpin, and Budworth fretted over the arrival of the wrong type of travellers, who flew from viewing station to station and from lake to lake with no appreciation of the finer points of the Picturesque (Andrews, 1989; Ousby, 1990). Gilpin, the great advocate of the Picturesque, also expressed his alarm that the Lakes were becoming 'the resort of gay company', the members of which were contaminating the 'simple people' of the locality by their taste for 'extravagance and dissipation' (Ousby, 1990). A particular focus of this concern for some, although not all, observers was the construction of what they regarded as unsuitable houses and grounds that threatened the integrity of a number of the stations and Picturesque sights. Joseph English's development of Belle Isle on Windermere (particularly his cabbage garden) engendered severe criticism, as did the melange of measures taken by Joseph Pocklington on the Derwentwater island he purchased in 1778. Pocklington's remodelling of the island through the construction of a house, a druid's circle and stone, a mock church and a fort persuaded influential voices of his lack of taste. Similar disquiet existed over his pioneering attempts to enhance the Lake District's portfolio of attractions through the provision of a mock hermitage and a druid's stone by the Bowder Stone (Ousby, 1990; Nicholson, 1955). These eighteenth-century extravagances were matched in the nineteenth century by the appearance of grand Gothic villas, as the district developed into a retirement and second home centre for the wealthy. Although Wordsworth fulminated against their incongruity with the landscape, it should be stated that, by the mid-nineteenth century, these monuments of bourgeois taste met with the approval of many of the guidebooks (Marshall and Walton, 1981).

The range and potency of the challenges to the Lakeland tourist industry increased as it developed through the nineteenth century. Much of this development, as we have seen, depended on the arrival of the railways, which encouraged the creation of other appendages of the industry such as the Lakes' steamers. Yet the relationship between the railways and the tourist industry was complex; a situation which again stemmed from the industry's reliance on the natural beauty of the area. The physical appearance and the noise and smell of the railways meant that many considered them to be an unsuitable form of transport in the inner sanctums of Lakeland. Thus although the mid-Victorian lines to Windermere, Coniston and Lakeside, and the route from the main line at Penrith to Cockermouth through Keswick, provided the access on which the holiday industry depended, proposals to build further lines that would press into the mountain fastness often met with fierce resistance.

Wordsworth first expressed the fear that railway incursions into the heart of Lakeland would do irreparable damage to its 'beauty and character of retirement' when he directed angry sonnets against any extension of the proposed Kendal and Windermere line to Ambleside and on to Keswick in the 1840s (Bicknell, 1991; Westall, 1991). By the late nineteenth century, there existed a substantial groundswell of opinion, influenced by Wordsworth's writings, which conceptualised the Lake District as a hallowed landscape. Attempts to achieve the extension feared by Wordsworth, and to build mineral lines elsewhere, thus foundered in the face of intense opposition (and, more importantly, on shaky economic prospects) in the mid-1870s, in 1883 and 1887, and again in the early 1920s. On all these occasions the protesters, whilst drawing out the moral need to avoid desecration of the landscape, laid much emphasis on the harm that it could do to the existing tourist industry, especially when accompanied by the expansion of mining and quarrying that would be necessary to generate lucrative twelve-month traffic (Marshall and Walton, 1981; O'Neill, 2001). The proposals in 1883 for new lines in Borrowdale (for slate quarrying) and Ennerdale (for iron ore) aroused particular wrath. Tourism could normally coexist with mining and quarrying, helped by the demise of the Coniston copper mines in the 1880s. When conducted on a limited scale these were unobtrusive and even interesting activities, with beetling quarry walls coming within the awe-inspiring canon of the 'sublime', although the Greenside mine above Ullswater came under increasing attack. By the same token, current pastoral agricultural practices were essential to the maintenance of the treasured landscapes, and tourism provided local markets that helped to prevent potentially damaging depopulation. But the proposals of 1883 threatened to transform the scale of extractive industry, and their promoters were damned as greedy, heartless speculators, bringing in the 'steam dragon of Honister' to ravish the virtuous damsel that was 'unspoilt' Lakeland. Cast as villains, faced with heavy parliamentary costs, and unable to counter these arguments on their own terms, the promoters of the railways withdrew their enabling bills (Marshall and Walton, 1981; Westall, 1991).

The campaigns to keep the heart of Lakeland free from railways were notable successes of the preservationist movement that grew up to defend Lakeland in the later nineteenth century, and which has continued in various guises to the present day. It developed such a reputation for power that the mountain railway schemes that came to the fore in Snowdonia and on the Isle of Man became almost unthinkable here. Whether it could have stood up to a determined assault by a major railway company remains open to question, however, and this movement has a less distinguished record in its attempts to prevent the use of the lakes as reservoirs. Notwithstanding energetic and sophisticated campaigns that again underlined the dangers to scenic beauty and the knock-on effects for the tourist industry, the preservationist movement has failed to prevent Manchester City Council from extracting water from major lakes in the district on a number of occasions. The first defeat occurred in the 1870s with the commencement of construction of a reservoir at Thirlmere, one of the prettiest lakes, where Manchester did not help its case by arguing that its landscaping works would actually improve the appearance of the area. The premium set on 'natural' beauty was so strong that this was greeted with derision (Marshall and Walton, 1981). This was followed in the inter-war years by development of a reservoir at Haweswater. In the 1960s, Manchester was eventually successful in securing parliamentary permission to extract from Ullswater, although the associated edifices were less obtrusive in this instance (Berry and Beard, 1980; Sheail, 2002). Other bodies have also looked to the Lakes for water supply. Barrow's attempt to extract water from the River Duddon in 1889 was foiled, but the towns of Workington and Whitehaven began extraction from Ennerdale and other western lakes in the nineteenth century. In the 1940s, Whitehaven town council received permission to re-embank and raise the level of Ennerdale. A subsequent delay led in the 1970s to this proposal being subsumed in the North West Water Authority's scheme both to raise the latter lake and to extract water from Wastwater. After a long and complex public hearing, these proposals were defeated as a result of opposition from both the Lake District Special Planning Board and various environmental organisations (Berry and Beard, 1980; Berry, 1982).

Other threats to the physical appearance of Lakeland in the twentieth century have stemmed from national government agencies. The Forestry Commission's policy after the First World War to acquire land in the district for conifer plantations provides a classic example. Plantations in Ennerdale and the Whinlatter Pass had raised initial alarm in preservationist circles. The Commission's acquisition of the Hardknott estate in Eskdale in 1934 prompted a determination amongst the leading societies to protect prominent hillsides in the district from the dark, geometrical blocks of planting favoured by the Commission, safeguarding the open, empty fells that characterised the treasured landscape. Despite some disagreements over tactics during protracted negotiations, the societies, which included the Council for the Preservation of Rural England, the National Trust and the Friends of the Lake District, eventually came to a compromise with the Forestry Commission in 1936. This involved the designation of 300 square miles in central Lakeland that would remain free from planting, with voluntary consultation procedures operating elsewhere. Since 1936, however, the development and management of woodlands outside the central area have remained a source of occasional conflict between the amenity societies, the National Park organisations and the Forestry Commission. What is notable here is the amenity societies' attachment to a particular landscape aesthetic that ruled out afforestation that might have been attractive to others, or in other locations (Sheail, 2002; Berry and Beard, 1980; Sandbach in Kain, 1981).

The introduction of electricity to the Lake District engendered a similar furore over the placement of pylons in the area. Plans published by the newly formed Central Electricity Board (CEB) in 1928 made it clear that the construction of the National Grid offered potential challenges to the integrity of the Lakeland landscape. To the preservationist societies the prospect of electricity pylons stretching across the area was deeply unattractive. They were quick both to point out the intrusive nature of the pylons in a place of natural beauty, and to remind the representatives of the tourist industry that such ugly contraptions were unlikely to captivate the educated visitor. The first dispute, centred around Keswick, erupted in 1929. The proposed line from Penrith to Cockermouth threatened to site pylons in the vicinity of the town. This provoked the creation of a local Anti-Pylons Committee, which included some of the major hotel-owners and landowners in the area. The committee emphasised the danger pylons represented to the local tourist industry and argued that in an area of such exquisite scenery the CEB had a moral duty to place the cables underground. Unhappy with the costs of this arrangement, however, the CEB began a long tactical battle over the issue that eventually drew in most of the preservationist societies concerned with the Lake District. The dispute became a national *cause célebre*, for it seemed to some to symbolise the defence of the aesthetics of the countryside against the more pragmatic imperatives of a modern, technological age. To *Country Life* it was 'the first trial of the legal claims of Old England versus the New'. After a series of manoeuvres and failed negotiations, however, the CEB eventually gave up the proposed line, citing problems of costs, while the preservationist groupings claimed victory (Luckin, 1990).

The Lake District was to host further disputes over electricity supply, however. The 1930s saw controversies about a proposed line from Kendal to Windermere and a line that was to serve Borrowdale and the Honister quarries. The preservationist societies managed to get part of the former line placed underground and the other section re-routed so that the pylons did not deface Scout Scar. A sustained publicity campaign also managed to delay the construction of an overhead line on 30-foot wooden poles in Borrowdale, and in 1939 the Electricity Commissioners ruled out the line on economic grounds. The post-war years saw continuing skirmishes, as the North-West Electricity Board modernised provision in the district. Arguments erupted over lines in Borrowdale, Patterdale, Martindale, Langdale and other Lakeland valleys. The preservationist societies maintained their preference for underground lines but this objective proved difficult to sustain in all cases. The picture since the war therefore has been a mixed one, with some lines placed underground but some carried on discreetly screened poles (O'Neill 2001; Berry and Beard, 1980).

In terms of sustainable tourism in Lakeland, the development of road transport has been a particularly thorny problem since the late nineteenth century. The car, the motor coach and the caravan have boosted the Lakeland holiday trade considerably, and thus they have always found their supporters in the region. What might be termed the mixed blessings of the car, however, have often raised preservationist hackles in an area renowned for repose and unblemished countryside. A range of complaints about the impact of motor transport emerged in the early twentieth century, including noise, dust, congestion in the resorts and instances of tar from roads seeping into the water courses and lakes. A further concern centred on the suitability of the larger motor coaches for the winding country roads of the district. In the 1920s, Westmorland County Council and other local government bodies sought to ban such vehicles from these roads. Worries about how to accommodate the impact of the motor vehicle have continued to exercise the minds of those concerned with protecting the Lake District to this day, of course. The remarkable growth in car and caravan ownership since the Second World War has placed intolerable congestion pressures on the region's honeypot sites, while generating anxieties about the landscape impact of car and caravan parks (O'Neill, 2001; Berry and Beard, 1980).

A related issue was that of road improvement. For some connected to the tourist industry, improved roads offered greater access and more widespread enjoyment of the pleasures of the district. For many preservationists, these improvements clashed with the character of the area and, by imposing straight lines and sterility on a fecund and intricate countryside, posed a threat to the main tourist asset. Proposals to open up the Lake District by improved road provision often found the proponents of these views at loggerheads. The first major scheme of this kind originated in the late nineteenth century when John Musgrave, an industrialist and landowner from Whitehaven, launched an unsuccessful attempt to persuade Cumberland County Council to build a new road over Sty Head Pass. The road, which promised access to Wasdale and the placement of new hotels in the valley, also offered quicker communication between Keswick and West Cumberland. These benefits ensured considerable local support but they also offended preservationist opinion, for the road threatened the solitude of perhaps the most secluded of the Lakeland dales. A boisterous campaign against the road judiciously warned of the threat of competition to existing hotel interests in the Keswick area, but (continuing an established theme) the scheme really foundered on the refusal of the County Council to countenance the costs involved (Marshall and Walton, 1981).

In spite of this reversal, dreams of improving the Lakeland passes continued to flourish in the twentieth century. The Musgrave family resuscitated the Sty Head Pass scheme in 1919 but again failed to convince the County Council that its benefits outweighed its costs. In the 1920s there followed two attempts to develop a road over Hardknott and Wrynose Passes, which engendered the usual propaganda barrages from both developers and preservationists. An apologist for the schemes argued that 'accessibility is the keynote of success in places of health and pleasure'. Opponents raised the spectre of the unsuitable effects of unbridled tourist development by picturing a Lake District with 'a vast system of boarding houses, after the style of some seaside resorts'. Whatever the impact of these wars of words, both proposals failed to secure the necessary interest from the County Council (O'Neill, 2001).

Much to the chagrin of the preservationist groups, this state of affairs only lasted until the 1930s, when Cumberland County Council put forward a scheme to develop a number of the passes in order to alleviate unemployment in West Cumberland. In 1934, the Council submitted plans and requests for government funding to the Special Area Commissioner to improve Styhead, Wrynose and Hardknott, Honister Hause, and two roads in the Duddon Bridge area. The bid, though, proved unsuccessful and only the Honister road came to fruition, paid for from the County Council's own funds. The Honister development, and insensitive work on widening and straightening the A591 from Keswick to Dunmail Raise, prompted the Friends of the Lake District to issue in 1939 its pamphlet, *A Road Policy for the Lake District*. In a carefully composed argument, the society recognised the need to improve access roads to Lakeland but sought to protect the character of roads internal to the district. This pamphlet became the basis of preservationist policy well into the period of the National Park. The 1960s, however, saw this policy confounded through the development of the A66 from West Cumberland to Penrith. Twenty-three miles of this road lay within the confines of the National Park, and many of these were composed of dual carriageway. Despite an enormous campaign against it, the government pressed ahead with the road in the early 1970s, largely to provide better transport links for the industries of West Cumberland. The creation of the A66 was a major defeat for the preservationist movement, but it has also had post-war successes in preventing unsuitable road improvements. In the 1970s, for instance, effective campaigns were maintained against proposals for a Barrow – Arnside link through the south of the region, and against a proposed bypass for Ambleside (O'Neill, 2001; Berry and Beard, 1980).

Road transport has thus played an ambivalent role in the development of Lake District tourism. It has underpinned the expansion of the industry in various ways and yet has been seen to threaten the 'natural' environment that is so critical to the district's attraction in the eyes of preservationists. Similar ambivalence can be found in other tourist activities that have developed over the years, particularly those that might be termed the playthings of the affluent. The lakes, particularly Derwentwater and Windermere, offer various examples of this trend. An early instance was the 'hydro-aeroplane' controversy, which divided the community in Windermere before the First World War. This conflict ranged the wealthier residents and larger hoteliers, who opposed the operation of seaplane rides from the lake, against the tradesmen, shopkeepers and other small businessmen that made up the majority of the Urban District Council (UDC), who saw the initiative as a boost for tourism. Unfortunately for the latter interest, the enterprise proved short-lived, as did another attempt just after the First World War (Walton in Westall, 1991; O'Neill, 2001).

The noise and speed of motor boats have also proved an enduring source of irritation to those worried about the lakes' reputation for repose. Recent conflicts over speed limits on Windermere have their echoes in the inter-war years, when the lake was the venue for various forms of power-boat racing. The early appearance of private motor boats and the craze for water skiing in the early 1920s provoked little concern in the resort. The use of the lake for an international power boat competition in 1926, however, was the catalyst for a disagreement that demonstrated once again contrasting perceptions about the nature of the tourist trade and the social divisions that could underpin these. A petition presented to the UDC against the power boats objected to 'the breach of guardianship' of the lake for 'sordid commercial reasons'. It contained the names of one hundred and fifty, mainly wealthy, residents and fifty non-residents, ostensibly to demonstrate the concern of the visiting public. The petition provoked furious responses from representatives of the tourist trade, who resented the interference of wealthy 'offcomers' and argued that visitors to Windermere needed to be entertained. The UDC seemed to back this judgement when they allowed various other events on the lake, including Henry Seagrave's fatal attempt on the world water speed record. But other actions by the UDC showed that its members also recognised the appeal of the serenity of the lake to many visitors. In order to reconcile the demands of sail and motor engines on the lake, the UDC in 1927 gained government permission to extend the area of the existing six miles per hour speed limit (O'Neill, 1994).

To the annoyance of the amenity societies the lakes remained the occasional focus of world water speed records, mainly through the efforts of the Campbell family. By the post-war years, moreover, the lakes were under more consistent pressure from the motor boats of more ordinary visitors. The car by this period guaranteed both readier access to Lakeland and the means by which to transport the motorboats and water skis that appeared on more and more of the district's waters. The Lake District Planning Board's concern over this situation prompted them to prohibit the use of motorised craft on 20 lakes and tarns in 1975. They also succeeded in 1978 in limiting the speed of such craft on Derwentwater, Ullswater and Coniston to ten miles per hour, so effectively banishing them from the three lakes. This did not end the matter, of course, and plans for similar speed restrictions on Windermere ensured that it remained a live issue at the turn of the millennium.

It was not just the lakes themselves that felt the impact of the leisure choices of a more affluent post-war society. The huge increase in the numbers involved in rambling and fell walking led to serious erosion of footpaths on the fells, a tendency accentuated by the development in the last decade or so of trail biking as a pastime. Such damage to the pristine landscape was particularly significant given the high expectations about 'unspoilt' beauty that prevailed. This situation prompted the National Park authorities to repair trails and footpaths through active schemes of upland management. Another dimension of this more affluent, leisure-oriented society was the proliferation of second home ownership, a trend with considerable impact on the character of communities and population decline in the district. Finally, mass car ownership has led to an explosion of day trips and picnicking that has brought problems of litter and the need to provide car parks and picnic sites to accommodate the demand (Berry and Beard, 1980).

Constraints on disruption

It can be seen that the multiplicity of demands on the Lake District countryside over the years has posed challenges to the concept of a sustainable tourism industry, especially given the high expectations attending this concept in a Lakeland setting. But several factors intrinsic to the historical development of Lakeland have served to limit the impact of these challenges. The fact that until the Second World War and after, the Lake District was primarily a relatively small-scale tourist destination catering primarily for more affluent holidaymakers has left the area comparatively free of the obvious environmental impact of concrete and suburban sprawl found in some of the seaside centres. Furthermore, most of these holidaymakers possessed the cultural capital that predisposed them to respect the district's aesthetic associations and treat the countryside in respectful fashion. This was true not only of members of university reading groups or of the middle-class walking clubs that tramped the fells in the early twentieth century, but also of many of the working-class visitors to Lakeland. Typical of this latter grouping were the clientele, often drawn from church groups, of organisations such as the Co-operative Holidays Association, whose activities are so evocatively described in T. A. Leonard's memoirs, or the Holiday Fellowship (Leonard, 1934).

The geographical configuration of the holiday industry has also alleviated the cumulative impact of the tourist hordes on the region's environment. Although the authors have commented on the expansion of the tourist trade into the dales through the farmhouse holiday and the all-encompassing reach of the motor car, it remains the case that throughout the period the great majority of visitors have tended to stay at the established towns, the old railheads and the most famous lakes. This was true even of those who came mainly to appreciate the scenery, as well as those whose ambitions lay more in fun and frolics on the lakes. This concentration of the visiting public, whilst creating its own problems of congestion, has reduced the pressure on other parts of the district, which are still relatively free of the noise and bustle of the crowd. Even the growth of camping and caravanning has made only minor changes to this overall picture.

It has been demonstrated that the character of tourist provision in the Lakeland resorts has mostly avoided the forms of artificial amusement that would compromise the region's place-image. True, the conceptual tension between Lakeland as an adventure playground and as a base for contemplation and serenity has occasionally led to conflict over suitable use of the landscape in the twentieth century; but most of the visitors to Lakeland have felt no need to experience the more hedonistic pleasures normally available at the seaside resorts. Entrepreneurs and municipal notables have therefore concentrated on exploitation of the natural attractions of the district, recognising not only that there was little demand for the funfair or the amusement arcade but also that such diversions would alienate the traditional market. An apt illustration of this occurred in Windermere in the 1920s, when, in response to a newspaper enquiry, local businessmen and civic leaders agreed that the resort was different from Blackpool because 'amusements and beauty of surroundings are not compatible' (O'Neill, 2001).

The prevailing model of tourism in the Lake District thus depended on the preservation of the landscape. This interconnection has been a major force both in containing the challenges to the holiday industry and in curbing unsuitable excesses within the industry itself. Resistance to inappropriate industrial and commercial development, for instance, started in the mid-nineteenth century and quickly developed institutional momentum. The Lake District Defence Society, founded at the insistence of Canon Hardwicke Rawnsley, the 'watchdog of the Lakes', in 1883 when it became apparent that the problems posed by the railway proposals of that year were going to keep recurring, and recruiting especially from members of the Wordsworth Society and from academics and public school teachers, was the first permanent organisation of this sort. Rawnsley, along with Octavia Hill and Sir Robert Hunter, was also a founder of the National Trust in 1895, and its policy of buying up land to protect it from development was applied in the Lake District from the turn of the century, although it did not gather momentum here until the inter-war and especially the post-war years (Marshall and Walton, 1981; Battrick, 1987; Murphy, 1987). It is important, however, to recognise the organisational and campaigning blueprints that these organisations drew up. Both bodies had a large leavening of wealthy and well-connected members, who were able to use their connections in parliament and the media to mount sustained campaigns against threats to cherished aspects of Lakeland. Their twentieth-century counterparts used similar tactics to further the 'defence of Lakeland' in the twentieth century.

The National Trust went on to great success in the twentieth century, but the LDDS had faded by 1914. In the inter-war years, however, a raft of organisations joined the Trust in campaigning for Lakeland. In 1919 Canon Rawnsley oversaw the foundation of the Society for Safeguarding the Natural Beauty of the Lake District (SSNBLD), a society composed of local property owners. The mid-1920s saw the formation of the Council for the Preservation of Rural England (CPRE), a national organisation which quickly became engaged in the various struggles that developed over Lakeland in this period. Finally, in 1934, a number of leading preservationists, dissatisfied with progress in defending the region, formed the Friends of the Lake District (FLD) with the express aim of gaining National Park status on a highly interventionist model. These organisations had their similarities but also their tactical differences, despite the fact that their membership often overlapped. All four organisations had wealthy and influential members, and all sought to use these connections to influence the government over issues such as afforestation and electricity in the Lake District. But their differences were apparent and sometimes caused conflict.

The National Trust, for instance, preferred its own method of purchasing land in the region as the best way of preserving the landscape. But this method attracted some criticism from leading preservationists, convinced of the need to concentrate on more active campaigning for a National Park. The CPRE and the SSNBLD were conservative organisations, happier with persuasion and behind-the-scenes compromises than the more thrusting FLD. This latter organisation believed in more radical action to pressurise the government of the day into proactive intervention in the Lake District. It disagreed strongly with the CPRE concerning the management of a number of Lake District disputes. It consistently mounted a more rigorous opposition to the variety of electricity-related threats to the district's landscape. The FLD also pursued a distinctive path during the afforestation controversy, seeking to use public opinion and petitioning to outmanoeuvre the Forestry Commission, whilst the CPRE preferred the route of a negotiated compromise. Characteristically, a Joint Informal Committee of the CPRE and Forestry Commission published compromise agreements on Lake District afforestation in 1936 and again in 1955 (Symonds, 1936; Joint Informal Committee, 1936 and 1955). Not surprisingly, the CPRE leadership preferred at the time to deal with the representatives of the SSNBLD, renamed the Lake District Safeguarding Society in the 1930s (Sandbach, 1981; O'Neill, 2001). Since World War Two better relations have existed between the amenity groups, and the FLD has become the driving force behind campaigns to protect and preserve the Lake District.

These differences in opinion and tactics should not blind us to the shared values that bound together the amenity organisations. Together they presented powerful moral and economic arguments for the preservation of the Lake District as a hallowed landscape, a jewel in England's crown. In the twentieth century, they were able gradually to integrate these sentiments into dominant cultural discourses. The inter-war period witnessed an efflorescence of literature designed to warn the British people of the existence of a multitude of environmental threats. *England and the Octopus* and *Britain and the Beast*, the first written and the second edited by Clough Williams Ellis, are perhaps the most famous of this oeuvre. The latter book contains a hard-hitting chapter by Kenneth Spence, a prime mover behind the formation of the FLD, which catalogued some of the pressures facing the Lake District. *The Times* during this period also contained frequent articles detailing the extent of these challenges to the countryside, many of which focused on the problems of the Lakes (O'Neill, 2001; Matless, 1998). In the post-war years, environmental and ecological ideologies have been more systematically propounded, although British governments, both Tory and Labour, have been slow to accommodate (or at least act upon) such arguments.

The increasing acceptability of environmental arguments over the course of the twentieth century has allowed the amenity societies to shame and rebuke potential developers who have transgressed the codes of conduct set for the Lake District by the preservationist interest. In dispute after dispute, it is possible to see the party of development, so to speak, having to come to terms with the enduring images of beauty and fragility associated with the area. Powerful organisations such as the Central Electricity Board and the Forestry Commission have had to compromise their original plans in the light of criticism of their insensitivity to the environment. Similarly, the company that operated the Greenside lead mine at Glenridding had to fight a long propaganda battle with the FLD from the 1930s to the 1960s over the milky effluent that ran into Ullswater down the local beck. In 1981, the Secretary of State for the Environment, Michael Heseltine, put forward 'damage to amenity' as the reason for his refusal to sanction the North West Water Authority's proposals for water extraction from Ennerdale Water and Wastwater (O'Neill, 2001; Berry, 1982).

A central feature of preservationist arguments before World War Two was the need for the Lake District to be given National Park status. The creation of such an entity would allow the development of the area to be planned as a whole. The economic uncertainties of the 1930s prevented the implementation of the Addison Committee's (1931) proposals for National Reserves, but the post-war Labour government finally granted the wishes of the amenity societies in 1951. The realities of the National Park authority in some ways disappointed the societies, for it was not given quite the power or levels of funding that they had hoped for. Nevertheless, it was still a significant initiative, introducing tighter environmental controls before the explosion of numbers and accompanying pressures that marked the tourism industry from the 1950s onwards. Since its inception, it has played a major part in curbing excessive development in the Lake District, whilst seeking to reconcile the demands of tourism, preservation and industry (Cherry and Rogers, 1996; O'Neill, 2001; Berry and Beard, 1980).

The National Park Authority's conception of its role of 'guardianship of the Lake District' has increased in sophistication over the years. The present-day authority maintains its familiar functions of planning and countryside management but its staffing base now includes ecologists, archaeologists, landscape officers, and forestry and estate teams in order to execute fully these functions in the early twenty-first century. One consequence of this has been a transformation in perceptions of the status of the remains of mining, quarrying and other industrial ventures in the district. The archaeological service of the Authority has preserved and interpreted a number of these features, such as the mine workings at Honister Hause, seeing them as integral parts of the area's history. A number of these sites are open to the public and thus the industrial past is now part of the portfolio of tourist attractions in modern-day Lakeland. This, of course, is a typical development of post-modern tourism, whereby the working practices of yesteryear become the leisure spectacles of today.

Sustainability?

This last point illustrates one of the ways in which ideas about what needs to be 'sustained' in the Lake District have changed over the period covered by this chapter. The desire to protect 'pristine' landscape (albeit recognised as a human creation in its present form, and associated with an idealised rural society) remains, and attachment to it has helped to place limits on the challenges posed by the rise of new levels and kinds of tourist demand, while the nature of the tourist trade and its perceived interests has also militated in favour of preserving the status quo as far as possible. But such interests and preferences have had to accommodate themselves to changing visitor needs and pressures, without sacrificing the core 'place-myth' around which the Lake District's international reputation has been constructed, and while accommodating the new attractiveness of 'industrial archaeology', especially (and perhaps ironically) preserved railways, mines and quarries. It should be clear from this historical introduction, however, that definitions of 'sustainability' and of what is to be 'sustained', with or without these explicit labels, have changed over time and varied between constituencies; and the resulting and continuing conflicts, in their current forms, will make up much of the meat, and the spice, of what follows.

References

Allen, R. with Linney, P. (1995) *Walking the Ridges of Lakeland according to Wainwright's Pictorial Guide Books Vols. 1-3*. London: Michael Joseph.

Andrews, M. (1989) *The Search for the Picturesque*. Stanford: Stanford University Press.

Bate, J. (1991) *Romantic Ecology. Wordsworth and the Environmental Tradition*. London: Routledge.

Battrick, E. (1987) *Guardian of the Lakes: a History of the National Trust in the Lake District from 1946*. Kendal: Westmorland Gazette.

Berry, G. (1982) *A Tale of Two Lakes*. Kendal: Friends of the Lake District.

Berry, G. and Beard, G. (1980) *The Lake District: a Century of Conservation*. Edinburgh: Bartholomew.

Bicknell, P. (ed.) (1990) *The Picturesque Scenery of the Lake District, 1752-1855: a bibliographical study*. Winchester: St Paul's Bibliographies.

Bicknell, P. (ed.) (1991) *The Illustrated Wordsworth's Guide to the Lakes*. London: Select Editions.

Bracey, H. E. (1970) *People and the Countryside*. London: Routledge.

Bragg, M. (1991) *The Maid of Buttermere*. London: Hodder and Stoughton.

Brennan, M. (1987) *Wordsworth, Turner and Romantic Landscape*. Columbia: University Press of South Carolina.

Brunton, J. (2001) *The Arts and Crafts Movement in the Lake District*. Lancaster: Centre for North-West Regional Studies.

Buzard, J. (1983) *The Beaten Track: European Tourism, Literature and the Ways to 'Culture', 1800-1918*. Oxford: Clarendon Press.

Capstick, M. (1972) *Some Aspects of the Economic Effects of Tourism in the Westmorland Cultural History of the British Experience, 1600-2000*. Basingstoke: Palgrave.

Cherry, G. E., and Rogers, A. (1996) *Rural Change and Planning*. London: Spon.

Collingwood, W. G. (1925) *Lake District History*. Kendal: Titus Wilson.

Corbin, A. (1994) *The Lure of the Sea.* Cambridge: Polity.

Countryside Commission and British Tourist Authority (1969) *Pleasure Traffic and Recreation in the Lake District.* (typescript report, 1969, in Lancaster University Library).

Dade-Robertson, C. (2000) *Furness Abbey: History, Romance and Culture.* Lancaster: Centre for North-West Regional Studies.

English Tourist Board (1973) *The Marketing and Development of Tourism in the English Lakes Counties.* London: P. A. Management Consultants Ltd.

Gilpin, Rev. W. (1996 edn.) *Observations, Relative Chiefly to Picturesque Beauty, Made in the year 1772 on Several Parts of England, Particularly the Mountains and Lakes of Cumberland and Westmorland.* Poole: Woodstock Books.

Griffin, A. H. (2000) *The Coniston Tigers: seventy years of mountain adventure.* Wilmslow: Sigma Leisure.

Hankinson, A. (1988) *A Century on the Crags.* London: Dent.

Hanley, K., and Milbank, A. (1992) *From Lancaster to the Lakes – the Region in Literature.* Lancaster: Centre for North-West Regional Studies.

Herbert, I. Lake District bid for heritage status is at risk. *The Independent,* 29 March 2001.

Jackson, H. and Jackson, M. (1980) *Lakeland's Pioneer Rock-Climbers.* Clapham, North Yorkshire: Dalesman.

Joint Informal Committee of the Forestry Commission and Council for the Preservation of Rural England (1936 and 1955) *Agreements on Afforestation in the Lake District.* London.

Kelly, S. F. (1991) *Victorian Lakeland in Old Photographs.* Shrewsbury: Swan Hill Press.

Kendall-Price, C. (1993) *In the Footsteps of the Swallows and Amazons.* York: Wild Cat.

Knowle, A. and Beech, G. (2001) *The Bluebird Years: Donald Campbell and the Pursuit of Speed.* Wilmslow: Sigma Leisure.

Leonard, T. A. (1934) *Adventures in Holiday Making.* London: Holiday Fellowship.

Luckin, W. (1990) *Questions of Power: Electricity and Environment in Inter-War Britain.* Bristol: Adam Hilger.

McCracken, D. (1984) *Wordsworth and the Lake District: a guide to the poems and their places.* Oxford: Oxford University Press.

Marshall, J. D. (1971) *Old Lakeland.* Newton Abbot: David and Charles.

Marshall, J. D. (1972) "Statesmen" in Cumbria: the Vicissitudes of an Expression. *Transactions of the Cumberland and Westmorland Antiquarian and Archaeological Society* 72, 248-73.

Marshall, J. D., and Walton, J. K. (1981) *The Lake Counties from 1830 to the Mid-Twentieth Century.* Manchester: Manchester University Press.

Martineau, H. (1855) *Guide to the English Lakes.* Windermere and London.

Matless, D. (1998) *Landscape and Englishness.* London: Reaktion.

Mitchell, W. R. (1984) *Wordsworth's Lake District.* Clapham, North Yorkshire: Dalesman.

Murphy, G. (1987) *Founders of the National Trust.* London: Croom Helm.

Nicholson, N. (1955) *The Lakers.* London: Robert Hale.

O'Neill, C. (1994) The Windermere tourist trade in the 1920s. *Local Historian* 24, 217-24.

O'Neill, C. (2000) Visions of Lakeland: Tourism, Preservation and the Development of the Lake District, 1919-1939. Ph.D. thesis, University of Lancaster.

Ousby, I. (1990) *The Englishman's England: Travel, Taste and the Rise of Tourism.* Cambridge: Cambridge University Press.

Ranlett, J. (1983) "Checking Nature's desecration": late-Victorian environmental organization. *Victorian Studies* 26, 198-222.

Ritzer, G. (1998) *The McDonaldization thesis: explorations and extensions.* London: Sage.

Roberts, W. (ed.), *Thomas Gray's Visit to the Lake District in October 1769.* Liverpool: Liverpool University Press.

Rollinson, W. (1981) *Life and Tradition in the Lake District.* Clapham, North Yorkshire: Dalesman.

Sandbach, F. (1981) The early campaign for a national park in the Lake District. In Kain, R. (ed.) *Planning and Conservation.* London: Mansell.

Sheail, J. (2002) *An Environmental History of Twentieth-Century Britain.* Basingstoke: Palgrave.

Shields, R. (1991) *Places on the Margin.* London: Routledge.

Simmons, J. (1985) *The Railway in Town and Country 1830-1914.* Newton Abbot: David and Charles.

Squire, S. J. (1985) Wordsworth and Lake District Tourism: Romantic Reshaping of Landscape. *Canadian Geographer* 32, 237-247.

Symonds, H. H. (1936) *Afforestation in the Lake District.* London: Dent.

Taylor, H. (1997) *A Claim on the Countryside.* Edinburgh: Keele University Press.

Urry, J. (1990) *The Tourist Gaze.* London: Sage.

Urry, J. (1995) *Consuming Places.* London: Routledge.

Victoria and Albert Museum (1984) *The Discovery of the Lake District.* London: Victoria and Albert Museum, exhibition catalogue.

Walton, J. K. (1983) *The English Seaside Resort: a Social History, 1750-1914.* Leicester: Leicester University Press.

Walton, J. K. (1998) Canon Rawnsley and the English Lake District. *Armitt Library Journal* 1, 1-18.

Walton, J. K. (2000) *The British Seaside: Holidays and Resorts in the Twentieth Century.* Manchester: Manchester University Press.

Walton, J. K. (2002) British Tourism between Industrialization and Globalization: an Overview. In Berghoff, H., *et al.* (eds.) *The Making of Modern Tourism.* Basingstoke: Palgrave.

Walton, J. K. and McGloin, P. R. (1981) The Tourist Trade in Victorian Lakeland. *Northern History* 17, 153-82.

Walton, J. K., and O'Neill, C. Numbering the Holidaymakers: the Problems and Possibilities of the June Census of 1921 for Historians of Resorts. *Local Historian* 23, 205-17.

Walton, J. K., and Wilcox, A. (eds.) (1991) *Low life and moral improvement in mid-Victorian England* .Leicester: Leicester University Press.

Wardale, R. (1986) *Arthur Ransome's Lakeland: a quest for the real Swallows and Amazons Country.* Clapham, North Yorkshire: Dalesman.

Welberry, K. (2000) "The Playground of England": A Genealogy of the English Lakes from Nursery to National Park, 1753-1951: Ph.D. thesis, La Trobe University, Melbourne.

Westall, O. M. (ed.) (1991) *Windermere in the Nineteenth Century.* Lancaster: Centre for North-West Regional Studies.

Wheeler, M. (ed.) (1995) *Ruskin and Environment.* Manchester: Manchester University Press.

Whyte, I. (1998) Wordsworth's *Guide to the Lakes* and the Geographical Tradition. *Armitt Library Journal* 1, 18-37.

Winchester, A. J. L. (1998) Wordsworth's "Pure Commonwealth"? Yeoman Dynasties in the English Lake District, *c.* 1450-1750. *Armitt Library Journal* 1, 86-113.

Yale, P. (1997) *From Tourist Attractions to Heritage Tourism.* Huntingdon: Elm.

Chapter Three

The Context of Tourism in the Lake District

Chapter Two discussed the historical evolution and development of tourism in the Lake District and demonstrated how some of the principles of sustainable tourism have been evident in the region from the 19th century. The previous chapter has also illustrated the complexity of developing sustainable tourism when different stakeholder groups with an interest in a geographic region have different priorities for the development of that region. What is evident, though, is that for the principles of sustainable tourism to be implemented there have to be 'champions' who take the lead in promoting the cause of sustainability. These champions in terms of the Lake District, were initially the influential writers such as Wordsworth and Ruskin, who were then followed by preservation societies such as the Friends of the Lake District.

A consideration of sustainable tourism has also to take into account the special characteristics of the region within which the tourism industry operates. The complex mix of the local population, economy, environment, and political processes for example will exert pressure on the priority that is given to the development of sustainable tourism. In certain regions such a mix will not lead to sustainable tourism being seen as a priority. In the case of the Lake District where the impacts of tourism on the landscape have been debated and discussed from the 19th century, the contemporary local context will be critical for the continuing management of the tourism industry on a sustainable basis. This chapter presents an overview of the socio-cultural, economic, political and environmental characteristics of the Lake District that provide the context for tourism. No study of sustainable tourism management would be complete without a consideration of the local resident communities, the tourist population, the physical and political environments within which they live, and the employment characteristics of the local economy. However, such a study is complex as any geographical region comprises a diverse, and dynamic set of factors that constitute the local population and the environments within which they live, work and play. One of the Lake District's most appealing features is its variety in terms of landscape and local communities. There are honeypot resorts such as Ambleside, Bowness, Keswick and Windermere that have large concentrations of tourist accommodation and tourist facilities, catering for the mass tourism market. At the other extreme there are quiet valleys with remote farms, small hamlets, and minor single track roads that receive fewer tourists.

The data presented in this chapter are the most up-to-date available, derived from a variety of official and commercial sources, including national sources such as the Office of National Statistics, as well as regional data compiled from Cumbria County Council, the Cumbria Economic Intelligence Partnership, and Locum Destination Consulting. The 2001 Census of Population statistics have been referred to wherever possible. However, key data from this survey are published incrementally, so reference is also made to earlier population surveys, as published by Cumbria County Council (see www.cumbria.gov.uk/aboutcumbria/district_profiles_2000).

Figure 3.0 *The complex mix of destination specific characteristics that influence sustainable tourism in the Lake District*

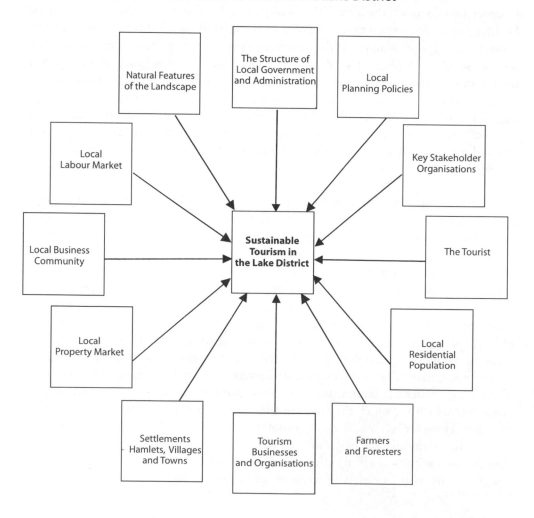

After the presentation of the data within this chapter, the key socio-cultural, economic, political and environmental characteristics of the Lake District will be established and the implications of this profile will be explained in terms of sustainable tourism management within the Lake District.

The Political Structure and Governance of the Lake District

As mentioned in Chapters One and Two, the Lake District National Park Authority is the local planning authority for the National Park and as such plays a major role in the economic and social development of the area. Chapter Five will discuss the role of the National Park Authority in more detail. There are six Local Authority Districts (LADs) within Cumbria: Allerdale Borough Council, Barrow-in-Furness Borough Council, Carlisle City Council, Copeland Borough Council, Eden District Council, and South Lakeland District Council. Each of these LADs works with Cumbria County Council to provide designated services for the local residential population as well as tourists, for example housing, education, social care, transport management, business and economic development support. The Lake District National Park falls within four of these LADs – Allerdale, Copeland, Eden, and South Lakeland, although the majority of the land area of the National Park falls within the jurisdiction of the latter. At a very local scale, wards within each LAD are represented by Parish Councils that comprise elected Councillors who are involved with taking decisions on issues relevant to the Parish.

It is not just the National Park Authority and the LADs that are responsible for the governance and administration of services and facilities within the National Park. A number of other organisations, funded by the public sector are also involved with the management of certain aspects of the development of tourism within the Lake District for example:

- ➢ Countryside Agency.
- ➢ Cumbria Tourist Board (designated as a regional Destination Management Organisation by the North West Development Agency in 2004).
- ➢ The Department for the Environment, Farming and Rural Affairs.
- ➢ English Nature and English Heritage.
- ➢ Environment Agency.
- ➢ Forestry Commission.
- ➢ Forest Enterprise.
- ➢ North West Development Agency.

In administering and developing tourism in the Lake District the agencies specified above work in partnership with each other, in partnership with private sector businesses and voluntary bodies to try and develop tourism in accordance with the principles of sustainable tourism. Developing successful and effective partnerships can be difficult and some of these challenges are discussed in Chapter Five along with an explanation of the role of some of these key organisations.

The National Park Management Plan (1999 & 2004) is an essential policy document that sets the framework for the development of tourism in the Lake District. This Plan is based on the Cumbria and Lake District Joint Structure Plan 1991 – 2006 (1995) and the Lake District National Park Local Plan (1998). The National Park Management Plan sets the policy framework for decisions that are taken in respect of all new planning proposals for the development and use of land and buildings requiring planning permission. The Lake District National Park Authority (1999:3) states that the Plan is vital "…in shaping the future of the National Park."

One of the major challenges in developing tourism in the Lake District is reconciling the contrasting positions and policies of each of the aforementioned stakeholders. Some of these agencies are clearly engaged in developing and promoting tourism (Cumbria Tourist Board and the North West Development Agency) while other stakeholders are required to conserve and preserve the Lake District for the enjoyment of future generations (Lake District National Park Authority). Until 2001 each of these stakeholders tended to operate relatively independently in terms of policy and strategy development. The Foot and Mouth disease crisis of 2001, however, acted as a catalyst, bringing these and other stakeholders together in order to develop a joint strategy to enable Cumbria and its communities to recover from the devastating impacts of the disease. Working in partnership to administer and govern tourism in the Lake District will be a feature of the role of these stakeholders in the future, but tensions and conflicts will still arise given the different aims and objectives of each stakeholder organisation.

The resident population of Cumbria and the Lake District

Cumbria is amongst the largest and most sparsely populated counties in England. It is home to just under half a million people (487,607) and has an average population density of 72 persons per square kilometre, compared to an England average of 381, and a North West regional average of 486 (Cumbria Economic Intelligence Partnership, 2002). The county of Cumbria accounts for 7 per cent of the population of North West England (ibid). Approximately 8 per cent of the population of Cumbria live within the Lake District National Park (43,000 residents), (Census of Population, 2001). Since 1991, the population of the National Park has risen by 0.7 per cent. Approximately 65 per cent of the residents of Cumbria live in the larger urban settlements, but 35 per cent, the highest figure in England, live in rural or deeply rural locations (Cumbria County Council, 2002).

Generally, low population densities can be problematic, for example segments of the population might be isolated from urban centres, and the services associated with them. Thus, social exclusion might arise as a result of not being able to easily access education, health, social, cultural, entertainment and retail services. However, in the Lake District, some members of the population might actively seek to be isolated from urban settlements in order to escape from society and to enjoy the natural beauty of the Lake District. These members of the population, who do seek to live in rural locations, will be particularly keen to see tourism in the Lake District managed and controlled so that their lifestyles are not adversely affected by large numbers of tourists.

In terms of the age composition of the Cumbrian population, when compared to the North West region, and the UK population, it can be seen that Cumbria has an above average retired population, "…2.6 percentage points above the regional and national benchmarks" (Cumbria Economic Intelligence Partnership, 2002:5). This is particularly marked in the districts of Allerdale, Eden, and South Lakeland, each of which has a land area within the Lake District National Park, see below. The above average elderly population is a result of inward migration, and the national trend towards an ageing population (ibid). The natural beauty of Cumbria and the Lake District acts as a magnate to affluent 'greying' members of society – "…South Lakeland has a very low proportion of pensioners claiming income support, at nearly half the English level, illustrating the influx of wealthy retirees into the Lake District" (Cumbria Economic Intelligence Partnership, 2002:70). On the one hand an influx of wealthy, retired people poses opportunities for a community – a resident population with money to spend on local services, and time to spend on leisure, cultural, and entertainment activities. But an influx of affluent, retired people will distort the property and labour markets. House price inflation will arise, preventing younger members of society from being able to afford to buy a house, and thus acting as a negative influence on the local labour market. Young people of working age will not be able to afford to live in the locality, and hence will migrate outwards, reducing the size and skills base of the local labour market.

These elderly residents will also be important opinion leaders within their local communities as it is likely that they will have retired from professional occupations and will be confident and articulate in expressing their views. Such residents when elected to local Parish and District Councils are likely to promote the views of preservation and conservation of the Lake District as opposed to promoting the further development of tourism and other sectors of the economy. They will seek to maintain the special characteristics of the Lake District rather than see new capital investment that might spoil the peace and tranquillity that has attracted them to re-locate there.

At the other end of the age scale, 16.7 per cent of the Cumbrian population falls into the 15-29 years age group, which is below the North West and the national average, both being 19.1 per cent. The below average younger age groups will have implications for the labour market, causing problems for tourism employers seeking to expand their businesses. The low proportion of younger people, as mentioned above, can partly be attributed to outward migration. Cumbria, although offering higher education opportunities to its resident population, does not have as yet its own dedicated university, although there are proposals to establish a University of Cumbria before too long. Thus, school and college leavers who are seeking a university education currently tend to leave the county, with just under half of them (48.9 per cent) selecting to study in the North West region. At the same time, the Cumbrian economy is not as diverse as in other regions of the UK, and has experienced recent decline in its traditional industries of shipbuilding, mining, manufacturing, and agriculture. As a result the number of career opportunities is restricted. So young people tend to leave the county to develop further their education, or to seek work, and do not tend to return because of the limited career opportunities. This 'brain drain' from Cumbria is problematic for the economy as a whole. The outward migration of young people is reducing the knowledge and skills base of the labour market, creating challenges for the development of the economy in the future. The decline in the skills base of the economy "…has implications for the ability of Cumbria to attract inward investors and/or generate indigenous growth" (ibid:8).

The above average retired population, and the below average under 30 years population have implications for tourism in the Lake District. Firstly, the elderly population, especially those living in the National Park, will have clear views on the way in which tourism should be managed and developed, and will be keen to see the scale of new developments not having detrimental effects on their quality of life. Indeed, as the Lake District population becomes increasingly elderly and increasingly dependent, the demand for improved health and social services will have to be addressed by the local authorities. This might result in an increase in the number of care homes being established, which could affect the aesthetic character of some of the urban centres. The outward migration of young people from the region is depriving the tourism industry of a local labour force. As will be mentioned later, tourism employers in the Lake District are finding it increasingly difficult to recruit staff which has implications for the continuing sustainability of some of the local tourism businesses. The effects of the local population on the development of sustainable tourism cannot be underestimated.

Resident population within the districts

As mentioned previously, Cumbria comprises six local authority districts and the Lake District National Park lies within four of these. In terms of the spatial distribution of the Lake District population, 56 per cent live in South Lakeland, 24 per cent in Allerdale, 11 per cent in Copeland, and 9 per cent in Eden (Cumbria County Council, 2002). In terms of population, South Lakeland is the most populous of these districts with a population of 102,306 (21 per cent of Cumbria's population), see Table 3.1.

Table 3.1   *Resident population of Cumbria 2001*

District	Males	Females	Total	% of County Total
Allerdale	45562	47931	93493	19.2
Barrow	35090	36889	71979	14.8
Carlisle	48729	52005	100734	20.7
Copeland	34542	34774	69316	14.2
Eden	24496	25283	49779	10.2
South Lakeland	49490	52816	102306	21.0
Cumbria	**237909**	**249698**	**487607**	**100**

Source: Office of National Statistics (2003)
NB: Figures may not sum due to rounding

Since 1991,although the population of Cumbria has been relatively static, only experiencing a 0.3 per cent decline, the populations of Eden and South Lakeland have increased by 8.2 per cent and 3.4 per cent respectively, while the populations of Copeland and Allerdale have declined by 3.7 per cent and 3.3 per cent respectively (Office of National Statistics, 2003). In Eden and South Lakeland, there has been inward migration of middle aged and retired members of society, whilst in Copeland and Allerdale, where traditional industries have declined, there has been an outward migration of people of working age.

The honeypot towns

Forty per cent of the Lake District National Park's population lives within the three honeypot towns of Keswick, Windermere and Bowness, and Ambleside. These larger towns, along with Coniston, Grasmere, and Hawkshead include a high proportion of the National Park's tourist accommodation, shops, restaurants and other visitor attractions and facilities. The population of these towns increases significantly during the main holiday season. The resident population statistics for these urban centres are given in Table 3.2:

Table 3.2   *Urban population of Lake District honeypot centres, 1991-2001*

Honeypot Centre	1991 Total Population	2001 Total Population	Numeric Change	Percentage Change
Ambleside/Grasmere	5310	4870	-440	-8.3
Keswick	4960	4860	-100	-2.0
Windermere & Bowness	8340	8020	-320	-3.8

Source: Office of National Statistics (2003)

Clearly, there have been quite significant declines in the populations of the main honeypot centres, and this can be attributed to the fact that these centres have elderly populations, and that the decline is accounted for by natural loss (more deaths than births), as opposed to outward migration. As can be seen from Table 3.3, nearly 25 per cent of the populations of Ambleside, Grasmere, Keswick and Windermere are over the age of 60 years.

Table 3.3   *Age structure of honeypot centres, 2000*

Age	Ambleside %	Grasmere %	Keswick %	Windermere %
0–14 years	12.5	15.3	15.3	14.1
15-29 years	29.7	24.9	17.7	22.4
30-44 years	15.8	19.6	18.0	17.8
45-59 years	17.7	15.4	17.9	17.4
60-74 years	15.1	15.2	18.2	16.9
75-84 years	7.4	7.5	9.7	8.3
85+ years	1.8	2.2	3.3	3.1

Source: Cumbria County Council, Ward Profiles, 2001

As well as considering the demographic profile of the resident population, attention has also to be given to the cultural associations and traditions of the population, as these clearly contribute to the distinctive appeal of an area. Chapter Four indicates how some of the literary cultural associations of the Lake District have been interpreted through the homes and writings of poets such as William Wordsworth, and writers such as Beatrix Potter. Preserving folk culture is essential, but it is difficult to achieve, as it lies outside the formal processes of tourism management and governance, resting with the passing down of traditions from one generation to another. As outward migration from an area occurs, and inward migration of non-local residents is experienced, the traditional folk culture of an area is eroded. The preservation of folk culture, as expressed in dialects, craft skills and pastimes is critical for the Lake District which has a long tradition of mankind interacting with a relatively harsh environment. Pastimes such as fell running, hound trailing and country sports such as Cumberland and Westmorland wrestling are still practised in the Lake District, but their future is uncertain with the outmigration of younger generations.

Craft skills that are indigenous to the Lake District are also under threat as the farming community de-populates. Traditional skills and crafts in dry stone walling, shepherding flocks of sheep on the high fells, coppicing and hedge laying, and building using local techniques need preserving, but the characteristics of the local population and the advent of new technologies makes this more problematic. To some extent, the preservation of the local culture rests with organisations such as the National Trust and other bodies involved with the conservation of traditional landscapes and communities – the Friends of the Lake District and the British Trust for Conservation Volunteers. It is also ironic that some of these traditional skills and crafts actually comprise part of the tourism product – skills in dry stone walling can be developed at the Lake District National Park Authority Visitor Centre at Brockhole, on the shores of Lake Windermere.

Case Study – Ambleside

Ambleside is situated at the heart of the Lake District, at the northern end of Lake Windermere, and is one of the most popular tourist towns in the Lake District. Many of the buildings are built with local green slate which contribute to the character of the townscape. The town has been involved in tourism for over 150 years, but the last 30 years have seen a major investment in the tourism facilities provided within the town. Market led demand for high quality accommodation and catering provision, supported by encouragement from the tourism development agencies has resulted in Ambleside's tourism superstructure being improved.

In addition to the demographic data presented above, the population of Ambleside can be broken down into five different segments, each with their own characteristics:

The Indigenous Population

Residents of Ambleside who were born in the town and work within the local or regional economy.

The Tourism Labour Force

This segment includes the entrepreneurs operating their own tourism business, as well as employees who work within the tourism industry in Ambleside.

The Retired

The 'greying' population who have moved to Ambleside for retirement. These members of the local community can often be seen as opponents to tourism as they move to Ambleside to enjoy the natural beauty and tranquillity of the landscape.

Tourists

The temporary residents of Ambleside who provide the income for the local economy.

Students

Ambleside Campus of St. Martin's College, Lancaster provides courses in teacher education, and so attracts a small number of students to the town.

When considering the different segments of the population that reside in Ambleside it is obvious that certain tensions will arise between the residents. The retired members of society will have contrasting needs to the students and tourists, while those residents engaged in the tourism industry will be keen to maximise the economic gains that can arise from the tourists. Resentment is bound to arise between the different segments of the local population. The tourism entrepreneurs will resent the views of the retired members of the population whose prime interest might be the protection of the town from further commercialisation.

In addition to the residents of Ambleside, other stakeholders will also have an interest in the development of the town. Those organisations engaged in the development and promotion of tourism will encourage further investment in the range and quality of services provided for tourists, which might be contradictory to the views and policies of those organisations whose role it is to conserve and preserve the town against inappropriate developments.

A number of issues arise for Ambleside as a result of the mix of different residents and stakeholders within the town:

➢ housing is overpriced as a result of wealthy retirees purchasing property in the town

➢ living costs are high as a result of inflated commercial property prices and the need of entrepreneurs to achieve a certain level of return on their investment

➢ an out-migration of younger people who cannot afford to purchase property, and who do not want to develop their careers in tourism.

Addressing these issues is extremely challenging, and little progress may actually be made in resolving them. This is because the local planning regulations prohibit the development of large numbers of new residential properties. There is little land on which to develop new businesses not engaged in tourism or related activities, which might help to diversify the local economy. And increasingly, at a district level, councils are being dominated by articulate retirees who are elected as councillors, and whose interest it is to preserve the existing townscapes and rural communities from further development and commercialisation. It would appear that Ambleside is part of a vicious circle from which it might be impossible to break out, especially given the trend towards early retirement in the United Kingdom and the interest of early retirees in re-locating from urban environments to smaller rural communities.

Housing

"Land which can be developed for housing without having a serious detrimental impact on the landscape of the National Park is severely limited", (Lake District National Park Authority, 1999:65). This is problematic because there is a shortage of housing stock for first-time buyers in the Lake District. As mentioned previously in this chapter, the influx of wealthy retirees has inflated house prices to the extent that young local people can no longer afford to buy houses in the National Park. This problem is further exacerbated by the number of holiday homes and second homes in the Lake District. The majority of these holiday and second homes are found in South Lakeland which provides nearly 65 per cent of the National Park total of second and holiday homes.

In terms of housing tenure within the honeypot centres there is very little housing for rent, either from the local authority or from private landlords. This compounds the difficulty of securing housing in the Lake District by young people who are just embarking on their careers and have limited disposable income to spend on residential accommodation, see Table 3.4.

Table 3.4   *Housing tenure and type in the honeypot centres, 1998*

Household Tenure	Ambleside %	Grasmere %	Keswick %	Windermere %
Owned out right	31.3	34.5	36.6	30.5
Buying	29.6	22.6	29.3	32.2
Local Authority rented	17.2	8.8	19.1	14.5
Housing Authority rented	5.1	8.0	4.2	2.6
Privately rented	13.3	16.6	8.2	16.8
Other	3.6	9.6	2.5	3.4

Source: Office for National Statistics, Policy & Research Unit, 2000

Car Ownership

Car ownership is often used as an indicator of affluence, but when considering the Lake District population, additional considerations have to be taken into account. The residents of the National Park tend to be car owners, which is not surprising given the rural nature of the area and the limited public transport provision. For many people living in the National Park, owning a car is not optional, but a necessity. Where public transport is limited or non-existent, owning a car is essential for commuting to work and accessing local services.

Table 3.5   *Car ownership in the honeypot centres, 1998*

Households	Ambleside %	Grasmere %	Keswick %	Windermere %
With no car	26.8	17.6	33.2	26.3
With one car	49.0	51.9	49.0	49.4
With two or more cars	24.2	30.3	17.8	24.3

Source: Cumbria County Council, Ward Profiles, 2001

The Lake District Economy

The economy of the Lake District has traditionally been based on agriculture, mining, quarrying and woodland industries. Of these traditional industries, the main employers in the 21st century are agriculture and woodland industries. These traditional industries have given the Lake District its "...local identity, dialect and events such as the valley shows" (Lake District National Park Authority, 1999:11). Tourism, now though, is the key sector of employment in the local economy. In the Lake District, tourism and agriculture are the main sectors of the local economy and both are associated with unsocial working hours, low pay, poor working conditions, and considerable disruptions to family and social life. Micro-businesses (10 or fewer employees) are especially important in the Lake District (accounting for 42 per cent of all firms), with life-style entrepreneurs assumed to be particularly important in the rural tourist industry. (Locum Destination Consulting, 2003). This is confirmed when the self-employment data are taken into account, which reveal that the proportion of working age people in self-employment in the Lake District is almost double the average for Cumbria, due to the importance of agriculture and tourism-sectors of employment (ibid). In terms of part-time working, 42.1 per cent of the Lake District's economically active population work part-time, compared to a Cumbrian average of 33.7 per cent. This again is a reflection of the local economy, where tourism and agriculture dominate, and both, due to seasonality, rely upon part-time seasonal employment.

Characteristics of tourism businesses

As mentioned above, the tourism sector in Cumbria and the Lake District is dominated by "...small independent, single unit, non-branded businesses" (Locum Destination Consulting, 2003: 5), with company turnover of less than £50,000 per year being the norm, and with 70 per cent of businesses employing 5 or fewer full time staff. Tourism businesses have a heavy reliance on part-time and casual labour, with these types of labour dominating some businesses. Locum Destination (2003:11) suggest that a fifth of businesses employ "...most or all of their staff seasonally." The serviced accommodation sector is characterised by hotels, inns, and guesthouses that operate with less than 10 letting bedrooms (ibid). With regard to visitor attractions, Cumbria and the Lake District is dominated by "...very small attractions" (Locum Destination Consulting, 2003:9), with 70 per cent of ticketed attractions receiving less than 20,000 visits annually. It was intimated in Chapter One that there are a number of dimensions to sustainable tourism, one being the challenge that some tourism businesses face in actually sustaining a viable business. Clearly, private sector operated businesses in the Lake District will also face this challenge but as demonstrated in Chapter Six, some accommodation providers in the region also implement sustainable environmental policies as part of their overall business strategy in order to improve profitability.

Employment

The proportion of people working full-time in the Lake District is below the county average – full-time male employment is below 40 per cent, with females accounting for nearly three-fifths of employment (Cumbria Economic Intelligence Partnership, 2002). Low economic activity rates arise for a number of reasons, but as indicated above, the Lake District is characterised by a prosperous, greying population, and one where there is an outward migration of younger people.

As already identified the distribution, hotels, and restaurants sector dominates employment in the Lake District, accounting for 48 per cent of the working population, with 11 per cent employed in agriculture, and 10 per cent in manufacturing (ibid). However, since 1991, the number of people employed in agriculture and manufacturing has been declining, (ibid), but farming still provides jobs in the countryside which help to sustain local communities. Another problem facing farming is the difficult physical conditions that farmers have to contend with, and the viability of some farms is frequently dependent on Government financial support. Financial support for farmers though is based upon European Union directives through the Common Agricultural Policy which is subject to review, and hence results in uncertainty on a yearly basis in terms of the level of a farmer's income. The Lake District National Park Authority and Cumbria Tourist Board are sympathetic to the financial problems faced by farmers and actively work with the farming community to encourage diversification into tourism and related areas.

The Cumbria and Lake District Structure Plan (1995) recognises the over-reliance on tourism within the local economy and provides for the diversification of the local economy by:

➤ identifying land that can be used for business/industrial uses;

➤ enabling the re-use of appropriate traditional buildings;

➤ protecting existing business/industrial sites from new uses which would adversely affect the range of job opportunities.

(Lake District National Park Authority, 1999:66)

However, planning applications for new tourism developments in the National Park occasionally lead to controversy with the organisation seeking planning permission feeling aggrieved when the National Park Authority does not grant planning permission. This is because the National Park Authority works within the framework of the Principles of Sustainable Rural Tourism. These principles ensure that new developments do not conflict with the special qualities of the National Park, are of a character and scale appropriate to the environment and that new developments are appropriate for the specific site identified for the new development. Clearly, the interpretation of these principles is prone to debate and discussion and can result in tension between the different parties involved with the planning application. There is an argument that suggests that the priorities of the National Park are incompatible with the need to diversify the local economy and to foster balanced local communities that will need a diversity of business and employment opportunities to be viable. The National Park Authority, however, would counter this view and recognises fully the need for local communities to be based on a sustainable local economy.

There was a national trend in the UK over the second half of the 1990s for unemployment to fall; this trend has been mirrored in the Lake District. Unemployment in the Lake District (1.4 per cent) is much lower than the Cumbria average, (3.9 per cent), which is lower than the North West average of 4.4 per cent (Cumbria Economic Intelligence Partnership, 2002).

Low unemployment creates a problem for the tourism industry which currently struggles to recruit a sufficient number of local people to work in the industry, resulting in the temporary employment of people from outside the region. As can be seen from Table 3.6, there is virtually full-employment (a labour shortage) in each of the honeypot centres, which indicates the employment challenges faced by tourism businesses that are seeking to expand. Low unemployment rates, combined with low levels of economic activity within the resident population, make it difficult for an area to attract new inward investors, or difficult for indigenous firms to achieve organic growth.

Indeed, in Cumbria, the hotels and restaurants sector is classified as one where job vacancies are hard-to-fill (Cumbria Economic Intelligence Partnership, 2002). When job vacancies in Cumbria are analysed, 43 per cent of all job vacancies were found to be in the distribution, hotels, and restaurants sector (ibid). Tourism is felt to be a low skills sector, paying low wages. This inhibits the recruitment of staff. Tourism employers, rather than tackling the fundamental issue of low wages itself, and hence attracting new employees into the sector, appear to accept the low-skills equilibrium, and the vicious circle that this results in: "there is a significant gap between the current skills levels of employees and the skills needed to meet business objectives" (Cumbria Economic Intelligence Partnership, 2002).

Table 3.6   *Unemployment in the honeypot centres, 2000*

Unemployed	Ambleside %	Grasmere %	Keswick %	Windermere %
Total	0.6	0.8	0.7	0.6

Source: Cumbria County Council, Ward Profiles, 2001

Particularly in tourism, it is felt that there are significant gaps in the core skills; personal, customer service, and communication. The tourism industry has a difficulty in addressing these skill gaps because of the low pay within the sector and the tendency towards seasonal and part time employment (ibid). Indeed, in the National Park, only 12.6 per cent of employers had a written training plan, and only 12.8 per cent of employers had a training budget. Clearly, there is a low commitment from Lake District employers to train their workforce, exacerbating the low skills equilibrium that is in place. This will have an effect on the quality of service provided to tourists, and in an increasingly competitive market, if tourists experience low quality service they frequently take their custom elsewhere. When tourism operators struggle to achieve a realistic return on their investment, the financial fragility, and hence sustainability of the business, can be adversely affected by staff who have inadequate skills.

Early retirement is also highest in the Lake District, when compared to other districts within Cumbria, but this is assumed to be for lifestyle reasons with the inward migration of wealthy retirees, as opposed to a lack of employment opportunities (Cumbria Economic Intelligence Partnership, 2002).

Earnings

The average wage rates in Cumbria tend to be 10 per cent lower than the national average, "…nearly three-fifths of full-time employees in Cumbria earn less than £350 per week, with around 30 per cent earning less than £250 "(Cumbria Economic Intelligence Partnership, 2002:31). Wages paid within the tourism industry are felt to contribute to the depressed average earnings levels in Cumbria. The payment of low wages results in double, or multi-jobbing, as people seek two or more jobs in order to bring their income levels up to a more realistic level.

Table 3.7 *Gross annual family income in the honeypot centres, 1998*

Income Band (£,000)	Ambleside %	Grasmere %	Keswick %	Windermere %
0-5	8.4	10.6	12.6	9.8
6-10	14.7	17.1	18.8	16.4
11-15	18.4	19.7	20.3	19.4
16-20	17.0	17.2	16.4	17.0
21-25	13.3	12.7	11.5	12.7
26-30	9.5	8.5	7.5	8.6
31-35	6.4	5.4	4.7	5.6
36-40	4.2	3.4	3.0	3.6
41+	8.1	5.5	5.1	6.7

Source: Cumbria County Council, Ward Profiles, 2001

The mean annual income for employed people in Cumbria in 2000 was £14,575, with self-employed people having mean incomes £2000 per annum higher (ibid). However, the mean annual full-time salary in the hotel and restaurant sector was £12,413 (ibid), which could account for high staff turnover figures within this sector, and the difficulty that such employers have in recruiting staff.

Social disadvantage

To provide an indication of the overall wealth of the resident population, CACI Ltd. used information from the 1991 Census to categorise households into one of the following groups:

A – **Thriving**: people established at the top of the social ladder – healthy, wealthy, and confident consumers, affluent greys, rural communities, prosperous pensioners.

B – **Expanding**: business people in better-off families – paying off mortgages, and bringing up children.

C – Rising: the young professionals and executives in towns and cities – working and studying to make their way up the career ladder, affluent urbanites, prosperous professionals, better-off executives.

D – Settling: the workers in the middle of the social spectrum – they have their homes and lead a steady lifestyle, comfortable middle-agers, mature home owning areas, skilled workers.

E – Aspiring: the people who are running hard to better their lot – buying their council homes and pursuing their goals, new home owners, white collar workers.

F – Striving: the people who find life toughest, older people, less prosperous areas, council estate residents, unemployed.

Source: Cumbria County Council, Ward Profiles, 2001

Table 3.8   *Social disadvantage in the honeypot centres*

Social Group	Ambleside %	Grasmere %	Keswick %	Windermere %	Cumbria %
A	75.5	100	57.9	65.2	25
B	7.7	0	0	0	6
C	0	0	0	0	1
D	16.7	0	8.9	28.7	35
E	0	0	18.3	6.1	16
F	0	0	15	0	16

Source: Cumbria County Council, Ward Profiles, 2001

As indicated in table 3.8, the honeypot towns are clearly skewed towards Social Group A, and Grasmere is totally given over to this type of resident confirming the pockets of great affluence that can be found in the Lake District. This contrasts strongly with those people who work in tourism or agriculture and whose level of income is considerably lower. The domination of the local communities of the Lake District by one segment of the population, probably with a common outlook, will clearly have major repercussions on how that community evolves and develops.

The tourist population of the Lake District

Studies to profile the tourist population of Cumbria and the Lake District have traditionally been commissioned by Cumbria Tourist Board. The data from these studies, when combined with findings from the United Kingdom Tourism Survey enable a profile of the tourist population of the Lake District to be established. Tourist profile data enable marketing strategies to be developed that can contribute to the management of sustainable tourism within the National Park. The most recent tourism survey that was commissioned by Cumbria Tourism Board was in 2002. The key findings from this research (Creative Research, 2002) and (Locum Destination Consulting, 2003a & b) will now be considered, although it should be noted that in certain cases the data refer to Cumbria as a whole, rather than to the Lake District.

Day visitors

Tourism in Cumbria is dominated by day visitors, in terms of the volume of tourists (Locum Destination Consulting, 2003a). The number of tourists who stay overnight in the Lake District has been static for the last decade. This is problematic for tourism in the Lake District, because it is the tourist who stays overnight who spends the most and hence represents the greatest value to tourism businesses.

Activities of tourists

Although the Lake District is an area of outstanding landscapes, and visiting the region for the natural beauty is a key motivational factor, for the majority of 21st century tourists less strenuous activities such as "...visiting towns, shopping, visiting restaurants and pubs and driving around by car" tend to be the main leisure activities pursued (Creative Research, 2002:10). If visitors do undertake some outdoor activity it is likely to be a walk of less than two miles, or visiting some form of tourist attraction whether that be a heritage or cultural site (ibid). Those tourists venturing into the fells tend to be in the minority, less than 10 per cent of the tourist population.

Demographic profile

A common perception of the tourist who visits the Lake District is that such tourists tend to be the more elderly members of society. This view was confirmed by (Creative Research, 2002), who concluded that visitors to Cumbria are likely to be aged 45 – 60 years, with most visitors being in a group of adults. However, more families visit the region during the school holidays. In terms of socio-economic profiles, Cumbria and the Lake District attract tourists from all socio-economic groups, but with a slightly 'up-market' profile.

Repeat visits

Cumbria and the Lake District have a relatively loyal tourist market. Approximately half of the tourists surveyed by (Creative Research, 2002) did not refer to any source of tourist information when planning their visit, and "two thirds of day visits were largely spontaneous, being planned in the week leading up to the visit" (ibid:14). This loyal market is problematic, however, because the region does not appear to be attracting any new visitors, and as a result the tourist market could be considered to be stagnant. If the quality of the tourism product declines, as suggested in the discussion on employment and labour force skills, then the viability of tourism businesses will be put further at risk.

Length of stay

It is interesting to note that the average length of stay of tourists in Cumbria and the Lake District tends to be 5.4 days (ibid). This suggests that holidays to the region tend to be 'medium stay' holidays. The era of the long-stay holiday to the Lake District is over, and although shorter break holidays are being recorded, the region attracts tourists to stay longer than the traditional short break of two – three nights.

Place of permanent residence

Of all tourists to Cumbria and the Lake District, 90 per cent are permanent residents of the United Kingdom, with the remaining 10 per cent residing overseas (mainland Europe, North America, Australia and South Africa being the key overseas markets) (Creative Research 2002). Of the United Kingdom tourists, the tendency is for them to live within three hours travel time of Cumbria (see Table 3.9). Thus, the majority of UK tourists are from the north of England and Scotland:

Table 3.9   *Origin of UK tourists to Cumbria, 2001*

Region	%
North East	9
North West/Merseyside	29
Yorkshire & Humberside	12
East Midlands	10
West Midlands	5
South West	4
Eastern	6
London	5
South East	7
Other UK	12

Source: Cumbria Tourist Board, 2002

Transport

Travelling by private car is the main form of transport used by tourists when travelling to the region – 83 per cent (Creative Research, 2002). Once in the Lake District, private transport is again the main form of transport, with only 10 per cent of tourists walking as their main means of travelling around. The problems created by an over reliance on car transport in the Lake District will be considered in Chapter 7.

Environmental Characteristics of the Lake District

In addition to explaining the socio-cultural and economic characteristics of the Lake District the natural environment that is the main attractant of tourists needs considering. The landscape of the Lake District has changed very little over the centuries. The fells are still relatively wild and offer the opportunity to walk across them, or to climb rock faces unhindered. Glaciers have left their legacy on the landscape in the form of mountain ridges (Striding Edge on Helvellyn and Sharp Edge on Saddle Back/Blencathra), deep valleys (Borrowdale), and lakes (Wast Water). These physical features offer a "…quality of scenery not found elsewhere in the country" (Lake District National Park Authority, 1999:11), and are one of the main reasons why the Lake District has been designated a National Park. These special qualities give the area its distinctiveness, not just in the United Kingdom, but also internationally.

The mountains, fells, limestone pavements, lakes, rivers and forests that attract tourists have other benefits for the local economy – farming, forestry, or supplying water. In terms of land ownership 25 per cent of the National Park is owned by the National Trust, with other large tracts of land being owned by the Forestry Commission, North West Water, local authorities, and a number of large private estates. Other, smaller tracts of land are owned by private individuals and conservation groups.

The physical characteristics of the Lake District have been shaped by a complex geology and glaciers over millions of years. A central prominent mountain dome is the basis for the radiation of streams and rivers to the valley floors and lakes. The landscape of the National Park varies considerably, incorporating coastline to the highest mountain in England – Scafell. The fells are an open landscape, with few boundary fences or walls, designated as common land, not owned by any organisation or individual "…and represent a cultural landscape of considerable interest and importance. Visitors and residents value the wildness, openness, tranquillity, and contrast with urban life which the fells provide" (Lake District National Park Authority, 1999:72).

The fells are home to a diversity of wildlife, and the European Union has designated parts of the fells as Special Areas for Conservation, for example Helvellyn and Fairfield in the centre of the National Park. Other tracts of fell have been designated as Sites of Special Scientific Interest. The fells are also home to a number of monuments that have been designated as Scheduled Ancient Monuments, for example prehistoric settlements and Roman settlements and forts, such as Hardknott Roman Fort.

The character of the open, high fells is preserved through the policies specified in the Joint Structure Plan and the Local Plan for the National Park which prohibit developments which would have a negative impact on the appearance of the open fells.

The landscape reflects farming practices over the centuries with distinctive patterns of fields, and farmsteads, many of which have been farmed by the same family for generations. Farming has had a major impact on the special qualities of the Lake District because much of the landscape is managed for farming – in particular the open nature of the high fells and the conservation of the dry stone walls that are a strong feature of the landscape. But farming families are struggling to survive – the income derived from farming has been reducing in recent years, and some families have a succession problem. Younger members of the family do not see their future in farming, and leave the land for jobs in higher paid careers. This de-population of farming communities will have implications not only for the physical landscape of the Lake District, but also the social and economic viability of some of the hamlets and villages which are so important for the tourist appeal of the Lake District.

Much of the Lake District National Park was designated an Environmentally Sensitive Area (ESA) in 1993. This scheme recognises areas where farming has shaped distinctive patterns in the landscape, and where wildlife and historic features need conserving. When ESA designation is achieved, certain benefits flow to the farming community, for example an upper limit on the number of animals that can be grazed on land, accompanied by grants to farmers to offset a resulting loss of income. Whilst attractive for the conservation of the landscape, farmers in the Lake District have been reticent to volunteer for the scheme – "some farmers have not entered the ESA scheme on the grounds that it offers insufficient incentives in relation to their business" (Lake District National Park Authority, 1999:19).

The valleys of the Lake District are a strong feature of the landscape with steep sides and a number of valleys in the central Lake District ending in cul-de-sacs. A network of single track roads, lanes, and footpaths provides access to some of these remote and relatively isolated valleys. The National Trust, a significant owner of land in the Lake District, has done much to conserve the character and features of the valley landscapes by encouraging its tenant farmers to adopt traditional skills in dry stone walling and hedging. Trees are important features of the valley landscape, providing shelter from the wind and weather for farmsteads and hamlets. Woodland provides a natural habitat for wildlife. "It is the pattern that these small areas of scrub, individual trees, small groups of trees and copses contribute to the landscape of the valleys which is important, not their precise location" (Lake District National Park Authority, 1999:88).

The natural landscape is home to a diverse range of habitats supporting a variety of aquatic species, animals, birds and plants. Bird life is a distinctive feature of the fells, where peregrine falcons, ravens, ring ouzels and small numbers of dotterel, golden eagle, osprey and merlin can be found. The Lake District has habitats of national and international significance – mosses and liverworts can be found in woodlands, lichen heaths on fell tops where near arctic conditions can prevail, and natterjack toads, bats, owls and red squirrels in forests. "The importance of the National Park for wildlife, geology and geomorphology is reflected in the extent and diversity of statutory sites designated for their importance for nature conservation" (Lake District National Park Authority, 1999:24). To conserve wildlife and habitats a Cumbria Local Biodiversity Plan has been produced. In addition the Council for National Parks has promoted the establishment of wild areas, where agriculture is excluded preventing farm animals from grazing the land enabling the natural regeneration of woodland and the natural succession of habitats to occur unhindered.

Obviously, the lakes, tarns and rivers are key features of the National Park's landscape, providing opportunities for a diverse range of recreational activities, as well as supporting a variety of aquatic plants and wildlife, and supplying water to the industrial conurbations of North West England. Three of the rivers in the Lake District are considered to be of international significance for nature conservation – the rivers Eden, Ehen and Derwent/Cocker. Windermere is the longest and most commercialised lake, whereas Wast Water is one of the most isolated and least commercialised, contrasting with Thirlmere which is a reservoir.

Each of the lakes has an individual management plan based on the special characteristics and features of the lake. Four of the lakes in the western fringes of the National Park: Wast Water, Ennerdale Water, Crummock Water and Buttermere have been designated Sites of Special Scientific Interest because of the communities of plants and animals associated with these lakes. Rivers flowing from Ennerdale Water, for example, are the only ones in the United Kingdom that spawn arctic charr. As a result the range of recreational activities permitted on Ennerdale Water is severely restricted, with boating only possible in canoes or rowing boats. Seven lakes have been identified by the National Park Authority as being especially important for nature conservation because their wildlife is felt to be particularly vulnerable to disturbances from recreational activity: Bassenthwaite Lake, Derwent Water, Esthwaite Water, Brothers Water, Elter Water, Rydal Water, and Windermere. Windermere has a long history of both commercial and recreational use because it is very accessible. As a result conflicts exist between the use of the lake as a commercial and recreational facility and the need to conserve and protect its features and wildlife. In 1981 a Windermere Management Plan was produced that led to the introduction of new byelaws "...including bans on the use of craft such as aircraft and hovercraft...and controls on sea boat toilets" (Lake District National Park Authority, 1999:116).

As indicated in Chapter Two, man has also left his mark on the landscape. Industrialisation in the north west of England in the eighteenth and nineteenth centuries saw valleys in the Lake District being dammed to form reservoirs – Thirlmere and Haweswater – with water being pumped to the commercial towns and cities of Lancashire. The demand for timber resulted in afforestation with large tracts of land being seeded for commercial forestry – Whinlatter forest, for example. The landscape in certain parts of the Lake District has been significantly changed by afforestation. "Between 1952 and 1975 the area under coniferous plantations more than doubled, as the Forestry Commission and private landowners responded to government policy to increase timber production" (Lake District National Park Authority, 1999:20). Since the 1980s, the national forest policy has changed to embrace sustainable forestry – balancing the economic gains to be realised from forestry with the need to conserve native woodlands, and at the same time providing public access to multi-purpose woodland and forest areas. Forests and woodlands account for nearly 12 per cent of the land area of the National Park with Forest Enterprise owning approximately 5 per cent of the National Park.

Forests and woodlands provide opportunities for a number of recreational pursuits. Whinlatter forest in the north of the Lake District is a good example of a multi-purpose forest. Tourist access is encouraged with walking and orienteering trails, mountain bike tracks, a childrens outdoor adventure playground, and a specially designed visitor centre. The forest is occasionally used for car rallying. The visitor centre incorporates a café, gift shop and an interpretation facility that educates visitors about the forest and its various roles, both as a commercial forest, a natural habitat, and a contemporary visitor experience.

Mining and quarrying have been features of the Lake District since Neolithic times with the extraction of minerals and rock from the landscape, for example the Coniston Copper Mines, Greenside Lead Mines, and Honister slate quarry. The role of these quarries and mines as contemporary tourist attractions will be discussed in Chapter Four. However, the prolonged effects of weathering over the centuries, and the lack of maintenance to some of these sites has resulted in unsightly scars being imprinted on the landscape. Additional problems include the pollution of the landscape from contaminated chemicals and the instability of some of the mine workings. However, such is the national importance of some of these landscape features that the Coniston Copper Mines and Greenside Lead Mines have been designated as Scheduled Ancient Monuments.

Hamlets, villages, and towns in the Lake District contribute to the quality of the landscape. The built environment comprises a great variety of buildings "…including medieval churches, fortified houses and halls, seventeenth century farmhouses and barns, formal houses of the late eighteenth and early nineteenth centuries and hotels and terraces from the Victorian period" (Lake District National Park Authority, 1999:31). The traditional farmsteads have a distinctive style using local stone and slate. Such buildings add to the attractiveness of the landscape with characteristic chimneys, porches, and galleries. These features can be seen at Dove Cottage in Grasmere, where William Wordsworth once lived. Dove Cottage and the other buildings in the hamlet have been preserved externally and internally in the style in which they were originally built. The Victorian era is evident in the honeypot town of Windermere where large Victorian houses dominate the townscape. Grand country houses such as Brantwood, built by John Ruskin, on the shores of Lake Coniston, and Rydal Lodge at Grasmere signify the wealth that was accrued by industrialists in the eighteenth and nineteenth centuries. "Each town, village and hamlet has distinctive combinations of buildings, open spaces, and important features which are worthy of particular consideration" (Lake District National Park Authority, 1999:11). There are some 1700 Listed Buildings in the Lake District, with 29 being of Grade 1 status indicating that they are of national significance.

In the 1960s with the growth in leisure time and increased wealth of the United Kingdom population there was a pressure within the Lake District for improved car parking, picnic sites, toilets, information boards and the development of additional tourist accommodation. The increasing number of tourists visiting the Lake District in the

1960s and 1970s resulted in buildings within the honeypot towns being developed or converted for tourism businesses such as hotels, guesthouses, restaurants, cafés, and gift shops. Such development detracted from the local character of traditional styles of architecture with extensions being built onto existing buildings.

In the 21st century pressures for development are constant – there is "…creeping urbanisation" as symbolised in "…street lights, kerbing and [a] clutter of signs. Roads are straightened, junctions modified, and safety barriers erected" (Lake District National Park Authority, 1999:15). The honeypot town of Bowness-on-Windermere in the height of the tourist season could be mistaken for a resort on the Costa del Sol with its road train. Cafés, restaurants, and public houses cater for the dietary requirements of the mass tourism market, and giftshops sell products more akin to seaside resorts such as Torremolinos and Blackpool.

Clearly, the pressures for change within the traditional villages and towns of the Lake District are strong, with neon lit signs in shop fascias and overhead wires reflecting the retail and development trends of modern times, but detracting from the ambience of the traditional architectural styles of the Victorian era.

The landscape of the Lake District is one of the main attractants of tourists to the Lake District but as indicated here is under pressure to change. The landscape as a feature of the contemporary tourism product will be explored in further detail in Chapter Four.

The Implications of the Demographic, Economic, and Environmental Characteristics of the Lake District for Sustainable Tourism

The purpose of this chapter has been to identify the special characteristics of the Lake District in terms of its political governance, population, economy, culture and landscape. It is evident that the relatively small geographic area of the Lake District provides many different contrasts, not only in its physical features, but also in its resident population. It is such diversity that makes sustainable tourism management not only very necessary, but also very challenging to achieve.

There is little controversy over the need to preserve and conserve the physical and cultural landscape for the enjoyment of future generations. The Lake District National Park Authority takes a lead role in this, working with Cumbria County Council to develop policies published as Structure Plans, and working with a number of partners on the implementation of such policies.

The greatest challenge though is probably reconciling the diverse needs of the local population. This chapter has identified the influx into the Lake District of an ageing, wealthy, retired population who are re-locating to enjoy the beauty and tranquillity of the landscape. Such an influx has a major impact on the local housing and local labour market. House prices become inflated, restrictions on the building of residential properties limits the supply of new houses, and young people just embarking on their careers are unable to afford to live locally. The over-dominance of tourism within the local economy restricts employment and career opportunities to the extent that young people tend to migrate outwards to other areas where housing and employment prospects are more favourable.

Tourism entrepreneurs and employers are adversely affected by the inward and outward migration of the population. Young people emigrating from the Lake District and elderly people retiring to the area reduces the size of the labour market, making it increasingly difficult for tourism businesses to expand or even to remain financially viable and hence sustainable. The influx of articulate, educated people with leisure time to devote to championing community issues means that the number of people opposing the further development of the tourism sector is expanding.

Tensions also exist between those agencies that are involved with the administration, governance, development and promotion of tourism within the Lake District. Local authorities and the regional tourist board are required to promote and encourage the economic contribution that tourism can make to the local economy. But these agencies do not have statutory rights over planning regulations within the Lake District – these are within the remit of the Lake District National Park Authority, whose main role is that of preservation and conservation of the landscape. On one hand there is strong pressure to develop tourism, but on the other hand there is strong resistance to such developments on the basis that they are detrimental to the environment.

As indicated at the beginning of this chapter no study of sustainable tourism management would be complete without a consideration of the special qualities and characteristics of the locality. This chapter has identified the special features of the Lake District that require conserving and preserving for future generations. At the same time this chapter has identified the tensions that exist between the various stakeholders who have an interest in the development of tourism, and those stakeholders who wish to see tourism even more strongly controlled than it is today. Muller (1994) defined sustainable tourism development as a pentagon with five points (see Chapter One). A subjective application of the pentagon to the Lake District, based on the content of this chapter would suggest that tourism in the region is starting to drift away from the ideal perspective presented by Muller. Although the economic health of the tourism industry in the Lake District is still relatively good, signs are starting to emerge that the quality of the tourism product is starting to deteriorate. Labour force skills which if not addressed will have a negative impact on the economic health, and hence sustainability, of the tourism industry. With regard to the subjective well-being of the locals this chapter has identified that tensions will exist within the local resident population. The local business community will wish to see the tourism industry promoted more heavily in order to increase their wealth. In contrast the retired population which does tend to dominate the settlements will lobby for no tourism growth in order to preserve the special qualities of the land and townscapes that have attracted them to retire to the region. Muller's third point of his pentagon – unspoilt nature, protection of resources – is probably the most undisputed aspect of sustainable tourism development in the Lake District. There are many policies in place, supported by legislation, to preserve and conserve the special natural features of the Lakeland landscape. Problems have started to appear with the fourth point of the pentagon – healthy culture. The outward migration of young people who have been born in the Lake District and the threat to the sustainability of farming families and hence farming communities will erode even further the traditional ways of life, dialects, customs and crafts. Although the local culture is preserved through the country fairs and shows that are held annually, as the native born population becomes increasingly elderly, there will be a decline in the indigenous population to continue such cultural traditions. The final point of Muller's pentagon relates to the optimum satisfaction of guest requirements. Tourists in the 21st century are becoming increasingly discerning, accustomed to modern high quality tourism facilities, incorporating state of the art technology and design. The tourism product of the Lake District is starting to appear jaded, in need of further investment to ensure it is able to compete with other world class destinations. Until such investment is made the Lake District will have a challenge in maintaining its current level of tourist numbers, let alone increasing its share of a highly competitive market – points to be developed further in Chapter Nine. Thus, although Cumbria and the Lake District has achieved the status of being the first tourist destination in the world to be accredited by Green Globe 21 as a sustainable tourist destination challenges will be faced in the future to maintain this accreditation, if a simplistic application of Muller's (1994) definition of sustainable tourism development is employed.

Perhaps the key lesson that can be drawn from this chapter is that the complexities and interweaving of the special characteristics of each tourist destination will have a major impact and influence on the attainment of the principles of sustainable tourism management. The constantly changing characteristics of each destination (demographic, economic, political administration and governance, for example) will either act as a catalyst or a deterrent to the attainment of these principles. No matter how well researched and written the destination's sustainable tourism strategy is, if there are unforeseen and uncontrollable changes occurring within the local community and economy, the principles of sustainable tourism may be difficult to achieve. Clearly though, effective tourist destination management should try to identify and assess these uncontrollable influences through thorough research. Strategies to develop sustainable tourism should be based on such research, and should be implemented through effective partnerships and collaboration. Chapter Five will discuss how the principles of sustainable tourism are implemented in the Lake District by the key agencies involved with the development of tourism in the region.

References

Creative Research (2002) *Cumbria Tourism Survey 2002 Report of Findings*. London: Creative Research.

Cumbria County Council, Ward Profiles (2001) accessed from www.cumbria.gov.uk/aboutcumbria/ward_profiles_2000.

Cumbria County Council and Lake District National Park Authority (1995) *Development for the 1990s: Cumbria and the Lake District Joint Structure Plan 1991 – 2006*. Kendal: Cumbria County Council and the Lake District National Park Authority.

Cumbria County Council (2002) accessed from www.cumbria.gov.uk/aboutcumbria.

Cumbria Economic Intelligence Partnership (2002) *An Economic Assessment of Cumbria*. Cockermouth: Cumbria Inward Investment Agency.

Cumbria Tourist Board (2002) *Facts of Tourism*. Windermere: Cumbria Tourist Board.

Lake District National Park Authority (1998) *Lake District National Park Local Plan*. Kendal: Lake District National Park Authority.

Lake District National Park Authority (1999) *Lake District National Park Management Plan*. Kendal: Lake District National Park Authority.

Locum Destination Consulting (2003a) *Cumbria Strategic Tourism Market and Development Forecasts, Market Trends Report – Final*. Haywards Heath: Locum Destination Consulting.

Locum Destination Consulting (2003b) *Cumbria Market Forecasts Study, Business Survey Final Report*. Haywards Heath: Locum Destination Consulting.

Muller, H. The Theory Path to Sustainable Development. *Journal of Sustainable Tourism* 2(3), 131-136.

Office of National Statistics, (2003), Policy & Research Unit.

Chapter Four

The Lake District as a Tourist Destination in the 21st Century

The Lake District is situated in north west England, approximately 450 kms from London and the south east. The region is easily accessible by road, rail and air. The M6 motorway and the west coast railway line run through Cumbria to the east of the Lake District and Manchester airport is just 160 kms to the south. Within two hours drive time of the Lake District are the major conurbations of Glasgow, Tyneside, Wearside, Greater Manchester, and Merseyside. However, despite good transport links to the rest of the United Kingdom (UK) and overseas, Cumbria only attracts 2.5 per cent of all domestic tourism trips, and 0.7 per cent of all overseas tourism trips to the UK (www.staruk.org.uk, 2003). This is a reflection of the highly competitive nature of tourism in the 21st century. Most regions of the world are now promoting themselves as tourist destinations, and with the advent of low cost airlines, it is as inexpensive and quick for UK tourists to holiday in mainland Europe, as it is to take a holiday at home (a point developed further in Chapter Nine). In addition, the Lake District is some four or five hours drive time from the populous south east of England, making it more difficult to attract short break tourists from the south east.

In terms of seasonality, like the UK as a whole, tourism to the Lake District is now more evenly spread throughout the year. Gone are the days when tourists just visited the region in June, July, August and September. Data indicate that tourists visit Cumbria in all seasons: 18 per cent of all domestic tourists visit in January, February and March; 22 per cent of visits are made in April, May and June; 35 per cent of visits in July, August and September; and 25 per cent of visits in October, November, and December (Cumbria Tourist Board, 2002). This pattern of tourist visitation is important as it helps to sustain the viability of tourist businesses throughout the year, having benefits for tourism entrepreneurs as well as their employees. This is particularly significant given the economic fragility of many tourism businesses, especially those that operate as micro-businesses (see Chapter Three).

A Classification of Tourist Facilities

To attract tourists to a destination region primary and secondary factors are required (Jansen-Verbeke, 1988). The primary factors include the destination's:

> ➤ cultural facilities – museums, art galleries, exhibitions, theatres, concert halls, cinemas;

> ➤ physical characteristics – ancient monuments and buildings, architecture, ecclesiastical buildings, parks and green areas, geomorphology, ecology, water, canals and riverfronts, marinas;

> ➤ socio-cultural features – local customs and costumes, dialects, folklore, friendliness, security;

> ➤ sports facilities – indoor and outdoor;

> ➤ amusement facilities – night clubs, amusement arcades, organised events and festivities.

The primary factors are those elements that actually attract tourists to the destination. Secondary factors are those elements that enhance the tourists' experience of the destination, or assist in attracting tourists:

> ➤ accommodation and catering facilities;

> ➤ shopping facilities;

> ➤ accessibility and parking facilities;

> ➤ tourist facilities – information centres, signage, tourist information.

This chapter focuses on the principal elements that constitute the Lake District as a contemporary tourist destination, with accommodation and transport issues being considered in Chapters Six and Seven respectively. However, when an analysis is made of the tourist attractions in the Lake District it is apparent that there is a relatively narrow base of attractions and tourist facilities. Using the Jansen-Verbeke typology of 1988, the Lake District relies heavily on its cultural and heritage attractions and its physical features (see Table 4.0). There are very few purpose built, greenfield, new tourist attractions in the Lake District National Park – apart from the Theatre by the Lake in Keswick and the Aquarium of the Lakes on the southern shore of Windermere. This is not to say that no new tourist attractions have been developed. On the contrary, new tourist attractions and facilities have been developed but the majority tend to be in converted buildings, rather than on new greenfield sites, for example the Home of Football in Ambleside and the Cars of the Stars Motor Museum in Keswick.

Table 4.0   *Examples of tourist attractions in the Lake District*

Classification	Examples
Cultural and heritage attractions	Eskdale Historic Water Corn Mill; Windermere Steam Boat Museum; Cumberland Toy & Model Museum; Ruskin Museum; Cumberland Pencil Museum; Beatrix Potter Gallery; Dove Cottage and the Wordsworth Museum; Threlkeld Quarry & Mining Museum; Cars of the Stars; Home of Football; Muncaster Castle; Brantwood; Dalemain Historic House & Gardens; Theatre by the Lake; Stott Park Bobbin Mill; Mirehouse; Rydal Mount & Gardens.
Arts and crafts	The Heaton Cooper Studio and Slapestones Gallery, Grasmere; Thornthwaite Galleries, Keswick.
Physical characteristsics	Lakes (e.g. Windermere, Ullswater, Wastwater); mountains (e.g. Scafell, Coniston Old Man, Helvellyn); valleys (e.g. Langdale, Ennerdale, Borrowdale); forests (e.g. Whinlatter, Grizedale).
Food & drink	Lakeland traditional inns; Grasmere Gingerbread Shop; Internationally recognised restaurants; fish & chip shops.
Transport related attractions	Windermere Lake Cruises; SY Gondola (Coniston); Ullswater Steamers; Ravenglass and Eskdale Railway; Lakeside & Haverthwaite Railway.
Sports facilities & outdoor pursuits	Low Wood Watersports Centre; Troutbeck Bridge Swimming Pool; golf courses; guided walking holidays; outdoor adventure specialists; fishing.
Shopping facilities	A Taste of Lakeland, Ambleside; Kirkstone Galleries, Ambleside; traditional glass and furniture makers; outdoor pursuit retailers; craft shops.
Animal and wildlife attractions	Aquarium of the Lakes; the Alpaca Centre; Lakeland Bird of Prey Centre; Trotters World of Animals.
Archaeological & architectural sites	The Bridge House (Ambleside); Ashness Bridge (near Keswick); Hardknott Roman Fort.
Tourist Information Centres	The Lake District Visitor Centre, Brockhole; TICs in the main tourist centres: Grasmere, Windermere, Keswick.
Special Events	Keswick Film, Jazz & Literature Festivals; Grasmere Lakeland Sports and Show; Borrowdale Shepherds Meet and Show.

The stringent planning regulations of the Lake District National Park Authority are one of the main reasons why very few new purpose built tourist attractions have been developed in the Lake District. The planning regulations, and the desire by a number of key organisations (the National Trust, the Lake District National Park Authority, and the Friends of the Lake District, for example) to conserve and preserve the distinctive features of the Lake District probably explains why tourism in the Lake District depends so heavily on its culture, heritage, and the natural landscape. Chapter Five provides further insight into the planning, management, and development of tourism in the Lake District and explains the contribution that the aforementioned organisations make to sustainable tourism management and development. Planning regulations clearly have a significant role to play in maintaining and preserving the natural features of the Lakeland landscape and preserving the traditional characteristics of towns and villages.

The planning regulations currently in place have further added to the development of sustainable tourism in the region by encouraging the dispersal of tourists away from the main honeypot towns of the Lake District to the sub-regions of Cumbria. A number of new tourist attractions have been developed in Cumbria in recent years that occupy large sites on the fringe of the Lake District National Park. Rheged – the Village in the Hill –

has been developed just outside the Lake District National Park boundary on the north eastern corner of the Lake District at Penrith. Rheged is Europe's largest covered building and is an all weather, all year round visitor centre. Housed within the site is an Imax cinema, the Helly Hansen National Mountaineering Exhibition and a range of retail and catering outlets. The Lakeland Sheep and Wool Centre is sited on the north west corner of the Lake District National Park at Cockermouth. This tourist attraction provides an opportunity to see 19 different breeds of sheep as well as experiencing some of the skills needed by shepherds. Neither of these two attractions would have secured planning permission to be developed within the Lake District National Park, but are both located on the fringe and help to draw tourists away from the central area of Lakeland. This has economic, social, and environmental benefits for the region and thus contributes to sustainable tourism management in the Lake District.

Gleaston Water Mill is located to the south west of Windermere. It is an example of a micro-business that not only contributes to sustainable tourism by using a former industrial site as a contemporary tourist attraction, but also demonstrates how such businesses need to consider their own financial sustainability. This is critical for their own survival, and in the case of Gleaston Water Mill has been achieved by the application of marketing strategy to identify and target key market segments.

Case Study – Marketing Gleaston Water Mill

Gleaston Water Mill is an independently owned and operated water powered corn mill located in a quiet rural valley on the Lake District Peninsula between Ulverston and Barrow. The site, in addition to the 18th century mill, offers Dusty Miller's café serving home made food, the Pig's Whisper country store – 'a paradise of all things Pig', a holiday cottage (converted from a pig sty) and the Barleycorn Suite – a fully equipped business suite. Gleaston Water Mill has been operational for eleven years and currently has one full-time and eight part-time employees.

Gleaston Water Mill fulfils the characteristics of an SME as posited by Schollhammer and Kuriloff (1979) in that: firstly, the scope of its operations predominantly serve local markets. Secondly the scale of operations limits market share and turnover. Thirdly it is owned and managed by a partnership to whom the operation is solely reliant; and finally, it conforms to a personalised style of management. These characteristics have an impact on the business in general, and marketing aspects in particular. They are compounded further by features specific to tourism such as high fixed costs, seasonality, product perishability and complimentarity.

Trading conditions have become increasingly difficult in Cumbria. Visitor numbers have been depressed in the last five years, a feature reflected in the decline in visitor numbers to the Mill over the same period, from a peak of 25,000 in 1997 to 17,500 in 2000 and to approximately 9,000 in 2001 – the direct result of significant happenings in the market such as Foot and Mouth disease. However, Gleaston Water Mill continues to provide a satisfactory return for its managing partners. This can be attributed to the attraction keeping a keen eye on market conditions, on-going development of a unique product theme and the continued desire to provide a high standard, value for money visitor experience.

The marketing activity undertaken by Gleaston Water Mill confirms the 'entrepreneurial' tag as stated by Dibb (1995) and the 'implicit marketing' tag devised by Carson and Cromie (1989, 1995). The market is broadly, yet clearly, defined with reference to the elements of the product portfolio. For example, the Barleycorn Suite is patronised by school groups, local companies (of various size) and other groups such as the local bee association and archaeological groups. Further detail is provided of a demographic, psychographic and geographic nature when describing the characteristics of the typical customer. Dusty Miller's café users tend to be middle-aged/elderly, many disabled and from the Morecambe Bay area and the Lake District. The holiday cottage customer tends to be middle-aged, has a sense of humour, uses the Internet, has family ties locally and therefore visits the area regularly. Whilst visitors are generated from all corners of the UK and abroad, the main generating areas are the Manchester region and the East coast of England. Whilst such a breakdown is relatively crude in nature, it provides evidence that an analysis of the product portfolio into market segments provides a basis for subsequent target market communication.

Some ad hoc marketing research is undertaken, recently focusing upon non-users, and is constantly supplemented by informal feedback. Additionally, complementary sources of information are gathered through the consortia groups of the Furness Tourism Partnership and the North West Mills Group, alongside membership of the Cumbria Tourist Board. The use of consortia in this way is a sensible method of improving marketing intelligence, a crucial element in the analysis phase of the strategic marketing planning process (McDonald, 1995). The Scottish Tourism Co-ordinating Group regard such collaboration as 'crucial to the minimisation of external threats and the maximisation of shared opportunities' (Fyall et al., 2001:212) and Whitehead (1999) asserts that visitor attractions must 'participate in local marketing exercises to become part of the total tourism package' (p.212). The view taken by Gleaston Water Mill that local competition within the visitor attraction sector is healthy for business acknowledges the notion that an enhanced visitor attraction offering draws greater numbers of visitors to the area and therefore benefits all stakeholders. The rural location of the Mill is, in part, dependent upon the visitor number inertia created in this way. Promotion of the site has also been assisted by the consortia. Interestingly, the major competitors were viewed as the nearby towns of Barrow and Ulverston who are working hard to attract people back into the town centre. Such a view raises the spectre that a collective approach by stakeholders that does not consider the whole tourism package of the local area may ultimately prove counter productive to an individual attraction such as Gleaston Water Mill.

Market intelligence has also played a significant part in the development of a unique product theme. The creation and development of the pig theme has established a unique selling point for the site. The cottage and retail store, as the central products of this theme, have the advantage of being accessible to a global market through the Water Mill websites (www.gleastonmill.demon.co.uk/millsite and www.watermill.co.uk). Indirect access is gained through links from other sites such as Cumbria Tourist Board (www.golakes.co.uk), the village of Gleaston (www.gleaston.org uk), and the consortia (www.lake-district-peninsulas.co.uk) thus potentially widening the customer base geographically and demographically.

Whilst the detailed strategic marketing planning approach as advocated by McDonald (1995) and Morgan (1996) cannot be observed in the practices employed by Gleaston Water Mill, the broad four stage concept of analysis, planning, implementation and control (Morgan, 1996) is evident, albeit with limited adherence to the final stage. Furthermore, the desire to 'continue to preserve the Water Mill' creates the assumption that future business sustainability is of key strategic intent. Analysis of competitors and customers, alongside market information and knowledge, plus promotion and price (although limited in explanation here), have enabled the Mill to confidently enter the planning phase of the strategic marketing planning model prior to implementation. This approach is on-going as the product continues to develop. The development of the site to date, arguably, has been a clever utilisation of strategic intent. The construction of a diversified product portfolio has enabled Gleaston Water Mill to continue to trade successfully through the recent significant effects of Foot and Mouth disease and the terrorist attacks in the USA. Having established a broad customer base, rather than being reliant on a single customer group, the Mill has maintained an income stream from markets less directly affected by continuing adverse conditions. This is clearly a salutary lesson for visitor attractions, and other small tourism enterprises, upon which to critically appraise their business. The effects of external factors in 2001 upon Gleaston Water Mill have nevertheless influenced a greater awareness of potential markets. The implementation of a radio advertisement across the nearby Morecambe Bay region was instigated to extend the local customer base. For this campaign, and all other promotional instances, the control phase of the strategic marketing planning process ought to be undertaken. Only then, with monitoring of the marketing effort, can the true value of marketing expenditure be assessed and the process of analysis, planning, implementation, and control become a cyclical and integrated benefit to business sustainability of the mill.

In conclusion, the observation of adherence to a basic strategic marketing planning approach (in three of the four identified phases) provides evidence of the occurrence of a strategic basis for marketing activity in this small visitor attraction. Two significant observations are evident in the strategic intent of Gleaston Water Mill. First of all the conscious decision to play a significant part in local and regional consortia networks which enable improvements in market intelligence information in the analysis stage and subsequently the opportunities afforded through such a network to plan and implement communication with target markets. Secondly, diversification of the product to enable a wider customer base and thus overcome any potential downturn in any one customer market. This strategic approach has ultimately assisted the sustainability of the site in the on-going difficult trading conditions in Cumbria.

The following sections of this chapter will investigate in more depth some of the natural, cultural and heritage features of the Lake District that make the region an important tourist destination. The place of sports and activity tourism will then be discussed before the position of the honeypot towns that draw the lion's share of visitors is considered. Examples will also be provided of how some of the tourist attractions featured in this chapter contribute to sustainable development through their own management strategies.

The Natural Landscape

As Chapter Two has already shown the distinctive Lakeland landscape has been widely appreciated as a tourist destination for the last two centuries (Urry, 1995). The vast array of literature testifies to this. The introduction to Talbot & Whiteman's *Lakeland Landscapes* typifies the beautifully produced full-colour approach of much of the literature:

> "Covering only thirty-five square miles, the diversity of the Lakeland landscape is remarkable: high peaks, wild fells, spectacular waterfalls, lush pastures, secluded villages, enchanting lakes, ancient sites, historic buildings, isolated farmsteads, remote villages and bustling towns" (Talbot & Whiteman, 1997:6).

The landscape itself has been heavily influenced by the underlying geology and physical geography of a region which owes much of its outstanding scenery to the activities of glaciers and ice sheets during the last Ice Age. The details of these developments have been covered fully elsewhere (Millward & Robinson, 1970; Boardman, 1996). In many ways the sub-heading 'natural' landscape is misleading, since the typical lakeland scene of today is the consequence of layer upon layer of human activity stretching back over centuries.

The landscape creates an impression of relative wildness, particularly in the higher central and northern fells, yet at the same time the seasonally changing tone and texture of woodland and farmland, along with the dominating presence of the lakes imbues the Lake District with photogenic qualities that make marketing simple, and keep visitor numbers high. Yet at the same time, the Lake District is a highly managed landscape, both manicured and gentrified. There are two principle causes for this; firstly, tight planning controls following designation as a National Park, and secondly, the large landowning presence of the National Trust (see Chapter Five). The National Trust holds far more land in the Lake District than in any other national park; a position which significantly increases its influence on the management of the landscape (www.cnp.org.uk). Alongside these two elements is the overwhelming desire of both local and national communities for the area to retain its perceived aesthetic purity (Urry, 1995).

A large number of elements together form a landscape of great attractiveness, appreciated by thousands of tourists each year. The fells, the semi-natural woodlands of the valley sides, the improved pastures of the intake land and the more intensively cultivated inbye land combine, with small villages and isolated farmsteads to produce an aesthetically pleasing rural landscape, made majestic by the glacial lakes that occupy the floor of many of the valleys.

The reality of this enduring landscape is in many ways quite different to the marketing. Indeed, it would be a mistake to consider this landscape as a static entity. For instance, changing economic circumstances in forestry led to the conversion of at least 1100ha of broadleaved woodland to conifers between the late 1940s and 1978, leaving a total of about 10,400ha. The swing in sentiment against regimented blocks of upland conifer plantations suggests that such changes are unlikely to be allowed in the future (Lake District National Park Authority, 1999). Even the lakes are not all quite what they seem. Thirlmere, as a supplier of water to Manchester, had its water level raised by over 15 metres following the construction of a dam in the 1890s, resulting in the inundation of several farms and the hamlet of Wythburn. Manchester was also responsible for the creation of Haweswater. In total, there are 17 reservoirs in the Lake District. Demand for water has not been the only cause of landscape manipulation. Tarn Hows, a beauty spot so popular that the National Trust has minimised associated road signs to prevent people finding it, began life as three natural tarns before being fashionably transformed at the end of the nineteenth century by the owner at that time. Ironically, the nineteenth century plantings that gave Tarn Hows its distinctive landscape are now having to be actively managed to prevent wetland from being smothered by conifers.

Active maintenance strategies are key elements of the work of the Lake District National Park Authority. For instance, over the period 1997-99, a combination of European Union funding (50 per cent) and National Park Authority funding (40 per cent) supported 35 local schemes ranging from village street enhancements to the conservation of local archaeological sites in that area of the national park eligible for Objective 5b funding. Details of some of these projects are contained in Table 4.1.

Table 4.1   *Funding to safeguard and enhance features of local landscape interest*

Consolidation of bee holes at Boon Crag, Coniston.
Repair of shared fence at High Yewdale Farm, Coniston.
Conservation and interpretation work at Myers Head Lead Mine, Hartsop.
Restoration of Dog Folly, Coniston.
Rebuilding traditional stone walls at Staveley and Hartsop.
Village car park improvement – Askham.
Conservation work on village greens – Askham.
Replacement of derelict roadside railings – Kentmere.
Conservation work to historic portals on a redundant bridge – Threlkeld.

Source: www.lake-district.gov.uk

The attraction of the Lake District for walkers is well known. But again, this involves significant landscape management issues. The Upland Access Group (a consortium including the National Trust and the Lake District National Park Authority) has received £1.46 million over 5 years from the Heritage Lottery Fund for an extensive programme of upland path repair and restoration (National Trust, 2002). With over one hundred seriously eroded paths, it has been estimated that a minimum of £2.5 million will be needed to rectify the problem (Lake District National Park Authority, 1999).

However not all of the Lake District scenery can be described as aesthetically pleasing. There are 30 mineral sites with planning permission, and quarrying remains a significant activity in several locations. Cumbria supplies more than 10 per cent of the UK output of roofing slate and a number of slate quarries are active in the National Park. In total, 220ha of land in Cumbria has planning permission for slate working (Richards *et al.,* 1995). Ironically, aesthetic demands for the use of appropriate, local building materials in the Park, ensures a guaranteed market for some of the quarries. Honister Slate Mine has turned this to its advantage as an industrial tourist attraction:

"Set in the heart of Lakeland, Honister Slate Mines have, for centuries, produced the beautiful green stone which is famous throughout the world. The mine offers underground tours and a visitor centre full of fascinating displays, historical information and souvenirs" (www.honister-slate-mine.co.uk).

Similarly, Kirkstone Galleries at Skelwith Bridge offer tea rooms and a shop alongside a quarry, while the National Trust has preserved Force Crag Mine as an industrial landscape, and disused quarries have been turned into car parks and climbing walls. Such variety definitely adds to the range of visitor attractions, but also helps to improve the visual features of the site with improved landscaping which is necessary in order to attract tourists. Again, the changing perceptions of quarry environments, along with new techniques for quarry reclamation are likely to impact on policies in the future (Gunn *et al.*, 1992).

A report in 1988 stated that "small traditional quarries, formerly worked by hand, are not intrusive but provide landscape features" whereas modern quarries "disfigure the landscape and require associated service roads, traffic and buildings" (Richards *et al.*, 1995). This tension between traditional and modern is set to continue, with bodies such as the Council for National Parks actively campaigning against further quarry developments (www.cnp.org.uk). Such a perception is not necessarily in line with local feeling, where slate quarries represent a way of life that has a longer tradition than tourism.

Clearly, the perceived landscape qualities of the Lake District are the principal factor in sustaining the region as a major tourism attraction. But, as seen earlier, such landscape qualities are far from simple and clear-cut, while perceptions vary between groups and over time. However, a successful tourist economy is rarely dependent upon a single factor. Attention will now be turned to other aspects of the area that reinforce its popularity as a tourist destination.

Literary Shrines

The importance of literary places in the tourist experience is well known, ranging from the inextricable interlinking of Shakespeare and Stratford upon Avon, to the creation of rather more recent tourist destinations such as 'Catherine Cookson Country' in north east England (Pocock, 1992) or indeed more tenuous connections such as the surge in tourist interest in Stamford, Lincolnshire, following the filming of George Elliot's Middlemarch in 1994 (even though the town had no connection with either the writer or the book) or the 'Tolkein Trail' brochure produced by Ribble Valley Borough Council on the basis of Tolkein's frequent visits to Stonyhurst College (Herbert, 2001; *Clitheroe Advertiser* and *Times*, 8th August 2002). Through these forms of tourist development, new meanings are imposed on landscape for economic gain (Squire, 1993). The importance of this area of heritage tourism is shown by the range of strategies implemented to attract visitors to such locations.

Herbert (2001) suggests there are four principal reasons for visits to literary places: firstly, to experience places that have connections with the lives of the writers. Secondly, to experience places that form the setting for novels; thirdly, for some broader and deeper emotions than the specific writer or the story; and fourthly, as a result of some dramatic event in the life of the writer. As will be seen, one might add a further set of reasons based around commercial appeal and consumer demands for a variety of often tenuously related products and experiences.

The Lake District is an area richly endowed with literary places and heritage-related tourism. Such tourism is particularly associated with the poetry of William Wordsworth, the writings of Beatrix Potter and Arthur Ransome and the cultural legacy of John Ruskin.

William Wordsworth (1770-1850)

As discussed in Chapter Two, the poetry of William Wordsworth is synonymous with the landscapes of the Lake District. Wordsworth's *Guide to the Lakes* was first published in 1810, had gone through 5 editions by 1835, the final text was published in 1906 and reprinted in 1930, 1970 and 1973 with a paperback being continuously available since 1977. Wordsworth's popularity as a poet has consistently enabled the Lake District to attract tourists to the landscapes he described. However, the very popularity and mythology of Wordsworth has enabled the poet himself to become a significant tourist attraction in his own right.

Wordsworth lived in the Lake District for most of his life and all three of his residences now constitute elements of the 'Wordsworth experience' (see Table 4.2).

Table 4.2   *The homes of William Wordsworth*

Date	Property	Current Use
1770 - 1778	Wordsworth House, Cockermouth	National Trust property. Rooms furnished in the Regency Style, personal effects of the poet, video showing in the stables, tea rooms, shop.
1799-1808	Dove Cottage, Grasmere	Owned by Wordsworth Trust. Guided tours of preserved cottage, Wordsworth Museum – manuscripts, books and paintings, special exhibitions, shop.
1813-1850	Rydal Mount and gardens	Owned by descendants of the poet, personal effects, extensive gardens.

Sources: www.wordsworth.org.uk : www.wordsworthlakes.co.uk

The importance of multiple attractions for tourist growth can be highlighted by contrasting tourist developments related to Wordsworth with the relative lack of development that has occurred in Lincolnshire concerning Wordsworth's equally popular successor as poet laureate, Alfred Tennyson.

John Ruskin (1819-1900)

John Ruskin was not a writer in the same sense as Wordsworth, Ransome and Potter; however, he was one of the greatest figures of the Victorian age; poet, artist, critic, social revolutionary and conservationist. His first impressions of the Lake District related to family holidays. Ruskin was appointed Slade Professor of Fine Art at Oxford University in 1869. He was a leading light in a group that included Hardwicke Rawnsley and Octavia Hill, two of the founders of the National Trust in 1896. Ruskin enthusiastically took up the cause of conservation, campaigning for town and country planning, green belts and smokeless zones. In 1871, he bought Brantwood on the shores of Lake Coniston. He was visited at Brantwood by many eminent Victorians, including Charles Darwin, Holman Hunt, Kate Greenaway and W. G. Collingwood, the house becoming; 'an intellectual powerhouse and one of the greatest literary and artistic centres in Europe' (Brantwood publicity leaflet). In 1877 he inspired William Morris to found the Society for the Protection of Ancient Buildings.

Ruskin died at Brantwood in 1900, and is buried in the churchyard of St. Andrew's Church in Coniston. A year later, W. G. Collingwood worked to set up an exhibition, now called the Ruskin Museum, at the back of the Coniston Mechanics Institute, as a place to preserve any Ruskin mementoes that could be found. In 1901 the building was opened by Canon Rawnsley, and now gets almost as many visitors as Brantwood itself. Interestingly, in the tourist literature, the museum is described as *'the village's* [author's emphasis] memorial to him' [www.lakedistrict.com].

The interlinking of tourist attractions can be clearly identified here. The National Trust uses a Victorian steam-powered yacht, the Gondola, which runs from Coniston to Brantwood jetty, providing an 'authentic' Victorian lake cruise, on a boat 'probably' used by Ruskin, from the honeypot village of Coniston to Ruskin's home. Commercial considerations are clearly to the fore in combining tourist activities through collaborative marketing. The Coniston Launch for instance, works 'closely with Brantwood to provide the very best way to experience a visit there. Buy your ticket on the launches and SAVE 50p.' (Coniston Launch leaflet).

Table 4.3   *Tourist activities related to John Ruskin*

Location	Attraction
Brantwood	Ruskin's home 1872-1900. Collection of Ruskin's watercolours, furniture. Craft gallery, bookshop and restaurant, outdoor theatre, art and craft centre, woodland walks.
Ruskin Museum, Coniston	Collection of Ruskin mementoes, linen and lace.
SY Gondola, Lake Coniston	Victorian steam yacht ('travelled on by Ruskin'), National Trust.
Armitt Museum, Ambleside	Section on John Ruskin.
St. Andrew's Churchyard, Coniston	Grave of John Ruskin.

Arthur Ransome (1884-1967)

Arthur Ransome, author of the 'Swallows and Amazons' series of books for children, is a further literary connection that has been actively promoted in Lakeland. The Arthur Ransome Society is based at Abbot Hall Museum of Lakeland Life and History in Kendal. The original 'Amazon' along with 'Esperance' (the model for Captain Flint's houseboat) can be seen at the Windermere Steamboat Museum at Bowness. As with Ruskin, Ransome's links to The Lakes began with summer holidays taken by his family from their home in Leeds, although he also attended preparatory school in Windermere. The settings for his books, with name changes, have been readily identified as various parts of the Lakes (see Table 4). It was only in 1925 that the Ransomes bought Low Ludderburn, an old farmhouse at the head of Cartmel Fell valley. His last house was Hill Top at Haverthwaite in south Lakeland.

Table 4.4   *Tourist activity and the writings of Arthur Ransome*

Name in Book	Lake District Location
Kanchenjunga	Coniston Old Man.
Lake (unnamed)	Coniston & Windermere.
Promontory where Swallows planned their first expedition	Near Nibthwaite on Coniston.
Wildcat Island	Peel Island, Coniston.
Museums and Galleries	
Ruskin Museum, Coniston	Section on 'Swallow and Amazons' country.
Abbott Hall Art Gallery & Museum, Kendal	Arthur Ransome room: memorabilia, sketches and drawings.
Windermere Steamboat Museum	Two of the dinghies Ransome used as models for the boats. Exhibition.

Sources: various including www.sndc.demon.co.uk/tars

The success of Ransome's children's writing has led to a further attraction for tourists. For instance, a book *In the footsteps of Swallows and Amazons* provides 19 walks covering the locations discussed in Ransome's book, while the Coniston Launch offers special interest cruises to Ransome's locations.

Beatrix Potter (1866-1943)

Although world famous as a writer of children's stories, Beatrix Potter was also a landscape and natural history artist, farmer and conservationist. She was responsible for the preservation of large areas of the Lake District through her gifts to the National Trust.

In 1905 Potter bought Hill Top, a small farm in Near Sawrey. In 1909 she bought another farm opposite Hill Top, Castle Farm, which became her main Lakeland base. In

1923 she bought Troutbeck Park Farm, and became an expert in breeding Herdwick sheep, winning many prizes at country shows with them. Beatrix continued to buy property, and in 1930 bought the Monk Coniston Estate – 4000 acres from Little Langdale to Coniston – which contained Tarn Hows, now Lakeland's most popular piece of landscape.

When she died on 22 December 1943, Beatrix Potter left fourteen farms and 4000 acres of land to the National Trust, together with her flocks of Herdwick sheep (for a detailed discussion of the role of the National Trust see Chapter Five).

The Beatrix Potter Phenomenon

Wordsworth, Ruskin, Ransome and Potter clearly had a love of the Lake District, but Beatrix Potter's generosity in leaving a substantial bequest to the National Trust was distinctive in creating a lasting impact on the subsequent development of both the National Trust and the National Park itself. Hill Top is the most visited literary shrine in the Lake District, receiving around 70,000 visitors each year, despite its spatial limitations and relatively difficult access, in itself a remarkable achievement for a moderately sized farm house left intact circa 1940. The National Trust clearly identifies the dilemma facing the organisation over how best to maintain the integrity of the property while affording maximum access to visitors.

> 'Hill Top is a very small house and a timed entry and booking system is operated. The number of visitors is monitored to avoid overcrowding and to protect the fragile interior. This is a unique and popular property, and visitors sometimes have to wait to enter. We regret that occasionally some visitors may not gain entry at all. School holidays are particularly busy and as a general rule, visitors are advised to come at the beginning or end of the season if at all possible' (National Trust, 2002: 277).

The National Trust is also active in its marketing of Beatrix Potter, including a *Beatrix Potter Properties Newsletter*, providing detailed information about Potter-related properties owned by the Trust (see Table 4.5).

Table 4.5   *Beatrix Potter related properties owned by the National Trust*

Property	Description
Hill Top, Near Sawrey	Farmhouse, former home of Beatrix Potter, containing all original interior.
Corner Shop, Hawkshead	Shop.
Beatrix Potter Gallery, Hawkshead	Former offices of Beatrix Potter's husband. Display of Potter's watercolours and drawings.

Source: www.nationaltrust.org.uk

What is more remarkable, however, is the commercial scale of subsequent developments, which sets Potter apart from the other three writers (see Table 4.6). The World of Beatrix Potter has the highest profile. Based at The Old Laundry, Bowness, and opened in 1991, the attraction comprises an exhibition of Potter characters in an 'indoor creation of the countryside' along with several video presentations, tea room and large shop selling Potter collectables, publications and memorabilia. It received the 1997 'Come to Britain' award from the British Tourist Authority. The Peter Rabbit and Friends chain of shops contain similar merchandise, with five stores in the Lakes (Keswick, Grasmere, Ambleside, Windermere and Bowness) along with an extensive internet mailing service and stores elsewhere in the country. A very large number of other shops in the principal towns and villages also sell an extensive range of 'Potter' goods. The celebration of the centenary of *Peter Rabbit* (2002) was followed by the centenaries of *The Tale of Squirrel Nutkin* and *The Tailor of Gloucester* (2003), with each offering a range of commercial and promotional opportunities (National Trust, 2002). Butler (1998:217) has argued that 'activities which could occur in urban areas assume greater significance and appear to give greater satisfaction in rural settings e.g. shopping, particularly for rural boutique items, wines and foodstuffs.' This observation appears to be confirmed by the existence of such a wide range of shopping opportunities in the Lake District and again relates to urban notions of rurality and the use of country areas as urban leisure facilities.

Table 4.6   *Beatrix Potter related tourist attractions*

Place	Current Use
World of Beatrix Potter	Exhibition of her life and characters including videos.
Armitt Museum and library, Ambleside	Collection of fungi, natural history and archaeological water colours and drawings, display of her life.
Hill Top, Near Sawrey, Ambleside	National Trust, Beatrix Potter's first house.
Beatrix Potter Gallery, Hawkshead	Collection of original drawings.
Keswick, Grasmere, Ambleside, Windermere, Bowness	Peter Rabbit and Friends Shops.

Sources: various including www.beatrixpottersociety.org.uk

Reinforcing these links has been an extensive series of publications relating Beatrix Potter to the Lake District (see Table 4.7). Hunter Davies' book *Beatrix Potter's Lakeland* is in many ways a classic example of the combination of biography and topographical writing, clearly with an eye to the tourist market, which reinforces existing links between author and landscape. Part biography, part geography, lavishly produced with stunning photography (by Cressida Pemberton-Piggott), it both captures the spirit of the Lake District and reinforces the importance of its literary connections. Commercial considerations are clearly important here, since the book is published by Frederick Warne & Co, the same publisher that, so Davies tells us, still sells 300,000 copies of *The Tale of Peter Rabbit* each year (Davies, 1998). Indeed, Warne & Co have taken a very pro-active line in continuing the promotion of the Beatrix Potter industry.

Table 4.7   *Sample publications connecting Beatrix Potter to Lakeland*

Author	Title	Year
H. Davies	Beatrix Potter's Lakeland.	1988
W. Bartlett & J. Whalley	Beatrix Potter's Derwentwater.	1998
A. Parker	Cottage and farmhouse detail in Beatrix Potter's Lake District.	1993
J. Taylor (Ed)	Beatrix Potter's farming friendship: Lake District letters to Joseph Moscrop, 1926-1943.	1998
J. Taylor	Beatrix Potter 1866-1943. The artist and her world.	1998
J. Taylor, J. Whalley & A. Hobbs	Beatrix Potter, artist, story teller and countrywoman.	1987
Beatrix Potter Society	Beatrix Potter Studies VII. Beatrix Potter and the Lake District.	1996

Sources: various including www.beatrixpottersociety.org.uk

Tourism related to Beatrix Potter has been seen as a largely female, middle class activity, where a significant part of the appeal lies in the marriage of Potter's depiction of rural life with the scenic reality of locations such as Hill Top. The two reinforce notions of Englishness and "are a means for people to live out, temporarily, a range of fantasies … one of these fantasies is about countryside and its role in modern, often urban culture" (Squire, 1994:204-5).

However, a closer analysis identifies other significant elements of what may be termed the Beatrix Potter phenomenon. Approximately one-third of all visitors to Hill Top are Japanese, signs in the house are in English and Japanese and the public house next door to the house even offers Japanese beer! These highlight the attractiveness of Beatrix Potter to the Japanese, as only 9 per cent of tourists to the Lake District are foreign visitors, and of that 9 per cent, only 8 per cent are Japanese. The number of Japanese visitors however, has steadily risen during the 1990s (Cumbria Tourist Board, 1998). In recent years, the Lake District has been much more involved in attracting Japanese visitors, to the extent that by 1999 it had replaced London and the Cotswolds as the most popular visitor destination for the Japanese. The Lake District Japan Forum, defined as: "A proactive private and public sector partnership dedicated to maintaining and increasing the numbers of Japanese visitors to the Lake District area" has been established with a dedicated web site in Japanese (www.japanforum.com and www.kosuichihou.com).

A range of strategies have been put in place to achieve and maintain this position. At both The World of Beatrix Potter and Hill Top, staff are able to speak essential Japanese, and the levels of satisfaction of Japanese visitors are considered to be very high. The home page of the Japan Forum website provides direct links to a wide range of Lake District attractions (see Table 4.8).

Table 4.8   *Website links on the Japan Forum home page*
(www.japanforum.com & www.kosuichihou.com)

Commercial activity	Web address	Japanese browser
English Lakes Hotels	www.elh.co.uk/japanese	Yes
The World of Beatrix Potter	www.hop-skip-jump.com	Yes
Wordsworth's Lake District	www.wordsworthlakes.co.uk	No
The National Trust	www.nationaltrust.org.uk	No
Windermere Lake Cruises	www.windermere-lakecruises.co.uk	No
The Mountain Goat	www.mountain-goat.co.uk	Yes
Cumbria Tourist Board	www.golakes.co.uk	No
Brantwood and Coniston Launch	ww.lakefell.co.uk	No
South Lake District Council	www.lake-district-breaks.com	No
Lake District National Park Authority	www.lake-district.gov.uk	No
Lakes Supertours	www.lakes-supertours.co.uk	Yes

It is no coincidence that the chairman of the Lake District Japan Forum is also the managing director of The World of Beatrix Potter. His explanation for the large number of visitors is clearly based on his own commercial experience:

> "Many people in Japan have learned English by reading Beatrix Potter books. But her popularity is slightly more subtle than that. It is also because cute cartoon characters are seen to be chic in Japan" (*The Guardian*, 8th November 1999).

Squire (1994) highlights the rather more mundane importance of shopping and the commercialisation of the Potter heritage with young Japanese women buying 'authentic' Peter Rabbit goods at Hill Top.

Approximately 25 per cent of visitors to The World of Beatrix Potter are from Japan, and they generally spend more money than British visitors. The arrival of a coach party of Japanese can have a considerable impact on the stock of shops such as those of the National Trust at Hill Top. The 'authenticity' of purchase is clearly of major significance here for Japanese visitors, as the range of trinkets available could be purchased by mail order or over the counter in Japan. Similar phenomena have been associated with the purchasing of football shirts relating to Fulham FC's Japanese star Junichi Inamoto, which are more valued if purchased from the club on a match day (*The Observer* 22nd September 2002). This observation clearly has resonance with Butler's (1998) observation about the relative satisfaction of purchasing in different circumstances (see above).

Additional reasons that were provided for visiting Potter sites referred to the quintessential Englishness of the locations, this being the case particularly at Hill Top, where rooms in the property match the illustrations provided in the books, thus reinforcing the authenticity of the experience.

This discussion of Japanese visitors and Beatrix Potter should not be seen in isolation however. The Japanese clearly regard the Lake District as a literary centre, and large numbers also visit the homes of Wordsworth at Rydal Mount and Dove Cottage, while the world-wide success of Arthur Ransome's books, including an Arthur Ransome Club in Japan, has also resulted in large numbers of Japanese tourists. The Lake District is not the only area where Japanese tourists are attracted by literary connections. Prince Edward Island, Canada, for instance, the location of the Anne of Green Gables novels of L. M. Montgomery is particularly popular with Japanese teenage girls (Butler, 1998).

The continued growth of 'cultural attractions' is likely to be encouraged. Cumbria Tourist Board (1998:23) cites the success of several theatres and jazz festivals along with the literary heritage. In its regional tourism strategy it states: 'There is considerable scope for extending the range of festivals and special events, particularly to support an extended tourist season and to encourage a wider distribution of tourism throughout the county.' Given that 65 per cent of visitors arrive during the months of April-September (Cumbria Tourist Board, 1998) there is clearly a potential for growth here, which by extending the season would provide more permanent, all-year-round employment.

Sports and Activity Tourism

The literary pilgrim might be conceptualized as a largely 'passive' tourist, content to gaze upon new places and capture images to re-experience when they return home (Urry, 1990; Herbert, 1995). However, as we have seen, definitions of a literary tourist are far from clear cut. By contrast, sports and activity tourism involve a far more proactive approach to the place visited. An 'active' tourist might be defined as one who wants to use the landscape; walking, climbing, power boat racing and so on (Herbert, 1995). In some senses therefore, the active tourist is using the landscape for the pursuit of a particular pastime or range of pastimes. The degree to which the landscape is merely the arena for the activity is difficult to determine. Clearly with an activity such as walking, the quality of the environment to be walked will be a crucial determinant in choice of walks; however with climbing or water sports, for instance, the nature of the rock face or the size of the lake may have a greater influence on the decision taken by the active tourist rather than any overall appreciation of the environment. The active tourist is likely to be urban in origin and sees the countryside as an opportunity for activities which are not readily available in urban areas. To some extent, therefore, the Lake District can be considered as an urban playground for the industrial towns and cities of the north and north west of England, with almost 25 per cent of all visitors to Cumbria coming from these regions (Creative Research, 2002). The increasing importance of day trips and short-stay holidays in the Lakes is likely to reinforce this situation – see Chapter Three.

As such, the 'active' tourist may have a range of impacts on the environment. In the case of the Lake District, the mountainous terrain, extensive woodlands and large lakes, the long tradition of allowing access together with public rights provide scope for many outdoor activities. There are over 3560km of public footpaths and bridleways in the National Park which are arguably the most important recreational resource (Lake District National Park Authority, 1998). Of the area's estimated 12 million annual visitors, as many as one in three take a walk of at least 4 miles during their stay (Lake District National Park Authority, 1999).

The multi-faceted characteristics of the tourism experience can be highlighted here by the importance of Alfred Wainwright (1907-1991), whose writings promoted walking in the Lake District and proved extraordinarily popular with walkers from the mid 1950s onwards, selling more than one million copies worldwide. Indeed, it is hard to argue with Mike Harding's comment on the jacket of Wainwright's final book that: "there can be few men who have made such an impact on people's relationship with a landscape as Alfred Wainwright". The recent creation of a 'Wainwright Society' (www.wainwright.org.uk) suggests that for future generations Wainwright might even move from the 'activity' tourism section of this chapter into the 'literary' tourist category.

The development of strategies to manage the 'active' tourist need to be seen in the broader context of a continually evolving national policy framework relating to recreational activities (see Chapter Five) where certain activities are clearly favoured over other activities. The 'outdoors' section of the Cumbria Tourist Board web site (www.lakedistrictoutdoors.co.uk) provides over 30 walking routes and over 20 cycling routes in the Lake District. Policies to increase the popularity of cycling are being implemented (see Chapter Seven). Cumbria County Council has established the Cumbria Cycle Way as a circular route around the county while the 'Coast to Coast' cycle route (C2C) has been established by Sustrans. The Ordnance Survey identifies "angling, boating and lake cruises, cycling, golf, riding and trekking, sailing, walking and watersports' as 'Sports and Activities" to be enjoyed in the Lake District, (Ordnance Survey, 1994:62) while the Cumbria Tourist Board website lists 27 pages of 'activity' holidays covering trekking, ballooning, cycle hire, equestrian events, climbing and a range of watersports.

At the individual level, entrepreneurs have utilized local resources to offer a range of activities. Farmers with fishing rights have successfully developed leisure activities not only for the angler but for the whole family, as at Esthwaite Water, where a range of angling styles are available to suit the entire competence range, from children and beginners to competition anglers. The multi-faceted nature of contemporary tourism is also on display, as the area incorporates barbeque stations ('to cook your catch'), picnic tables and an organic farm shop ('to buy your tea') (www.fishlink.com/hawkshead). Former industrial landscapes have been, on occasion, turned to recreational uses for the active tourist. For instance, the Hodge Close Quarry in Tilberthwaite is a popular location for activities such as rock climbing, abseiling and sub-aqua diving.

Again, such a range of activities are not without their problems. The National Park Local Plan (1998) categorically states that new golf course and driving ranges will not be permitted because of their landscape impact, considering that the five existing courses are sufficient for the needs of the local population. Such a policy provides a significant contrast with those areas where golf course provision is seen as an integral part of a strategy to encourage tourist development. The approach to equestrian development in the Lakes is rather more ambivalent – new proposals will be permitted where it can be demonstrated that there will be no harmful impact on the landscape. Effectively, existing buildings will have to be utilised and any all-weather surfaces, jumps and fencing must not be intrusive on the landscape (Lake District National Park Authority, 1998). The approach to both golf courses and horse riding can be seen as an attempt to ensure that the National Park retains its distinctive character at a time when much of the open countryside of the urban fringe appears to be turning into a playground for the suburban middle classes.

The Lake District National Park Authority Management Plan notes that

"Pursuits such as war games, car rallying, motor cycle tracks, trail riding, driving on unsealed roads and tracks, and paragliding need to be restricted to particular places and/or times in order not to harm other people's enjoyment or interests, or wildlife to a significant degree" (Lake District National Park Authority, 1999:60).

Mountain biking has been subject to significant public criticism, largely because of trespass onto footpaths and lack of consideration to walkers.

Over the last 10 years or so, the Lake District National Park Authority has become concerned about the apparent increase in recreational green road driving, both in 4 Wheel Drives (4WDs) or on motorbikes. Long-standing clubs such as the Cumbria Group of the Trail Riders Fellowship, North Lakes 4X4 Club, and Cumbria Land Rover Owners Club have been supplemented by commercial safari organisations, and the increase in sales of new and used vehicles has resulted in what appears to be a burgeoning activity. The Council for National Parks has been unequivocal in its condemnation: "Four wheel drive recreational use of green lanes is causing terrible damage to many National Parks" (www.cnp.org.uk).

The use of recreational vehicles in the countryside is an emotive issue for many people with noise, pollution, erosion and conflicts with other users among the areas of concern. It was the popularity of a number of 'green roads' in the Park and their subsequent deterioration in condition that prompted the Lake District National Park Authority, along with other organisations, to initiate the Hierarchy of Trail Routes Experiment. This is an attempt to manage the current level of activity on green roads through voluntary restraint rather than statutory legislation (see Chapter Five).

The aim of the Hierarchy is not to promote or stop use but to eliminate irresponsible use. Four categories of use have been designated; *free use* – those routes open to all recreational traffic at all times of the year; *privileged use* – those routes to be used by members of the Land Access and Recreation Association affiliated clubs only; *no use*

4WDs – those routes that are unsustainable for 4WD vehicles but can be used by motorcycles; *no use* – those routes that are unsustainable for any recreational vehicles or are dead ends with no links to other parts of the network. However, the Management Plan is unequivocal, if "the trail route hierarchy proves inadequate in particular localities, legal solutions and enforcement will have to be pursued" (Lake District National Park Authority, 1999:24). In the most extreme case of Bethecar Moor, restrictions on vehicles have been imposed through a Traffic Regulation Order and repair work has been undertaken on the damaged route (Lake District National Park Authority, 1999).

The decision to approve a 10mph speed limit on Windermere, with effect from March 2005, is a clear indication of changing national opinion on appropriate forms of activity tourism for areas such as the Lake District. In this instance, the clear focus has been on power boats and water skiing, as the ban is not expected to extend to sailing boats travelling faster than 10mph (*Guardian* 1st March 2000). Tensions over this issue are still evident with a threatened challenge in the European Court of Human Rights and local businesses complaining about reduced spending by wealthy power boat owners and the loss of jobs in local boat yards (*Guardian* 1st June 2001). In the opposing camp, the Council for National Parks was delighted to report: "Quiet enjoyment of Windermere will now be possible thanks to the 10mph speed limit" (www.cnp.org.uk). Restrictions have been placed elsewhere on water-based activities. At Haweswater and Wet Sleddale reservoirs, only shore-based angling and occasional sub-aqua activities (without boats) are permitted, as it was felt that boating would undermine the wild character of Mardale, in the vicinity of Haweswater, while increased access to Wet Sleddale would conflict with farming and wildlife interests (Lake District National Park Authority, 1999).

Activities with a less obvious environmental impact can also be subject to restrictions, as with climbing on crags which may be restricted geographically, or seasonally as at Chapel Head Scar where it is essential to avoid disturbing peregrine falcons (Lake District National Park Authority, 1999).

In this discussion of 'activity' tourism, there are the same dangers of oversimplification as with the earlier discussion of literary tourists. To categorise tourists as either 'literary' or 'activity' is to deny the multi-faceted nature of much modern tourism. The single most popular paying visitor attraction in the Lake District (and the 9th most popular in the UK in 2001) was a cruise on Windermere, perhaps a rather passive form of activity tourism! (www.englishtourism.org.uk) Indeed more than one in four of all visitors take a boat trip at some point during their visit (Lake District National Park Authority, 1999). If we add in the one-in-three that take a long walk, it becomes clear that many visitors wish to experience a range of activities.

This has led to sustainable tourism activities being developed, with an appropriate case study being the integration of a cruise on Windermere, being combined with a visit to either, or both, the Aquarium of the Lakes, and the Lakeside and Haverthwaite Railway in southern Lakeland.

Case Study – Windermere Lake Cruises

Windermere is the longest lake in England and is currently classified as a public highway. In the 19th century steam ships carried passengers and cargo between the main settlements on the shore – Ambleside, Bowness, and Newby Bridge. The ferry service connected with road and rail transport, enabling passengers and cargo to combine different modes of transport on their journey. In the 21st century, such combinations of transport are still possible, and are actively promoted to reduce traffic congestion on Lake District roads. Windermere Lake Cruises currently operates regular sailings along the length of Windermere and offers joint ticketing with Stagecoach, the Lakeside and Haverthwaite Steam Railway, First Northwestern Trains, Mountain Goat Coaches, and the Aquarium of the Lakes at Lakeside. Indeed, the Aquarium of the Lakes chose its site at Lakeside for the development of its facility as it saw the opportunity to work closely with Windermere Lake Cruises and the steam railway to provide a cluster of tourist attractions in southern Lakeland. Tourists can arrive at the Aquarium by ferry, train, public transport, in their own cars, on bikes, and by walking. Not only is the Aquarium a tourist attraction in its own right, but so too is the mode of transport especially if the tourists arrive by ferry or train, helping also to reduce traffic congestion.

Windermere Lake Cruises promotes and provides 'green public transport', and the company encourages tourists to "leave their cars behind and to use boat, bus and train" (Windermere Lake Cruises, 2003:1). The company provides all year round ferry services linking Ambleside, Bowness, and Lakeside, with connections to other tourist attractions in southern Lakeland (the Lake District Visitor Centre, Brockhole and the World of Beatrix Potter, for example). A 'park and ride' facility is available at Bowness, which also provides tourists with the opportunity to catch a bus to Hilltop (Beatrix Potter's farmhouse) and to Hawkshead. To encourage tourists to leave their cars behind, they can transport cycles and wheelchairs on board the steamers. Careful attention has been paid to the launch and steamer timetables so that the ferries, buses, and trains operating in the Lake District all work to co-ordinated schedules. This enables tourists to travel easily within the Lake District on public transport, without having lengthy waiting times between the different modes of transport used. As a result there is an integrated transport system in operation, which clearly contributes to sustainable tourism development.

Windermere Lake Cruises also "believes in and actively embraces the principles of sustainable tourism by employing local people, providing secure jobs, offering first class working conditions, career opportunities and professional skill training", (ibid:1). The company's commitment to sustainable tourism is also evidenced through its relationships with the local community – whenever possible local goods and services are purchased for use by the company, even if a premium price has to be paid for such inputs. Employees of the company are representatives on a number of groups involved with transport management in Cumbria: Cumbria Tourist Board's Sustainable Travel Development Steering Group, Cumbria County Council's Public Transport Forum, the Lakes Line Rail Users Group and Traveline, (Windermere Lake Cruises, 2003a). All upgrading work on Windermere Lake Cruises fleet of launches and steamers is done by its own skilled craftsmen.

In August 2002 Windermere Lake Cruises was recognised as "meeting the Responsible Tourism Standard" – a scheme operated in the Lake District by the Lake District Tourism & Conservation Partnership and Cumbria Tourist Board. To be accredited, Windermere Lake Cruises had to demonstrate that it:

➢ cares for the environment
➢ supports the local economy and community
➢ promotes local culture and services
➢ encourages clients and employees to become involved with Responsible Tourism.

The Honeypot Towns

While it is undoubtedly the landscape which draws tourists to the Lake District, the reality of the tourist experience for many is likely to be centred on the principal towns of the area, as it is these towns which contain much of the tourist infrastructure of hotels, guest houses, restaurants, public houses, shops and attractions (see Table 4. 9). Forty per cent of the population of the National Park live in the three towns of Keswick, Bowness and Windermere, and Ambleside (Lake District National Park Authority, 1999).

Table 4.9   *The honeypot towns of the Lake District*

Town	Attractions
Ambleside	Cinema, library, museum, garden centre, glass works, The Homes of Football, lake trips.
Bowness and Windermere	Lake cruises, sailing, rowing, motor boats, pitch and putt, theatre, Steamboat museum, World of Beatrix Potter.
Coniston	Ruskin Museum, lake cruises, sailing, rowing, Copper Mines, SY Gondola, Coniston Brewing Company.
Grasmere	Dove Cottage, Rydal Mount, Heaton Cooper Art Gallery, Gingerbread Shop.
Hawkshead	Beatrix Potter Gallery.
Keswick	Cumberland Pencil Museum, sailing, fishing, canoeing, windsurfing, Theatre by the Lake, art gallery, Cars of the Stars Museum, boat trips, park with bowls and tennis, indoor swimming pool.

The marketing of the towns and larger villages of the Lake District shows clear similarities, with an emphasis on historic environments, stunning scenery and easy access to the lakes. This is combined with a sound awareness of the commercial possibilities for the services available for the tourist.

The Ambleside website (www.ambleside.org.uk), for example, boasts a Japanese web browser and highlights the historic and literary links that the town possesses. It also states categorically:

> "Because we are a small town, we have not been colonised by High Street chain stores. But because we cater for millions of tourists, retailers here have been able to develop successful shops selling a wide range of goods not easy to find elsewhere.
>
> Also, because our visitors generally appreciate high standards, both in our Lakeland landscape and in our catering and hospitality, the range of goods on offer in our shops is remarkable in its quality and value.
>
> Not only that – many goods are unique to this area, being craftsman-made in Ambleside and nearby towns and villages."

This claim is certainly supported by the number of shopping opportunities provided by a small town with less than 3,000 inhabitants – there are 81 retail outlets in Ambleside, with gift shops and other tourist related retailers accounting for some 30 per cent of all retail outlets.

The description of Bowness and Windermere on the lakedistrict.com website emphasizes the attractions of the honeypot towns.

> "Bowness. Adjacent to the larger town Windermere. Popular with tourists, it has developed into an attractive town centre. Neighbouring Windermere is the slightly busier town of Bowness-on-Windermere with a vast range of shops and attractions. There you could go on a cruise with Windermere Lake Cruises (and even make a trip to the Aquarium of the Lakes at Lakeside, on the western side of Windermere), enjoy a production at The Old Laundry Theatre, visit the Windermere Steamboat Museum or marvel at an indoor re-creation of the Lake District countryside at the World of Beatrix Potter™ Attraction.
>
> At the junction of our road is the famous Beatrix Potter Exhibition and Old Laundry Theatre. Strolling down the shopping street past the Parish Church brings you directly to Bowness Bay, one of the Lake District's most popular scenes where all types of sailing, rowing and motor boats can be enjoyed. Take a cruise on England's largest lake. In and around Bowness there is an abundance of attractions to visit whilst being located in the Lake District National Park, an area of outstanding natural beauty which will enchant you."

A significant number of the attractions cited here are only indirectly dependent on a location in the Lake District. They provide a range of additional tourist experiences that might be located anywhere which receives large numbers of visitors. To illustrate this, the English Tourist Board visitor survey of 2001 ranked the Adrian Sankey Glass works in Ambleside as the 10th most visited workplace with 150,366 visitors. A broad definition of tourist attraction is obviously needed to ensure that the multi-faceted nature of contemporary tourism is fully explored.

It is to the larger settlements that future growth in purpose built tourist attractions is likely to be directed. This is because of the stringent planning regulations laid down by the Lake District National Park Authority – see Chapter Five. Given increasing pressures of tourist numbers, it is likely that policies to restrict access and developments in quieter areas such as the Western Lakes will be strengthened, thus polarising new investment in tourist attractions in the honeypot towns in central Lakeland.

Conclusions

As Pocock (1992:236) stated, "expectation is a crucial component in the experience of place". Plans for the future development of tourism in the Lake District are being driven by the desire to sustain an environment that is attractive to the tourist yet is not being made less attractive by the activities of tourists. This is the essential paradox at the heart of the founding principles of the English national parks. As this chapter has shown, there is far more to the tourist experience than simply the environment. It is interesting to note the absence of 'shopping' from the list of 'principal attractions' stated previously. Clearly the reality of the tourist experience might be quite different to the perceived character of place. As Urry (1995:203) has rightly observed: "in the making of the Lake District there is an increasing coalescence of the cultural and the commercial." These issues raise a range of questions as to the nature of the authenticity of the tourist experience in the Lakes.

The future direction of tourism within the National Park is extremely difficult to predict. However, the stated intentions of the Lake District National Park Authority Management Plan do provide an indication of the planning priorities that relate to visitors. These priorities include enhanced access to footpaths and bridleways, with better signs, new routes and links in existing networks to improve safety and opportunities for pedestrians, cyclists and horse riders, as well as effectively implementing the 'right to roam' legislation. At the same time, fewer noisy pursuits will be tolerated, and active management of conflicts between different activities is likely. Policies towards accommodation are likely to focus on improving the quality and range of accommodation available, in line with the stated aim of attracting a larger proportion of visitors from the more affluent social classes (Lake District National Park Authority, 1999).

These priorities, coupled with a clearly stated intention of "less damage being caused to the environment by recreational activities" (Lake District National Park Authority, 1999:203) suggests that the sports and activity tourist is less likely to find the Lakes as biddable a playground as it has been, on occasion, in the past. Planning policy and the regulatory framework are likely to lay greater emphasis on the peaceful enjoyment of the Lakes. However, given the commercial pressures of increasing visitor numbers, and the seemingly insatiable demand for 'authentic' retail experiences, one is tempted to ask whether the National Park will be left standing Canute-like as the waves continue their relentless motion.

References

Boardman, J. (1996) *Classic Landforms of the Lake District*. Geographical Association.

Butler, R. (1998) Rural recreation and tourism. In B. Ilbery (Ed). *The geography of rural change*. Harlow: Longman.

Carson, D. and Cromie, S. (1989) "Marketing Planning in Small Enterprises: A Model and Some Empirical Evidence", *Journal of Marketing Management*, 5(1), 33-49.

Carson, D., Cromie, S., McGowan, P. and Hill J. (1995) *Marketing and Entrepreneurship in SMEs*. Harlow: Prentice Hall.

Creative Research (2002) *Cumbria Tourism Survey 2002 Report of Findings.* London: Creative Research.

Cumbria Tourist Board (1990) *A Vision for Cumbria.* Windermere: Cumbria Tourist Board.

Cumbria Tourist Board (1998) *Regional Tourism Strategy for Cumbria.* Windermere: Cumbria Tourist Board.

Cumbria Tourist Board (2002) *Facts of Tourism.* Windermere: Cumbria Tourist Board.

Davies, H. (1998) *Beatrix Potter's Lakeland.* London: Penguin/Warne.

Department of Culture, Media and Sport (1999) *Tomorrow's Tourism: a growth industry for the new Millennium.* London: DCMS.

Dibb, S. (1995) "Understanding the Level of Marketing Activity in the Leisure Sector". *The Service Industries Journal*, 15(3), 257-275.

Dulgarn, G. (2000) '*Lake District National Park, Beatrix Potter and the Japanese Tourist*' Edge Hill College, BA dissertation.

Fyall, A., Leask, A. and Garrod, B. (2001) "Scottish Visitor Attractions: a Collaborative Future". *International Journal of Tourism Research*, 3, 211-228.

Gunn, J., Bailey, D. and Gagen, P. (1992) *Landform Replication as a Technique for the Reclamation of Limestone Quarries.* London: Department of the Environment.

Herbert, D. (1995) Heritage places, leisure and tourism. In D. Herbert (Ed) *Heritage, Tourism and Society.* London: Mansell.

Herbert, D. Literary places, tourism and the heritage experience. *Annals of Tourism Research* 28(2), 312-333.

Jansen-Verbecke, M. (1988) *Leisure, Recreation and Tourism in Inner Cities.* Amsterdam: Netherlands Geographical Studies No.58.

Kendall-Price, C. (1993) *In the Footsteps of Swallows and Amazons.* Los Angeles: Wild Cat.

Lake District National Park Authority (1998) *Lake District National Park Local Plan.* Kendal: LDNPA.

Lake District National Park Authority (1999) *Lake District National Park Management Plan.* Kendal: LDNPA.

McDonald, M. (1995) *Marketing Plans – How to Prepare Them – How to Use Them*, Oxford: Butterworth – Heinemann.

Millward, R. and Robinson, A. (1970) *The Lake District.* London: Eyre and Spottiswoode.

Morgan, M. (1996) *Marketing for Leisure and Tourism*, Harlow: Prentice Hall.

National Trust (2002) *North West News.* Autumn.

Ordnance Survey (1994) *Lake District Ordnance Survey Leisure Guide*: Ordnance Survey.

Parker, G. and Ravenscroft, N. (2002) Tourism, national parks and private lands. In R. Butler and S. Boyd (eds) *Tourism and National Parks: issues and implications.* (pp 95-106) Chichester: Wiley.

Pocock, D. C. D. (1992) Catherine Cookson Country: tourist expectations and experience. *Geography* 77, 236-243.

Richards, Moorhead & Laing Ltd. (1995) *Slate waste tips and workings in Britain.* London: HMSO.

Schollhammer, H. and Kuriloff, A. H. (1979) *Entrepreneurship and Small Business Management*, New York: J. Wiley.

Shank, M. (1999) *Sports Marketing: A Strategic Perspective.* New Jersey: Prentice Hall.

Squire, S. J. Valuing countryside: reflections on Beatrix Potter tourism. *Area* 25(1), 5-10.

Squire, S. J. (1994) Gender and tourist experiences: assessing women's shared meanings for Beatrix Potter. *Leisure Studies* 13, 195-210.

Talbot, R. and Whiteman, R. (1997) *Lakeland Landscapes.* London: Wiedenfeld & Nicholson.

Urry, J. (1990) *The Tourist Gaze.* London: Sage.

Urry, J. (1995) *Consuming Places.* London: Routledge.

Whitehead, T. (1999) Visitor attractions in the new millennium from a local government perspective: In Fyall, A., Leask, A. and Garrod, B. (2001) "Scottish Visitor Attractions: a Collaborative Future". *International Journal of Tourism Research,* 3, pp.211-228.

Websites.

www.staruk.org.uk

www.visitbritain.org.uk

www.honister-slate-mine.co.uk

www.lake-district.gov.uk

www.cnp.org.uk

www.golakes.co.uk

Chapter Five

The Planning and Management of Tourism in the Lake District

This chapter investigates the ways in which tourism is planned and managed in the Lake District. A number of different agencies and organisations are involved in this complex process. "Government and public bodies are important partners with private business and with voluntary organisations in the mixed economy of tourism" (Callaghan *et al.*, 1994:161). Tourism is administered and governed through a variety of legislation, public policy and the work of agencies and organisations charged with the planning, management and development of tourism.

Bramwell and Lane (2000:1) state that "the importance of involving diverse stakeholders in tourism planning and management is receiving growing recognition". This chapter will identify the diverse range of stakeholders who influence the development of tourism in the Lake District. What will become evident to the reader, though, is that each of the organisations and agencies featured in this chapter recognises the importance of working effectively with partner organisations and agencies. Such collaboration has had a long history in the Lake District, and can be traced back to the formation of the preservation societies identified in Chapter Two. As indicated in Chapter One, partnerships and collaborations are becoming increasingly important in developing and implementing tourism policies. "Stakeholder collaboration has the potential to lead to dialogue, negotiation and the building of mutually acceptable proposals about how tourism should be developed", (ibid). The benefits of such collaboration are felt to be shared ownership of policies, operational advantages, and ultimately an enhanced tourism product. The UK government strongly supports such collaboration and partnership, see the UK government's tourism policy document, *Tomorrow's Tourism* (DCMS, 1999). Perhaps the Lake District is an example of best-practice in how such collaboration and partnership has contributed significantly to the development and management of sustainable tourism in the region.

However, before discussing the role of each of the key stakeholders involved in planning, managing and developing tourism in the Lake District, a brief introduction will be provided to landuse planning in the United Kingdom.

Landuse Planning in the United Kingdom

Local government in the UK is primarily responsible for landuse planning – determining how a particular parcel of land can be developed and used. Central government stipulates that each local authority in the UK has to produce and publish a development plan, which must "conform to national planning guidelines which provide statements on policy on nationally important landuse and other planning matters" (Howie, 2003:165). European Union directives have also to be taken into account within the planning framework. "The UK planning system is a well-established and statutory approach for the reconciliation of objectives in environmental planning and landuse and the approach is broadly similar elsewhere in western Europe and other social democratic countries" (Howie, 2003:159). Most planning systems invlove two elements. Firstly, controls that are specified by the authority responsible for managing the rural and urban landscapes in the geographic area being considered. Controls that are put in place by the planning authority will vary according to the developmental needs of the geographic area. In highly sensitive environments such as national parks, the planning controls will be very stringent prohibiting developments that will adversely affect the traditional characteristics of the settlements and landscape. Planning controls will cover a multitude of elements, for example whether redundant farm buildings can be converted for other uses (such as self catering holiday accommodation). Whether new access routes can be provided to settlements and the size and location of car parks. Whether 'green field' investments such as a new hotel or a new tourist attraction can actually be permitted on a previously undeveloped plot of land. Planning controls can also relate to the materials used for building new developments, for example the type and colour of roof-tiles and window frames to be used. Planning controls can be very stringent and the developer has to adopt all requirements of the local planning authority for planning permission to be granted.

The second element of a planning system is the actual plan that is published by the planning authority to indicate what type of development can take place in specific geographic areas. Plans are of two types, a Structure Plan for a large geographic area such as a region, and Local Plans for a smaller geographic area such as a local authority district. Most plans (whether Structure or Local) identify development zones where certain types of investment will be encouraged, for example agricultural, extractive, manufacturing, residential, retail, tertiary, or tourism development. The plan is then rigidly applied when new planning applications are considered by the planning authority. If the proposed development does not conform to the requirements of the designated zone then it will be rejected. The aim of the plan is to ensure that development takes place in a structured and ordered manner so that the specific developmental needs of the geographic area under consideration are respected.

In the United Kingdom there is a considerable amount of legislation that influences planning controls and local plans. The local planning authority has to ensure that all new developments that are approved conform with this legislation. This is known as an 'interventionist' style of planning (Howie, 2003:160) where "the planner 'intervenes' on behalf of the 'wider community of interests' or the other stakeholders". Howie continues by saying that there are many different interests and perspectives to be taken into account in any planning proposal. The challenge for the local planning authority is to "attempt to satisfy them all" (ibid), but clearly this has to be within the planning controls and regulations that are in place for the specific geographic area. If the developer gains planning permission for the development, building work can commence, but the actual construction or renovation work will have to comply with another set of regulations referred to as 'building controls'. These controls relate to the detail of the internal and external building works to ensure that the development conforms to safety and legal specifications.

It has already been identified that tourism is a significant sector of the economy in Cumbria and the Lake District (see Chapter Three). As a result a number of different agencies and organisations are involved with the planning, management and development of tourism. Each of these organisations develops and implements policies that reflect their ethos and mission. There is a certain degree of overlap in the mission, objectives and strategies of some of these organisations with some duplication of activities. However, it is the totality of the work of these organisations that results in tourism in the Lake District being planned, managed and developed sustainably. The rest of this chapter will explore the roles and activities of some of these agencies.

Figure 5.0   *The key contributors to the planning, development and management of sustainable tourism in the Lake District*

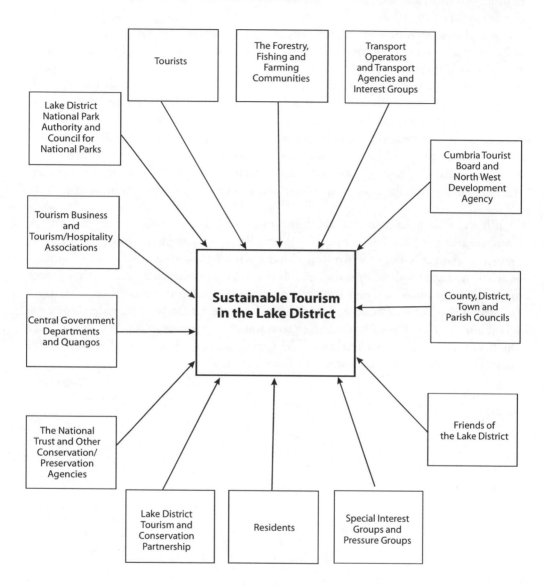

Town and Parish Councils are the smallest units of civil administration in England, and provide the statutory tier of local government closest to the resident population. The role of Town and Parish Councils is varied, including:

➢   the maintenance of community buildings and land;

➢   the provision of bus and other roadside shelters and seats;

➢   the power to make byelaws;

➢   the authority to work with other agencies in crime prevention;

> ➤ providing entertainment and support for the arts;

> ➤ the maintenance of footpaths and bridleways;

> ➤ power to provide litter bins in streets and in public places;

> ➤ power to provide parking places and public conveniences;

> ➤ the right to be notified of planning applications;

> ➤ the power to contribute to the encouragement of tourism.

Source: adapted from Cumbria Association of Local Councils, 2003

Town and Parish councils also raise issues on behalf of the communities they represent. At a very local level they are able to influence the development of tourism within their area of jurisdiction by supporting or objecting to, proposals for new tourism developments and facilities and representing the views of the local community. The local authority responsible for the area is heavily involved not only in helping to develop the tourism industry by providing services for tourists and tourism businesses, but also by developing and operating specific facilities for tourists. In addition, the local authority plays an important role in the marketing of the area as a tourist destination. Cumbria Tourist Board and the North West Development Agency have a strong remit to develop and promote tourism in the region for the benefit of the regional and local economies and for the benefit of the regional and local resident communities. Cumbria County Council and the Lake District National Park Authority develop the Structure Plan for the Lake District, with the National Park Authority being the planning authority for the Lake District. Cumbria County Council also has a major role to play as a provider of services, many of which benefit tourists. VisitBritain at a national level promotes the Lake District as a tourist destination to domestic and overseas markets.

All of the aforementioned agencies are statutory bodies that have a role to play in the planning, management and development of tourism. In addition, there are other organisations that do not receive public funding, but also have an influence on the management of tourism in the Lake District. Two of these organisations are the National Trust and the Friends of the Lake District. The National Trust is a major landowner in the Lake District and has a central role to play in the conservation of the landscape and the preservation of local communities. The Friends of the Lake District, a registered charity, was established to represent the views of those people who are particularly concerned about the conservation of the special characteristics of the Lake District. It influences the development and management of tourism through lobbying and expressing its views on key planning issues.

This chapter will explain the role of five of these organisations in the planning, management and development of tourism in the Lake District:

> ➤ the Lake District National Park Authority;

> ➤ the National Trust;

> ➤ the Friends of the Lake District;

> ➤ Cumbria Tourist Board;

> ➤ the local authorities whose area of influence includes the Lake District.

The purpose of this chapter is to introduce some of the tourism planning, management and development issues that these agencies and organisations are involved with, and to show how each of these organisations contributes to sustainable tourism management in the Lake District. A case study will also be provided of the Lake District Tourism and Conservation Partnership that was established in the 1990s as another means of enabling public, private and voluntary sector organisations, with support from tourists, to work together on conservation projects within the Lake District.

The Lake District National Park Authority

Under powers given by the 1949 National Parks and Access to the Countryside Act, the Lake District Planning Board was established in 1951. Though administratively a part of the three Shire Counties that embraced the designated area (Westmorland, Cumberland and Lancashire), the Board was given independence of action. In 1974 the Board became the Lake District Special Planning Board (LDSPB) and was established as the unitary planning authority for the National Park (using powers granted under schedule 17 of the Local Government Act 1972). The LDSPB was dissolved in 1997 to make way for the National Park Authority. The earlier Boards were established to manage people's expectations of the area and protect its fragile and special qualities; they were a response to the pressures created by nature and by other interests. The need for sustainable management was recognized in part. Controlling the impact of urban development and the visitor upon the landscape was the driving force. Few powers to influence land management decisions were created, as farmers and foresters were seen as the custodians of the Lake District. In 1949, little thought was given to the possibilities of landscape change by farming or forestry.

The purposes of a National Park and the role of a National Park Authority are now defined by the Environment Act 1995. The Lake District National Park Authority is the statutory local government body set up by Parliament to care for the National Park on behalf of the nation and is primarily responsible for the conservation and enhancement of the area. Its role is to secure the purposes of National Park designation (see below). In 2002, the English National Parks became the responsibility of a new Ministry, the Department for Environment, Food and Rural Affairs (Defra). Defra Ministers published a review of the English National Park Authorities in 2002 in which it was stated that 'the National Park Authorities are at the heart of the Government's need to develop the rural economy'. Ministers have made it very clear that national priorities must be achieved (Defra, 2002).

The purposes of National Park designation:

> "to conserve and enhance the natural beauty, wildlife and cultural heritage of such areas; and to promote opportunities for the understanding and enjoyment of the special qualities of these areas by the public" (Environment Act 1995 – Section 61).

A duty placed upon a National Park Authority:

"Whilst [*and only whilst – authors note*] pursuing these purposes, the National Park Authority has a duty to seek to foster the economic and social well-being of local communities within the Park but without incurring significant expenditure" (Environment Act 1995 Section 62). Government Circular 12/96 instructs National Park Authorities to focus their funds on the two purposes of designation and not to compete with those authorities charged with securing the socio-economic well being of communities (Department of Environment, 1996). This approach has been continued under the Local Government Act 2000 whereby National Park Authorities are not required to produce 'community strategies', these fall to the District, County or Unitary Authorities. The National Park Authorities are expected to work in partnership with such bodies in order to secure the National Park purposes (Defra, 2002).

The duties placed upon all public bodies:

> "In exercising or performing any functions in relation to, or so as to affect, land in a National Park, any relevant authority shall have regard to the purposes specified and, if it appears that there is a conflict between those purposes, shall attach greater weight to the purpose of conserving and enhancing the natural beauty, wildlife and cultural heritage of the area" (Environment Act 1995 – Section 62).

This second part of Section 62 is an interesting aspect of the Environment Act. The intent is clear but there is no mechanism for monitoring its application and so it is little understood. The Government has recently called for more reporting and policing of this paragraph and is clearly expecting the National Park Authorities to play a key role both as a mentor and a guardian (Defra, 2002).

The operation of the National Park Authority

The Lake District National Park Authority's stated vision is "to enhance the natural beauty and heritage of the National Park; help people to appreciate its special qualities; and work with others to ensure it remains England's finest landscape".

The national taxpayer funds the Authority with a budget in the order of £7 million pa (2002 base year). The Authority has 26 executive members, each appointed by either local or central government. The majority are elected members of local government. Seven are drawn from district councils, seven from Cumbria County Council, five from Lakeland parish councils and seven individuals are appointed by the Secretary of State.

The Authority employs a team of around 200 staff working across land use planning, park management, visitor management and administration. Over 300 trained voluntary wardens support its work.

Many presume that the National Park Authority has draconian powers, including the nationalization of land, to enable it to achieve the purposes of designation. In fact, the Authority has few powers at its disposal. It secures the purposes by influencing the actions of others and by working in partnership. It must nurture relationships and gain respect. Much of its work is about consensus building and conflict resolution.

The planning and management of sustainable tourism

Statutory Powers

The Authority must prepare a statutory National Park Management Plan and review it every five years (Lake District National Park Authority, 1999). The Management Plan is a statement of the National Park Authority's policy for managing and carrying out its functions in relation to the Park and as such it should:

➢ be a plan for the future of the National Park (not just the activities of the National Park Authority);

➢ promote an integrated approach to management, and stimulate and co-ordinate action by many agencies, organisations and individuals; and

➢ provide the basis for bidding for funding from Government and other sources (DoE ,1996).

The Authority is empowered to state the future vision for the area and define its special/fragile characteristics. The current plan follows the principles of sustainable tourism established by the Countryside Commission and others (Countryside Commission, *et al* 1995). The Government is now seeking the inclusion of an explicit sustainable tourism strategy within the plan (Defra, 2002). The plan is developed in consultation with all who care for the National Park.

In 2003 consultation commenced with a wide variety of stakeholders on the review of the Lake District National Park Management Plan published in 1999. A revised Management Plan was produced by the Lake District National Park Authority, its partners and interest groups, and distributed to stakeholders in July and August 2003 for comment and discussion. The intention of the consultation process was to include as many stakeholders as possible in the development of a new Management Plan to ensure that the plan did have shared ownership. Comments were encouraged by the National Park Authority from "everyone with an interest in the Lake District National Park," (LDNPA, 2003:3) – for example, partner organisations, residents, tourists, farmers, the business community, and politicians. At the end of the consultation period some 183 responses had been received with approximately 1,400 individual comments being made. At the time of writing, these comments are being considered by the National Park Authority before the agreed Management Plan is published in Spring 2004. All stakeholders who support the vision for the Lake District National Park and the policies contained within the 2004 Management Plan will be asked to actually endorse the policies by being signatories to the published plan.

The National Park Authority is the sole local planning authority for the National Park with a role in planning which combines those undertaken by the County Council and the Districts (Environment Act 1995, Section 67). It can control development (as defined by the Town and Country Planning Act 1947) by the preparation and adoption of the statutory Development Plan, which today consists of a Structure Plan produced jointly with Cumbria County Council (CCC/LDNPA, 1995) and a Local Plan which incorporates a Minerals and Waste Plan (LDNPA, 1998). There is a perception that planning policies within the National Park are being interpreted too strictly and inhibiting rural enterprise. In fact, the Authority typically deals with over 1,000 applications for development each year, more than any of the other National Parks. It receives a greater number of applications per 1000 population than the District Councils within Cumbria. Approval rates are similar, at around 90 per cent. The policies reflect national planning policy guidance, which gives strong support to the need to protect the area's outstanding landscape. They also give priority to meeting the needs for housing in particular localities and diversifying the rural economy.

The Authority has been given the power to employ rangers and wardens. These teams not only help land owners maintain and enhance the landscape, they also help visitors to understand and enjoy the special qualities of the National Park in such ways that conflict with other users and residents is minimized. As an example of the principles of sustainability in action, patrol vehicles (both on land and water) are powered by liquid petroleum gas.

National Park Authorities were given the power to create byelaws for the recreational management of navigational waters within their areas in the Countryside Act 1968. There are four navigable waters in the Lake District: Coniston Water, Derwent Water, Ullswater and Windermere. All are subject to National Park byelaws, policed by water-borne rangers. On Windermere this task is shared with South Lakeland District Council who owns the bed of the Lake. It was in 1957 that the use of powerboats was first debated. 1978 saw the Three Lakes Byelaw Inquiry that ended recreational speed boating on all waters except Windermere. Following extensive debate and a public inquiry, the Government confirmed on the 29 February 2000 a maximum speed of 10 mph for all powered craft on Windermere (DETR, 2000). The grounds for the restriction were held to be the incompatible use between speeding boats and the many other interests on the water.

The Authority is allowed to own land and run businesses. What is not always understood is that over 85 per cent of the land in the National Park is in private ownership or management. The National Park Authority only owns about 4 per cent of the designated area. Some of this land was bought to create public access, manage public access (e.g. the siting of car parks), remove eyesores or to use as good practice demonstration sites. The UK's first national park visitor centre was opened here, at Brockhole, in 1966. Other land has been given, either in lieu of death duties or by individuals and charities (such as the Friends of the Lake District), in order for the land to be managed in accordance with National Park purposes.

The Authority runs commercial ventures such as pay and display car parks, a cafe, retail sales, accommodation and boat hire (all powered boats are electric in order to conserve water quality and aid tranquility), educational courses and events. It owns two farms and runs a network of information centres. In some of these ventures the Authority has partners and tenants. The Authority is clearly a part of the tourism industry, as well as being central to its management and development.

The Countryside and Rights of Way Act 2000 (CRoW) made National Park Authorities responsible for managing access to mountain, moor, registered common land and heath. An Access Land Map is expected to be published in 2004. Interestingly, the Government has not yet indicated when the public will be given the right to use these Open Access Areas. However, Ministers have directed the National Park Authority to manage the area's access obligations. An independent Lake District Local Access Forum has been appointed, representing a wide range of interests, including tourism, to advise the Authority on access management issues. (This Forum will also have an advisory role on the development of Rights of Way Improvement Plans). In the Lake District, landowners and managers have happily tolerated trespass for centuries yet the public had few rights – as they found during 2001, when the Foot and Mouth Disease led to the widespread closure of the fells and commons. When the CRoW Act comes into force, the public will enjoy the right to walk across almost a half of the National Park. Their right will be limited to walking and there will be no right to other recreational activities except with the permission of the landowner. There will be rules on keeping dogs under control. Furthermore, at times (as defined by the Act) landowners, English Nature and other bodies will have the power to remove or limit the rights. It will fall to the National Park Authority to keep the access map up to date and make the information available to the public at the time they need it. No simple task!

Delegated powers

Other agencies and organisations give some powers to the Lake District National Park Authority. Cumbria County Council has agreed that the National Park Authority should act as its agent on some rights of way matters:

> ➢ Maintaining footpaths and bridleways.
>
> ➢ Signposting and way-marking routes.
>
> ➢ Reviewing the definitive rights of way map.
>
> ➢ Traffic Regulation Orders.

National Park Authority staff walk and map every right of way to make sure that the Definitive Map is up to date and that all the routes can be enjoyed by the public without let or hindrance.

There are approximately 3,100 kilometres of rights of way within the National Park. This represents one of the single most important recreational assets for the area and is a vital part of the tourism package. The National Park Authority has taken on the liability of maintaining and enhancing these rights of way but it is supported by a number of partners in this work, especially the National Trust and some tourism businesses. Together they ensure that the public's use of the rights of way does not lead to the degradation of the landscape. In addition, the Authority seeks to develop local skills and employment opportunities in the placing of maintenance contracts.

Influence

The National Park Authority is but one body, and a relatively small body, operating in the Lake District. If it is to achieve its statutory purposes then it must influence the actions of others. There are a number of ways to gain such influence. Active partnerships with defined aims can be created (which are considered below) but the Authority does not have the resources to be involved in every action. Much can be gained by helping others to make decisions in accordance with national park purposes. The prime tool for influencing the actions of others is the National Park Management Plan (see section on statutory powers), for if others choose to adopt the policies advocated then co-ordinated action will automatically follow. The difficulty is nurturing a sense of ownership of that plan amongst all the key players. Other actions are required. The Authority offers grant aid and provides information to others, either in the form of surveys, reports or as advice.

It is not the Authority's policy to divert a high percentage of its budget to grant aid as there is less than a million pounds a year of unallocated spend. The policy is to use small sums to pump prime schemes that achieve the National Park Management Plan policies and are likely to attract significant sums from other sources. An example is the European Union funded Lakeland Village Landscapes enhancement programme, which has had a significant impact upon the tourism sector. The Authority has been able to offer grant aid to local communities, chambers of commerce or other councils to devise and implement village design plans. The Authority also gives the time of specialist staff. By ensuring a high quality of design and presentation in the built environment, communities are better able to attract and retain the visitor. Many villages and towns have benefited from the sensitive use of paving, signage and lighting. Where appropriate, pedestrianised areas have been introduced in order to support commercial centres. The latest schemes include Keswick town centre and Ravenglass whilst more mature schemes are to be found in Ambleside, Bowness on Windermere, Grasmere, Hawkshead and Pooley Bridge.

National Park staff work on a wide range of committees and working groups established by others (such as the County Council or Voluntary Action Cumbria) where they share information and expertise. In particular, time is given to ensure that statutory guidance produced by others takes into account the requirements of the Environment Act 1995. Staff are very active in the development of regional planning guidance and economic or tourism strategies so as to ensure that sustainable policies are in place for all. There are times when the Authority has to use its national position to influence the regional or local agenda. After all, the designation is national, not regional or local. To undertake this work the Authority joins with the other UK National Park Authorities under the umbrella of the Association of National Park Authorities or, at a European level, as a part of the Federation of Nature and Natural Parks of Europe (known as the EUROPARC Federation). The Federation is a private body that brings together some 500 national parks (which includes the Lake District), nature parks and biosphere reserves. These two bodies lobby governments on behalf of the National Parks by direct representations or by the publication and promotion of papers and reports. Tourism and sustainable development has been the subject of a number of such initiatives.

Partnerships

The Lake District is relatively remote and has a very dispersed population, see Chapter Three. The management and development of tourism in the National Park has often needed the combined forces of a number of agencies to make progress. The Lake District continues to show the benefits of the collaborative approach, not least in the rural recovery following the Foot and Mouth epidemic in 2001, and the National Park Authority is a partner in both the Cumbria Rural Action Zone '*Next Steps*' programme and the North West Regional Development Agency's regional recovery action plan, '*Rural Renaissance*' (CRAZ Steering Group 2002 & NWDA 2002). Much can be achieved by joining forces with other bodies that are prepared to share common aims and there have been many successes.

The local tourism industry has traded on the Lakeland landscape for a century. The Foot and Mouth epidemic was a shock to many local businesses. Before the outbreak very few people thought about the relationship between their income and the landscape. The landscape was taken for granted and no one had to worry about its supply but in 2001 access to the land was denied. Some businesses had already made the link. The Lake District Tourism and Conservation Partnership brought together organisations such as the National Park Authority, National Trust, Cumbria Tourist Board and tourism businesses. The partnership is discussed later in this chapter but its main aim is to raise funds from businesses and their customers to maintain and enhance the Lake District. Through this partnership the industry not only puts something back into the National Park, it actually enhances the park.

Its forerunner could be said to date back to 1990. The Upland Cumbria Initiative brought together the Cumbria Training and Enterprise Council, 16 local authorities and other agencies (including the National Park Authority) to fund conservation work. That work was to be carried out by farmers, local contractors and individuals on projects identified and managed by local conservation organisations.

The Upland Path Initiative has been developed by the National Park Authority in partnership with the National Trust, supported by the Friends of the Lake District and local businesses. Its purpose is to raise lottery funds to be used for the enhancement of the upland paths and the training in crafts for the maintenance of rights of way. The greatest recreational resource the Authority can offer the visitor is good access to viewpoints and lakeshores. With 22 million recreational trips to the National Park each year (Countryside Commission, 1995) it is not surprising that there is considerable erosion on the more popular routes. The visitor presumes that the landscape is natural, though in reality it is all a managed landscape, and objects to obvious 'engineering' solutions to the restoration of paths on the open fells. The partners wish to develop traditional techniques so as to preserve Cumbrian crafts and enhance the landscape. Unfortunately, these skills have been lost over time and there are few contractors who can undertake the work. Hence, an important part of the scheme is to give new skills to Lakeland residents. They will then have the opportunity to gain new employment within the hills and see a direct benefit from helping the visitor enjoy this special place.

Using LEADER+ funding (a European Union fund) a partnership of Voluntary Action Cumbria, the National Trust and the National Park Authority is exploring ways of taking this concept further by developing 'Fell Farming Traineeships'. Much of the attraction of the Lakeland landscape arises from the built features, such as walls and the scattered agricultural buildings. These features are labour intensive to maintain, and modern farming in the National Park no longer supports ancillary workers. There is a need to nurture a new workforce skilled in a modern interpretation of traditional crafts. Both Defra and the Government Office North West has indicated their interest in the project.

Access to the hills can cause difficulties other than the erosion of the land. Remote communities can be damaged by unmanaged access. An extreme example is the popularity of the 'Three Peaks Mountain Challenge' run for charitable sponsorship. The aim is to reach the summit of the highest peaks in England (Scafell), Scotland (Ben Nevis) and Wales (Snowdon) in 24 hours, usually mid-day to mid-day. Unfortunately for the Lake District, Scafell is between the other two peaks and so it attracts the participants during the night time. Many thousands of people can descend upon the small communities around Scafell each night, accompanied by lights, rescue vehicles and dozens of coaches. There are regular problems with traffic congestion, noise, litter, foul waste and damage to property. The National Park Authority and the Institute of Fundraising has drawn up a code of practice for running such events and the Institute works hard to guide people towards other activities.

With good management, access to special sites can give benefit to all. An interesting example is the Osprey Project being run by the Forestry Commission, National Park Authority and the Royal Society for the Protection of Birds. In 2001, the first pair of Ospreys to breed in the wild in England since 1850 was found around Bassenthwaite Lake (a National Nature Reserve owned by the National Park Authority). These are rare birds in England and deserve the highest protection but they are fascinating to the public and offer the potential of a large tourist market in their own right. The partnership works to protect the birds whilst establishing safe viewing points linked to facilities where local traders can serve the visitor. One aim is to develop public transport links to reduce private car miles and develop eco-tourism initiatives within the local town, Keswick.

Some issues to be tackled are not as easy to resolve. Many of the wild tracks across the fells have motorized vehicular rights along them. A number of businesses have developed green-road adventure holidays and experiences in the Lake District. Because of their status these routes are not surfaced. Indeed, visitors (including green-road drivers) would object to an urban approach to their maintenance. Unfortunately heavy use by 4x4 vehicles can cause severe erosion, which is both unsightly and restricts access by those on foot or horse. Not all erosion arises from recreational use; the farming community has to use these tracks for their access to the fells. Where erosion is caused by recreation it falls to the Authority to limit and repair the damage. The highway authority can impose road traffic orders on routes that either restrict or ban vehicle access but these are difficult to enforce and, in any case, result in a plethora of road signs in the open countryside. The Authority has preferred to work in partnership with the recreational green road drivers in an attempt to manage the situation through voluntary restraint and voluntary repair parties. The Hierarchy of Trails Project was set up in 1999 in conjunction with Cumbria County Council and the Land Access and Recreation Association (LARA). Its purpose was to survey 115 unsealed unclassified roads and 7 byeways open to all traffic and to identify those not suitable for off-road use and those that should have a 'licensed' use. The scheme ran for two years with general success except for a few very popular routes, where voluntary restraint has not solved the problems. With reluctance, the Authority has to resort to the road traffic orders on these few routes, such as the experimental order proposed for Gatescarth. Time will tell if the road traffic orders are successful. The Authority has called for the government to review how the road traffic regulations are applied to open countryside, as a solution suitable to a suburban residential street is not suitable to the high Lakeland fells.

It is not just the high fells that attract attention in this respect. Since 1993 there has been a partnership considering the movement of vehicles and people through the National Park known originally as the Lake District Traffic and Transport Management Initiative (currently the Lake District Transport Strategy) (Cumbria County Council, 1996). There is a perception that since the M6 motorway was opened in the 1960s traffic growth in the Lake District has down graded the quality of life of local residents. Increased car ownership by National Park residents since the 1960s may also be a contributory factor. Although this is debatable. The initiative is made up of Cumbria County Council, Countryside Agency, Highways Agency, Government Office North West, Cumbria Tourist Board and the National Park Authority. The District Councils attend the committee meetings but do not contribute financially. The initiative has ensured that there is a traffic and transport strategy for the National Park. The strategy considers road design, traffic management, signage and public transport provision. Significant cycle routes and bus services have been introduced but the Government's wish to explore large scale 'park and ride' schemes for the National Park is proving difficult. Nonetheless, there are active area committees that include all local communities and business interests who are developing a series of action plans to resolve local issues. Solutions can be simple, such as speed restrictions or changes to traffic flow. Others are more complicated, such as calls for the pedestrianisation of large parts of towns and villages (e.g. Keswick and Windermere Town) or computer linked buses. When fully implemented, the Lake District will have some protection from one aspect of tourism that threatens a sustainable future – transport. Chapter Seven provides more detail on the management of transport in the Lake District.

Education tourism has a role to play in sustainability. The National Park Authority, with its business partners the Field Studies Council and the water company United Utilities, is finding that demand outstrips supply. Together, these partners run both residential courses and short modules based on their own properties or in conjunction with the Youth Hostel Association or others. The principal market is school and university based but individuals of all ages do take part. The aim is to ensure that there is a greater understanding and appreciation of the special qualities of the National Park and the needs of its communities.

Other partnerships have been developed to run facilities. The Tourist Information Centre (TIC) in Keswick is run by the National Park Authority but owned by Allerdale Borough Council and managed by a joint advisory committee made up of Allerdale Borough Council, Keswick Town Council, Keswick Tourism Association and the National Park Authority. This arrangement works very well and ensures co-ordinated action for the benefit of the visitor and local tourism businesses. The Authority supports South Lakeland District Council in their running of the Broughton TIC, a similar arrangement.

Thus, as can be seen from the above discussion the Lake District National Park Authority has a central role to play in the planning, management and development of tourism in the Lake District. It has a critical role to play in ensuring that the principles of sustainable tourism are adopted and implemented. The next organisation to be considered is a special interest group that has charitable status and works actively to promote the sustainable development of the region – the Friends of the Lake District.

The Friends of the Lake District

The Friends of the Lake District (FLD) was established in 1934 with the aim of creating a National Park for the Lake District. When this was achieved in 1951, the objectives of the charity were widened to the protection and conservation of the landscape and natural beauty of the Lake District, and to work with other bodies having similar interests or objectives. In 1978, FLD took on the role of the Cumbria Association for the Council for the Protection of Rural England (CPRE) representing them throughout the whole of Cumbria. There are approximately 7000 members of FLD, many of whom are tourists to the area, and others who operate tourism businesses in Cumbria. FLD is a constituent member of the Council for National Parks, a Commercial Member of the Cumbria Tourist Board, and also a member of Tourism Concern.

Friends of the Lake District and tourism

The creation of National Parks both for protection of the landscape and their appropriate enjoyment suggests that tourism has always been central to the National Park concept. Friends of the Lake District (FLD) have had a long standing interest in tourism issues, but its stance has never been as basic as either for, or against it. In 1996, at the request of the South Lakeland Tourism Partnership, FLD published its Tourism Policy, which clearly set out the charity's general views on tourism issues. Specific tourism issues and proposals are considered separately in the light of their individual circumstances. The Policy is widely available, and was revised in 2002.

The Policy sets out FLD's vision for tourism in Cumbria:

> "FLD's vision for the tourism industry in Cumbria is one where tourism is based on and is sensitive to the intrinsic and special qualities of the area, and where the industry strives to protect these qualities against harmful tourism development and growth. The industry should operate within a long term perspective which not only contributes to the economic and social well being of local communities but provides a sustainable future for both the industry and the unique and precious environment of Cumbria."

The Policy contains FLD's views on key issues such as:

- ➢ sustainable tourism;
- ➢ the need for the industry to adopt a long term perspective;
- ➢ tourism development;
- ➢ local and community support;
- ➢ marketing and interpretation;
- ➢ large scale enterprises;
- ➢ transport;
- ➢ the winter season;
- ➢ the geographical distribution of tourism;
- ➢ partnerships.

It also contains examples of good practice/criteria for success, and notes the recommendations of FLD's research into sustainable tourism (see below).

FLD sees tourism in the Lake District as appropriate where it is based on the natural beauty, special qualities and cultural heritage of the area, it is small scale, reflects local distinctiveness, locally owned businesses, utilises existing buildings, and builds on activities which are based on quiet and appropriate enjoyment. However, not all areas of the Lake District are considered appropriate for all forms of tourism. It is important to retain quiet and unspoilt areas which people should be able to discover rather than be 'led' towards; these are essential for the diversity of the character of the area.

In the late 1990s, FLD decided to commission independent external research into the sustainability of tourism in the Lake District. The intention was to adopt a proactive stance, and provide a working document that showed where the industry is, in terms of sustainability, but also to give recommendations and encouragement for directing the future of the industry. Before the consultants began work, all the key players were consulted on the research brief, including Cumbria Tourist Board.

The research resulted in the short summary report *Green Horizons* (2001), and a longer report published by the consultants at Glasgow Caledonian University. The short report lists key findings, conclusions, 39 recommendations, and a tear off guide illustrating steps that tourism businesses could take to make a better environment.

How Friends of the Lake District interpret Sustainable Tourism

FLD fully recognise the three legs of sustainability – the environment, the economy and the social. However, where FLD may differ from other organisations is the relative weight given to each of these legs. The stance adopted by FLD is that the environment must come first, and that from a healthy environment will come economic and social benefits. Nothing that would inextricably harm or degrade the environment or its special qualities should be allowed, because once that damage is done, it is done for eternity. This reflects the 'Sandford Principle' in the Environment Act 1995 for National Parks where, if conflict between conservation and public enjoyment cannot be avoided, the former must prevail. This also reflects the sustainable development principles of the prudent use of natural resources and the precautionary principle. Many in the industry suggest that it is a healthy economy that is essential and from that will come the environmental and economic benefits. Over the last fifty years or so, the Lake District has had a relatively healthy economy and tourism has boomed, but there have not been corresponding good fortunes for the environment, and much landscape and environmental harm has occurred, e.g. footpath erosion, deterioration of water quality, and inappropriate new development.

Issues that Friends of the Lake District face in relation to tourism

FLD's work covers a multitude of issues, basically anything that may have an impact on the landscape of Cumbria. This includes subjects such as planning, transport, agriculture, quarrying, water resources, forestry and renewable energy. Tourism issues overlap into many of these subject areas, and as such, tourism is linked directly or indirectly to much of FLD's work. Issues that relate to tourism include:

> ➤ *Sustainable development:* How can an integrated approach to rural development in general be assured, building on many good examples and initiatives that have already been undertaken? Rural tourism can play an important role in supporting rural economies.

How can the tourism industry be encouraged to adopt a sustainable approach and improve its environmental performance?

➢ *Land use and planning:* all planning applications throughout Cumbria are monitored by FLD. Tourism issues include large extensions to hotels and guesthouses in the open countryside and caravan site extensions which may be detrimental to the landscape or result in significant traffic generation. Each application is considered on its merits, and generally FLD raises no objections to developments in towns or villages. In the open countryside, the consideration is whether or not the proposals are in scale with their surroundings, enable people to enjoy the special qualities of the landscape, how visible or intrusive developments may be, the level of traffic generation and the quality of the building design.

➢ *Traffic issues:* This is one of the big issues raised by tourism. Increasing pressure from private cars can result in further pressure for more car parks, road improvements, road signage and so on, and these in turn may have detrimental impacts on the landscape. To alleviate these problems, how can a greater number of visitors be persuaded to use public transport, both to come to the area, and perhaps more pragmatically when they arrive?

➢ *Agriculture and local products:* Agriculture has shaped much of the current landscape of the Lake District, and it is this landscape that is at the heart of tourism in the area and is one of the main reasons most people visit the area. Issues relating to agriculture and tourism include: how can the tourism industry use more local products that can help ensure that agriculture in the Lakes is viable? Will modern farm buildings and the loss of traditional buildings such as barns affect the landscape, and hence have an adverse impact on the visitor experience? Are there some elements of farming that represent the true cultural landscape the visitors come to see, e.g. Herdwick sheep on the uplands? How can these be maintained, particularly when they are often economically unviable? It is however important to recognise that some aspects of agriculture can reduce the quality of the landscape, and the challenge is to try and overcome this whilst still enabling viable agriculture.

➢ *Use of resources:* As tourism in the Lake District increasingly becomes all year round, there is more pressure on the use of resources, e.g. electricity, local sewage systems, and water. This can lead to the need for more infrastructure to provide these services. This raises issues of the impact of this infrastructure on the landscape. For example a new overhead wire from Troutbeck to Keswick in order to provide higher levels of service to Keswick during the winter months as tourist numbers increased, might be detrimental to the aesthetics of the landscape. Furthermore, it needs to be determined whether the tourism industry can be more efficient in its use of resources, demand reduction and recycling.

> *Access and enjoyment:* How can the visitor have maximum enjoyment from their trip to the area, but at the same time not spoil the experience for others? Some visitors value a lot of interpretive material, but in some locations this can be intrusive and impact on other people who enjoy a voyage of self discovery. Are there some activities that are not appropriate within the National Park, and are contrary to the purposes of the National Park, spoiling enjoyment for the majority of people?

> *Adopting a long term perspective*: How can the tourism industry be encouraged to adopt a long term perspective and holistic approach to its development, rather than looking at short term development (3-5 year plans) and determining success in purely quantitative terms? FLD's *Green Horizons* report gives examples of good practice and benchmarks for sustainable tourism which could form alternative measures of success. How can we ensure that the traditional reliance on market forecasting does not develop a self-fulfilling prophecy?

> *Local and community support*: Can the industry build further on its existing support for the local economy in order to preserve the local culture, distinctiveness and skills of the area for future generations?

> *Distribution of tourism*: In seeking to prevent further growth in the quantity of tourism in the Lake District, the policy of the industry is to encourage it to other areas, such as West Cumbria, the Furness Peninsula and the North Pennines. How can it be assured that these areas can benefit from tourism, but at the same time that their special qualities and distinctiveness are maintained and enhanced?

The role of Friends of the Lake District in influencing others

FLD's role in tourism management and development is largely through influence, persuasion, and demonstrating good practice. FLD works with a range of stakeholders on tourism issues. The main challenge for the future is to open up communications with the tourism industry. Consultations on tourism plans and issues from the National Park Authority, the District Councils and the County Council are now mainstream and occur on a regular basis. Working with the industry is more challenging as there appears to be less of a history of consultation between those inside and outside the industry, and also rather more suspicion. The Cumbria Tourist Board have consulted FLD previously on its Regional Tourism Strategy, but rarely on other initiatives or plans. There is often a suspicion amongst the industry of consulting with other organisations, particularly those dealing with the environment, because it is feared that such organisations will always object to tourism plans and proposals. This may be because the tourism industry has shorter term aims than the environmental bodies who adopt a longer term perspective. Whilst there may be objections, these are the exception rather than the rule, and FLD are keen to work with others, either in the industry or outside it, to find solutions to problems and ensure that the future for the area is a healthy one. FLD support the recommendation from the Cumbria Foot and Mouth Inquiry that suggested the formation of a Cumbria

Tourism Forum, with an independent Chair from the private sector. The Forum would facilitate the different sectors of the industry and create a framework within which the industry can define its priorities and seek consensus.

Examples of how FLD have worked with others to help change things for the better and how they seek to influence them are given below. In general the work of FLD relates more to environmental work and landscape protection than to the tourism sector per se, except that maintaining a quality landscape is essential to the future of tourism in the Lake District.

➤ *Partnerships and communication*: FLD seek to be as open as possible about their views on tourism and fully support partnership working where appropriate. For example, a joint pilot project with United Utilities is being undertaken to investigate saving water in tourism businesses, following a recommendation in the Green Horizons report. FLD has previously joint funded schemes with the Lake District Tourism and Conservation Partnership and hope to continue to do so. The FLD web site is being built up and a recent addition is a page advertising local products and services. Commercial membership of the Cumbria Tourist Board facilitates an understanding of how the Board operates.

➤ *Public Transport*: The main form of transport by most tourists to the Lake District is the private car. FLD try and support public transport and encourage a greater awareness of the options to use public transport, working with Cumbria County Council and the Lake District National Park Authority. As such, several bus services have been funded, for example the Kentmere Rambler Bus Service, and every year FLD contributes to the funding of public transport information.

➤ *Removing road sign clutter*: FLD has worked with two Parish Councils in the Lake District National Park near Ullswater to audit unnecessary road signs. A grant was provided to help pay for redundant signs to be removed and for other signs to be combined. This has helped to not only reduce the overall number of signs in a very attractive rural part of the National Park, but also has removed confusing signs that led visitor traffic along the wrong road.

➤ *Access and enjoyment*: FLD have a long history of campaigning for greater access to the countryside across Cumbria. The aim is to try and ensure that as much access as possible is available, it is in good condition, and that if diversions are sought they do not result in a poorer quality experience for the users. Several new bridges have been funded, footpath repairs on the high fells have been paid for, helping to create footpaths for less able people, and also some interpretation leaflets have been funded. Less directly, FLD tries to prevent inappropriate development, which would make the Lake District less desirable as a tourist destination. This is all part of work to ensure that the National Park and Cumbria can be enjoyed by visitors and locals, reflecting the second purpose of the National Park.

➢ *Promoting understanding*: FLD have funded several National Park Authority leaflets that highlight the special qualities of the Lake District. A two year project has just commenced with English Nature called 'Flora of the Fells'. This sets out to show the importance of fell flora to the upland landscapes of Cumbria and develop a vision for the future.

➢ *Landscape enhancement*: Each year through FLD's Environmental Improvement Grants scheme, grants amounting to around £50,000 each year are awarded to small scale landscape enhancement schemes (e.g. restoring village features). Larger schemes have also been funded, for example a grant of £10,000 was given to the Forestry Commission to remove unsightly trees from the summit of Dodd, near Bassenthwaite Lake. All these grants help to ensure that the landscape is enhanced for future generations and for all to enjoy. FLD is therefore conserving and enhancing the basic resource upon which tourism depends.

FLD, therefore, is a very influential organisation on the development of tourism in the Lake District. For 70 years this charity has been active in the cause to conserve and preserve the natural environment of the region so that it can be enjoyed by future generations. Such an ethos and mission is also shared by the National Trust.

The National Trust

History of The National Trust in the Lake District

The need to safeguard the Lake District was an enormous influence on the founding of the National Trust. One of the three founder members, Canon Hardwicke Rawnsley, vicar of Wray and then Crosthwaite, near Keswick, was a determined crusader, keen to protect the Lake District and in particular the countryside around Keswick. Whilst living at Wray he had become a close friend of John Ruskin who lived nearby at Brantwood. Canon Rawnsley turned to Ruskin for support when he learnt that a syndicate of quarry owners was planning to build a railway along the shores of Derwentwater to take slate from Honister to Keswick. Ruskin's response was: "You may always put my name, without asking leave, to any petition against any railway anywhere. But it's all of no use. You will soon have a Cook's tourist railway up Scawfell, and another up Helvellyn, and another up Skiddaw. And then a connecting line, all round".

Fortunately Rawnsley did not give up on receiving these pessimistic words, rather they stiffened his resolve to launch a successful campaign which not only defeated the Borrowdale railway, but also proposals to extend railways to Ennerdale and Ullswater. The concept of sustainable tourism was alive and well in those early days. The next campaign, also successful, was Canon Rawnsley's fight to keep open the rights of access for the local people to Latrigg Fell, at the foot of Skiddaw, against the owners' wishes. His passion for conservation campaigns of this sort earned him the nick-name "the most active volcano in Europe".

A renewed threat to Derwentwater finally brought together Hardwicke Rawnsley, Sir Robert Hunter, solicitor to the Commons Preservation Society, and Octavia Hill, a social reformer who was keen to protect the countryside for the benefit of the urban poor. And so, in 1895 the National Trust was founded, as a registered charity and independent of government, to preserve places of historic interest or natural beauty permanently for the nation to enjoy.

It was not until 1902 that the Trust acquired its first property in the Lake District, Brandelhow Park, 43 ha on the shores of Derwentwater, and largely again through the efforts, including fundraising, of Canon Rawnsley and Octavia Hill. One hundred years later the Trust owns or protects 55,000 ha within the Lake District National Park, approximately one quarter of the total area, including England's highest mountain- Scafell Pike, the deepest lake- Wastwater, and over 90 farms. Almost all of the central and western fell areas are now owned or leased by the Trust, together with 24 lakes and tarns and just under 3,000 ha of woodland. It also owns over 200 houses and cottages including four that are open to the public either in the Lake District- Hill Top and Townend, or just outside the National Park boundary- Sizergh Castle and Wordsworth House in Cockermouth (see Chapter Four).

In 1907 the National Trust was incorporated by an Act of Parliament. The Act granted the Trust the unique power to declare its land inalienable. Such land cannot be sold, mortgaged or compulsorily acquired against the Trust's wishes without special parliamentary procedures.

The National Trust as a Property Manager

Owning such a diverse range of properties brings challenges of its own, not least to find an acceptable balance between protecting and conserving those properties and to provide access to them. In practice the Trust has always taken the approach that where the conservation of a property is threatened by inappropriate levels of access then conservation must take precedence. The following examples help to demonstrate the issue:

> ➤ In the early 1970s the pressure from visitors at the well known beauty-spot, Tarn Hows, was causing erosion problems on the steep descent path from what was then the main car park to the water's edge. A number of different treatments were tested on different plots of the worst affected area, which was fenced off to exclude the public for the duration of the experiment. A year later, when the site had apparently recovered, it was reopened but within two weeks the erosion was as bad as at the outset on all the plots. As a result of this unsuccessful experiment it was decided that the only solution was to close the car park above the Tarn and to create an enlarged car park at the same level as the Tarn so as to reduce the pressure on the

slope. This proved to be the right solution and today Tarn Hows can accommodate the 250,000 or so visitors who go there each year, with minimal effect on the landscape.

➢ Visitor numbers to Hill Top, Beatrix Potter's house, were averaging around 80,000 in the 1990s. The pressure on this small house was so intense at certain times of the day that a visit could be spoilt by the need to queue along the roadside in order to buy a ticket, and by the number of visitors in the house at any one time which created conservation problems of its own. A timed ticket facility was introduced to even out the visitor flows and the situation today is much improved.

In the early 1970s, it was not just Tarn Hows that was suffering from the effects of too many human feet- large areas of the fells were beginning to show signs of wear and tear. The Trust, as owner of some of the most popular routes to the summits of the Lakeland fells, decided to use some of its resources to improve the surface of these paths by "pitching" them.

This method, dating back to Roman times, was "rediscovered" by the Trust and has proved most effective. Basically the process is to lay large stones at a slight angle to the horizontal to provide a solid pathway which drains freely and is comfortable to walk on. Adequate drainage channels are put in, at an angle across the paths, at regular intervals to prevent large volumes of water from flowing down the paths so causing the stones to wash out. As many as 16 people in 4 teams have been regularly employed by the Trust at any one time to carry out this work which is both rigorous and demanding.

Today many of the worst scars on the landscape have been eliminated by this process and almost all the walkers and climbers are content to see and use these "manufactured" paths instead of the deeply eroded gullies which they replaced. There are many other facets to the Trust's work as a manager, many of which are related to maintaining the natural and cultural environment of the Lake District for the benefit of the local inhabitants and the visitors. The following examples help to illustrate this:

➢ *Buildings*. Where possible the Trust will use traditional materials and methods in the construction of new buildings and the restoration of old ones in the National Park.

Inevitably it is considerably more expensive than modern treatments but that is a price that has to be paid to keep the area as visitors and locals expect to find it. It is arguable whether it should fall on the Trust to meet the extra resources however – a point that is regularly made.

➢ *Forestry*. The majority of the Trust's woodlands are managed for amenity reasons rather than commercial ones. As a consequence they produce little or no income. Nevertheless they have to be maintained which involves felling trees that might be a danger to the public, clearing small areas to allow for natural regeneration to take place and ensuring the walls and fences are stockproof. Where commercial forestry is the expedient then the more traditional methods of thinning, felling and replanting are used

➢ *Wardening.* The Trust employs a number of wardens and estate workers whose job it is to maintain the lowland paths, fences and drystone walls; to erect stiles, gates and signs; to plant and maintain new hedgerows; to provide a service to the general public and a link with the local communities and schools, and many other roles besides.

The Property Management Plan

Each property in the Lake District, which may constitute a single valley or a number of valleys, has a Property Manager responsible for the day to day running of the property. One of the key tasks for the Property Manager is to produce an up-to-date Management Plan. This requires, at the outset, a Statement of Significance to be written describing what is particularly special or significant about the property. To achieve this a consultation process is adopted whereby the staff and local community are invited to give their views. In many cases the process goes wider to other organisations and stakeholders.

The Property Manager will then assimilate all the information and draw up a short Statement of Significance. This provides the basis upon which the Objectives for the future management of the property can be formulated and so the Management Plan can be written. The Plan thus becomes the focus for all future management decisions. In drawing up the Plan the Property Manager and team will, inter alia, take account of the conservation needs and the appropriate levels of access to the property.

When considering the conservation requirements the Property Manager will draw on in-house expertise e.g. from the nature conservation and archaeological advisers. He or she will also discuss with the customer services department how access may need to be restricted to parts of the property, or managed to reduce pressure on sensitive areas. Once the plan is finalised an annual work programme will be drawn up for the benefit of the staff at the property and for budgetary purposes. The Management Plan is normally reviewed every three years.

Public benefit

Public benefit, one of the National Trust's key commitments, is not solely about access. There are many other ways in which the Trust provides benefits to the public:

➢ *Campsites-* the Trust runs three campsites in the Lake District, two of which are at the head of the valleys of Wasdale and Great Langdale. The question is sometimes asked as to whether it is appropriate to have campsites in such sensitive places and whether it would not be better to site them at the lower end of the valleys. In each case the campsites are well screened and barely visible.

In the case of Langdale it is worth reflecting on the situation in the late 1960s before the site was built. At that time almost all the Trust farms at the head of the valley had their own unscreened campsites, run by the farm tenants. None of these had proper facilities. Walkers in Great Langdale were confronted with a hotch-potch of fields containing an array of coloured tents which most people considered an eyesore. The decision was taken to create a formal campsite with modern facilities and to abandon the ad hoc arrangements that had previously existed. This was achieved through negotiation with each affected farm tenant and a rent reduction was agreed commensurate with their loss of income from camping. By this means the Trust had control over the amenities on site, the necessary screening and the appropriate number of pitches.

➤ *Holiday Cottages* – With such a large portfolio of houses and cottages it would be all too tempting to let them as holiday homes. In fact the Trust took the decision some years ago to restrict the number to those which, in most cases, would be difficult to let to local people, either because they were too remote or too expensive to bring up to modern day standards. One of the holiday cottages still has an earth closet! There are only 16 houses and cottages let for holiday purposes.

➤ *Basecamp*- the Trust built the Basecamp at High Wray in 1969, the first of its kind in the Trust. This has been in use ever since, providing basic facilities for those wishing either to spend their holidays doing voluntary work for the organisation or merely as a base for exploring the Lake District. Volunteers have priority when booking, followed by disadvantaged groups seeking an activity holiday, before it is offered more widely.

➤ *Shops and restaurants*- most properties, particularly houses open to the public, will have a shop or restaurant or both, according to the annual number of visitors. In the Lake District there are a few shops in the 'honey pot' villages, such as Hawkshead and Grasmere, which are owned and run by the Trust. All net income deriving from such enterprises is used for the conservation of the properties.

➤ *Education* – With thousands of hectares of countryside, a huge range of habitats and wildlife, historic buildings and gardens, archaeological sites and industrial monuments, the National Trust is one of the biggest educational resource banks in the world. Education is now a vital part of the Trust's work. Education staff work to provide learning opportunities to all ages; primary and secondary school children, further education colleges and universities.

In the Lake District there are a number of 'Guardianship' schemes, which enable strong links to be established between a certain property and a local school. Children learn about their local environment and how to be its 'guardians'. Learning does not end at school or university. It occurs continually throughout our lives. So the Trust runs events, courses, exhibitions, trails and workshops, and offers interactive experiences to encourage discovery and learning about houses, gardens and the countryside.

> ➢ *Interpretation* – This is the term used to describe any communication tool that interprets the 'resource'. It helps visitors to leave with a better understanding and appreciation of the site. Interpretation has to be balanced with the atmosphere, experience and protection of the place. It would be a huge mistake to site a large panel at the summit of Great Gable (one of the highest mountains in the Lake District) for example; better by far that such interpretation is restricted to focal points such as car parks. Techniques that are used include signage and waymarking, storytelling, costumed characters, leaflets, guidebooks, audio guides and labelling.

The Trust as a landlord

Besides the 90 or so farm tenancies there are other tenants renting small areas of bare land. The Trust is also landlord to some commercial enterprises such as public houses, caravan sites, hotels and cafés, and numerous residential lettings. The Trust works closely with, and supports, its tenants, recognising that the relationship with its agricultural tenants is vital to the success of its conservation work. The 2001 Foot and Mouth crisis brought that relationship into close focus and the Trust did much to help its farmers, in providing emotional and financial support, to try to minimise the worst effects.

A major current initiative is the development of Whole Farm Plans, which help to establish mutual business and conservation objectives for the Trust and its farm tenants and their families. An example of a close working relationship with a farming tenant and his family is at Yew Tree Farm in Borrowdale. It is let to Joe and Hazel Relph who have an excellent track record in farming and Bed and Breakfast. In 1996 the Relphs decided to develop their business and, with support from the Trust, opened a small tearoom – The Flock-In. This was so successful that they expanded again two years later, specialising in Herdwick recipes- the Herdwick being the indigenous breed of sheep in the Lake District known for its excellent flavour.

Encouraged by enthusiastic responses to the Herdwick dishes in the tearoom, the Relphs decided to sell meat directly to the public, offering joints, vacuum-packed and oven-ready, together with Cumberland sausage and 'Herdi-burgers'. The response was so overwhelming and demand for the products so high that the Relphs now buy in Herdwick meat from their neighbouring National Trust farm tenants.

Working towards sustainable tourism

The National Trust today is a significant player in the tourist industry welcoming nearly 12 million visitors to its pay-for-entry properties and an estimated 50 million visits to its coast and countryside properties annually in England, Wales and Northern Ireland. As well as balancing its statutory responsibilities for conservation and access, the Trust also has to ensure that it is sensitive to the life of the local community.

The Trust believes that the primary objective of any tourism strategy must be to protect the environment on which that tourism depends. If tourism impacts too much on the environment, visitors may degrade the very thing they are coming to enjoy. A sustainable approach must also embrace the social and economic effects of tourism ensuring that visitors enjoy their visit, local economies benefit, living standards are protected and the skills of the local people are harnessed. The National Trust's approach is in line with the 'wise' growth strategy for tourism outlined in the Government's *Tomorrow's Tourism* White Paper.

The White Paper placed special emphasis on sustainability and included many new initiatives. The Trust believes that if sustainable tourism is to be achieved, it will be necessary to:

➤ *Promote regional characteristics:* Tourism strategies should respect and nurture local and regional characteristics. The rich diversity of Britain's landscapes and local culture, including dialect, language and events is one of the UK's greatest assets, and nowhere more so than in the Lake District, drawing as it does, visitors from Britain and abroad. Safeguards are needed to ensure these characteristics are not adversely affected by tourism and profits from tourism should be applied to identify and encourage diversity. The Trust's programme of producing Statements of Significance for each property showing what is special about them will help to promote regional characteristics.

➤ *Provide improved public transport:* In order to balance conservation with accessibility, the Trust is actively encouraging alternatives to the car such as walking, cycling, horse riding and public transport. In the Lake District it provides minibuses to transport visitors on Landscape Tours, and schools to visit particular properties. It also runs a free bus service at weekends from Keswick to Watendlath, and Hawkshead via Tarnhows to Coniston from where visitors can embark on the Trust's steam yacht – S. Y. Gondola – for a trip around the lake. Alternatively they can disembark on the other side of the lake at John Ruskin's house- Brantwood – and return on a later service.

➤ *Support local economies:* National Trust restaurants and shops stock local produce wherever possible. 60 per cent of the produce used in Trust restaurants is sourced locally. In each one in Cumbria, Herdwick lamb from National Trust farms is on the menu.

➤ *Educate:* The Trust believes the key to encouraging more sustainable tourism is to promote greater understanding of the issues involved. Public awareness should be raised regarding sustainable tourism and what individuals can do to help. Sustainable tourism and management of the environment should also be included at all levels of formal education from schools to leisure and tourism courses.

➤ *Support the environment:* All money raised by the National Trust is used to support its work. For many years the Trust has been running a successful Lake District Appeal for funds to support its landscape conservation work such as the footpath pitching and the extra costs of using traditional materials in new buildings. A total of £6.5 million has been raised since the launch in 1986. A large proportion of that money has come from Trust members, of which there were 3 million at the end of 2002, either in the form of donations or legacies.

But the tourist industry should put a proportion of its profits back into the environment since it is that very environment upon which the industry depends. It was with this principle in mind that the Lake District Tourism and Conservation Partnership was founded in 1993 and which established the Visitor Payback scheme whereby guests staying in some hotels, self catering accommodation or other facilities would be invited to contribute a small proportion of their bill to the upkeep of the landscape or a specific project. Further information on the Lake District Tourism and Conservation Partnership is provided later in this chapter. (See case study)

➤ *Increase access:* The Trust believes that sustainable tourism should be inclusive in its practice, providing access opportunities for people who are less affluent and for people with particular needs, including those with disabilities, families with young children and the elderly.

There are many examples in the Lake District where the Trust has upgraded access provision to meet this principle, such as the paths around Tarn Hows or along the western shore of Derwentwater which are able to be used by those in wheelchairs. At Aira Force there is a 'Blind trail': here it is possible to collect an audio tape describing the walk to the falls, from the staff on site, and use a wooden rail as a physical guide.

Working in partnership

The activities of a large number of other organisations and agents in Cumbria are also instrumental in supporting the local economy. In recent years, working with and through others has become a priority for the Trust. It is through co-operation with such partners that the land is managed to best effect so that the many millions of visitors who come each year can enjoy it and benefit from it.

Partnerships will continue to be an essential element of the Trust's work in the Lake District, not least in delivering both the Cumbria Rural Action Zone (RAZ) strategy, produced in the wake of the 2001 Foot and Mouth crisis, but also the key rural objectives in the North West Development Agency's *Strategy Towards 2020*. Perhaps one of the most effective partnerships is the Lake District Tourism and Conservation Partnership, see below.

Two of the key partnerships for the Trust are those with the Lake District National Park Authority and Cumbria Tourist Board. The aims of the National Park Authority are broadly similar to those of the Trust, but as owners of approximately one quarter of the Park, the Trust needs to work closely with it to ensure that the respective strategies, aims and objectives are as mutually supportive as possible.

A rather different approach is necessary with the Cumbria Tourist Board. Here the Board seeks to encourage, on behalf of its members, tourists to visit the region by marketing the product in order to fill the hotels, guesthouses and B&B's. On the other hand the Trust has to balance the conservation and access needs of its properties, whether open for a fee or not. Clearly open dialogue is essential to ensure that the sensitive sites are not over-exploited and, in practice, this works well.

Case Study – The Lake District Tourism and Conservation Partnership

Established in 1993 the Lake District Tourism and Conservation Partnership's (LDTCP) aim is to raise funds from visitors, tourism and related businesses and others in order to maintain and enhance the Lake District landscape. For the first time, a means had been created whereby visitors, tourism businesses and other related organisations, and the conservation bodies that protect the landscape were connected. The founding organisations were the Cumbria Tourist Board, the National Trust and the Lake District National Park Authority. Initial pump-priming support was also provided by the Cumbria Training and Enterprise Council and the Rural Development Commission (now part of the Countryside Agency).

By 1997 LDTCP had become an independent, non-profit distributing company limited by guarantee. Personal and financial support has been secured from important individuals and essential organisations that form its Board of Directors. Both the Cumbria Tourist Board and the National Trust are represented at Director level. The National Park Authority and English Nature act as advisers to the Board and there are a further eight members, including the Chairman, representing the tourist industry. Core funding is received annually from the Corporate Members as well as from an Associate membership scheme. The Associate scheme has been purposefully set up as a tiered scheme allowing the smallest of tourism businesses to play an active part in supporting their local environment; 70 per cent of funding comes from the private sector. Other funding avenues identified for particular projects have included grants from the North West Development Agency, English Tourism Council, the Countryside Agency, as well as European funding.

The role of the Lake District Tourism and Conservation Partnership

The foundation of the LDTCP arose out of the realisation amongst the tourism industry that it has a responsibility to help maintain the environment upon which the industry depends. At the same time the conservation organisations were aware that they had insufficient resources to carry out all the necessary work. External research supported by practical projects showed that visitors to the Lake District were willing to contribute towards landscape conservation work. The difficulty in the past had been that there was no means whereby the visitor could contribute, except to the National Trusts's own Lake District Appeal which was specifically for work on Trust land. LDTCP provides the conduit with innovative fundraising schemes, commonly known as visitor payback. These schemes include a voluntary contribution in the overall cost of the visitors' stay. There are two types of payback, opt-in and opt-out. Opt-in operates when the visitor requests *inclusion* in the scheme ie there is an opportunity to donate £1 or more to a project and the customer has to tick the box signifying agreement. Alternatively there is an opt-out scheme whereby the visitor has to request *exclusion* from the scheme, ie the customer has to tick the box to indicate that he or she does not wish £1 on the bill to be donated. Other fundraising methods used are donation boxes, percentage of sales income and proceeds from events.

There is ownership of the particular project the business has adopted (see Chapter Six for examples) and the Partnership itself as it is non-political, proactive and an exemplar of how sustainable tourism can be promoted through the combined energy of its main stakeholders. The LDTCP is recognised in the UK as a centre for excellence and is emulated throughout the UK and beyond. It continues to be cited as an example of best practice by VisitBritain, the Countryside Agency, Cumbria Tourist Board, the National Trust and the Lake District National Park Authority. It is referred to in both the Government's Tourism Strategy and the Rural White Paper.

➤   **Responsible Tourism**

The year 2002 saw the launch of 'Responsible Tourism', an accreditation scheme for small tourism businesses – a first for Cumbria. With the help of Cumbria Tourist Board, LDTCP designed, delivered and administered the scheme that recognises good practice amongst tourism initiatives and fosters improved business performance through responsible action. Over 50 businesses have entered the scheme and are keen to take their commitment forward.

➤   **Corporate Responsibility**

LDTCP also provides the opportunity for visiting conference groups and businesses in Cumbria, to become actively involved with 'hands on' conservation. In conjunction with the British Trust for Conservation Volunteers, projects such as clearing rhododendron or scrub are designed. These conservation days are then marketed through events companies within the region and have attracted corporate groups such as KPMG and Bolton Wanderers Football Club.

➤   **A Success Story**

The LDTCP is a successful pioneering partnership. Over 85 practical conservation projects have been supported since 1995 and in excess of £300,000 has been raised proving that small contributions from tourism businesses and visitors can make a difference. These projects range from repairs to high fell footpaths, bridge restoration, hedge laying and dry-stone walling, to habitat protection, interpretation and education. These practical tasks enhance not only the visitors' experience but also improve the landscape for the rural communities. Visitor payback has now become part of the vocabulary of tourism management. LDCTP is a proven player in sustainable tourism and is recognised as such within the UK, Europe and beyond. The sharing of best practice extends as far as Holland, Greece, and Indonesia.

Until three years ago LDTCP employed one member of staff. As private sector interest has increased, coupled with financial assistance from Europe, the number of employees has grown to three. This will in turn allow increased funds to be raised to support further conservation work throughout Cumbria. LDTCP has demonstrated how the economic benefits of tourism can maintain and enhance the Lake District landscape. This has been recognised internationally as the partnership received, for the second time, the British Airways Tourism for Tomorrow Highly Commended Award in November 2002.

The organisations discussed so far in this chapter are all primarily engaged in the conservation and preservation of the distinctive features and special qualities of the Lake District. The Cumbria Tourist Board has been the Regional Tourist Board for the Lake District for over 20 years and has been actively engaged in helping the tourism industry to develop, as well as being heavily involved in promoting the region as a sustainable tourist destination. In 2003-4 the Cumbria Tourist Board will evolve into a new destination management organisation for Cumbria as part of the North West Development Agency's tourism strategy for north west England.

Cumbria Tourist Board

Cumbria Tourist Board (CTB) is a non-departmental public body, a form of Quango – a quasi-autonomous non-governmental organisation. Its role has been to ensure that national and local priorities for tourism are reflected in the development of tourism in Cumbria. In the 1990s, the national priority for tourism development was enhancing the quality of Britain's tourism product through "product development, investment in human resources, and improvements to the transport network; and on improving Britain's performance as an international tourism destination" (Cumbria Tourist Board, 1998:3). These national priorities are reflected at a regional and local level through "…a framework of documents which influence the development of tourism in Cumbria" (ibid:3) for example the Structure and Local Plans, economic development strategies, and CTB's Regional Strategy for Tourism in Cumbria (1998).

CTB in 2001 – 2002 received modest Partnership Funding of £653,087 from the English Tourism Council, Cumbria County Council, the six local authorities in Cumbria, and from membership subscriptions (Cumbria Tourist Board, 2002). For the same financial year, the Board administered a further £3,657,434 primarily to help the region recover from the devastating effects of the 2001 Foot and Mouth crisis. CTB's mission in recent years has been to be the "voice of tourism for Cumbria" (ibid:8). CTB saw its role as providing:

> "Vigorous marketing and promotion
> Objective measurement and research
> Integrated development of sustainable tourism
> Continual drive for higher standards and value
> Eloquent representation of the Industry"
>
> *Source:* Cumbria Tourist Board, 2002

Each of the above elements of CTB's mission will now be briefly explained.

Marketing and promotion

Developing brand awareness of Cumbria and the Lake District is a key task of CTB. However, the Board has a limited budget to spend on marketing and promotion, (£1m in 2003-2004). Most expenditure tends to be invested in the design, print, and distribution of hard and soft copy promotional literature such as:

Cumbria – the Lake District Holiday Guide, 400,000 copies, which is the lead publication produced by CTB.

Spring into Summer, 200,000 copies, *and Autumn and Winter,* 100,000 copies, special seasonal brochures, distributed to a specially targeted set of tourists on CTB's data base, those who had previously expressed an interest in short break holidays to the region.

Bed and Breakfast Touring Map 80,000 copies.

Group Travel Guide for incoming tour operators and coach companies.

Camping and Caravan Guide.

www.gocumbria.co.uk

www.golakes.co.uk

www.lakedistrictoutdoors.co.uk

New tourist guides in 2004 include:

Hidden Treasures of Cumbria 2004.

The Taste District 2004 (food and drink guide).

Flora & Fauna of Cumbria.

Fishing Guide 2004.

www.hiddentreasurescumbria.co.uk

www.lastminutelakedistrict.co.uk

Each of the above publications is targeted at a specific market segment, with all elements of the marketing strategy combining to form an integrated and comprehensive national multi-media campaign, www.gocumbria.co.uk (2003). In addition to the above guides and websites, CTB also works with the media to publicise and promote tourism to the region. Holidays in Cumbria and the Lake District are regularly featured on television programmes (the BBC Holiday programme, for example), and as editorial copy in newspapers and magazines.

Market segmentation and product positioning

In 1995 CTB commissioned a major piece of research, see Cumbria Tourist Board (1996), to collect data to inform the development of a revised and updated Regional Tourism Strategy for Cumbria. As a result of the research CTB was able to identify four target markets that were felt to be the priority markets for Cumbria and the Lake District:

➤ Get away from it all tourists – this market segment was looking for relaxation in attractive surroundings while staying in high quality accommodation. This tourist typically arrived by car, was in the 45 to 65 age group, and in the ABC1 socio-economic group.

➤ Activity tourists – these tourists enjoyed sports and outdoor leisure activities, or indoor pursuits based on hobbies and special interests, and were generally in the 15-54 age group.

> ➤ Culture and heritage tourists – these tourists were in the ABC1 socio-economic group and generally aged 35+ years. This was felt to be a growing market segment taking more frequent holiday breaks around a heritage/cultural theme.

> ➤ Fun-seeking tourists – typically this segment was dominated by families with children aged 4 to 16 years in the C2DE socio-economic groups.

Source: Cumbria Tourist Board (1998:48)

With the identification of the above four target markets, positioning strategies were then developed for each segment – the key values and images which ideally each target market should hold about the Lake District. A common theme of the positioning strategies developed in the 1990s was the use of Lakes and Mountains as key attributes of the tourist experience, which obviously reflected the images that most people held about the Lake District. Conceptualising a brand identity is to some extent relatively easy, through the use of photographs and images that portray mountains and lakes, and incorporating these images in all promotional material. The challenge, though, was communicating the brand identity with limited financial resources – Cumbria Tourist Board and the other organisations involved with the marketing and promotion of tourism in the Lake District had very small budgets to devote to direct advertising activities. Most of the communication and development of the brand identity occurred through the publication and distribution of guide books and accommodation guides. However, the use of the same brand values and brochure designs each year helped to reinforce the message, but probably with existing repeat tourists as opposed to new first time visitors who might require some form of media advertising to make them aware of holiday opportunities in the Lake District.

An analysis of two Lake District guidebooks helps to illustrate the above point. *Cumbria The Lake District Holidays and Breaks 2003* was CTB's main guidebook in 2003. It featured a photograph of a peaceful and tranquil Grasmere on the front cover, with not one tourist in sight. Turning to the first page of the brochure the scene was again of lakeland tranquility with the sun rising over a mist shrouded Windermere. Thus the brand identity of lakes and mountains was being portrayed. On the second page of the brochure one of the other core values of the Lake District – a world class sustainable environment – was signified by the prominent positioning of the Green Globe 21 logo, promoting the Lake District as the world's first Green Globe destination (see Chapter One). Turning the page of the brochure again, the reader saw a photograph of Derwentwater with surrounding fells and mountains, but again without a single tourist in site and no sign at all of any commercial activity. The subsequent pages of the brochure were designed to communicate information to the aforementioned target markets, and to encourage them to visit. The photographs of peace and tranquility will have appealed to the 'get-away-from-it-all' visitors. Six pages of the brochure were devoted to the history and culture of the region, four pages highlighted activities for families, and throughout there were indications of the outdoor and indoor pursuits that were on offer in the Lake District. Photographs and images of the Lake District that portrayed the high quality of the region were used in the brochure to signify a high quality tourism product for the ABC1 socio-economic groups. *Keswick Heart of the Lake District 2003* was the visitor information and accommodation brochure produced to promote tourism to the northern lakes. It adopted a similar design style to the CTB brochure with a photograph of Derwentwater and the mountain of Skiddaw on the front cover with the text on the second page describing the "boundless opportunities to explore the mountains, valleys and lakes in this peaceful northern part of the Lake District National Park."

The marketing of the Lake District as a tourist destination – 2004 and beyond

Cumbria Tourist Board uses market research to devise its marketing strategy. In 2002 it commissioned a major study to provide data to help inform the design of a new tourism strategy for Cumbria, see Locum Destination Consulting (2003). Locum Destination Consulting whilst agreeing with the importance of segmenting the tourism market did not support the notion of categorising people too precisely into very specific market segments as they believed that most tourists will actually participate in a range of different activities and leisure pursuits. However, the research report does identify six distinct product/market segments that have been used to form the basis of a new marketing strategy for Cumbria and the Lake District:

> Seaside and Countryside Holidays – fairly traditional, primarily long stay holidays for young families and retired members of society that are focused on the Cumbrian coast and the central Lake District, attracting tourists from the CD socio-economic groups living in the Midlands and the North of England, and staying in bed & breakfast guesthouses, independent hotels, and holiday villages.

> Rural Getaways – short to medium break holidays for families and couples from the ABC1 socio-economic groups, some of whom enjoy serious walking, but also those who like a diverse range of leisure and cultural activities in a quiet and beautiful environment.

> Sophisticated Short Breaks – affluent pre- and post-family tourists, the majority living in urban environments, who enjoy taking short breaks in high quality hotels.

> Active Outdoors – tourists who visit Cumbria for serious physical activity, especially walking.

> Conferences and Exhibitions – business tourism.

> Overseas Visitors – dominated by tourists from North America and Australasia, normally staying for short periods in serviced accommodation.

Source: Locum Destination Consulting (2003:88)

Locum Destination Consulting (2003) as well as identifying new product/market segments to be developed also advocated the adoption of regional branding rather than the proliferation of a number of sub-regional brands. This is because tourists when going on holiday tend to travel quite extensively within a region, rather than confining their holiday to a geographic area that might replicate the boundary of a local authority district. The proliferation of sub-brands results in the duplication of scarce marketing and promotion budgets, and by concentrating on major regional brands such scarce resources can be better utilised. One of the recommendations made by Locum Destination Consulting (2003) was that the Lake District brand should be refined and developed further as it is widely known, invokes images and impressions of the region, and generates positive perceptions. Chapter Nine will explore further the future marketing strategy of the Lake District.

Objective measurement and research

Cumbria Tourist Board represents the regional tourism industry on a variety of policy, strategy, and regulatory issues (www.gocumbria.co.uk 2003). It works with key stakeholders on the formulation of new policies and strategies (Cumbria County Council, North West Development Agency, Lake District National Park Authority, and Local District Councils, for example). Part of CTB's role is also to identify potential funding streams from Government Offices, and organisations such as Urban and Rural Regeneration Companies. In order to represent the views and issues facing the regional tourism industry effectively, and to identify realistic funding opportunities, CTB adopts an evidence – based approach. That is to say, that CTB is a research-led organisation – it commissions a variety of different research studies each year to provide data to inform the strategic and operational development of tourism in the region. The final research reports are made available for purchase by the various stakeholders of CTB and members of the public. For example, research findings on the volume and value of tourism in Cumbria and the Lake District are essential when the CTB and other agencies seek funding from the EU, central government, or the North West Development Agency.

Research is also undertaken to provide data on other key issues affecting the development of tourism in Cumbria such as studies to investigate the adoption of environmental management practices by tourism organisations, and research into the local labour market for tourism. The CTB also provides funds to assist partner agencies and organisations to undertake research, and offers a range of research services to tourism businesses. An example of this is the "Demograf" system that can assist tourism businesses in targeting their marketing activities more effectively, www.gocumbria.co.uk (2003).

Integrated development of sustainable tourism

A variety of different strategies are being implemented by CTB to develop sustainable tourism in the region. CTB fully realises the importance of the Lakeland landscape and Lakeland communities in attracting tourists to the region. In the 1990s it embraced fully the notion of sustainable tourism as being central to the success of the Lake District's tourism industry, both from a product and market perspective. CTB was a founding partner of the Lake District Tourism and Conservation Partnership. It was the CTB that was the lead body in gaining Green Globe 21 accreditation for the Lake District. Sustainable tourism became a central element of the promotional strategies implemented by CTB to attract tourists to the region. Research was commissioned to provide baseline data on the sustainable management strategies implemented by tourism businesses in the region, with the intention of increasing the number of businesses devising and implementing such strategies. With regard to assisting with the financial sustainability of individual tourism businesses, during the 2001 Foot and Mouth crisis CTB provided advice and support to businesses who were facing severe difficulties as a result of lost bookings. A major achievement of CTB has been raising the awareness of sustainable tourism with a variety of different stakeholders in Cumbria and the Lake District, and encouraging and supporting these stakeholders to devise and implement sustainable tourism practices in their day-to-day operations. An example of the support the CTB provides for tourism businesses is the 'Sustainable Travel Friendly Audit & Action Plan' (STFAAP).

The STFAAP scheme is for accommodation providers and tourist attractions and is a means to raise awareness of how that business can encourage more of its guests and visitors to travel by public transport, or by other modes that do not involve travelling by car. The aim is to help reduce traffic congestion, pollution, and visual intrusion in the Lake District. CTB's Sustainable Travel Co-ordinator conducts a travel audit of the business, and helps to devise an action plan that will encourage more of that business's customers to leave their car, and travel by more environmentally appropriate modes of transport.

A challenge facing the sustainable development of the Lake District's tourism industry is that of workforce development. It was indicated in Chapter Three that there is a labour market imbalance in the Lake District, too many economically inactive residents, and an out migration of economically active young people. To help address this problem CTB has been funding a number of initiatives to assist tourism businesses to recruit and retain young people within their workforces.

Funding has been secured from the 'Sustainable Regeneration through Tourism Single Regeneration Budget' (www.gocumbria.co.uk, 2003) to employ three full-time members of staff to encourage Cumbrian people to work in tourism. CTB attends careers exhibitions in schools, provides career advice to job seekers, advertises job vacancies on its website, and hosts community events to raise the profile of working within tourism. Through the implementation of such measures it is hoped that more local people will consider tourism as a career, and hence assist tourism businesses to become more sustainable.

CTB also recognises that tourism businesses will become more financially sustainable if they improve the skills and capabilities of their workforce, and has embarked on a major strategy to encourage this, with funding from the North West Tourism Skills Network and the Learning and Skills Council – Cumbria.

Continual drive for higher standards and value

Improving the quality of the visitor experience is fundamental to the success of any organisation. In tourism, this can be challenging given the high level of human interaction between tourism workers and their customers. CTB actively promotes the Welcome Host courses that are designed to improve customer service skills of people working in tourism. Investment is also made to improve the services offered to tourists through tourist information centres, especially developing the communication information technology skills of staff, and ensuring that the centres are fully networked to the latest software and databases.

Each year, CTB organises the Cumbria for Excellence Awards that recognise achievements by tourism businesses operating in the region, with awards being presented to each major sector of Cumbria's tourism industry.

Eloquent representation of the industry

As mentioned above CTB sees itself as the voice of tourism, not only within the region, but also nationally and internationally. CTB communicates regularly with its membership through seminars and newsletters. At a national level, particularly during the 2001 Foot and Mouth crisis the CTB was involved with meetings with Prime Minister Tony Blair, senior government ministers, and Members of the European Parliament. Strong relationships have also been established with other key agencies such as the Confederation of British Industry.

Structure and strategy

To undertake its work the CTB in 2002 employed an average of 31 people, organised into two main Departments, Marketing and Development Operations, and Financial & Administrative Services. To realise its Mission, CTB produces and implements a Regional Tourism Strategy for Cumbria (Cumbria Tourist Board, 1998). The 1998 Strategy had 12 key objectives:

1.   To develop the tourism industry in areas where there was the need and potential for growth.

2.   To identify needs and opportunities for tourism development and stimulate that development.

3.   To encourage investment in appropriate tourism projects.

4.   To seek the protection and enhancement of the environment and heritage of Cumbria as the mainstay of its tourism industry, and to promote good visitor management to minimise the pressure of visitors on the environment.

5.   To seek the maintenance and development of those farming practices and rural industries which make an important contribution to visitors' enjoyment of Cumbria.

6.   To safeguard and improve the transport system to and within the region and to promote effective traffic management.

7.   To encourage people from Britain and overseas to visit Cumbria by effective marketing.

8.   To extend the tourism season to improve income and increase the number of permanent jobs.

9.   To ensure the provision of comprehensive and up-to-date information for visitors.

10.   To improve the quality and value for money of accommodation and other facilities for tourists and ensure fair and consistent descriptions in publicity.

11.   To encourage higher standards of training throughout the tourism industry.

12.   To increase public awareness of the importance of the tourism industry and to justify resources for implementing this strategy.

Clearly, the CTB with its limited resources (staffing and finance) is unable by itself to implement all elements of its Regional Tourism Strategy for Cumbria, and explicitly stated "implementation of the policies ...will require the involvement of everyone associated with the tourism industry" (Cumbria Tourist Board, 1998:65). It listed as its partners:

➤   Commercial operators.

➤   Local Authorities and the National Park Authority.

➤   Government Departments and other agencies (for example: Government Office for the North West, Department of Environment, Farming and Rural Affairs, Department of Trade & Industry, Business Link, Cumbria Careers Ltd., England's North Country – to name just six potential partners).

➤   National Tourist Boards.

➤   Other organisations (for example: the National Trust, West Cumbria Groundwork Trust, East Cumbria Countryside Project).

As well as working directly with some of these organisations on the implementation of the Regional Tourism Strategy for Cumbria, CTB commended these organisations to be fully aware of the policies contained within its strategy document so that they can be taken into account when the partners are "... reviewing and implementing their own policies"(ibid:65).

The above discussion has demonstrated that CTB plays a major part in supporting the management and development of the tourism industry in the Lake District on the principles of sustainable tourism. To secure Green Globe 21 accreditation for Cumbria and the Lake District as a tourist destination that is committed to the principles of sustainable tourism management, CTB will have followed the six steps proposed by Weaver (2000:302):

Step 1 – define goals and objectives for sustainable tourism;

Step 2 – establish planning and management parameters;

Step 3 – select appropriate and feasible indicators of sustainable tourism;

Step 4 – measure and monitor performance against the indicators;

Step 5 – determine whether the sustainable tourism goals have been achieved;

Step 6 – implement remedial action.

Clearly, achieving Green Globe 21 accreditation for the Lake District was a major achievement and reflects the commitment that CTB has to conserving and preserving the special qualities of the Lake District so that they can be enjoyed by future generations.

The Local Authorities

"Throughout the UK exists a comprehensive cover of directly-elected, multi-functional local authorities" (Callaghan *et al.*,1994:169). As mentioned in Chapter Three, there are six local authority districts in Cumbria as well as Cumbria County Council. Four of these local authorities include segments of the Lake District within their geographic areas: Allerdale Borough Council, Copeland Borough Council, Eden District Council, and South Lakeland District Council. Local authorities are required to produce a Local Economic Development Strategy to comply with the provisions of the 1989 Housing and Local Government Act. Such strategies are set within the context of the local authority's Corporate Plan. Although local authorities do not have a statutory duty to become engaged in the management and development of tourism, all of the local authorities in Cumbria do invest resources to ensure that the tourism sector is able to contribute to local economic development on a sustainable basis. This is achieved by providing staff expertise and revenue expenditure to assist with the development and promotion of tourism. The local authority's Economic Strategy will specify how the council will contribute to the development and promotion of tourism, indicating clearly what the priority areas for development are, and how they are to be achieved, and by when.

Each local authority will have a role to play in providing direct and indirect support to the tourism industry. This is manifested through the local authority's responsibilities for planning regulation, the provision of local infrastructure, the management of visitor attractions, and the provision of tourist information and other services for tourists, including:

➢ libraries;

> art galleries;

> arts centres;

> museums;

> heritage centres;

> theatres;

> concert halls;

> leisure and sports centres;

> swimming pools;

> golf courses;

> country and urban parks;

> camping and caravan sites;

> tourist information facilities;

> car and coach parks;

> festivals and special events.

The local authority will also be engaged in providing additional support to encourage the development of tourism. Each local authority will identify opportunities for new investment in tourism facilities, in keeping, of course, with the provisions made within the Local District Plan on sustainable development and grant opportunities. The tourism officers of the local authority will be able to provide advice to potential investors in relation to the development potential of specific sites and properties. With regard to existing tourism businesses the local authority will have an important role to play in encouraging improvements to the range and quality of the existing tourism facilities, accommodation, and attractions so that they may realise their full potential and benefit from opportunities arising from the evolving tourism market. Where appropriate, the local authority will be the lead organisation in identifying national and European Union funding opportunities for the local tourism industry. This will include identifying funds to improve the skills of the local labour market, or funds to encourage the development of tourism in rural areas as a means of local economic diversification.

Another key role of the local authority is to promote tourism and to provide visitor information. The local authorities work closely with Cumbria Tourist Board to ensure that tourism businesses have up-to-date data and information on the key market segments to target, and the profiles of those market segments. The local authority publishes hard and soft copy accommodation guides listing serviced and non-serviced accommodation as well as guides to the towns, villages, and hamlets within its jurisdiction. Through these publications the brand identity that the local authority is promoting will be communicated. Extensive use of communications information technology is made through the local authority's own website, with links to other tourism websites. Key providers of visitor information are the Tourist Information Centres (TICs), many of which tend to be funded and managed by local authorities. TICs are key facilitators of the tourism experience providing information on accommodation and offering an accommodation finding and booking service. They also distribute information about attractions and special events that are being organised in the locality, as well as providing items for sale: maps, guidebooks, tickets and souvenirs. The siting of TICs is crucial, some being at gateway entry points to the region, or at transport nodes, or in the heart of honeypot towns. Other promotional activities of local authorities involve liaising with the media in order to raise the profile of the area through press publicity and television programmes. The local authorities play an important role in visitor management, especially within the urban centres, by providing and co-ordinating signage to key visitor attractions and other tourist facilities, and contributing to the management of tourist flows around the honeypot towns. Throughout their work the local authority will be aiming to improve and enhance the quality of the visitor experience so as to generate repeat visits and word-of-mouth recommendations to promote further tourist visits to the area.

In devising and implementing their tourism strategies, officers of the local authorities work in partnership with officers from a variety of organisations. These include the other local authorities in Cumbria, staff and executives of the National Park Authority, Cumbria Tourist Board, English Heritage, the National Trust, Cumbria County Council and other relevant national and regional agencies as well as the voluntary and private sectors.

Multi-agency Management of the Planning and Development of Tourism

The introduction to this chapter suggested that there are considerable benefits to be gained from the collaboration of agencies in the planning and management of tourism. Bramwell and Lane (2000:7) suggest that some of these benefits include:

> ➢   the democratisation of the planning and management process – those stakeholders involved with, and affected by, tourism are involved in the decision making process, are able to influence it, and as a result should feel ownership of the decisions that are made. This should facilitate the implementation of tourism plans;

> ➢   multi agency involvement in the planning and management of tourism can lead to the social acceptance of tourism plans within the wider community enabling tourism plans to be implemented with the support of the resident population;

> ➢   collaboration of different agencies in tourism planning should reduce tension between the different agencies, particularly when each agency will have its own mission, objectives, and strategies. As a result of collaboration constructive progress should be made in producing a tourism plan that is acceptable to all stakeholders;

> ➢   as in all cases of team working, the collective views of all participants will be greater than the views and ideas of each individual. From a tourism planning perspective, operating in a collaborative multi agency context will enhance the quality of the decision making process and the outcomes of the planning process should be more feasible and appropriate;

> ➢   collaboration and multi agency operations will result in each of the partner agencies having a much deeper understanding and awareness of the mission, objectives and strategies of the other agencies. This should result in improved co-ordination of the policies and activities of each of the partners;

> ➢   multi agency collaboration will ensure that a variety of different perspectives are taken into account in the tourism planning and management process. In a geographically varied region this will ensure that the economic, environmental, social, and political complexities of both the urban and rural communities will be considered in the decision making process;

> ➢   collaboration can also result in the pooling of resources, especially at the strategy implementation stage. This can result in an increase in both financial and human resources, each of which tend to be in short supply when agencies are reliant upon public sector funding.

As discussed in this chapter there is a long history of the organisations involved with the tourism industry in the Lake District working together on a collaborative basis. This perhaps is the key to successful sustainable tourism management in the region. Each of the organisations involved with the Lake District tourism industry is fully aware of the need to conserve and preserve the special features of the Lake District that have been attracting tourists for over 200 years. This shared mission firmly draws together the activities of quite varied organisations, and actually requires them to work in partnership. By working in partnership the benefits identified by Bramwell and Lane (2000) above are realised, and the ultimate beneficiaries will be future generations who also will be able to visit and enjoy a highly distinctive natural and cultural environment. Although there are key players in the management and development of tourism in the Lake District each organisation recognises that it, alone, cannot be the champion of sustainable tourism, there is a strong realisation that partnerships and collaboration are the key ingredients for implementing the principles of sustainable tourism.

Multi agency collaboration though, is not necessarily easy, and does pose challenges that have to be faced and addressed in order to ensure that the benefits of collaboration outweigh the limitations. Bramwell and Lane (2000:9) identify some of these challenges:

> ➢   the partners in the collaboration process may find it difficult to work together because their mission and vested interests as an organisation will differ considerably from the mission and interests of other partners;

> all partnerships and collaborations will be affected by the internal politics that are present in the association that is developed. Some of the partners might have a stronger power base than others and are able to influence the discussions and decisions that are made more effectively than a partner that might not be quite so influential;

> the internal politicking of the partnership might be counter-productive; one partner might use its influence and authority to coerce other partners to accept a decision that might not be the most appropriate decision to take;

> each of the public agencies involved in the collaboration will have its own means and measures of accountability; these may be different to other partners and will have an influence on the degree to which mutually acceptable outcomes can be achieved;

> some individuals or groups within the local community might be formally excluded from becoming members of the partnership because of its constitution. This might result in resentment and dissatisfaction from the excluded groups and individuals;

> establishing the administrative structure and organisation of the partnership might be difficult – who will be the Chair and members of the Executive Committee? – clearly such individuals will have an influence on the direction and work of the partnership;

> collaborations and partnerships work through consensus; reaching consensus on policies and strategies may prove to be difficult, and might even stifle potentially innovative ideas that arise through the involvement of a diverse range of stakeholders in the decision making process;

> the actual administration and management of the process of collaboration will inevitably be costly and time consuming and this might hinder and restrict the progress that the partnership can actually make.

Clearly the limitations to collaborative working are quite significant and it will take the various partners time to establish an effective working relationship with each other. It is likely that the partners will pass through the accepted stages of group development: storming, norming and performing. That is to say that a group will not operate and perform effectively until initial disagreements on modus operandi have been addressed, and norms and routines of group behaviour have been established and agreed.

Each of the different organisations that has been discussed in this chapter will have its own mission, aims, and objectives but most will also have an element of its strategy that formally recognises the need to work with other partners. To some extent this is inculcated into the modus operandi of these organisations; there is a clear expectation at a strategic and operational level that each organisation will operate in collaboration with others. Indeed, there will be multi-representation and collaboration to such an extent that an executive might find her or himself contributing to a number of different committees, all comprising a similar membership. From a practical perspective, networking frequently with executives from other agencies and organisations will help to develop effective working relationships so that some of the limitations to collaborative working as identified by Bramwell and and Lane (2000) do not become significant. However, it will be inevitable that tensions and disagreements will arise at some stage in the collaboration process between the different partners. Some of these tensions and disagreements will be quite fundamental, arising from the mission and objectives of each organisation differing to such an extent that no compromise can be reached on the way forward. Clearly in the Lake District there is a difference between those agencies that are primarily engaged in the preservation and conservation of the landscape and local communities, and those that see tourism as a key contributor to local economic development. Agencies that see tourism as a key contributor to economic development will wish to see the tourism industry in the Lake District developed and promoted further. This could be contradictory to the views of those agencies whose remit it is to conserve and preserve. Special interest and pressure groups also contribute to the management and development of tourism in the Lake District through publicising their views on tourism development issues, and lobbying those organisations who have decision making authority. On some issues it will not be possible to reach a consensus and at times these different perspectives will be problematic. Failure to reach an agreed perspective on the way forward will result in a sub-optimum decision being reached.

In working together collaboratively the various agencies described in this chapter are fully aware of each partner's different perspective on developing and managing tourism in the Lake District. Indeed when a new strategy is being developed, multi-agency consultation is the norm before the definitive strategy is published. However, it is the general understanding that it is the Lake District's outstanding environment that is the key to the success of tourism in the region that leads to collaboration. The need to protect and conserve this resource for the benefit of all stakeholders and future generations is the catalyst in ensuring partnership and collaboration between those organisations involved with the management and development of tourism in the Lake District.

The establishment of the Lake District Tourism and Conservation Partnership is one example of how the various agencies responsible for the management and development of tourism in the Lake District have worked together successfully for the benefit of sustainable tourism. The establishment of the Cumbria Rural Action Zone following the 2001 Foot and Mouth crisis is another. The Foot and Mouth crisis had a devastating impact on agriculture and tourism in the Lake District. It did result, though, in many organisations throughout Cumbria, working together on a regular basis in order to devise medium and long term recovery strategies that at their heart reflected the principles of sustainable development and sustainable tourism.

Lessons to be learned about the management and development of sustainable tourism

This chapter has reinforced the view that the tourism industry in the Lake District is managed and developed on the principles of sustainable tourism. Bramwell and Lane (1993) identified four principles that need to be present for sustainable tourism:

> ➢ holistic planning and strategy making is necessary;
> ➢ the essential elements of the ecological process have to be preserved;
> ➢ human heritage and biodiversity have to be protected;
> ➢ productivity has to be sustained for future generations.

The combined work of those organisations discussed in this chapter leads to the above four principles being attained. There is a comprehensive set of plans and strategies in place to manage the natural and built environment of the Lake District. Plans and strategies exist at a regional, sub-regional and local level. There are considerable measures in place to preserve the areas of special scientific interest in the Lake District – fells, lakes, forests, and rivers where the natural ecology would otherwise be threatened. The need to preserve the distinctive human heritage is well understood and efforts are made to encourage the continued use of traditional crafts and skills. In the early years of the 21st century all those organisations involved with economic development are fully committed to developing a tourism industry in the Lake District that is financially sustainable, as the fragility of the industry was clearly demonstrated during the 2001 Foot and Mouth crisis.

So what lessons can be learned about developing sustainable tourism from the above? In the case of the Lake District it is apparent that it is the concerted efforts of a wide range of stakeholders that is enabling tourism to be developed sustainably. Each of these stakeholders, while being independent from one another, all share a common vision of how tourism needs to be managed and developed in the Lake District. There is considerable partnership and collaboration in devising strategies and policies for the tourism industry, and subsequently on the implementation of strategies. Not-for-profit organisations and increasingly private sector companies are also involved in the development and implementation of these strategies ensuring that there is a strong commitment to the principles of sustainable tourism from all elements of the tourism industry. This perhaps is the most important lesson to be drawn from this chapter – if the principles of sustainable tourism are to be achieved then all stakeholders have to be committed to the cause. No single stakeholder can implement the principles of sustainable tourism alone, it requires the concerted efforts, over a long period of time of all those involved with, and influenced by the tourism industry.

References

Association of National Park Authorities (2000) *Approaching a Model of Sustainable Rural development.* Hexham.

Association of National Park Authorities (2002) *National Parks: models for sustainable rural development.* Cardiff.

Bramwell, B. and Lane, B. (Eds) (2000) *Tourism Collaboration and Partnerships.* Cleveland: Channel View Publications.

Callaghan, P., Long, P. and Robinson, M. (1994) *Travel and Tourism, 2nd Ed* Sunderland: Business Education Publishers.

Countryside Act 1968, HMSO.

Countryside Commission (1995) *1994 All Parks Visitor Survey.* Cheltenham: Centre for Leisure Research and JMP Consultants Ltd.

Countryside Commission, Department of Natural Heritage, Rural development Commission, English Tourist Board (1995) *Principles of Sustainable Rural Tourism: opportunities for local action.* CCP 438 Cheltenham: Countryside Commission.

Countryside and Rights of Way Act 2000, HMSO.

Cumbria Association of Local Councils (2003) www.calc.org.uk – accessed 9/4/2003.

Cumbria County Council (1996) *A strategy for Transport in the Lake District.* Carlisle: Cumbria County Council.

Cumbria County Council/LDNPA (1995) *Development for the 1990s, Cumbria and Lake District Joint Structure Plan 1991–2006.* Kendal: Cumbria County Council & Lake District National Park Authority.

Cumbria Rural Action Zone Steering Group (2002) *Next Steps: Cumbria Rural Action Zone Strategy.* Carlisle: Cumbria Rural Action Zone Steering Group.

Cumbria Tourist Board (1996) *Tourism Market & Development Forecasts Study.* Windermere: Cumbria Tourist Board.

Cumbria Tourist Board (1998) *The Regional Tourism Strategy for Cumbria.* Windermere: Cumbria Tourist Board.

Cumbria Tourist Board (2002) *Annual Report and Accounts 2001-2002.* Windermere: Cumbria Tourist Board.

DCMS (1998) *UNESCO World Heritage Sites,* a consultation paper on a new United Kingdom tentative list of future nominations. London: Department for Culture, Media and Sport.

Defra (2002) *Review of the English National Park Authorities.* HMSO.

Department for Culture, Media and Sport (1999) *Tomorrow's Tourism. A Growth Industry for the New Millennium.* London: DCMS.

DETR (2000) Windermere Byelaw decision letter to Lake District National Park Authority, www.lake-district.gov.uk.

DoE – Department of the Environment Circular 12/96 HMSO, 1996.

Environment Act 1995, HMSO.

EUROPARC Federation (2001) *Protected Areas and Tourism*, the European Charter, Grafenau.

EUROPARC (2002) *Sustainable Development in the Protected Landscapes of Europe* – Conference paper adopted by EUROPARC Federation in Llandudno, Wales.

Fishwick, A. (1985) Planning and Management responses to recreational pressures in the Lake District National Park. In N. G. Bayfield and G. C. Barrow (eds) *The Ecological Impacts of Outdoor Recreation in Europe and North America*. Recreation Ecology Research Group Report No 9.

Friends of the Lake District (2001) *Green Horizons. An Assessment of the Sustainability of the Tourism Industry in the Lake District*. Kendal: Friends of the Lake District.

Glasgow and Associates, (1991) Tourism in National Parks.

Griffin, T. and DeLacey, T. (2002) Green Globe: Sustainability accreditation for tourism. In R. Harris, T. Griffin and P. Williams (Eds) *Sustainable Tourism a Global Perspective*. Oxford: Butterworth Heinemann.

Hind, D. W. G. (1994) The Marketing of Travel and Tourism. In P. Callaghan, P. Long, and M. Robinson (Eds) *Travel and Tourism*. Sunderland: Business Education Publishers.

Howie, F. (2003) *Managing the Tourist Destination*. London: Continuum.

LDNPA (1998) *Lake District National Park Local Plan*. Kendal: LDNPA.

LDNPA (1999) *Lake District National Park Management Plan*. Kendal: LDNPA.

LDNPA (2003) *Lake District National Park Management Plan. Part One Policies. Consultation Draft*. Kendal: LDNPA.

Local Government Act 1972, HMSO.

Local Government Act 2000, HMSO.

Locum Destination Consulting (2003) *Cumbria Tourism Market Forecasts*. Haywards Heath: Locum Destination Consulting.

National Parks and Access to the Countryside Act 1949, London: HMSO.

North West Regional Development Agency (2002) *Rural Renaissance: the regional recovery plan,* Manchester: NWDA.

UNESCO, (1978) The World Heritage Site Convention leaflet, edited by Incafo SA, Madrid.

Weaver, D. (2000) Sustainable Tourism: Is it Sustainable? In B. Faulkner, *et al* (eds). *Tourism in the 21st Century Lessons from Experience*. London: Continuum.

Website

www.gocumbria.co.uk

Windermere at Ambleside *Courtesy of Friends of the Lake District*

Ravenglass and Eskdale Railway *Courtesy of Friends of the Lake District*

S Y Gondola, Coniston Water *Courtesy of Friends of the Lake District*

Traditional Lakeland Farmhouse *Courtesy of Friends of the Lake District*

Open Top Bus – Route 599 *Courtesy of Friends of the Lake District*

Low Wood Hotel, near Ambleside *Courtesy of Friends of the Lake District*

Fell Walking on Designated Paths
Courtesy of Friends of the Lake District

Erosion caused by Off-Road Vehicles
Courtesy of Friends of the Lake District

Chapter Six

Accommodation Providers: Towards Sustainability

This chapter aims to examine the concept of sustainability in the accommodation sector of the tourist industry in the Lake District and Cumbria. The serviced and non-serviced sectors are described in terms of their size, structure and distribution, and there is a discussion of farm accommodation specifically. This description of the supply of accommodation is followed by the demand from visitors discussed in terms of occupancy rates. There follows an examination of the three elements of sustainability (economic, environmental and social) as they apply to the accommodation providers. A number of 'live' case studies are then described which demonstrate sustainable practices. Finally, some conclusions are presented.

The accommodation sector has the greatest significance, in economic terms, to tourism, both in the UK, and Cumbria specifically. Accommodation spend in the UK accounted for 25 per cent of tourism-related expenditure by UK residents, which was the highest category of expenditure. For Cumbria, 37 per cent of UK resident's expenditure was on accommodation (British Tourist Authority, 2002). In the Lake District too this was the largest proportion of tourist spend.

There are over 2.1 million employees, including self-employed, in tourism related industries in the UK; this is around 7 per cent of all people in employment. Over 410,000 work in hotels and other tourist accommodation. In Cumbria, out of a total of 25,600 employees in tourism-related industries, 9,600 work in hotels and other accommodation (Office for National Statistics, 2000). Accommodation provision is diverse and includes hotels, guest houses, inns, self catering cottages, youth hostels, camping barns and camping and caravan sites. In addition, outdoor centres and university campuses provide accommodation serving a specific market, as do boats, timeshare property and religious centres.

The wide variety of accommodation establishments arises from historical, cultural, geographical and political influences (Youell, 1998). The diversity of such properties in the Lake District, built of local stone or slate, and often of traditional design and appearance, plays a part in the creation of a local identity, and sense of place, thereby contributing to the sustaining of local culture. Furthermore, although the essential role of accommodation is to fulfil the needs of sleep, it can be noted that a hotel or guesthouse is part of a psychological product, and may, therefore, also include "some of the psychological apparatus of the home environment" (Voase 1995: 21).

Classification of the diverse range of accommodation is inexact because distinctions between each category are not always clear, and there is sometimes overlap. Youell (1998) identifies six ways of categorisation; serviced or self-catering, charged or free, chain or independent, static or mobile, urban or rural, and by purpose of visit. The discussion in this chapter is first based upon the serviced and non-serviced categories of accommodation, because much of the relevant literature uses this classification. However, due to the level of agriculture in the area, the provision of both serviced and non-serviced accommodation at many farms, and the often unique and solitary position they occupy in rural communities, farm accommodation is also examined in its own right.

Table 6.1   *Accommodation stock in Cumbria's predominant districts*

	Allerdale	South Lakeland	Cumbria
Non-serviced accommodation			
Non –serviced accommodation -units	1037	2050	**4077**
Non-serviced (caravan & camping) parks			
- total sites	42	65	**176**
- total pitches	4205	7881	**18165**
Holiday parks	2	0	**3**
- total units	8	0	**792**
- total capacity	223	0	**4323**
Group accommodation			
- number of establishments	20	28	**72**
- bedrooms	186	460	**960**
- bedspaces	868	1624	**3444**
Serviced accommodation			
Serviced accommodation -establishments	385	717	**1676**
- bedrooms	3088	6296	**14664**
- bedspaces	6244	13112	**29925**

Source: TRIPS Database, Dec. 2002

As shown in Table 6.1, the accommodation stock is unevenly distributed across the county. South Lakeland is predominant with almost half the stock and Allerdale holds around a quarter of the stock. The remaining districts of Barrow, Carlisle, Copeland and Eden share the remaining provision between them. When the serviced and non-serviced sectors are compared, 50.3 per cent of the non- serviced accommodation units are located in South Lakeland, and 25.4 per cent situated in the district of Allerdale. Similarly, 43 per cent of the serviced accommodation establishments are in South Lakeland, and 23 per cent are located in Allerdale. (As noted in Chapter Three, the National Park lies within Allerdale, Copeland, Eden and South Lakeland – the majority of land in the latter.)

The Government's tourism strategy has identified, as one of its objectives, a new grading scheme for all hotels and guest houses (DCMS, 1999). Thus, in order to give holiday-makers consistent quality, the three major schemes (AA, RAC, ETC) previously in use, have been harmonised. The tables below give the proportions of Cumbrian stock graded by the new Quality Assurance Scheme, but should be viewed with caution as a large element of stock is not registered. Based on 1999/2000 figures 62 per cent of self-catering establishments, 47 per cent of serviced accommodation, and 41 per cent of caravan parks are included in the scheme (English Tourism Council, 2002).

Serviced Accommodation

The new harmonised grading scheme distinguishes between hotels and bed and breakfast establishments. In terms of the grading of hotels, Table 6.2 indicates the proportions of hotels classified at the various grades. As indicated, there is a predominance of 2 and 3 star-rated accommodation. Furthermore, compared to the national average there are more of Cumbria's hotels in the 1 and 2 star categories, but less with 3, 4 and 5 star ratings.

Table 6.2   *Hotel grades (Cumbria and England)*

	Cumbria %	England %
1 Star	5	3
2 Star	57	45
3 Star	36	43
4 Star	2	8
5 Star	0	1

Source: Cumbria Tourist Board/Locum Destination Consulting, 2003

Table 6.3 shows the percentages of bed and breakfast premises and guest houses which are classified at the various grades. As indicated, there is a predominance of accommodation in the 3 and 4 diamond range. Additionally, Cumbria's stock appears to be slightly higher quality than the national average.

Table 6.3   *Bed and breakfast/guest house grades (Cumbria and England)*

	Cumbria %	England %
1 Diamond	5	3
2 Diamond	57	45
3 Diamond	36	43
4 Diamond	2	8
5 Star	0	1

Source: Cumbria Tourist Board/Locum Destination Consulting, 2003

Nineteen per cent of serviced accommodation in Cumbria operates under a national or international brand (Cumbria Tourist Board, 2003). This suggests the sector is highly individualised. This may lead to variable standards in quality and consistency that can affect customers. However, individuality may retain distinctive Cumbrian character and personal hospitality that can enhance the guest experience. Similarly, over 80 per cent of serviced accommodation establishments do not belong to a group, again suggesting considerable individuality. Membership of a group however, does not necessarily indicate a tendency towards homogeneity. For example, the 20 Cumbrian hotels in the Best Western group are all independently owned and operated, they are graded 2, 3 or 4 star, and range from 21 beds at the Tufton Arms, Appleby to 110 beds at the Low Wood, Ambleside (Thistle Hotels, 2003).

Non-Serviced Accommodation

This sector of the tourist industry is, inevitably, fragmented. Many self-catering accommodation units have individual owners with different motivations for ownership. Some will operate their properties as purely commercial concerns, seeking to maximise the return on their investment. Other owners will let their second homes, or perhaps their main homes, with the aim of covering some or all of their running costs (Cumbria Tourist Board, 1999). Personal use for pleasure would account for some periods of the year when there would be no income.

Differences in the motivations of owners will lead to differences in their management and marketing skills, so the success of a particular self-catering business may be more to do with the expertise and motivation of the owner than the type of facility or its location (Cumbria Tourist Board, 1999).

Entry into the self-catering business is relatively easy as long as there is adherence to planning and fire regulations, and health and safety legislation. This ease of entry results in the very diverse provision in terms of quality, type, size and location of properties on the market. There is diversity, too, in the camping and caravanning provision in the Lake District. All sites are registered with the local authority, but this still allows provision to range from cheaper basic pitches for tents on farms, to more expensive static caravans and chalets on purpose-built holiday villages.

There will also be variation in the quality of self-catering accommodation available. Where an independent unregistered provider offers their unit to the market, no quality control measures are in place. For registered properties, an annual inspection takes place which guarantees a minimum standard. Furthermore, only 2 per cent of non-serviced accommodation operate under a national or international brand (Cumbria Tourist Board, 2003) so this sector is overwhelmingly independent and individualised. Similarly, 83 per cent of non-serviced accommodation do not belong to a group (Cumbria Tourist Board, 2003). However, 17 letting/management agencies in Cumbria have been identified and approximately 40 per cent of registered self-catering units in Cumbria are operated through such agencies (Cumbria Tourist Board, 1999). This registration requires adherence to the quality standards of each agency. These will, of course, vary.

Farm Accommodation

Farm accommodation forms an element of farm tourism. Farm tourism has been defined as "the provision of facilities for tourists on working farms" (Denman, 1994:50). As such, it can range from the farm and its associated activities forming an interactive tourist attraction, to the farm as a provider of accommodation and hospitality, where the working environment merely provides the visitor with a passive appreciation of agriculture as a "backcloth to the tourism experience" (Clarke, 1999:27).

Records of existing farm accommodation are incomplete, and estimates vary. The ETC TRIPS database includes over 3,500 farms nationally, but this omits many smaller seasonal operators. The *Farmers' Voice* survey puts the figure at over 10,000 (Morris, 2002). In Cumbria there are 366 known farms offering accommodation (Lawrence, 2001) but it seems likely that this number is increasing because, following the Foot and Mouth epidemic, an increasing number of farmers indicated that they wanted to diversify into tourism- related business (Morris, 2002).

Tourism brings opportunities to increase the visitor's understanding of the countryside (Morris, 2000). With specific reference to farm tourism, Paynter (1991) states that many farmers want to be more involved with visitors to improve the public perception of farming practices. Shields (2003) reports that her guests really enjoy talking to her farming husband about agriculture while he serves their evening meal at Tarn House, Ravenstonedale. She also points out that many of their visitors know 'nowt about hill farming'.

In rural areas, and particularly in some of the remote communities of the outlying parts of the Lake District, an isolated farm may be one of only a few businesses scattered locally and, if it is sustainable, then this also sustains the local community and cultural landscape (Organisation for Economic Co-operation and Development, 1994). Marketing is crucial if a farm guest house such as this is to sustain itself, however, according to Lane (1994) most rural tourism businesses invest relatively little in marketing. Furthermore, a single farm with few resources of its own, has much to gain from collaborative marketing (Clarke, 1999) but is relatively helpless on its own. Morris (2002) believes there is a need for a national generic marketing campaign based on what he sees as a strong farm tourism brand.

Collaborative marketing effort under a farm tourism brand can be seen in Farm Stay UK which was established in 1983 as The Farm Holiday Bureau with support from the Agricultural Development Advisory Service (ADAS), the Royal Agricultural Society of England, the National Tourist Boards and the trade magazine *Farmer's Weekly*. The functions of Farm Stay UK are

➤ to promote the concept of farm tourism in the UK;

➤ to help members expand their businesses through proactive marketing/sales support;

➤ to assist farmers in broadening their income base through diversification.

Membership of Farm Stay UK is open to any accommodation provider where there is a source of income from agriculture. The accommodation may be a farmhouse bed and breakfast or self-catering cottage, converted farm building, camping barn, caravan park or campsite. The benefits to each member include entry in the annual guide and entry on the Farm Stay UK website, with options of individual web page links. Farms also benefit from press and media coverage, exhibitions, and the right to use the high profile brand of Farm Stay UK. Thus, Farm Stay UK, through economies of scale, provide national and international exposure for the individual farm member.

The majority of the 1000 members also belong to local Farm Stay groups each of which works together to provide advisory and referral services. There are 94 such groups across the UK. In Cumbria the three local groups which existed before the creation of the Farm Holiday Bureau and which formed part of the pilot scheme in 1983, have now become five in number: Carlisle and the Borders, Hadrian's Wall, South Lakeland, Eden Valley and North Pennines, and Central Lakes. With a post -Foot and Mouth Disease grant from Cumbria Community Foundation Recovery Fund, the Eden Valley and North Pennines Group, under the name Eden Country Holidays, with over half their members affiliated to Farm Stay UK, have produced their own brochure containing 26 entries of farm accommodation. Also included are advertisements of various businesses in the immediate area, together with a listing of the local farmers' markets. As well as the brochure, the Eden Country Holiday group have created their own website, and they operate a referral arrangement in an attempt to fill vacancies collaboratively (Wilson, 2002).

It is worth noting here the role of the Northern Uplands Farm Tourism Initiative (NUFTI). Set up in 1997 under Objective 5b with European funding of £2.6 million over 5 years, NUFTI was a partnership of the four Regional Tourist Boards of the North of England (Cumbria, North West, Northumbria and Yorkshire). Capital grants for barn conversions were awarded to farmers diversifying into tourism, and farm tourism was publicised by the inclusion of 400 farms in the *Stay on a Farm* guide. Although NUFTI has now ceased to exist, much of its function continues through the work of the North West Development Agency (Bendelow, 2003).

Occupancy Rates

A crucial measure of the success of an accommodation provider is their occupancy rate, both in terms of how full the premises are on a given night, and the level of occupation enjoyed over a year. Cumbria Tourist Board use two calculations to show this activity; room occupancy and bed space occupancy ratios.

Not all parts of Cumbria experience the same occupancy rates, with some districts being much more popular than others. South Lakeland achieved the highest room occupancy rates of all districts in 2001, recording an average of 52.6 per cent, with July, September and October over 60 per cent, and August at 74.9 per cent. In comparison, Eden's average was 36.9 per cent, with an August high of 55.8 per cent (Cumbria Tourist Board, 2001).

As well as there being occupancy rate variation by district, there is also a difference according to whether hotels and guest houses are inside the National Park. Average room occupancy inside the National Park in 2001 was 47.2 per cent, with an August high of 66.6 per cent. For accommodation providers outside the Lake District National Park the average room occupancy was 43.4 per cent, with a high in August of 59.2 per cent. These figures are evidence of the popularity of the Lake District as a tourist destination.

The size of accommodation establishment appears to influence its occupancy rate, with average room occupancy levels increasing relative to the size of establishment. Businesses with 1-3 rooms averaged 24.7 per cent room occupancy, 4-10 rooms averaged 39.5 per cent, 11-25 rooms 46.3 per cent, 26-50 rooms 59.4 per cent and hotels with a capacity of 51-100 rooms 65.2 per cent average room occupancy (Cumbria Tourist Board, 2001).

In 2001, the Foot and Mouth crisis seriously affected agricultural areas, and rural rights of way. This had an impact on tourist activity, particularly in the months of March to July. The tourism infrastructure varies across Cumbria's districts, as does the level of agriculture, but even in South Lakeland, where the tourism infrastructure is arguably more robust, there was a 1.3 percentage point decrease in average occupancy rates from 2000 to 2001 (see note 1). Included in this figure is a 14.7 percentage point decrease in April. All districts show a downturn with the exception of Carlisle (+ 1.9 percentage points) that is accounted for by the vets and Defra officials who stayed in the city during the crisis (Cumbria Tourist Board, 2001).

Economic Sustainability

Employment is a key component of economic sustainability and Cumbria's accommodation sector is a major employer. Out of a total of 25,600 employees in Cumbria's tourism-related industries, 9,600 work in hotels and other accommodation (Cumbria Tourist Board, 2000). The nature of this employment and its contribution to sustainability varies. Obviously full time permanent employment gives greater income and job security than part-time casual work and results in greater local economic gain. However, part-time and casual employment is of value to people with limited hours to offer. Flexible part-time opportunities may suit women wanting to return to work after having a family (DCMS, 1999). Additionally, research by the Hospitality Training Foundation suggested that women working in hospitality stand a better chance of reaching managerial positions than in other industries (DCMS, 1999). It is also worth noting that staff are sometimes recruited from some distance away from their employer (see Derwentwater Hotel case study).

As shown in Table 6.4, the accommodation sectors (serviced and non-serviced) in Cumbria have similar proportions of businesses employing all or a majority of their staff on a part-time basis (12.2 per cent and 9.5 per cent respectively). In relation to full-time employment, serviced accommodation (23.3 per cent) is again only slightly higher than non-serviced (18.5 per cent). Arguably, seasonal work is of least value to the local economy, often with low wages, low skill requirements and little long-term security. Furthermore, it has been claimed that seasonality may act as a deterrent to attracting skilled and professional workers to some jobs (DCMS, 1999). The seasonal employment figures for the serviced and non-serviced accommodation in Cumbria (6.7 per cent and 6.0 per cent) are similar to all other sectors except visitor attractions which have the highest figure of all the sectors (14.2 per cent).

Forward-thinking tourism businesses are aware that greater success is likely to occur if they invest in their staff (DCMS, 1999) (see Oasis Whinfell Forest case study). Additionally better trained and qualified personnel will undoubtedly have more opportunities for job satisfaction and career prospects, and this may result in better quality service to guests. However, the perception of the industry as a whole has been damaged by poor management and employment practice. Low rates of pay, unsocial working hours and skills shortage are the most common reasons given by employers for difficulties in recruiting staff (DCMS, 1999). In response to these concerns the Hospitality Training Foundation is aiming for 500 hospitality employers to work towards the Investors in People Award. Also, companies are encouraged to include human resource information in their annual reports, such as percentage of employees who have achieved NVQs, and how the company stands in relation to National Learning Targets. With reference to customer care specifically, the Welcome Host programme is a training course aimed to improve customer service and product knowledge. Nationally, bed and breakfast establishments have the highest number of staff who are Welcome Host trained (795 units) (see Derwentwater Hotel case study). Inns have the lowest number with 126 (ETC, 2003).

Table 6.4   Indicators of economic sustainability for Cumbria

	Non-Serviced Accommodation % (n=114)	Serviced Accommodation % (n=256)	Food and Drink % (n=265)	Professional Services % (n=58)	Retail % (n=63)	Transport % (n=54)	Visitor Attractions % (n = 165)
plan to upgrade facilities	48.1	55.4	36.5	42.5	27.5	39.6	52.1
plan to expand facilities	15.9	14.3	12.9	27.2	22.4	24.2	31.3
all/majority full-time jobs	18.5	23.3	10.9	31.9	30.4	32.8	27.6
all/majority part-time jobs	9.5	12.2	30.2	11.3	7.7	13.9	14.7
all/majority casual jobs	15.6	9.5	14.3	1.6	6.3	4.9	4.9
all/majority seasonal jobs	6.0	6.7	2.8	2.0	2.2	0	14.2
do not employ staff	33.9	32.8	18.3	31.0	32.4	44.4	13.4
no staff training	5.3	5.4	4.3	0	8.2	12.9	2.8
induction training	56.4	50.0	37.3	66.6	57.5	37.5	71.0
on the job training	78.6	82.6	90.9	92.1	80.4	74.0	85.1
internal training courses	35.0	19.6	8.1	54.9	26.0	7.2	48.3
external training courses	40.4	33.5	13.9	70.7	27.6	12.5	64.5
day release for formal training	15.1	23.3	9.6	36.1	14.1	14.3	29.4
> 50% goods/services sourced in Cumbria	19.7	22.4	25.4	14.7	9.6	2.7	19.4
> 25% sales (by value) carry local branding	2.2	4.5	7.3	4.9	6.6	0	7.1
organic food for sale	2.2	2.1	2.8	0	2.2	4.0	5.4
organic products for sale	4.1	6.7	6.5	0	2.2	0	11.5
organic meal options	4.7	6.1	5.0	2.0	2.2	0	3.5

(See note 1)   *Source:* Cumbria Tourist Board/Enteleca, 2000

Other forms of staff training have been measured by Cumbria Tourist Board (see Table 6.4). Non-serviced accommodation compares favourably to serviced accommodation in relation to induction training, external courses and particularly internal courses. The serviced accommodation provider performed slightly better in 'on the job' training and day release. With reference to the other sectors, professional services show the highest proportion of businesses providing 'on the job' training (92.1 per cent), and visitor attractions recorded the highest percentage of businesses providing induction training (71 per cent). However, it is suggested that such comparisons should be made with caution because each sector of the industry has its own specific staff training needs and modes of delivery.

New business investment can be seen as an indicator of the health of a business. Continuing investment suggests improved quality of service to guests and stronger competition in the market. The sustainability of the accommodation sector may, in part, be judged by the percentage of providers who intend to upgrade their facilities. This might be in the form of refurbishment, decoration, upgrading of furnishings, grounds improvement, provision of disabled access, renewal of equipment or improved energy utilisation. As shown in Table 6.4, the serviced accommodation sector has a slightly higher proportion of its businesses planning to upgrade facilities than the non-serviced sector. More importantly serviced accommodation has the highest figure for all sectors. However, in terms of businesses planning to expand their facilities, both accommodation providers show less intended activity than most other sectors.

Another element of economic sustainability is the use of local goods and services (see YHA and Derwentwater Hotel case studies). Such use benefits the local economy as tourist-spend is recirculated. Other advantages of local sourcing have been identified as reduced transport costs, lower freight mileage, and enhancement of visitors' sense of place and enjoyment (Cumbria Tourist Board, 2000). With reference to goods/services sourced in Cumbria, both accommodation types perform well when compared to the industry as a whole, with only food and drink scoring higher. Further research is required to determine the range of goods available to hoteliers locally. In terms of micro-breweries there are several in the area, including Great Gable Brewery at the Wasdale Head Inn, Barngate at the Drunken Duck and Bluebird at Coniston.

In terms of locally branded goods, and organic products, the marketing of these can enhance associations of individuality and quality with the destination, and help generate a positive identity of a place (Cumbria Tourist Board, 2000). These benefits may be of particular relevance to farm accommodation where guests staying on a working farm may have an enhanced experience through local organic food and meal options. It can be seen from Table 6.4 that, like most other sectors, the percentage of accommodation providers offering organic goods is extremely low. All sectors are in the 0-6.7 per cent range, with the exception of visitor attractions, of which 11.5 per cent sold organic products.

Case Study - Derwentwater Hotel

Set in 16.5 acres of wetland on the shore of Derwentwater, a large proportion of the grounds are in a natural state, with some limited formal gardens. Ducks reside in the estate, and deer and pheasants are seen regularly. Red squirrel feeders have been installed.

The formal gardens and wetlands of the Derwentwater Hotel. (*Photo: Derwentwater Hotel*)

When guests arrive at the hotel, they find a 'go green' card in their room which asks them to regulate the heating as required, turn off lights and television when not in use, and to place towels that require washing in the bath.

Derwentwater Hotel employs approximately 50 staff, of which 80% are full-time, and 20% part time. All are permanent. Around 20 staff live-in, and a mini-bus collects staff from as far afield as Maryport, and other outlying areas at various pick-up points, making the return trip later in the day. On the job training is provided, some of which leads to formal qualifications, such as the Food Hygiene Certificate, and NVQs. Some training is organised collaboratively, with employees from neighbouring hotels joining the Derwentwater staff in-house. Most front of house staff are Welcome Host trained. Some of this training has been supported by Cumbria Tourist Board.

The hotel sells locally branded goods. Blue Bird beer from the Coniston Brewery, and Cumberland Ale from the Jennings Brewery at Cockermouth are sold in the hotel bar. The kitchen uses locally sourced food products and groceries where possible. With the exception of meat and fish, all food is bought from one of two local grocers. The local Allerdale cheese is usually on the restaurant's menu. The hotel uses a local printer for most purposes.

Reduced flush toilet cisterns are in use, as are low energy light bulbs and double glazing. Environmentally friendly cleaning products are used.

Recycling facilities are available where the local community can recycle paper and cans. Glass and used vegetable oil is collected regularly by an external party (Leighton, 2002).

Environmental Sustainability

The prudent use of natural resources, and the protection of the environment are two of the Government's objectives in their vision for sustainable tourism (DCMS, 1999). Responsible approaches to tourism such as these can be seen in the establishment of the International Hotels Environment Initiative. Some of the major players in the global hotel industry are involved in this initiative aimed at raising awareness of responsible practice amongst government bodies, tour operators, suppliers and the hotel industry itself.

Large multi-national hotel chains have shown that significant savings can be made through energy efficiency measures. For example, Inter-Continental Hotels and Resorts have made net reductions of 26 million US dollars in water and energy over 10 years (IHEI, 2003). Savings such as these can be facilitated by the use of benchmarking. With funding from Biffaward, the IHEI and the World Wildlife Fund have recently developed a benchmarking tool which allows all hotels to monitor their energy management, freshwater consumption, waste management, waste water quality, purchasing programmes, community relations and biodiversity improvement (IHEI, 2003).

To demonstrate this improved environmental practice to the market the tourism industry uses a variety of green labels and awards. There has been a proliferation of these awards with an estimated 75 currently in existence (see note 3). This has led to the claim that there is "an increasing clutter of environmental awards and labels in tourism" (Font and Tribe, 2001: 9). The most common reasons for companies applying for green labels have been identified as; cost savings, a genuine commitment to improving green credentials and image, an aim to broaden market appeal, and a genuine commitment to protect the resources of the destination (Hawkins, 1997).

In Cumbria green tourism action can be seen in the Responsible Tourism Scheme which is co-ordinated by Cumbria Tourist Board in conjunction with the Lake District Tourism and Conservation Partnership. The project is part of a pilot phase for a national sustainable tourism scheme, and is funded by the English Tourism Council and the North West Development Agency. The scheme consists of tourism businesses registering with the partnership initially, followed by a self-assessment against a range of green criteria. A site visit is then carried out on which an assessor reviews documentation including environmental policies, targets and action plans, records of use of resources (energy, water and waste) and action to reduce such use. In addition, the assessor interviews staff to determine their knowledge and application of policies and practices. A random selection of locations at the site are scrutinised to assess water saving devices, use of energy, and recycling of waste. A sample of telephone interviews may also be conducted with other parties such as neighbours, the local tourist boards and the local authority. Cumbria Tourist Board and the Partnership make the final decision on the provider's accreditation and provide a written report on findings and suggestions for further improvements. A certificate, valid for 2 years, is issued, and the accommodation gains added marketing exposure through separate listings on CTB and the Partnership websites, as well as inclusion in CTB's marketing activities.

Table 6.5 Indicators of environmental sustainability for Cumbria

	Serviced Accommodation % (n = 256)	Non-Serviced Accommodation % (n = 114)	Food and Drink % (n=265)	Professional Services % (n = 58)	Retail % (n = 63)	Transport % (n = 54)	Visitor Attractions % (n = 165)
use lower energy light bulbs	75.7	66.1	38.5	23.2	36.2	13.5	48.8
use double glazing	51.1	47.8	15.3	32.3	14.6	21.5	30.2
invested in energy efficient equipment	47.8	40.6	29.6	13.1	10.2	17.5	29.5
use dual flush toilets	20.0	15.2	9.8	6.9	3.6	0	8.3
use reduced capacity toilets	29.9	19.9	14.7	7.7	8.1	8.0	24.3
re-use towel and linen	41.0	22.7	12.3	10.1	6.2	12.0	16.3
use rain barrels	27.8	27.6	10.9	9.7	11.6	4.0	17.4
use unpackaged goods	25.4	13.7	17.5	15.6	12.1	0	22.6
replacing individually wrapped portions	29.4	4.7	8.9	7.8	4.4	0	8.4
use recycled paper	42.4	35.0	28.3	30.9	30.7	8.0	44.6
use environmentally friendly cleaning products	38.5	39.5	27.0	31.2	24.4	17.4	41.5
sort waste	42.9	47.6	32.9	37.6	38.0	20.4	39.8
provide recycling for guests	7.7	42.5	5.7	13.0	0	0	7.8
any use of composting	17.4	41.9	6.9	8.9	10.2	8.0	24.9

(see note 1) *Source*: Cumbria Tourist Board/Enteleca, 2000

Cumbria Tourist Board have identified a number of energy efficiency measures which allow the monitoring of environmentally responsible practices (see Table 6.5). Both accommodation providers are the two best performers in Cumbria's tourism industry in relation to the use of low energy light bulbs, the use of double glazing, and investment in energy efficient equipment. Furthermore, they out-performed all other sectors by a margin of at least 17 percentage points.

Water efficiency is another measure of environmental sustainability. Although the Lake District is the wettest part of England, with average annual totals exceeding 2000 mm (Meteorological Office, 2003) any complacency should be avoided because matching supply with demand without damaging the freshwater environment has been identified as a key issue (Cumbria County Council, 2002). Supplies in West Cumbria are not sufficiently reliable and dry up quickly without rainfall. There is also a serious deficit anticipated in the Carlisle supply zone by 2005 as a result of industrial demand increasing, and new home construction. Sustainable management of the water resource is therefore imperative, and one of the required measures is the efficient use of water (Cumbria County Council, 2002).

Hotels and self-catering units can make a significant contribution to saving water in the way they adopt water efficiency measures. In Cumbria, both accommodation providers show considerable activity in this area. Specifically, they performed better than all other sectors of the tourism industry in relation to their use of dual flush toilets, and the use of rain barrels. Also a high percentage of serviced accommodation providers (41 per cent) operate a re-use towel and linen scheme (see Derwentwater Hotel case study), suggesting a good level of acceptance of this sustainable practice by customers.

Sustainable purchasing policies can save a considerable amount of waste, and the associated costs of disposal. This problem can be tackled from both ends; encouraging suppliers to use less packaging, and users recycling as much packaging as possible (see YHA case study). Indeed, there is a symbiotic relationship between the two. Hoteliers can only use unpackaged goods if suppliers are able to provide them.

In Cumbria, serviced accommodation providers show higher levels of using unpackaged goods than non-serviced accommodation (25.4 per cent compared to 13.7 per cent). Additionally, 29.4 per cent of serviced accommodation providers have a policy of replacing individually wrapped portions with unpackaged alternatives, compared to 4.7 per cent of non-serviced accommodation businesses. However, it may be the case that individually wrapped portions are much less a feature of the self-catering establishment than the hotel and guest house.

With national waste increasing by 3 per cent p.a. and almost 60 per cent of UK waste sent to landfill sites, central government has set local authorities tough recycling targets. Cumbria County Council for example are requested to recycle at least 14 per cent of household waste by 2003-4, increasing to 21 per cent by 2005-6 (Cumbria County Council, 2002). As a local authority with a considerable proportion of rural areas, higher waste collection costs are incurred, as well as lower collection rates, and longer haulage distances than more urbanised areas. These factors were believed to contribute to Cumbria's figure of 2 per cent recycled household waste, compared to a national figure of 4 per cent (based on 1990 figures) (Cumbria County Council, 1997). Furthermore, Cumbria County Council identify the improvement of recycling as an objective under Best Value. There is, therefore, clearly a need for Cumbria's district councils to locate recycling sites throughout the county, including the less accessible remote areas. To facilitate this a number of accommodation providers, in partnership with their local council, place recycling facilities for use by the local community in their grounds e.g. Derwentwater Hotel, Portinscale, the National Trust's Great Langdale campsite, and Buttermere Youth Hostel.

As shown in Table 6.5, there is a reasonable level of activity in both the serviced and non-serviced accommodation sectors in terms of their sorting of waste. With reference to providing recycling facilities for guests, there is a considerable difference between the two sectors, which is perhaps accounted for by the different nature of their relationship with guests, and differences in guest behaviour while staying in each type of accommodation.

Social Sustainability

If tourism is to be sustainable, lasting benefits should accrue to the local community and the quality of life of local residents should not be adversely affected. In extreme situations, the impact of tourism can be negative and put a host community under severe stress. Narrow roads become very congested at peak times, and normal life of local people can be disrupted. For example, the instance of a local resident being forced to keep her child off school for the day due to severe congestion on local roads when the Network Q Rally took place in the forests near Llanidloes, a rural community in mid-Wales (Blakey *et.al.*, 2000).

The creation of 'ghost hamlets' by a predominance of holiday homes, many of which may be empty for long periods of the year would also have an adverse, but more enduring effect on the local community. Such a practice also results in making it difficult for young local people to buy their own home within their community due to inflated property prices (see Chapter Eight). However, there are also positive social impacts of tourism. It has been claimed that, in some larger settlements, tourism has helped to sustain local services such as buses, GP practices, cottage hospitals, post offices and banks (Countryside Agency, 1996). It is also the case that tourists attend events organised by local clubs and associations, and some may become long-term members of these groups. For example, the current President of The Cumberland Geological Society was, for many years a regular visitor to Keswick, and active member of the group (Smith, 2003).

When a hotelier improves his/her estate, the local neighbourhood can also be the beneficiary. Improvements may take place to the property itself or the grounds. This is sometimes in the form of developing habitats for wildlife (see Oasis Whinfell Forest case study). For example, in Cumbria the non-serviced accommodation providers show

Case Study - CenterParcs: Oasis Whinfell Forest

Oasis Whinfell Forest is a CenterParcs village situated 5 km from the NE boundary of the Lake District National Park. Set in 400 acres of forest, the village is comprised of 718 lodges, 79 apartments, 14 restaurants and bars, eight shops, a family centre, an entertainment centre and a sub-tropical swimming paradise.

Having acquired the development in September 2001, CenterParcs immediately began to integrate Oasis Whinfell Forest into its corporate environmental philosophy by implementing their ecological monitoring and management system. This aimed to bring the village to ISO 14001 accreditation by August 2003. Included in this process was the drawing up of a biodiversity action plan externally verified by independent consultants, and English Nature. Emergency measures were implemented where necessary. For example, in order to preserve the population of great-crested newts, pond water levels were stabilised and a species and habitat management regime was established.

Initial biodiversity surveys were completed within 18 months, revealing 320 species of flora, including 2 nationally and locally scarce varieties. 518 species of fauna have been identified, including 26 which are locally scarce, 17 which are nationally scarce, and one variety of lauxiniid fly which is internationally scarce and classed as an endangered species.

Oasis is one of the best places to see red squirrels in Britain and a number of measures are in place to protect this beleaguered animal:

1. A special nature tour has been designed called the 'Squirrel Walk'.

2. Guests receive information about inappropriate feeding on lodge patios.

3. 57 feeders are provided and a supplementary feeding programme is carried out from May to September.

4. Rangers survey all dreys to monitor the current population.

5. Sightings are recorded.

6. Rope bridges have been erected across roads to give all squirrels safe crossing.

7. Oasis Whinfell Forest are members of the North West Red Alert Group, part of the National Conservation Team.

8. A marksman is used to destroy any grey squirrels sighted.

9. Nest boxes are provided at approximately one to every two hectares.

Other measures to promote the diversity of wildlife at Oasis include; badger gates to allow movement along established pathways, 20 bat nurseries erected, 200 bird boxes of various types provided to preserve blue tit, great tit, coal tit, chaffinch, robin, spotted flycatcher, tree creeper, nuthatch and tawny owl. National conservation scheme support can be seen in the RSPB Species Champion for the bullfinch, which involves CenterParcs sponsoring Ph.D. research into the decline of this species.

An audit has been conducted into the efficiency of the lodges, both in terms of gas and electricity usage, and water conservation. An action plan is in place which monitors heating levels and thermostats. All external lighting uses energy saving lightbulbs, and these are installed internally as replacements are required. There is some limited double-glazing at present. Environmentally friendly cleaning products are used. Hippo bags are in alternate toilets. (Water flow levels prohibit further use of this devise). Rain-water from the dome roof of the sub-tropical swimming pool is recycled to maintain the very high quality of water in the lakes and ponds, and also to stabilise water levels which significantly enhances the habitat of all aquatic life.

Rainwater from the roof is recycled (*Photo: CenterParcs*)

Oasis Whinfell Forest employs 1,165 local people of which 61 per cent are full-time and 39 per cent are part-time. In accordance with the Investors in People Award, training needs are reviewed annually, and staff development opportunities supported as appropriate. These range from NVQ level 1 to Masters Degrees.

With reference to public transport, this is publicised at the village, and some staff use this daily as their means of getting to work. The village itself is a car-free environment, so guests always walk or cycle within the village. Walking and cycling from the village into the local area is encouraged by maps and leaflets. There is also full disabled access.

Guests are encouraged to recycle their waste through information in their pre-arrival pack. Facilities are provided in the village for the recycling of glass, paper and card.

In relation to the use of packaging, and individually wrapped portions, CenterParcs, by means of a free company seminar programme, actively encourage its suppliers to improve the sustainability of the supply chain. If suppliers adopt more sustainable practices, small local independent accommodation providers will also benefit.

Local craft stalls are located within the village complex providing shopping opportunities for guests. Some of these stalls sell organic products.

As part of National Energy Week, in October 2002, the village ran a New Leaf event, aimed at energy saving in the home. This included trade stands, staff and guest competitions, and free samples of 'hippo' bags and energy saving light bulbs for guests to take home. As well as a high staff involvement in the competitions, and two winners in the art national final, a reduction of 4.1 per cent of total energy usage was achieved for the week.

In refurbishing the villas at Oasis Whinfell Forest, CenterParcs apply a rigorous 're use' policy which demonstrates commitment to their social responsibility, articulated in their social policy. Uniforms are re-used in Africa, through Christian Aid. Over 7000 articles of furniture have been donated to the homeless charities throughout Cumbria. Additionally, through the Inside Out Trust, bicycles and computers are recycled through local prisons. Prisoners gain NVQ qualifications for stripping down and servicing bicycles that are then given to charities throughout eastern Europe and Africa. Similarly, computers are converted to Braille and given to the visually impaired (Drury, 2003).

Bicycle repairs lead to NVQ qualifications. (*Photo: Inside Out Trust*)

Repaired bicycle arrives in Kenya. (*Photo: Inside Out Trust*)

considerable activity in encouraging wildlife through planting and setting aside areas for wildlife (see Table 6.6). Similarly this sector is active in providing floral displays and public seating. The serviced accommodation sector is also very active in providing floral displays on their premises. These will often be visible externally and, aesthetically at least, enhance the local community. A number of hotels and guest houses acting in a similar way can, collectively, have a considerable impact to the benefit of tourists and locals alike.

Table 6.6 Indicators of Social Sustainability for Cumbria

	Serviced Accommodation % (n = 256)	Non-Serviced Accommodation % (n= 114)	Food and Drink % (n=265)	Professional Services % (n = 58)	Retail % (n = 63)	Transport % (n = 54)	Visitor Attractions % (n = 165)
encourage wildlife through planting	21.6	34.8	5.1	12.8	12.4	1.9	37.6
setting aside areas (for wildlife)	17.2	43.8	2.9	5.0	7.4	9.8	34.6
creation of new habitats	6.7	25.1	1.6	5.8	6.2	1.9	21.7
provide outdoor public seating	25.9	33.8	23.2	4.2	8.8	4.0	30.0
provide floral displays on premises	69.5	52.0	43.3	24.2	33.2	13.7	43.5
full disabled access	13.3	11.5	17.4	20.6	27.0	7.0	34.6
partial disabled access	26.0	29.6	25.7	20.2	24.1	11.8	40.9
public transport information in premises	60.5	48.3	16.3	19.1	13.9	9.5	31.7
collect visitors from stations	40.5	26.8	2.5	7.9	0	32.6	14.9
promote public transport activity prior to visit	18.1	22.9	1.7	20.2	2.2	9.8	24.0
promote walks from premises	61.4	57.8	8.8	21.1	11.7	5.5	33.1
promote local cycle hire	49.3	38.5	6.1	24.9	7.3	0	13.7
promote local horse riding	39.7	43.2	4.5	19.0	3.6	0	12.2
drying rooms	53.0	32.9	0.9	2.0	0	0	5.3
covered storage area for cycle	47.9	33.1	2.9	7.1	0	0	5.0

(see note 1) *Source:* Cumbria Tourist Board/Enteleca, 2000

Another aspect of social sustainability relates to the widening access of tourism. Keeling and Thomason (2001) describe a disabled-friendly hotel on the shores of Grienerick Lake, Germany. Built by a Berlin-based disabled charity concerned by the lack of accessible holiday facilities for disabled people, this 108 bed-roomed pioneering project includes extra wide corridors, wheelchair accessible bedrooms and a reception desk at wheelchair height. In the UK, the Hotel for All brand has been launched, aimed at, but not exclusively for, the disabled market.

The new National Accessible Scheme ensures a level of standards in meeting the needs of disabled people (ETC, 2003). There is only an extremely limited amount of tourist accommodation registered under this scheme (3.7 per cent of total stock -2000 figures) but there has been an increase from 1999 (2.9 per cent) and almost 100 per cent increase in disabled access on caravan parks from 1999 to 2000 (ETC, 2000). However, disabled access is much more widespread than this registration scheme suggests. In Cumbria, as shown in Table 6.6, over one third of both serviced and non-serviced accommodation businesses provide full or partial disabled access.

Traffic is a major element of tourist activity that can seriously impact on local communities. This issue, and the use of public transport, is fully discussed in Chapter Seven. Some points relating to Cumbria's accommodation providers specifically can be made here. First, 40.5 per cent of Cumbria's serviced accommodation providers offer to collect their guests from local bus or train stations (an echo of a horse-drawn practice from the 19th century – see Chapter Two). By this measure, and that of providing public transport information on the premises, this sector is the most active across the industry (see YHA case study). Additionally, only around 20 per cent of both accommodation providers promote public transport or car free activities in brochure material sent out prior to the visit (see STFAAP, Chapter Five). Arguably this material could have an influence on guests' intentions at the planning stage of their visit, particularly with reference to their decision to travel from home to the Lake District by public transport. Furthermore, car free activities while on holiday in Cumbria may also be more likely to occur if planned in advance.

When guests have arrived at their place of stay, both accommodation sectors are generally good promoters of car-free activities (see YHA case study). Over half actively promote walks from their premises, and over a third promote local horse riding, and cycle hire. Morris (2000) claims that concerns for health and fitness, and the provision of new walking and cycle routes have stimulated increased demand for walking and cycling in the countryside. Clearly such activities can be encouraged by the provision of appropriate facilities. Thus such behaviour becomes more established and sustainability is improved. In Cumbria, around half the serviced accommodation businesses provide drying rooms, and a covered storage area for cycles. These facilities are provided by approximately one third of non serviced accommodation businesses.

The Lake District Tourism and Conservation Partnership has over 120 registered organisations that support the process of funding conservation through tourism. Most of these are accommodation or hospitality providers, which operate one or more schemes that raise funds from visitors to directly support local conservation projects. The prime example of this is the Visitor Payback scheme (see The Lake District and Conservation Partnership Case Study Chapter Five). The scheme is flexible and can therefore satisfy a range of providers' aspirations. For example, the Lindeth Howe Hotel has used a £2 opt-

Case Study – Youth Hostel Association (England and Wales)

The YHA is a major provider of tourist accommodation, operating 228 Youth Hostels in England and Wales, for the benefit of over 300,000 members. Hostels provide comfortable, budget, self-catering accommodation with some hostels supplying meals and packed lunches as an alternative option for guests. There are 27 hostels in the Lake District ranging from the small and remote Black Sail Hostel at the head of Ennerdale (16 beds) to a large urban hostel in the centre of Ambleside (245 beds). The remaining hostels vary from between 20 and 109 beds.

Founded in 1930 with 73 Youth Hostels based on donations of money, buildings and goodwill, the YHA was part of the 'outdoors' movement. As such, the organisation has always had a strong emphasis on the countryside and the environment. The YHA Environmental Strategy, developed from the International Youth Hostel Federation Environmental Charter of 1992, consists of objectives in the following 5 areas:

1. Purchasing and Consumption

The YHA has committed itself to seeking suppliers who can provide environmentally friendly products, and to encouraging its hostel managers to do the same. Also managers are asked to utilise a wide range of methods that are environmentally friendly: buy free-range eggs; use less harmful cleaning materials; use less packaging; buy locally; grow herbs and fruit trees in hostel grounds; use half-flush toilet cisterns; use less paper, re-using paper where possible.

In Lake District hostels many of these methods are utilised. The Coniston (Holly How) hostel uses local suppliers for all products for which YHA does not have a National Purchasing Contract, so fresh meat, fruit, vegetables, milk and bread are bought locally (Kruger, 2002). The Elterwater hostel is among those buying free-range eggs. Also their suppliers are encouraged to use less packaging and two suppliers take back their packaging (Owen, 2002). At Holly How, minimum cleaning materials are used through trigger spray bottles wherever appropriate, and recycled paper products are purchased. At Elterwater, 'hippo' bags are used in toilet cisterns to reduce water consumption.

2. Recycling

The National Office is in the process of putting pressure on local authorities to provide recycling facilities. This is particularly significant to those local authorities containing National Parks because there is a high concentration of Youth Hostels in these areas. Also, it is worth noting that hostels can play the role of recycling centre for the local community. Again, this is particularly relevant to the Lake District, where many small settlements may be quite remote and some distance from the nearest Civic Amenity Site. Clearly the YHA working with the local authority can make a difference in these situations. For example Buttermere Youth Hostel has a community recycling facility for glass, and Derwentwater Youth Hostel has community recycling facilities for glass, paper, cardboard and cans. In urban areas too, community recycling facilities may be located in hostel grounds. Ambleside Youth Hostel, for example, has community recycling facilities for glass, cans, paper, textiles and shoes.

Hostels are encouraged to provide recycling bins for their own use and many hostels in the Lake District do this. Elterwater has bins for recycling newspapers/magazines, glass and cans. Here, some newspapers are recycled twice; once in the drying of wet footwear, then secondly through the lighting of fires. At Holly How and Buttermere some food waste is composted.

It is suggested by the YHA that re-cycling bins are provided for guests and that these are colour-coded, and with multi-lingual labels. The YHA recognises its role in environmental education as being unique in encouraging guests to continue environmental good practice back at home, school or the workplace. Further research is required to determine whether such behaviour occurs.

3.   Energy Conservation

Hostel managers are asked to utilise a variety of energy conservation measures. These include: turn off electrical appliances, turn down thermostats, use time switches, use low energy lighting and appliances, increase insulation, use radiator reflection panels, use pull down cloth-towel dispensers, 'zone' hostel in relation to heating/lighting, separate staff and guest water and central heating systems.

Again, many of these operations occur at hostels in the Lake District. Elterwater's water boilers are on time-switches; Holly How and Elterwater both use low energy lighting throughout the hostels. Some of Elterwater's radiators have reflection panels, and the lights in the showers, washroom and drying room are on p.i.r. switches. There is some 'zoning' of heating and lighting.

Black Sail and Ennerdale Youth Hostels are situated in the valley of Ennerdale which has no mains electricity. To supplement the gas supply at these hostels Black Sail has a small windturbine and solar panels, and Ennerdale, using a nearby mountain stream, has its own hydroelectric power supply.

4.   Transport

Members are encouraged, through the hostel guide, and timetable information provided in each hostel, to use public transport. Also, without being 'anti-car' youth hostelling has a culture of travelling by foot, cycle or public transport. At Windermere Youth Hostel there is cycle hire on site, and at Ambleside a local cycle hire arrangement. At Holly How, through a display, 'car-free' days are actively promoted with a variety of itineraries for days out using public transport (buses, lake launches) and by foot. In the Lake District this is further encouraged through the publication *The Lake District Youth Hosteller's Walking Guide* (Hanks, 1997). This gives detailed diagrammatic maps with various pedestrian and cycle routes between each hostel. In addition, single maps are available at the hostels, and they can be obtained in advance of the guest's arrival. Furthermore, there is a free shuttle bus service between Windermere Rail Station and the hostels in the South Lakes area. During Spring, Summer and Autumn this service meets most trains until the early evening. Also, many hostels encourage guests to share transportation costs and offer lifts to each other.

5.   Nature Conservation

The YHA encourages its managers to plant wildlife friendly gardens at its hostels, to resist the use of pesticides and herbicides, and grow herbs and fruit trees in hostel grounds.

At Elterwater, the hostel has its own small herb garden and there has been planting of native beech and oak trees in order to provide an undergrowth with feeding opportunities. Some grass areas are mown only once a year to encourage wild flowers to self-seed. Two areas of the Holly How grounds are kept 'wild' to encourage wildlife. Roe deer, foxes, brown hares, hedgehogs and over 50 species of bird have been sighted. At Elterwater small areas are left to provide habitats for slowworms, toads and hedgehogs. There are also foxes, woodpeckers, and a small colony of bats. Guests can borrow a bat detector to listen to the bats feeding.

Many hostel buildings are quite old and their design makes it difficult to implement some of the guidelines in the IYHF Environmental Charter. However, there is clearly a concerted effort towards 'greener' tourism, and as hostels are refurbished, appropriate energy saving mechanisms are installed.

out scheme, Heart of the Lakes and Cottage Life match fund every £1 raised from the 'opt-in' with 50 pence from their own resources. Langdale Leisure Ltd. launched their scheme in 1994 with a £5 opt-in on the Timeshare Management Fees. This has recently been increased to £10. Other mechanisms used take the form of donation boxes and fundraising events.

The examples below clearly demonstrate the direct link connecting visitors, via the accommodation provider and the Partnership, to local conservation projects:

➤ The Regent Hotel at Waterhead is supporting the restoration of an ancient damson orchard in Howe Ridding Nature Reserve on Whitbarrow Scar.

➤ Red Alert North West, which is aiming to halt the decline of the native red squirrel, has been supported by the Derwentwater Hotel, Lindeth Howe Hotel, Linthwaite House Hotel, Matson Ground Estate Company, and Cleughside Farm B & B.

➤ Fallborrow & Limefitt Caravan Parks raised almost £9,000 to support the repair of footpaths in Kentmere.

➤ The Burn How Hotel achieved their £2,500 target for improvements to footpaths on Post Knott, Bowness.

➤ The Derwentwater Hotel supported the completion of Howrah's Footpath, a popular link route between Portinscale and Keswick.

➤ Footbridges and paths in the Borrowdale Valley have been restored with the help of £1,300 raised by Cumbria House, Keswick.

➤ Improvements to access and footpaths on Summer House Knott have been supported by Newby Bridge Country Caravan Park.

➤ The path which circumnavigates Stickle Tarn, Langdale, is being restored with aid from Wheelwrights Self Catering Cottages.

➤ The paths along the shore of Grasmere are being repaired with funds from The Bridge House Hotel, The Gold Rill, Broadrayne Farm, The Moss Grove, The Red Lion and The Rothay Garden Hotel.

➤ Drystone wall and footpath repair projects in the South Lakes have been helped by fundraising by Lakeland Holidays.

➤ The Wild Boar Hotel, Crook has provided funding for repairs to walls at Docker Nook Bridleway Bridge in Longsleddale.

➤ Hedges and dry stone walls at Torver and Hawkshead have been restored with funds provided by The Waterhead Hotel.

➤ Habitats on the banks of the River Esk have been restored with support from Brockwood Hall in the Wicham Valley.

➤ Habitats for dormice in the Duddon Valley have been restored with funds from the Low Wood Hotel.

➤ Bassenthwaite Lake Lodges has supported a new telescope for habitat and species monitoring on Bassenthwaite Lake Nature Reserve.

➤ The Lindeth Howe Hotel has provided £2,500 for the restoration of Coniston Dog Folly.

➤ Stepping Stones at Blelham Tarn have been supported by Highfield Country House.

Arguably, the demonstration of support for conservation schemes such as these can play a part in fostering a positive attitude in the local community towards tourism generally, and accommodation providers specifically.

Case Study – The Langdale Estate

Situated on the site of a gunpowder works dating back to 1832, the Langdale Estate and Country Club was established in 1981. Replacing the existing caravan park, which had been there since 1932, the 50 acre woodland site comprises of 80 Scandinavian lodges, a 59 bedroomed hotel and country club, together with a converted barn, 4 cottages and a country house. The development has won a Civic Trust Award for its design being in sympathy with the environment (Langdale Leisure, 2002).

In 1996, as Scottish and Newcastle Breweries were rationalising their assets, Langdale plc was formed as a holding company which floated a share offer to existing timeshare owners who could purchase one share per week of ownership. A Board of Directors was established consisting of managers, owners and external industry leaders who have sustainable tourism "close to the heart of the Langdale Management Team" (Langdale Leisure, 1999). This is borne out by a number of sustainable practices in operation at the Langdale Estate:

1. As the founder of the "Our Man At The Top" scheme in 1994, Langdale Estate guests and owners have supported the funding of a member of the National Trust's footpath repair team for a number of years. Now part of the Responsible Tourism Scheme co-ordinated by the Lake District Tourism and Conservation Partnership, owners are encouraged to add a £10 donation to the payment of their annual management fee.

Helicopter drop. (*Photo: Langdale Leisure*)

Our Man At The Top, footpath repair. (*Photo: Langdale Leisure*)

2.   Similarly, Langdale Estate promoted a scheme to raise funds to repair the footpaths on Harrison Stickle. This mountain is visible from the complex, and guests and owners donated £50 to sponsor a metre of footpath. In return they received a certificate and grid reference of their metre

3.   The 50 acre site contains a nature trail, and there have been sightings of red squirrel, badger, roe deer, barn owl, kingfisher, heron and dipper.

4.   There is monitoring of red squirrels in the grounds and a regular article in the newsletter. Special feeders have been installed which are too small for the grey squirrel (Langdale Leisure, 1998).

5.   The estate is self-sufficient in fresh herbs, grown in their own herb garden.

6.   The local 'Co-op' shop, which is managed by a committee of local people, and whose annual dividend is shared by its 550 members has been featured in the newsletter, and, situated next to the Estate, is used by guests.

7.   Wainwright's Inn, the local public house owned by Langdale Estate, sells beer brewed three miles away at the Barngate Brewery, based at the Drunken Duck Inn, Tarn Hows.

8.   South Lakeland District Council provide facilities on the Estate for the local community to recycle their glass and paper.

9.   Local artists, poets, and foods are featured in newsletters, and members asked to vote for their favourite.

10.   The estate mascot, Larry Langdale, is a life-size stuffed replica of a local Herdwick sheep.

11.   Staff accommodation has recently been upgraded to a high specification.

12.   A programme of talks by Langdale residents, takes place in the Country Club. This has covered mountain rescue, farming and conservation, natural history and rock-climbing.

13.   When the 2001 Foot and Mouth crisis prevented access onto the fells, Langdale was active in creating some alternatives for guests such as new walking routes, cycle rides and a 'Langdale Loop' circuit, combining map, local history, eating out and shopping.

14.   Langdale have recently achieved the Business Mark Award for their work in the local community.

As the new timeshare centre of Underscar, Keswick nears completion, the Langdale management team has been employed as consultants. Arguably, therefore, some of the sustainable tourism practices from Langdale will be replicated there. Furthermore, Fredericka Johns, a director of Langdale, has recently been appointed a Green Globe assessor.

Case Study – YMCA National Centre, Lakeside

The lakes, rivers, forests and mountains of the Lake District provide an environment which is ideal for a wide range of outdoor adventurous activities, from canoeing, sailing and windsurfing, to rock climbing, mountain walking and orienteering. Many visitors pursue these activities independently, but there are several specialist residential outdoor centres which provide adventure for their guests.

In Cumbria there are over 70 adventure providers registered with the Adventure Activities Licensing Authority. However, many of these are small operators without their own specialist site. There are probably only around 20 centres in the Lake District and outlying areas which provide accommodation. The biggest of these and indeed Europe's largest is YMCA National Centre, Lakeside. This centre has been operating since the early 1930s when young boys from Everton cycled some 70 miles to Lakeside for a weekend in the outdoors, combined with bible studies. In 1952 Lakeside was opened as a permanent year round centre, originally given to Britain by South Africa to express their gratitude for assistance in the Second World War.

Today, environmental responsibility forms part of Lakeside's mission statement. Situated on the west shore of Windermere, and set in 400 acres of woodland with one mile of shoreline, YMCA Lakeside is a major provider of adventure activities, outdoor education, leadership and instructor award courses and management development. Accommodation is in two residential wings of Somervell House, lodges in the woods and, from April to September, a tented village at South Camp (YMCA, 2001).

The extensive grounds of mixed vegetation, woodland, meadow, shoreline and small crags provide a rich and varied location for numerous activities, including pond dipping, 'earth walk', ropes course, obstacle course, 'king swing', orienteering, archery, rock climbing, aerial runway, initiative challenges, raft building, canoeing and sailing. The pressures of 12,000 visitors per year, many of whom participate in these activities, have caused a number of environmental problems for Lakeside management and staff. These are:

1.   Footpath proliferation, erosion and widening.

2.   Removal of vegetation cover by trampling.

3.   Lack of tree and shrub regeneration due to trampling and grazing.

4.   Litter.

5.   Damage to trees.

6.   Disturbance of wildlife.

In response to these problems, a number of measures have been taken. First, in Parks Wood:

1.   The erection of extensive wooden fencing to control movement through the woods.

2.   The upgrading of major pathways with hard-core surfacing and edge lining.

3.   The re-siting of orienteering markers to avoid further proliferation of paths and prevent deviation from existing paths.

4.   An extensive tree planting scheme, protected by fencing, to restore woodland.

5.   The provision of nest boxes for a variety of birds and bats.

Second, a number of measures have been taken in Brows Woods:

1.   Major reconstruction of footpaths, including the building of stone steps, footpath repairs, drainage and blocking of some minor pathways.

2.   Hedge-laying along road boundary to discourage random crossing.

3.   Restricted access to quiet areas to encourage wild life. Installation of deer hide for observation.

In addition, extensive parts of Low Parks Wood, and Burrow Croft, are seldom used for activities, with the woodland remaining largely untouched (YMCA, 2002).

Conclusions

An holistic approach to sustainability involves equal importance being given to economic, environmental and social factors. In practice, however, it would appear that economic considerations have priority. This is reflected, for example, in the predominance of research into the economic impacts of tourism and the paucity of literature relating to social and environmental impacts.

Clearly the economic, environmental, and social elements of sustainability are not mutually exclusive. The creation of wildlife habitats has environmental benefits, but if it adds to the quality of life of the local community there can be social benefits too. Similarly, the use of low energy light bulbs is a practice that is both more environmentally and economically sustainable. As stated previously, the serviced and non-serviced accommodation sectors show considerable activity in the use of these bulbs, together with the installation of double glazing, the use of energy efficient equipment, the use of dual flush or reduced capacity toilets and the use of rain barrels. As hoteliers are charged for water and electricity used, there is a financial advantage from the use of these measures. In relation to other aspects such as the visitor payback scheme, the creation of wildlife habitats, on-site promotion of public transport and car-free activities, and the use of recycled paper, Cumbria's accommodation providers again show considerable activity. However, in these cases, although the environmental benefit is clear, commercial gain is less evident. Here, the critical factor in relation to the adoption of more sustainable practices may ultimately be the personal commitment of the owner/manager. In an establishment where green elements such as these are absent, Middleton's (1997:13) description of the worst businesses having "no commitment to the environment on which they trade" may be appropriate.

Cumbria's Responsible Tourism Scheme is designed to encourage providers to adopt more sustainable practices and demonstrate this through the satisfactory completion of a green audit. The hotel's accreditation under this scheme reflects a commitment to greener tourism and the environment itself. However, it is probably the case that these green credentials are largely unrecognised in the external market and, if so, Font and Tribe's (2001:19) description of green labelling as "a suppliers' game, an internal competition between limited core players" is appropriate.

At a national level, if customers are becoming more discriminating of green practice, the accommodation providers need to move towards eco-labelling which is valued and recognised, at home and abroad. A green grading system, from 1 to 5 leaves for example, could be designed and implemented by VisitBritain and each provider awarded the grade appropriate to their green credentials. In Cumbria, membership of the Lake District Tourism and Conservation Partnership and the associated contributions to local conservation projects could be part of the green assessment. As a national scheme, the other regional tourist boards would set up their own mechanism for visitors to contribute to conservation, and, with their own priorities, decide upon local projects eligible for funding.

Each accommodation provider will have it's own requirements in terms of staff training. This will be in the form of internal or external courses, either of which may lead to formal qualifications. Where the training is conducted on the premises, the practice by Derwentwater Hotel (see case study) of in-filling its own training programme with employees from neighbouring hotels is obviously an efficient and cost effective delivery mode which contributes to the economic sustainability of the many independent hotels. The implications of this are clear; collaboration between small- sized businesses is crucial; education providers and training agencies need to be flexible in their delivery and perhaps include distance-learning packages; there is a role for Cumbria Tourist Board to play in coordinating training needs.

To make progress towards more responsible tourism, all existing practices of the industry need to be challenged in order to determine whether a more sustainable approach can be adopted. Cumbria Tourist Board gathered a comprehensive set of indicators (see Chapter One) from across all sectors (Cumbria Tourist Board, 2000) and this data provides an opportunity to scrutinise all customary practices. Such scrutiny needs to bear in mind the structure of the accommodation sectors, as well as the nature of their relationship with guests. Based upon these considerations, and notwithstanding possible changes to the structure of the sectors, priorities for targeted action can be identified. For example, as shown in Table 6.6, a large number of accommodation providers do not send out public transport information prior to their guest's arrival.

Green Tourism in the accommodation sector can be split into two parts; 'going green' operationally, and encouraging green behaviour in guests (and perhaps the local community) (Evans, 1990). Hoteliers and self-catering providers need green confidence in their customers if they are going to adopt practices that directly impact upon guests and their behaviour. On the operation's side, low energy light bulbs and double glazing probably go unnoticed but the guest is directly involved in decisions concerning, for example, the re-use of towels. As stated earlier, there would appear to be considerable acceptance of this practice, and hoteliers may therefore be encouraged to adopt other green measures which have a direct impact on guests.

The gradual building of green confidence can be nurtured by the sharing of green practice. This can be facilitated by Cumbria Tourist Board at their quarterly Members' meetings where green leaders such as local youth hostel managers could be guest speakers and a suppliers' seminar programme, such as that organised by CenterParcs, could be embraced and shared with much smaller operators. Green practice, particularly if it is shown to be of commercial benefit, can also be featured in Cumbria Tourist Board's newsletter *Viewpoint*.

There is an oversupply of accommodation which could lead to tighter regulation controls in the future in order to limit the supply and it seems likely that this will raise standards. Furthermore, some providers may reposition themselves to cater for the local population in the form of a care home for the elderly or flats for local first time buyers.

The accommodation sector can potentially play a hugely influential role in developing more sustainable tourism. As a major sector of the tourism industry it could collectively bring pressure to bear on suppliers to deliver greener goods and services. As host to the tourist, accommodation providers are in a position to deliver subtle but poignant messages to a captive audience staying in beautiful but fragile areas. This may result in changes in the tourist's current or subsequent behaviour. Holistically accommodation providers are well-placed to have an influence across a range of measures of economic, environmental and social sustainability.

Notes

1. Such a comparison also needs to take account of depressed occupancy rates in the later months of 2000 due to a fuel crisis, rail disruptions and flooding, as well as the attack on the World Trade Center on September 11th 2001.

2. When comparisons are made between different sectors it needs to be borne in mind that the sample size of each sector varies, and some sample sizes are small.

3. For a full examination of 'eco-labelling' see Font, X. and Buckley, R. (eds) (*Tourism Eco-labelling: Certification and Promotion of Sustainable Management.*) Wallingford, UK: CABI Publishing.

References

Bendelow, C. (2003) Personal communication with Farm Tourism Manager, Cumbria Rural Enterprise Agency.

Blakey, P., Metcalfe, M., Mitchell, J. P., and Weatherhead, P., (2002) Socio-Cultural Impacts of Visitors to the Network Q Rally of Great Britain on a Rural Community in Mid-Wales in S. Gammon and J. Kurtzman (eds.) (2002) *Sport Tourism: Principles and Practices.* Brighton: Leisure Studies Association.

British Tourism Authority (2002) *Key Facts of Tourism in Cumbria 2001* [Retrieved June 18, 2002] On WWW at http://www.staruk.org.uk//webcode/contents.

Clarke, J. (1999) Marketing Structures for Farm Tourism: Beyond the Individual Provider of Rural Tourism. *Journal of Sustainable Tourism* 7(1), 26-47.

Cumbria County Council (1997) *State of the Environment. Audit of Cumbria.* Carlisle: Cumbria County Council.

Countryside Agency (1996) *The impact of tourism on rural settlements.* Research notes RDR 21/S [Retrieved October 12, 1999] On WWW at http://www.countryside.gov.uk/research/notes/rdr21.

Cumbria County Council (2001) *Best Value. Performance Plan 2001/2.* Carlisle: Cumbria County Council.

Cumbria County Council (2002) *Managing Quality of Life in Cumbria.* Carlisle: Cumbria County Council.

Cumbria Tourist Board (1999) *Self Catering Accommodation in Cumbria.* Windermere: Cumbria Tourist Board/CRED.

Cumbria Tourist Board (2000) *Cumbria Sustainable Tourism Baseline Survey.* Windermere: Cumbria Tourist Board/Enteleca.

Cumbria Tourist Board (2001) *Cumbria Services Accommodation Occupancy Survey 2001 Report.* Windermere: Cumbria Tourist Board.

Cumbria Tourist Board (Dec. 2002) TRIPS database.

Cumbria Tourist Board (2003) *Business Survey Report.* Windermere: Cumbria Tourist Board/Locum Destination Consulting.

Denman, R. (1994) Farm tourism market. *Insights* A67-74.

Department of Culture, Media & Sport (1999) *Tomorrow's Tourism.* London: DCMS.

Drury, S. (2003) Personal communication with UK Environment Manager, CenterParcs UK.

English Tourism Council (2003) *National Sustainable Tourism Indicators.* London: ETC.

Evans, M. (1990) Green Tourism: a hoteliers view. *Insights* D9-11.

Farm Stay UK (2002) *Information Pack.* Stoneleigh: Farm Stay UK.

Font, X. and Tribe, J. (2002) Promoting green tourism: the future of environmental awards. *International Journal of Tourism Research* 3(1), 9-21.

Hanks, M. (1997) *The Lake District Youth Hosteller's Walking Guide.* Ashbourne: Landmark.

International Hotels Environment Initiative (2003) *International Hotels Environment Initiative* [Retrieved March 10, 2003] On WWW at http://www.ihei.org/csp/csrwebassist.nsf.

Keeling, A. and Thomason, L. (2001) Here to stay: new hotel products in the UK. *Insights* A67-74.

Kruger, S. (2003) Personal communication with Manager, Coniston (Holly How) Youth Hostel.

Lane, B. (1994) Sustainable rural tourism strategies: A tool for development and conservation. *Journal of Sustainable Tourism* 2, 102-111.

Langdale Leisure (1997) *Views. The Newsletter of the Langdale Owners' Club.* Langdale: Langdale Leisure.

Langdale Leisure (1999) *Views. The Newsletter of the Langdale Owners' Club.* Langdale: Langdale Leisure.

Langdale Leisure (2002) *Langdale Estate Information Pack.* Langdale: Langdale Leisure.

Lawrence, C. (2001) *A Strategy for the Future. A report to the NUFTI partners.* Windermere: Cumbria Tourist Board.

Leighton, D. (2003) Personal communication with Manager, Derwentwater Hotel.

Meteorological Office (2003) England: rainfall. On WWW at http//www.met-office.gov.uk/climate/uk/location/England/index.

Middleton, V. S. (1997) Fouling the nest? Environmental impact of small businesses. *Insights* D13-19.

Morris, H. (2000) Holidays in the countryside. *Insights* B1-16.

Morris, H. (2002) The Farm Tourism Market. *Insights* B67-84.

Office for National Statistics (2002) *Employment in Tourism.* [Retrieved June 18, 2002] On WWW at http://www.staruk.org.uk/webcode/contents.

Organisation for Economic Co-operation and Development (1994) Tourism Policy and International Tourism in OECD Countries 1991-1992. In J. Clarke (1999) Marketing Structures for Farm Tourism: Beyond the Individual Provider of Rural Tourism. *Journal of Sustainable Tourism* 7(1), 26-47.

Owen, N. (2002) Personal communication with Manager, Elterwater Youth Hostel.

Paynter, J. (1991) Farm attractions. *Insights* B49-64.

Shields, H. (2003) Personal communication with owner/manager, Tarn House, Ravenstonedale.

Smith, A. (2003) Personal communication with President of The Cumberland Geological Society.

The Lake District Tourism & Conservation Partnership (2002) *Information Pack.* Ambleside: The Lake District Tourism & Conservation Partnership.

Thistle Hotels (2003) *Highlife Breaks.* Leeds: Thistle Hotels.

Voase, R. (1995) *Tourism: the human perspective.* London: Hodder & Stoughton.

Wilson, L. (2002) Personal communication with secretary, Eden Valley and North Pennines Group, Farm Stay UK.

YMCA (2001) *Information Pack.* Lakeside, Windermere: YMCA.

YMCA (2002) *Staff Handbook.* Lakeside, Windermere: YMCA.

Youell, R. (1998) *Tourism: An introduction.* New York: Longman.

Youth Hostel Association (2003) *Go. 2003/4 Accommodation Guide.* Matlock: YHA (England & Wales).

Chapter Seven

Sustainable Transport Management and Cycle Tourism

This chapter initially discusses the process of creating a Transport Strategy for the Lake District National Park in conjunction with Cumbria County Council's Local Transport Plan, and highlights the implementation of Local Area Action Plans and more strategic initiatives which impact on the wider geographical area of the National Park. Progress in developing public transport initiatives within the National Park form part of this evaluation.

The first case study on 'Green Road Driving' outlines the problems associated with the increased use of 4 x 4 vehicles and other forms of transport on the labyrinth of un-surfaced roads and tracks within the National Park. Later in the chapter there is a discussion of the introduction of the National Park Authority's Hierarchy of Trail Routes Initiative, and an evaluation of its success, principally as a form of a voluntary restraint programme. This is followed by an analysis of responses to freight movement and then an evaluation of the success of the Transport Strategy as a policy instrument for developing sustainable transport initiatives within the National Park.

The second case study initially discusses linkages between cycle tourism and the exemplification of principles of sustainability, and highlights how within Cumbria and the National Park, cycle tourism provision is viewed as making a considerable contribution to the promotion of sustainable tourism. In particular the development of the Sustrans 140 mile linear Sea to Sea Route (C2C) which partly traverses the National Park, is investigated as a 'flagship' development which promotes the use of the bicycle as a form of sustainable transport and tourism initiative within Cumbria and the National Park.

The Context for Sustainable Transport Strategies within the Lake District National Park

The statutory purposes for National Parks incorporated in the National Parks and Access to the Countryside Act (1949) (see Chapter Five) gave them the purposes of "preserving the natural beauty of their areas" and also to "promote their enjoyment by the public". It was only when car ownership expanded rapidly that the conflict between these purposes became apparent. If "promoting enjoyment" means support for improved roads and car parks to accommodate visitors the natural beauty, far from being preserved, comes under threat; yet if the facilities are not provided the result is likely to be congestion, tailbacks and adverse environmental impacts.

The History of Policy Development

Concern at the impacts of traffic first became widespread from the 1960s onwards. Weal (1968) proposed a Park and Ride system for Langdale, a possibility also discussed in the first National Park Plan (Lake District Special Planning Board, 1976) alongside other options such as selective road closures and one-way schemes. However, enthusiasm waned and no action was taken until the late 1980s when continuing traffic growth and the developing environmental agenda brought new pressures. Meanwhile, as in other parts of the UK, the public transport options declined considerably. The only rail line crossing the National Park, from Penrith to Keswick and Workington, closed in 1970. The 1986 deregulation and privatisation of bus services was accompanied by major reductions in the revenue support given by Cumbria County Council (CCC) to bus operators. Annual subsidies exceeding £1m in the early 1980s fell to £141,000 in 1990/91, the lowest of any English county and used almost entirely to fund bus services outside the National Park. Understandably services were reduced and even key routes such as Ambleside to Coniston and Penrith to Keswick came close to total closure.

Against this background the forerunner of the current Transport Strategy was set up in the form of a Working Party with membership from Cumbria County Council, the Lake District National Park Authority (LDNPA), the Countryside Commission and Cumbria Tourist Board (CTB). After looking at a number of options the group chose a project in Borrowdale, where increased parking charges would be used to fund a frequent bus service (CCC and LDSPB, 1990 and 1992). However, objections from the local community and the National Trust, whose support as a major landowner and car park provider was vital, led to abandonment of the proposal (Lake District Herald, 1991). The Working Party was then formalised as a Traffic Management Initiative employing a Project Officer whose report, published in 1995, recommended a road hierarchy under which through traffic would be excluded to varying degrees from roads according to their status (Lake District Traffic Management Initiative, 1995). Regrettably the extent to which traffic would be restricted was exaggerated in the media (see in particular *Daily Telegraph*, 1995), again raising considerable local hostility and threatening to bring about withdrawal of the CTB from the consortium.

The Creation of a Transport Strategy

It became evident from these problems that community support was essential to achieve progress, reflecting the fact that, unlike some countries, the UK's National Parks are places where people live and work. Views are strongly held that traffic problems are confined to specific times and places, and that "blanket" restrictions would be unnecessary and damaging to the local economy. Nonetheless, as with all National Parks, over 90 per cent of visitors arrive by car (Countryside Commission, 1995 and 1996) and, in the absence of positive action, this can only be expected to increase. The Transport Strategy that emerged recognised that an objective must be "to enable the local community to go about its normal business". Its other objectives were to:

1. Improve the accessibility of the LDNP to all people regardless of income or disability.

2. Ensure that the LDNP remains accessible for quiet enjoyment.

3. Maintain the tourism industry and assist it to become sustainable.

4. Offer alternative modes of transport to the car.

5. Tailor traffic to the ability of existing roads to cope.

6. Reduce traffic impact on the environment.

7. Reduce traffic and parking congestion.

(CCC, 1996).

The management of the Strategy was entrusted to CCC's arms length traffic consultancy Design and Business Services, which in 2000 was transferred to the Capita PLC group as Capita*dbs*. Capita's Strategy Co-ordinator and a small team report to a Strategy Advisory Group with representation from the original members (who provide core funding for the Strategy's work), the Highways Agency and District Councils. Implementation is carried out through the County's Local Transport Plan (LTP), funding being sought through the LTP process and other opportunities as they arise, such as Rural Bus Challenge.

The LTP document (CCC, 2001) identifies four targets to be achieved within the LDNP through the Strategy:

➤ An annual rate of traffic growth of 0 per cent by 2006.

➤ An increase in public transport use of 15 per cent compared with 1999 levels.

➤ An increase in frequency on the Windermere rail line to half hourly by 2005.

➤ Achievement of hourly public transport services linking main settlements and attractions, and on approach routes, by 2005.

Implementation takes place at two levels – strategic actions intended to affect the whole or a large part of the LDNP, and through a series of Area Action Plans which feature local community representation. The LDNP has been divided into 14 of these Areas, with plans being developed on an incremental basis; to date seven of the plans have been rolled out. Much of the work involves localised traffic engineering (e.g. pedestrianisation in Keswick and re-routing of traffic in Windermere) and this chapter will therefore concentrate on some of the strategic actions.

The South -East Approaches

The most popular route by which traffic approaches the central and southern Lake District is by the A591 dual carriageway, which by-passes Kendal on its western side but then becomes a single carriageway as it approaches Windermere, Ambleside and Grasmere. This, therefore, is where most of the Park's traffic problems occur.

The A591 is paralleled by the only remaining rail line entering the Lake District National Park from the east. This is a branch to Windermere from Virgin's West Coast Main Line (WCML) at Oxenholme on which an hourly service is provided by First North Western Trains, alternate journeys running through to Manchester Airport. A plan was originally conceived for a multi-modal interchange which would provide for Park and Ride with possible transfer to both bus and rail. However, this is less attractive than it appears because:

(i)   Rail only gives access to the town of Windermere which, contrary to the expectations of many, is not directly on the lake of the same name.

(ii) An interchange including rail would limit the choice of sites to one or two which would create their own environmental problems.

(iii) A traffic study for Kendal being conducted simultaneously by Capita*dbs* also indicated Park and Ride as a solution. While the major traffic problems in Kendal occur on weekdays, Lake District demand peaks on Sundays (together with school holiday periods).

On cost-effectiveness grounds, therefore, a case exists for locating the "Strategic Gateway" so that it can serve both Kendal and the central Lake District. Short-listing of sites against this criterion has taken place, but the locations were deemed unacceptable on landscape grounds by LDNPA. An alternative site for Kendal alone has been identified (Feb 2004), after which its suitability for Park and Ride within the National Park will be considered. A further "Strategic Gateway" in the form of an inner interchange is developed from an under-used car park on the edge of Bowness. The latter caters for visitors who prefer to take their cars to a central location, but Rural Bus Challenge funding has been granted for a shuttle bus service connecting it to other destinations in the area.

One of the weaknesses of the rail line is that it is single track and run on the "one engine in steam" principle, which limits the service to once hourly. Engineering improvements to allow a doubling of frequency are being pursued through Rail Passenger Partnership funding. A further proposal envisaged a direct summer Sunday service from York, but this would require support from a number of train operating companies together with Network Rail; recent events in the rail industry make this a low priority project and it has been deferred.

The Penrith -Keswick Corridor

The railhead for Keswick and the northern Park is Penrith on the West Coast Main Line. Following privatisation of the UK bus industry in 1986, most local and inter-urban bus services in Cumbria came into the hands of the Stagecoach group, whose local subsidiary followed a vigorous policy of commercial development. Although Stagecoach restored a connecting bus service that was previously close to abandonment, the possibility remained of up to an hour's wait between train and bus. The Strategy team therefore sought and obtained Rural Bus Challenge funding to operate an additional service, which would be run with new low-floor vehicles and give a combined half-hourly frequency. The impact of Foot and Mouth Disease (FMD) on visitor numbers in 2001 was such that it could not be justified and was withdrawn, but it was reintroduced from 2002 onwards.

A private proposal also exists for re-opening of the rail line between Penrith and Keswick. However, inevitably over 30 years much of the trackbed has been adopted for other uses, including highway improvement and popular walking and cycling routes, while many bridges have been removed. For a small proportion of the estimated capital cost of £35m a frequent high-quality free bus service could be provided, and thus while the restoration of a rail service must be desirable it cannot be given high priority.

Public Transport Promotion and Publicity

The Strategy inherited a fragmented public transport system with little common publicity and less in the way of integrated fares. Stagecoach already published a free newspaper-style brochure showing its services for each summer season, but this included no other operators. Its quality has been improved to include full colour and attractive photography; it is now supported financially by CCC, the LDNPA, the Countryside Agency and Friends of the Lake District together with a number of ferry operators and the National Trust, all of whom provide leisure-oriented services. CCC also publishes a *"Getting Around Cumbria and the Lake District"* timetable and map, including all public transport services in Cumbria, with support from Stagecoach, the LDNPA and Windermere Lake Cruises.

A feature of the Stagecoach *Lakeland Explorer* booklet is the inclusion of bus-based walks. The LDNPA also encourages leisure use through its "Car Free Care Free" programme which suggests itineraries in publicity available from Information Centres, while a jetty at its Brockhole Visitor Centre allows visitors to arrive by ferry as an alternative to road. Admission to the Centre itself is free but parking is charged for, encouraging visitors to travel by bus or ferry and so avoid this charge. Roadside information displays are now of a high standard, with measurable benefits in bus awareness and use; however, the County has long had an interest in IT applications and also pioneered the use of both screens at major terminals and a "Journey Planner" interactive information service. Personal information and booking facilities present a challenge, because none of the major operators has an office or staff based within the LDNP, and the burden therefore tends to fall on Information Centres. The LDNPA has set itself the target of being able to carry out public transport bookings through the Internet by 2005.

Joint and multi-modal tickets have been developed on an incremental basis. The Strategy team is currently supporting CCC in a Rural Bus Challenge project to develop 'smartcards' which, being developed with local authorities in Lancashire, is intended to give an inter-modal and inter-operator facility. It would include school journeys by public transport, local authority concessionary schemes and standard or promotional fares, and it could work on a stored value or stored journey basis. Following a pilot scheme in the Ulverston area, implementation is planned for 2004/5.

Hill Top

In the village of Near Sawrey near Hawkshead, the National Trust owns Hill Top, the farmhouse associated with Beatrix Potter's stories and illustrations (see Chapter Four). Many of its 70,000 visitors each year are Japanese – because Beatrix Potter stories are used to teach English to Japanese children. The whole village is a Conservation Area, lies on a minor road that leads to the natural barrier of Windermere in one direction, and has limited parking availability. Many visitors arrive on organised coach tours, but this is not universally popular because large coaches can cause severe problems on the narrow and twisting roads, and dedicated coach parking exists only in Hawkshead two miles away.

An enterprising "Boat and Goat" facility was set up in 2001 by Windermere Lake Cruises and the specialist local tour operator Mountain Goat. From Bowness visitors can buy an inclusive ticket to cross Windermere by launch, connecting with a minibus shuttle to Hill Top and Hawkshead. Despite the 2001 Foot and Mouth Disease crisis, which prevented Hill Top (still a working farm) from opening until late in the season, the operators were sufficiently happy with performance in 2001 to extend operation to some winter weekends. For 2002 the LDNPA secured Countryside Agency funding for a "B4" network (Boat, Bike, Boot and Bus) which incorporates the "Boat and Goat" as part of a wider project including walking and cycling.

Recreational Green Road Driving

The LDNP is criss-crossed by many minor unsurfaced roads and tracks. These tracks are either Byeways Open to All Traffic (BOATs) or Unclassified County Roads (UCRs). BOATs are the only rights of way on which vehicular use is allowed and while UCRs have no proven vehicular rights, motorised vehicles as well as horse and carriage have used them for recreation and business for the last century or more.

The LDNPA has become concerned about the apparent increase in recreational green road driving, both in 4 wheel drives (4x4s) or on motorbikes. Long-standing clubs such as the Cumbria Group of the Trail Riders Fellowship (TRF), North Lakes 4x4 Club, Cumbria Rover Owners Club *etc.* have been supplemented by commercial safari operators and the increase in sales of new and used vehicles has resulted in what appears to be a burgeoning activity.

The use of recreational vehicles in the countryside is an emotive issue for many people with noise, pollution, erosion and conflicts with other users among the areas of concern. It was the popularity of a number of 'green roads' in the LDNP and their subsequent deterioration in condition that prompted the LDNPA, along with other organisations, to examine ways of managing the activity.

The LDNPA is opposed to recreational green road driving (LDNPA, 1998) but realises that it is a legitimate activity that requires management. Current advice from central Government (DETR, 1997) is for local authorities to pursue management solutions first rather than more stringent statutory controls. The LDNPA has followed these guidelines with the Hierarchy of Trail Routes approach which is evaluated later within this chapter.

Prospects for traffic restriction

Eckton (2002 and 2003) studied attitudes to road pricing, with provision of an alternative free bus service (although it would be necessary to pay a car parking fee in Ambleside), in the context of Great Langdale. Separate surveys were conducted of visitors, local residents and businesses, using a Contingent Valuation approach which identified car users' willingness to pay (WTP) at times of high demand.

The *visitor* survey found that 52.7 per cent of respondents were willing to pay some charge from 0.01p upwards, with 23.6 per cent willing to pay £5; the mean stated WTP was £2.22. However, 27.0 per cent of respondents recorded a "zero protest" bid, indicating that they would not visit Langdale at all, as opposed to the alternatives of using the bus or arriving outside the restricted hours. At a £2 entry charge, the number of visitors intending to continue using their cars would fall by 52.1 per cent; however, 68.6 per cent would continue to visit, using either cars or the bus. If these results represent the true outcome of a road pricing scheme, it is clear that, while a substantial reduction in traffic would be achieved, there would also be a substantial effect on the local economy.

The *resident* survey unsurprisingly identified a lower willingness to pay (9 residents from 47) although 36.2 per cent thought visitors/tourists should have to pay. Residents were invited to rank alternative options for traffic demand management, with the following results:

1st choice: - increased provision/reduced cost of public transport.

2nd choice: - increased parking charges.

3rd choice: - a ban on private vehicles.

4th choice: - road user charges.

5th choice: - widening/improvement of roads.

This order of preference is perhaps predictable because the first and second, in Eckton's words, would "have least impact on residents' current mobility patterns". Public transport solutions frequently score well in surveys but are not good indicators of actual outcomes because those surveyed see them as options to be taken up by others, leaving their own car use unaffected or indeed made easier. It might also be expected that residents would enjoy an exemption from user charges. Eckton points out that residents are typically responsible for a disproportionate number of car journeys in their home area, and that an exemption would both limit the effect in traffic reduction and usage of the alternative bus.

Businesses were predictably also opposed to a charge, although the sample was small; ten responses were received from 24 forms circulated, only one of which supported a charge. This group again favoured improvements and cost reduction in public transport as a demand management strategy.

Overall, Eckton's findings are a useful indicator of the implications of a possible course of action, although with limitations. It was recognised that a survey conducted early in the season following the 2001 outbreak of Foot and Mouth Disease, which had a disastrous effect on rural tourism in Cumbria, might bring more **negative** responses than at a more favourable time. It was concluded that the bus service could not be self-supporting from user charge income, especially if charging was limited to a shorter period than originally proposed, and would therefore require external funding. However, Eckton's estimates of bus operating costs may be on the high side, and it can be assumed that the existing Langdale bus service would be integrated into the scheme, so reducing the additional cost. Furthermore, if the charging period were reduced, it would concentrate on the period when visitor numbers were highest and the bus would not operate outside these times, with the result that the deficit would fall rather than increase.

The Cumbria Tourist Board has set its face against any actions restricting traffic until public transport offers a satisfactory alternative and, as it recognises, this is far distant:

> "Whilst we fully support all efforts to improve public transport and encourage residents and visitors to use alternative means of transport to the car, we continue to resist all efforts to penalise car use as long as the alternatives are so woefully inadequate. To do otherwise could only be damaging to the local economy, and to our industry" (CTB, 2000:11).

Cumbria County Council has prioritised the need for regeneration along the industrial western coastal strip of the county, while the business impact of FMD in 2001 understandably reinforced calls to avoid any action which might damage the tourism industry's recovery. The case for "sticks" to balance the "carrots", in the form of congestion charging or traffic restriction, is therefore difficult to make, and there is reluctance even to limit traffic to essential use in side valleys where congestion has become a regular feature. Cumbria is politically a highly marginal county, with all three major parties having areas of strength; from 1997 to 2001 the majority party was Labour, after which control passed to a Conservative/Liberal Democrat coalition. Such marginality makes for nervous local politicians and a reluctance to take radical steps for fear of voter retribution at the next election.

Concern also exists as to whether the Strategic Gateway proposal is the right way forward. There are fears on one hand that it would simply create space for more visitor cars, leading to an unsustainable increase in total visitor numbers. This is balanced by a view that the call for Park and Ride itself sends out a deterrent message of traffic problems which, it is argued, are limited in time and location (CTB, 2001).

Yet there is surely a need to do something. The lesson is probably one which applies across the UK and much of the western world. Government (at all levels) must be prepared to put far more into both capital investment and revenue support for high quality alternatives to the car, while using its powers of persuasion to increase acceptance of priorities and congestion charging.

Freight

The Strategy also contains a freight element. Many communities have lost their village shop and one Area Action Plan has considered the setting up of a centralised distribution system for inhabitants without cars. However, it is recognised that public attitudes to freight, especially in sensitive areas, are overwhelmingly negative and that local authorities have a limited perception of its role. A danger exists of imposing controls such as vehicle weight limits, routing and delivery restrictions without considering the impact these would have on operators and the businesses to which they deliver. Research is under discussion that would study those impacts and identify opportunities for making retail deliveries both more efficient and more environmentally friendly. For example, in the small towns that characterise National Parks, a high proportion of businesses are sole outlets (e.g. clothing and gift shops) which sometimes lack the benefits of centralised distribution enjoyed by larger groups.

What can the Strategy Achieve?

The Strategy Implementation Document (Lake District Transport Strategy, 2001) claims:

> "The Transport Strategy will over ten years fully integrate national and local economic, environmental and social policy to improve the quality of life in a dispersed rural area and stand as a national demonstration of integrated transport."

Fine words, it is said, "butter no parsnips": can the Strategy achieve its targets? It has at least succeeded in avoiding the 'reefs' on which its predecessors foundered: it has presented an image of partnership and unity which has secured Government support and funding above what could otherwise have been expected. The question is whether this is at a price of compromise and lowest common denominator that will limit its achievement. Its philosophy is based on choice, with residents and visitors able to reduce car use through the greater availability of alternatives. Certainly survey work (see for example Friends of the Earth, 1990, 1991) has shown that some motorists are willing to change mode if an alternative is provided, but the habitual car user often has no reason to be aware of its existence, still less to make the change to use it.

Secondly, if the inducement to change is to be based on "carrots" rather than "sticks", the carrots must be juicy ones. Yet the role of rail can never be more than marginal, and despite much improvement in both commercial and subsidised bus services, their availability – especially during the winter months – remains thin. Cumbria County Council's revenue support, at £1.42 per head of resident population, is still one of the lowest in the UK, and it forms only 3.2 per cent of the total transportation budget (Local Transport Today, 2002). Ninety five per cent of services are provided commercially by Stagecoach, and while the company has been energetic and innovative, potential users are largely dependent on what it finds viable to provide. For example, the last daily journey on the "core" service 555 through the Central Lakes, connecting Windermere, Grasmere and Keswick, leaves Kendal at 1635 hrs. The vulnerability of reliance on a thin commercial network was demonstrated in late 2002 when a deteriorating financial performance by Stagecoach led to abandonment of some critical inter-urban routes everywhere else in Cumbria. Nor has it been possible to solve practical problems like the failure of First North Western's Windermere trains to wait even a few minutes at Oxenholme for late running Virgin arrivals from London and the south.

Case Study – The Hierarchy of Trail Routes

The Hierarchy of Trail Routes (HoTR) is an attempt to manage the current level of activity on green roads through voluntary restraint rather than statutory legislation. Under the Wildlife and Countryside Act 1981, plus amendments under the Countryside and Rights of Way Act 2000, highway authorities assess evidence from users as to whether a right of way should have higher or lesser rights than shown on the Definitive Map. This is time consuming and costly, it does nothing to help manage use on the ground and it does not apply to unclassified roads (UCRs) as these are not included on the Definitive Map.

In 1995 the LDNPA met the Land Access and Recreation Association, which represents motorised recreational users, and Cumbria County Council (as highway authority) to discuss the management of 4WD and motorcycle activity in the LDNP. It was from this and future meetings that the HoTR Experiment evolved. The aim of the Hierarchy is not to promote use or stop the activity but to eliminate irresponsible use. Between 1995 and 1997 over 100 unsealed UCRs and BOATs were identified and surveyed by LDNPA Rangers and local users. The information gathered from these surveys was then used to classify the routes into different categories of voluntary restraint. The criteria used in the evaluation included overall condition of the route, likelihood of conflict with other users, proximity to buildings and livestock, narrowness of the route *etc.* The original voluntary restraints included:

➢ Free use routes – those that were thought to be sustainable for all users at all times.

➢ Privileged use routes – those that required a greater degree of skill and responsibility to drive or ride and should therefore only be used by members of LARA affiliated clubs.

➢ No use 4x4 routes – those that were thought to be unsustainable for 4x4 use.

The first model of the Hierarchy of Trail Routes ran as an experiment for two years between 1999 and 2001. During this time surveys were carried out on both levels of use, compliance with the voluntary restraints and route condition. Advisory signs were erected on site and a Green Road Code of Conduct was produced and distributed to 4x4 drivers and motorcyclists. Interim and final results of the Experiment were reported to a Trails Management Advisory Group (a body set up by the LDNPA comprising all user groups, land managers, local authorities and pressure groups) and the LDNPA's Park Management Committee.

The Experiment showed that motorcycles are the dominant vehicular user on trail routes in the LDNP, accounting for two-thirds of recorded use. Use is concentrated in the south-east of the National Park and of the 108 routes in the Hierarchy, only 20 to 25 are regularly used. Complaints reported to the LDNPA decreased by 50 per cent after the erection of the advisory signs with a marked reduction in incidents involving large convoys of vehicles. However compliance with the voluntary restraints varied from route to route with less notice being taken of restraint on the well known and more heavily used routes. The privileged use category of voluntary restraint was not a success: use did not decrease as was anticipated if only members of LARA affiliated clubs used the route, and it was impossible to identify whether users were members of clubs or not.

Traffic Regulation Orders (TROs) have been used on a number of routes across the National Park. They are a form of statutory control and can be made under legislation from the Road Traffic Regulation Act 1984. They can prohibit, restrict or regulate traffic for the following reasons:

➢ Preventing danger to persons or other traffic using the road.

➢ Preserving the character of the road for use by persons on foot or on horseback.

➢ Preserving the amenity of the area through which the road runs.

➢ Preventing damage to the road.

➢ Preventing the use of the road by vehicular traffic of a kind which is unsuitable having regard to the existing character of the road.

However, in open and remote locations, they have not proved effective in controlling use. The breaching of a TRO is regarded as a minor traffic offence and Cumbria Constabulary will not afford it any priority. Vehicular users, especially motorcyclists, know they can use the route without the fear of being caught.

Given the numbers of motorcycles recorded during the Experiment, it can be assumed that the majority of users do not belong to LARA or one of its associated clubs. Indeed the LDNPA has pinpointed the low profile of LARA and its relatively small sphere of influence as a problem that needs to be addressed if a culture change amongst all vehicular users is to be attained.

Twenty-four routes were chosen for detailed condition survey. They showed that lack of maintenance is a primary reason for route deterioration and that upland fell routes are the least sustainable to vehicles. This is due to a combination of lack of maintenance, recreational pressure, higher slope angles, thinner soils and higher drainage density. Lower level 'agricultural' type routes tend to have a stone cobbled surface and are robust enough to withstand higher levels of vehicular use.

From the summer of 2002, a substantially amended form of the Hierarchy of Trail Routes was embarked upon. The new scheme was based on the outcomes of the review of the HoTR Experiment (LDNPA 2001). The principles of voluntary restraint still apply but have been simplified into a three-colour code system. The codes are:

Green routes: These are assessed as being sustainable for recreational motor traffic at all times. Recorded use is minimal and no problems or valid complaints over vehicular use have been identified. Some green routes may be short dead end routes where no or little use has been recorded and turning round may be a special problem. The management policy here is one of non-intervention unless problems arise, when consideration may be given to moving a route into another category. Green routes are not signed but the advice contained in the Green Road Code still applies.

Amber routes: Amber routes are subject to moderate levels of use by recreational motor vehicles and a greater degree of sensitivity and responsibility is necessary to drive or ride them. They may also be used by a significant number of walkers, cyclists and horse-riders, pass by houses, go through farmyards or close to stock pens, or the surface of the route may mean that use by recreational motor vehicles is not sustainable in all weathers. Amber routes are signed for voluntary restraint specific to each route, and additionally general green road code information is provided.

Red routes: Red routes experience significant use and attract the greatest number of valid complaints regarding vehicular use. They are under the greatest pressure and are subject to the greatest conflict between different classes of user and between users and the environment. Some of the routes cross the high fells and are badly eroded. For these reasons red routes need more active management. Recreational vehicle users are asked to comply with a variety of voluntary restraint controls. For example 4x4 drivers are advised not to use certain routes, one way traffic is recommended on others, or users may be asked not to use a route between holiday dates when it is heavily used by walkers and horse-riders. Red routes are signed and advice specific to each route as well as general green road code information is provided.

Concern was expressed that signing routes would encourage and increase vehicular use of these routes. However the erection of the original HoTR signs showed that these concerns were unfounded and the LDNPA is of the opinion that these new signs will not cause any increase either.

The Green Road Code of Conduct has been revised and re-printed and the new advisory signs were erected at the end of 2002. Certain routes and types of users are being targeted over the next two years. The LDNPA will liaise with local and regional 4x4 and motorcycle dealers and garages, commercial users, national manufacturers and media in an effort to raise awareness of the sensitivities of recreational green road driving among the non-club element who participate in the activity.

The HoTR Experiment has been monitored on a national level. This type of management approach has been quoted in the Institute of Public Rights of Way Officers Good Practice Guide (IPROW 2002). The findings of the HoTR Experiment have also been used in the on-going revision of the DETR document, Making the Best of Byeways. Officers from the LDNPA have also represented the Association of National Park Authorities at meetings of the Rights of Way Review Committee and the Local Government Association. The LDNPA has been at the forefront of managing vehicles in the countryside and has a wealth of experience and expertise that has been and will continue to be called upon in the future.

Cycling and Sustainable Tourism in Cumbria and the LDNP

Richards (1996) reminds us that sustainable development is perceived as a policy objective that should be pursued, with Jackson and Morpeth (1999:1) arguing that "it is to implementation, rather than enunciation and further clarification, that both analysts and the tourism industry must turn regarding sustainability". In terms of achieving sustainable transport scenarios, Page (1999:276) provides a similar view, asking whether transport options can "really be put into practice or do they remain a stated policy objective of environmental planning which is little more than a paper exercise". Consistent with transport policy advocacy to identify sustainable forms of transport, Tolley and Turton (1995:370) noted that "if genuine sustainability is to be achieved, the bicycle – or something very like it – has to occupy a much more central role than the car in future transport policy".

Given the on-going process of attempting to implement sustainable transport initiatives which re-orientate the use of motor vehicles within the LDNP, this section highlights contemporary applications of cycle tourism as an alternative to the use of the motorcar for tourism exploration within the LDNP, emphasising in particular that the CTB and CCC, in conjunction with Sustrans, are in the process of operationalising wider dimensions of sustainable tourism through emerging strategic developments in cycle tourism. The Draft 'Cycle Tourism Strategy for Cumbria' (2004-09), highlights how the quest for sustainable tourism, is consistent with The Regional Tourism Strategy for Cumbria (1998), which positions cycling as an ideal form of sustainable tourism, and which is a particularly suitable activity for the special landscape qualities of the LDNP.

Whilst cycle tourism is recognised as a quintessentially environmentally form of sustainable tourism, it also 'respects' the integrity of social and cultural resources, and furthermore has the potential to provide economic benefits for local communities (see for example Jackson & Morpeth,1999). In particular this section illustrates how the emergence and the on-going development of the Sustrans inspired Sea to Sea Cycle Route (C2C) (which is supported by 14 local authorities, the LDNPA, the North Pennines Tourism Partnership and East Cumbria Countryside Project) is making a substantial contribution to operationalising and 'establishing' different dimensions of sustainable tourism within Cumbria and the LDNP.

Historical antecedents to developing cycle tourism rural locations

The on-going initiatives to expand cycle tourism in Cumbria and the LDNP provide a timely reminder of the status that the bicycle has previously enjoyed. In the latter part of the 19th and early 20th centuries the bicycle was a significant form of transport for utility, leisure and tourism. It was Patmore (1983) who provided a wider social commentary on the use of the bicycle as an affordable transport mode, which enabled cycle tourists with limited financial means to explore and discover natural landscapes outside of industrialised and urban environments. Patmore (1983:34) described how the national cycling organisation, the Cycling Touring Club, had stimulated mass participation in cycling with over 60,000 members in 1899. This was emblematic of the role of the bicycle in "renewing the urban acquaintance with the countryside", maintaining its popularity into the early part of the 20th century despite the "growing ubiquity of the car". Therefore bicycle touring, referred to interchangeably as cycle tourism, has a long lineage as a leisure and tourism form within the UK. It has enjoyed a renaissance in demand by a diverse group of cyclists, and associated provision by both commercial operators and public policy makers who recognise cyclings' credentials as a sustainable tourism form.

In terms of defining cycle tourism, Simonsen and Jorgsen (1996) and Ritchie (1998) suggest that there is a spectrum of cycle tourists, ranging from 'occasional cyclists' who combine cycling with the main elements of a holiday and 'cycling enthusiast' 'living their holiday' through the bicycle. More specifically Lumsdon (1995:2) highlights the highly fragmented nature of the market for recreational cycling, focusing on the following broad categories and sub-segments which include: Independent day cyclist, Day cycle hirers, Short break tourer, Cycle holiday: independent, Cycle holiday: group and Solo Mountain Biker (ibid.). In particular, the popularity of mountain biking has heralded a new generation of cyclists, melding off road adventure with youth culture and fashion. This has wider implications for the management of 'hard' adventure tourism within the National Park boundary, with the need to educate off-road 'trail-blazing' cyclists through the introduction of codes of conduct (it is worth noting that the International Mountain Bike Association UK (IMBA UK) was partly established in 2003 to address this issue).

Given the former boom in cycling activity, the latter part of the 20th century witnessed a retreat in transport terms of the status of the bicycle in relation to motorised use of transport networks, not least in rural areas. This was demonstrated by the headline 'Go by bike to save the countryside', which accompanied an article in *Countryside* (the newspaper of the Countryside Commission, July/August 1992, Number 56), which highlighted that the Transport Studies Unit at Oxford University advocated that the private motorcar should be used more selectively in rural locations. The article cited the need for greater availability of public transport, linked to opportunities for walking and cycling. In a similar vein the National Trust in 1995, in response to the Royal Commission Environmental Pollution report on road traffic (1994), urged the Government to curtail car use and improve access to public transport, advocating that there should be greater use of the bicycle (*The Guardian*, June 27, 1995).

Within the context of Cumbria and the LDNP, Cotton (1995:8) highlighted the perennial challenge for cycle tourists in overcoming the dominance of the motorcar suggesting that

> "much of the central area of the Lake District, unless one is highly selective about the time and the season, is unsuitable for cycling – the roads, even the small lanes, are clogged with cars and caravans and off-road many of the bridleways in the heart of the fells are either too steep, too rocky, too boggy, too vague, too full of people".

He was nevertheless optimistic that cyclists could find excellent cycling routes on the fringes of the LDNP boundary within Cumbria. Consistent with these safety fears expressed by Cotton, Sustrans (1996a: 8) (a UK based national sustainable transport charity) identified that the development of a National Cycling Network (NCN) "will begin to change cycling culture by helping to remove the greatest barrier to recreational cycling – the fear of traffic".

The concept of a Sustrans inspired NCN was bolstered by the creation of a National Cycling Strategy (1996), a significant policy document which elevated the status of cycling as a form of sustainable transport. The introduction of this strategy represented a paradigm shift in transport thinking in the UK in identifying

> "the need to manage the existing road network more efficiently (and that) Cycling has a clear role to play within this policy framework. Sustainable transport options are needed for both utility and leisure trips, offering practical alternatives to the private motorcar" (1996: 2).

This strategy signalled the growing national status of cycling in the UK, recognised by Central Government as an environmentally – friendly form of transport which exemplified sustainability principles. The National Cycling Strategy provided targets for increasing cycling use in line with the UK Royal Commission on Environmental Pollution (1994). Targets, emphasising in this respect the key role of the public sector in stimulating increased cycle use, highlighted that there should be a quadrupling in cycling to 10 per cent of all journeys by 2004. Within the context of Cumbria and the LDNP there have been a number of strategic responses to recognising the significance of cycle tourism as an exemplar of sustainable tourism.

Strategic Responses to Cycling and Cycle Tourism within Cumbria and the Lakes

Arguably, since the inception of the Cumbria Cycle Way in 1980, there have been incremental initiatives for cycling and cycle tourism which have now been superseded by a more strategic planning approach to cycling and cycle tourism. This incremental and ad hoc approach to the development of an infrastructure for cycling and cycle tourism was characterised initially by the Lake District Transport Strategy which recognised the need to respond to the specific needs of visitors such as fell walkers and non-car users, but no overt reference was made to the role of the bicycle within this initiative. However, there is now growing evidence of key strategic documents which recognise the growing status of the bicycle as a sustainable form of transport within Cumbria and the LDNP.

The Cumbria and Lake District Joint Structure Plan (1991-2006) within the chapter on 'Transport and Communication' highlighted a 'headline' policy which encouraged greater use of public transport and also advocated increased cycling and walking. The development of a network of cycling routes was also intended as a policy instrument for reducing 'transport pressures', and as such encouraging the development of a sustainable form of transport. This 'headline' policy is echoed within the Local Transport Plan (2001-2002/2005-2006) which in response to the guidance of a Cycling Panel consisting of local stakeholders, created a Strategic Cycling Network. As part of this network CCC in partnership with CTB and the LDNPA (and as part of a 'Enjoy Cumbria's Great Outdoors' promotion), identified 23 cycling routes within the Western Lake District, Keswick and the Northern Lakes, Central and the Southern Lakes and the Eden Valley and the North Pennines.

The emphasis on the coherence of this network was partly to link rural and urban settlements for utility cycling, but also to provide more extensive routes for leisure and tourism usage. Additionally, CCC's Local Agenda 21 Strategy acknowledges the need to integrate the strategic transport aims of the Structure Plan and the Local Transport Plan, in order to prioritise access (and to not be reliant on the motorcar) to local services and facilities for 'mobility-deprived' groups (see for example Tolley & Turton, 1995). The CTB is now taking a strategic lead in creating new cycle routes, with significant route development of the Eden Valley Circular Cycle Way and the Eskdale Trail, which incorporates travel on a miniature railway, the Ravenglass and Eskdale Railway.

Indeed, there are wider exciting contemporary strategic developments by the CTB in conjunction with CCC and the Rural Regeneration Company in commissioning consultants to produce a draft document 'Delivering Its Potential: A Cycle Tourism Strategy for Cumbria' (2004-09) which builds on existing cycle tourism initiatives within Cumbria and the LDNP. It is important to stress that this document is still at a discussion stage and that likely intended strategic outputs discussed within this chapter may change before the strategy is fully implemented.

This draft strategy document emphasises the wider strategic importance of cycle tourism, as a sustainable form of tourism, not just within Cumbria and the LDNP but with a wider regional context of the North West of England (2004:8). Indeed both The Tourism Vision for England's North West and The Strategy for Tourism in England's NorthWest make claims of the capacity of cycle tourists to engage with 'world class countryside' and cycle tourism contributing to the 'renaissance of the Lake District' (ibid.).

The draft 'Cycle Tourism Strategy for Cumbria' (2004-2009) (CTSC), document recognises the multi-faceted nature of cycle tourism, characterising cycle tourism as an essentially leisure based activity, which attracts different market segments. This document builds on previous seminal work on cycle tourism, which recognises the complex and fragmented nature of the market characteristics of cycle tourists (see for example Lumsdon, 1995; Simonsen and Jorgsen, 1996; Ritchie, 1998) but similarly recognises that cycle tourists have core product requirements which include safe, stimulating and coherent routes, supported by a range of services and information. These services include cyclist-friendly accommodation, visitor attractions, hospitality and support services which include transport providers who offer opportunities for cycle carriage on buses, boats and trains, and also opportunities for secure parking (Draft CTSC, 2004).

Services and information will be targeted at mountain bikers, cycle tourists and local cyclists, recognising that people might visit Cumbria and the LDNP as day visitors or as holiday cyclists, who have either planned to cycle or decide spontaneously to cycle. Planned cycle holidays might be centre-based, independent or provided as a 'packaged' experience by a holiday operator. The provision of routes and services recognise the different, demographic, lifestyle and lifecycle characteristics of cycle tourists (Draft CTSC, 2004).

Cycling and sustainable tourism

Global policy advocacy of cycle tourism as a sustainable form of tourism recognises that cycling not only mitigates against negative environmental impacts in the countryside of car borne tourism but that in a positive sense it has economic, social and cultural benefits. Underpinning the highlighted benefits of developing cycle tourism within the draft strategy document are key themes underpinned by dimensions of sustainability which might provide discernible benefits for both the human and physical geography of Cumbria, and the LDNP, and are intended to enhance the quality of the tourist experience (Draft CTSC, 2004:6). Specifically, environmental benefits centre on holiday trips which are pollution free and improve air quality, and do not add to over congested roads. As such it is anticipated that cycle tourism can help to maintain long-term, the unique and fragile quality in particular of the National Park landscape, and stimulate use of under-used resources of quiet country lanes and disused railway lines.

The economic benefits of cycle tourism are well documented (see for example Sustrans, 1995; Cope *et al.*, 1998), and the continuing success of the C2C long distance cycle route, which partly traverses Cumbria and the LDNP, demonstrates the economic benefits to tourist-focused SMEs, and local communities, particularly in marginalised rural settlements, as well as established tourist destinations. The draft 'Cycle Tourism Strategy for Cumbria' (Draft CTSC, 2004-09) recognises that even in advance of strategically-led development within Cumbria, the economic benefit annually of cycle tourism is estimated to be approximately £48 million. Additionally, it was estimated that 23,000 dedicated cycle tourist holidays are taken in Cumbria annually, although it is important to note that 88 per cent of visitors to Cumbria arrive by car (Draft CTSC, 2004).

It is also anticipated within this draft strategy document that cycle tourism can help to overcome problems of the spatial and temporal concentration of visitors, which is such a feature of 'honey-pot sites' within the LDNP, by encouraging cycle tourists to stay longer in a variety of locations (Draft CTSC, 2004). The anticipated social and community benefits are consistent with CCC's Local Agenda 21 Strategy, and Sustrans (1996b) linkage between the creation of a National Cycling Network and Local Agenda 21 strategies, in so far that, there are synergistic health and access benefits in the creation of cycling infrastructure which would advantage both communities and tourists. Likewise, it is anticipated that the cultural benefits to communities 'servicing' the C2C cycle route, is both in the cultural interaction with a different type of tourist in cycle tourists, and in the sense of community ownership of cycling infrastructure, which provides new access routes into rural communities. It is also anticipated within the draft strategy document that these cultural benefits can be extended to other cycling routes within Cumbria and the LDNP (Draft CTSC, 2004).

In line with recognition of the principles of sustainable tourism being acknowledged through the 'Green Globe Destination' designation, CTB interpret the management of sustainable tourism as balancing the needs of local communities and visitors. Consistent with this message of sustainability, CTB promotes cycling as an activity which is 'sympathetic' to the natural environment and which provides economic benefits.

The philosophy of CTB in relation to cycle tourism is that if its potential is to be fully realised then a quality supporting infrastructure is required which recognises that local accommodation providers, attractions, hospitality outlets, and cycle shops and cycle hire businesses, have an important role in servicing the needs of cycle tourists. To assist local SMEs in supporting cycle tourism, the CTB has been instrumental in arranging workshops and seminars to highlight the economic and community benefits of getting involved in responding to the needs of cycle tourists. The CTB is confident that the basis of an effective cycling service sector exists which incorporates an established cycle retail sector and cycle holiday sector, and a network of emerging cycle friendly accommodation providers (Draft CTSC, 2004). It is worth noting that the CTB has agreed in principle to be part of a CoAg and VisitBritain pilot scheme which is trying to introduce a national cyclists welcome accreditation scheme.

It is clear that the CTB in conjunction with CCC, Sustrans and other organisations and agencies are now creating a county-wide infrastructure for leisure and tourist based cycling with a labyrinth of different surfaced routes, which includes 1200 miles of bridleways and cycleable rights of way routes with the capacity to attract mountain bikers. Quiet and unused country lanes are viewed as having the capacity to attract a range of cycle tourists (Draft CTSC, 2004).

Other key organisations and agencies within Cumbria and the LDNP have been innovative in offering opportunities for cycle tourism. In particular, Youth Hostel Association properties within the LDNP have introduced a bike hire scheme, and their shuttle buses have the capacity to carry bicycles. Likewise, National Trust properties around Coniston Water are developing cycle networks, consistent with their policy nationally of introducing cycle hire facilities which enable a wide range of groups to engage in cycle tourism on their sites.

Consistent with national Forest Enterprise initiatives for designated mountain bike trails, the Grizedale and Whinlatter forests in the LDNP, provide scope for off-road cyclists to engage in more adventure based cycling. There is also evidence of local cycle networks being integrated with wider non-car based transport systems with the Cross Lakes Shuttle Service operating between Windermere and Coniston calling at the Grizedale Forest. With the Mountain Goat minibuses, Windermere Cruises and Coniston launches all being adapted to carry cycles, cycling has an elevated status in the transport hierarchy within the LDNP.

Consistent with the view of the shifting image of contemporary cycling, characterised by Beioley as a transformation from "wicker baskets, cycle clips and plastic capes, replaced by figure hugging lycra" (1995:17), the CTB view cycle tourism as more of a mainstream tourist activity rather than specialist or niche market for tourism within Cumbria and the LDNP. In this respect the CTB 2004 'Official Guide' has successfully integrated images of cycling as a 'mainstream' tourism activity, and has linked the benefits of cycling with walking as a form of activity tourism.

The CTB also recognise the significance of the role of cycling as a key element in integrated transport initiatives within Cumbria and the Lakes, highlighting its inter-modality with the rail hubs of Carlisle and Penrith, which provide access to the Northern Lakes and the Eden Valley, and Oxenholme for the Southern Lakes. There is scope for these rail hubs to provide the starting point for cycle touring, offering links with outlined cycling routes, not least the Sustrans inspired C2C 140 mile linear route from Whitehaven (and Workington) in Cumbria, to Sunderland (and Tynemouth in North East of the UK) which incorporates a significant part of the route within the LDNP (Whinlatter to Penrith in the Northern Lakes).

Recreational Trails and Sustainability

It is important to note that there are important historical antecedents to the development of linear recreational routes, which provide a model for the C2C route to stimulate policy development for cycling as an exemplar of sustainable tourism. In 1972, A.Wainwright unveiled the 'Coast to Coast Walk', an 'unofficial' 190 mile long-distance walking route, from St. Bees Head in Cumbria to Robin Hood's Bay in North Yorkshire. This route traverses the Lake District and the Pennines, Swaledale, the Cleveland Hills and the North York Moors, with two-thirds of the route traversing three National Parks. It symbolised the stimulation of a latent demand for long-distance walking routes within the UK, which had previously been popularised by the Pennine Way and a network of long-distance routes designated by the Countryside Commission (now the Countryside Agency). However, Wainwright was cautious about the emergence of a plethora of 'official' long-distance routes and the 'too-popular parade' of walkers causing erosion of over-used landscapes advocating the need for durable and sustainable recreational routes.

Nevertheless, trails have wider utility, with Lane (1999) highlighting how trail development is viewed as having environmental, transportation, health and economic benefits, with more specifically Rail Trails, a form of Greenway, creating multi-purpose recreational trails which are used for walking, horse riding and cycling (see also Ryan, 1993). Lane (1999) noted that trails offered specific opportunities for cycle hire, and the scope for new forms of interpretation and theme development. The concept of a nation-wide matrix of footpaths and bridleways forming continuous and linear recreational routes is the hall-mark of the work of Sustrans.

Sustrans

The visionary work of Sustrans was initially based on the conversion of in particular 'Rail Trails' principally for use for utilitarian cycling. In this sense they have successfully constructed traffic-free paths, catering for walkers, people with disabilities and cyclists since the early 1980s. Their initial aim in partnership with local authorities and other organisations and agencies, was to create a 2,000 mile national network of traffic free routes, which would link urban centres throughout the UK. Routes combined traffic-calmed roads with traffic free-paths, utilising disused railway lines and river and canal paths.

With the boost of £42.5 million of funding from the UK Millennium Commission in 1995, Sustrans working in conjunction with local authorities, have accelerated the creation of a 6,500 mile National Cycle Network (NCN) (now extended to 10,000 miles) linking each urban area of the UK. The initial rationale for route development is to enable local communities of approximately 20 million households to be a 10 minute cycle ride from the NCN. A key aspect of Sustrans UK vision for a NCN, is that it should provide improved mobility and environmental benefits of reduced traffic, on a local level for communities who want an alternative to car borne travel (Sustrans, 1996b).

However, the use of the NCN for cycle tourism has become an increasing priority for route development, with Sustrans estimating that cycle tourism will generate £150 million in tourism receipts annually in the UK, creating 3700 jobs (Sustrans, 1995a). Indeed the growing importance of the cycle tourism potential of Sustrans 'created' routes, has seen the appointment of a designated Cycle Tourism Officer based in Sustrans Headquarters in Bristol.

The focus of their work is not purely on a national basis, and they have been instrumental in co-ordinating developments in cycle tourism in a European context in collaboration with the European Cyclists Federation, and the creation of a Pan European cycling network (see Sustrans, 1995b and 'LFI Noordzeeroute'). However it is in a UK context that Sustrans has been instrumental in developing innovative routes for cyclists such as the C2C route, with Page (1999: 281) stressing that "the C2C route illustrates the generative effect which new cycle routes can have on tourism". It is anticipated by the CTB that in addition to this 'flagship' cycle tourism route, the development of a Hadrian's Wall Cycle Way, and a route from Barrow to Sunderland (both due to open in 2005), will stimulate more local cycling route development within Cumbria and the LDNP. These routes will add to the critical mass of NCN cycle tourism routes in Cumbria, which include the 150 mile 'Reivers Cycle Route' from Whitehaven to Tynemouth (with 90 miles of the route in Cumbria).

The Sea to Sea Route (C2C)

In 1995 this Sustrans inspired 140 mile route (developed in conjunction with local authorities, tourism organisations and the LDNPA) was officially opened. It provided the opportunity for cyclists to link the peripheral areas of Cumbria, with central areas within the LDNP, and linkages to the high Pennines to the east of the National Park boundary. Four per cent of the route is on main roads, 50 per cent on minor roads, 46 per cent on cycle paths, off-road and rail trails, providing the prospect of a safe and durable recreational route. The 'start' and 'end' of the route incorporates two urban regions of post-industrial decline, with the greater part of the route traversing rural areas which traditionally have been peripheral and satellite tourist areas in comparison to the 'dominant' tourist area of the LDNP. This is consistent with the observation of Lane (1999) who argued that leisure and tourism trails can be used as a management tool for directing the flow of tourists in specific underused and overused localities. In this case linking the peripheral parts of West Cumbria with the LDNP.

The C2C route was a significant marker in the evolution of the Sustrans inspired 10,000 mile NCN, and symbolised a re-orientatation in the focus from principally utilitarian cycling, to promoting the leisure and tourism potential of route development. Amplification of the sustainability credentials of this route occurred in 1995, when Sustrans received the British Airways sponsored, 'Tourism for Tomorrow Global Award'. This was followed in 1998, by the Smithsonian Environment Award, in recognition of "the lasting contribution to protecting the environment" (1998:5) and then the plaudit in 1999, of a silver medal in the Green Transport Category in the ETC 'England for Excellence Award'.

In terms of the monitoring of cycle trails, the C2C in particular became the focus for academic scrutiny, with Cope *et al.* (1998) undertaking survey work using a combination of automatic field counters, field interviews, and telephone interviews in 1996 and 1997. They established that in 1996, between 12,000 to 15,000 cyclists used the route, spending between £1.07 and £1.85 million, and estimated that 11,000 cyclists used the route in 1997. The evidence from a 2000 Sustrans survey reveals that the C2C has sustained and indeed increased the levels of route usage identified within the 1996 and 1997 surveys. Within the LDNP, Sustrans highlight that automatic cycle counters (supported with data from self-complete questionnaires) on the Threlkeld railway path reveal an increase from 31,197 cyclist using the route in 1996, to 40,226 in 2000. Sustrans (2000) suggest that in 2000 between 12,000 and 12,500 cyclists cycled the whole route spending on average 3.75 days on the route (with the likelihood of one full day with overnight accommodation being spent within the LDNP). With the route generating between £1,350,00 and £1,635,000 during 2000, and over a 5 year period since monitoring began, it is estimated that the route has generated £7,000,000 for 'relatively deprived' rural economies.

Sustrans previously highlighted accommodation and hospitality outlets that have benefited. The owner of the Langley House guest house in Penrith stated in 1996 that "virtually all of my visitors this year have arrived on bicycle – no problems with parking and such friendly people" (Sustrans, 1996 c).

Similarly the indication from micro-tourism accommodation businesses within Keswick, in the 'heart' of the LDNP (and a significant 'first accommodation centre' on the C2C route) is that they are receptive to providing cycle friendly facilities of safe parking and drying rooms. A small scale survey indicated that the development of the C2C was not necessarily the main motivation for providing these facilities, but it is hoped that these facilities might encourage cyclists to stay more than one night in Keswick as a base for cycle touring (Morpeth, 2003). Sustrans are keen to identify circular routes within the LDNP to encourage cyclists to take advantage of guesthouse and Bed and Breakfast accommodation. Methodologically there is scope to extend such a survey to investigate the response of local village communities with associated small businesses to feedback the benefits of the C2C route.

This information is helpful in planning for future route developments and improvements and to enable effective route management. For example a concern about the growing popularity of the route, is that cyclists en route would be followed by support cars, however the anecdotal evidence from Sustrans is that this has not materialised. This might be in part due to the emergence of a cycle (and rider) shuttle bus that has minimised the need to combine bicycle and car usage. However, the limitation of public transport linkages to Whitehaven and Workington means that motorcars are used to transport cyclists to the start (and are available for cyclists at the finish).

The draft 'Cycle Tourism Strategy for Cumbria' (2004-09) is confident that Cumbria and the LDNP will be the pre-eminent destination for cycling within the UK, and that the prospects for growth in the cycle tourism market are good, with the NCN experiencing year on year growth since 1996, and generating an estimated £300 million for Cumbria's local economy between 2004-2008, with an estimated 32,000 jobs being generated (Draft CTSC, 2004). Furthermore, the strategic management of cycle tourism highlighted within this strategy, is viewed as offering innovation in transport which can realise the goals of sustainable transport, offering sustainable benefits for Cumbria and the LDNP. The implementation challenge lies ahead for a Cycling Cumbria Steering Group, comprised of the CTB, LDNPA, Yorkshire Dales National Park Authority, CCC, West Lakes Renaissance/Rural Regeneration Company, and representatives from working groups on Business Development, Cycle Touring, Local Cycling, Mountain Biking and Research and Monitoring.

Conclusions

In terms of achieving the goal of sustainable mobility within the LDNP it is tempting to paraphrase Tolley and Turton (1995:351): "Policy for sustainable development: no examples yet!" Undoubtedly the changing morphology of the transport network and the unique topography of the LDNP, present different problems and challenges for residents and visitors. The response and solutions that have emerged from a range of policy makers within Cumbria and the LDNPA have been highlighted within this chapter. The Lake District Traffic Management Initiative exposed the pitfalls that piecemeal approaches to complex transport problems result in. The willingness to forgo car travel has to be met by substantial opportunities to take advantage of public transport. For example Eckton's (2002) study which explored the prospects for traffic restriction providing free public transport alternatives to car use in Great Langdale, revealed that in broad terms visitors showed a greater propensity to pay than residents, with local businesses largely opposed to car charging. The CTB was concerned that restricting car use without viable public transport provision would be likely to damage the local economy. Perhaps crucially with local political volatility, it was suggested that local politicians of all persuasions would be unwilling to support schemes which would curtail car usage in Cumbria and the LDNP. The suggestion was that the regeneration of the industrial western coastal strip of the county would take priority over sustainable developments within the LDNP. However, the case study of cycle tourism and the C2C policy initiative highlights the positive sustainability benefits of promoting non-motorised tourism.

In this sense the success of the Lake District Transport Strategy will be judged against the ability of both national and local politicians to maintain policy momentum in finding collaborative and sustainable solutions to over-reliance on the use of the motorcar and its association with economic growth rather than its environmental dis-benefits.

The Hierarchy of Trails Initiative demonstrates the complexity of combining legislation and voluntary restraint, as providing an effective policy vehicle for the management of recreational vehicular use over the labyrinth of green lanes within the LDNP. The introduction of a colour code scheme supported by informative signage provides the prospect at least of educating vehicle users. The case study on cycle tourism and the Sustrans' initiative of the C2C demonstrates the growing status of the bicycle with the capacity to address the negative environmental impacts of car usage, and demonstrates that cycle tourism can provide significant economic, social and cultural benefits for a largely rural region. Undoubtedly route awareness and effective marketing of the route by Sustrans have helped to maintain its popularity. There are encouraging signs through the draft 'Cycle Tourism Strategy for Cumbria' (2004-9) of a strategic pro-bicycle planning philosophy which benefits both residents and visitors. The future of rural transport strategies within Cumbria and the Lake District are dependent for their success on the collaboration between agencies which are sensitive to the mobility needs of rural communities and visitors.

In the words of MacEwen and MacEwen (1982:145) the key policy challenge is that road "hierarchies remain largely on paper and the public and shared transport services that provide a theoretical alternative to the private car play a much bigger part in publicity than they do on the ground. This is not for lack of enthusiasm (for National Park Authorities have been outstanding in their efforts to pioneer public bus and rail transport) but it is due to lack of means and powers and the public's overwhelming commitment to the private car". The development of the C2C route at least symbolises scope for the reorientation in the 'centre of gravity' of mass tourism, and provides an alternative means of enjoying the special landscape and culture of the LDNP.

References

Beioley, S. On yer bike- cycling and tourism. *Insights* 1995 (September), B17-B31.

Cope, A., Doxford, D., & Hill, T., (1998) Monitoring Tourism on the UK's First Long-Distance Cycle Route. *Journal of Sustainable Tourism* 6(3), 210-223.

Cotton, N. (1995) *Cycle Tours: 24 one-day routes in Cumbria and the Lakes*. London: Hamlyn.

Countryside Commission (1992) *Countryside* July/August. Number 56. 1992 p.1.

Countryside Commission (1996) *Visitors to National Parks: Summary of the 1994 Survey Findings*. CCP 503. Countryside Commission: Cheltenham.

Cumbria County Council and Lake District Special Planning Board (1990). *Lake District Traffic Congestion Review. Working Party's Interim Report.* Nov 1990. Carlisle: Cumbria County Council.

Cumbria County Council and Lake District Special Planning Board (1992). *Lake District Traffic Review. Working Party's Second Report.* Aug 1992. Carlisle: Cumbria County Council.

Cumbria County Council (1996) *A Strategy for Transport in the Lake District. Dept of Economy and Environment.* Carlisle: Cumbria County Council.

Cumbria County Council (2001) Local Transport Plan. Carlisle: Cumbria County Council.

Cumbria County Council, Cumbria Tourist Board, Rural Regeneration Cumbria (2004) Unpublished Draft- *'Delivering Its Potential: A Cycle Tourism Strategy for Cumbria* (2004-9). Carlisle: Cumbria County Council.

Cumbria Tourist Board (2000) *Annual Report 1999-2000.* Windermere: Cumbria Tourist Board.

Cumbria Tourist Board (2001) *Minutes of Executive Board and General Tourism Council. July 2001.* Windermere: Cumbria TouristBoard.

Cumbria Tourist Board (2002) *Official Guide.*Windermere: Cumbria Tourist Board.

Daily Telegraph (1995) *Huge Traffic Curbs Planned for Lake District.* 1 May 1995, p9.

Department of Transport (1996) *National Cycling Strategy.* London: DETR.

DETR (1997) *Making the Best of Byways.* London: DETR.

Eckton, G. (2002) *Great Langdale Valley, Cumbria: An Analysis of the Viability of Friends of the Earth (1990-1991) Transport Survey of Visitors to South Lakeland.* South Lakeland: Friends of the Earth.

Eckton, G. (2002) Road User Charging as a Demand Management Tool for Motor Vehicle Dependent Recreation. MA Dissertation, University of Central Lancashire. Preston.

Eckton, G. (2003) Road User Charging and the Lake District National Park. *Journal of Transport Geography* 11, 307-317.

Friends of the Earth (1990 and 1991) *Transport Survey of Visitors to South Lakeland.* South Lakeland: Friends of the Earth.

Guardian (1995) *Government told to end car culture.* Tuesday, June 27, 1995. p.6.

Jackson, G. & Morpeth, N. (1999) Local Agenda 21 and Community Participation in Tourism Policy Planning: Future or Fallacy. *Current Issues in Tourism.* 2(1).

Lake District Herald (1991) *Victory for Locals over "Park and Ride".* 2 February 1991.

Lake District Special Planning Board (1976) *Lake District National Park Plan Review.* Traffic and Parking. Kendal: LDSPB.

Lake District Traffic Management Initiative (1995) *Traffic in the Lake District.* Kendal:

Lake District Transport Strategy (2000) T*ransport Strategy Implementation Plan: Stage One, 2000-2005.* Carlisle.

Local Transport Today (2002) *Merseyside Tops Local Authority Spending.* Table. 6 Sept 2002, p3.

Lumsdon, L. (1995) *Cycle Tourism a Growth Market.* Conference For Cycle Tourism: A Growth Market, Staffordshire University, Friday 24th February.

MacEwen, A. & MacEwan, M. (1982) *National Parks: Conservation or Cosmetics.* Allen & Unwin: London.

National Parks and Access to the Countryside Act (1949). London: HMSO.

Page, S. (1999) *Transport and Tourism.* Harlow: Longman.

Patmore, A. (1983) *Recreation and Resources.* Oxford: Blackwell.

Richards, G. (ed.)(2001) *Cultural Attractions And European Tourism.* Oxon: CABI Publishing.

Ritchie, B. (1998) 'Bicycle tourism in the South Island of New Zealand: planning and management issues': *Tourism Management,* 19(6), 567-582.

Royal Commission on Environmental Pollution's Report (1994) *Transport and the Environment.* Oxford University Press: Oxford.

Ryan, K. (ed.) (1993) *Trails for the Twenty-first Century: Planning, Design, and Management for Multi-Use Trails. Rails-To-Trails Conservancy.* Washington: Inland Press.

Sustrans (1995a) *The National Cycle Network: Update One.* Bristol: Sustran.

Sustrans (1996a) *LF1 Noordzeeroute: cycling between Den Helder and Boulogne-sur-Mer.* Bristol: Sustrans.

Sustrans (1996b) Local Agenda 21 and the National Cycle Network: Routes to Local Sustainability. Sustrans: Bristol.

Sustrans (1996c) *Network News.* Autumn. Bristol: Sustrans.

Sustrans (2000) Monitoring tourism on the C2C cycle route during 2000 – a summary. Unpublished study.

Tolley, R. & Turton, B. (1995) *Transport Systems Policy And Planning: A Geographical Approach.* Harlow: Longman.

Weal, F. (1968) Traffic in the Country – a Strategy for Protection of the Lake District. In *Architect's Journal,* 28 Aug 1968, 358-370.

Wainwright, A. (undated) *A Coast to Coast Walk: A Pictorial Guide*. Kendal: Westmorland Gazette.

Chapter Eight

The Impacts of Tourism in the Lake District

It has been demonstrated throughout this book that the development of tourism inevitably has impacts on destinations. The nature of such impacts is, of course, highly variable; they may be either positive or negative – or, more usually, a combination of both – and the extent to which they are manifested or perceived is largely dependent on a number of factors, including the socio-economic and environmental characteristics of the destination, the type and scale of tourism that it attracts and supports, and the stage of tourism development (Mathieson and Wall, 1982; Burns and Holden, 1995). Thus, in some contexts, the impacts of tourism may be relatively minor; in others, particularly where tourism is a dominant activity and/or occurs in relatively fragile physical or social environments, such as national parks or other protected areas, its consequences are likely to be more significant (FNNPE, 1993). Chapter Three has presented the context upon which tourism in the Lake District is based, and the discussion that follows reflects these special characteristics.

Irrespective of the degree of impact, however, it has been recognised that, since the emergence of tourism as a mass leisure activity in the 1960s, its consequences or impacts should be carefully managed or controlled. At that time, tourism was seen somewhat simplistically as an environmental threat (Budowski, 1973; Dowling, 1992) and the focus was, therefore, very much on attempting to minimise the deleterious outcomes of tourism development. In effect, the purpose was to protect destinations *from* tourism (or, more precisely, mass tourism) – very much as Wordsworth had suggested much earlier in both proposing the Lake District as a 'national property' in his *Guide to the Lakes* and, subsequently, in 1844, arguing against the construction of the railway to Windermere (see Chapter Two). In the context of the countryside in general, the rapid increase in tourism in the 1960s – referred to by Dower (1965) as the 'fourth wave' – was similarly seen as a threat to fragile rural destinations. As a result, the planning philosophy of the day was not to manage but to contain the threat by diverting demand to newly-created facilities, specifically country parks developed closer to major centres of population (Sharpley, 1996).

More recently, however, the effective management of tourism's impacts has assumed a more positive role as a fundamental element of sustainable tourism development. In other words, it has become more broadly synonymous with optimising the longer-term benefits of tourism to local communities, to the environment and to tourists themselves, rather than with the specific concern of environmental protection. Thus, Miss Harriet Martineau, who settled in Ambleside in the mid-1800s, certainly held enlightened and contemporary views when, in contrast to Wordsworth, she described the railway as "the best as well as the last and greatest change in the Lake District" (Martineau, 1855, cited in Berry and Beard, 1980: 2). That is, she foresaw the economic and social advantages that the railway, and the tourists it carried, would bring to the Lakes.

The purpose of this chapter, therefore, is to consider the impacts of tourism in the Lake District within the context of sustainable tourism development in the region. In so doing, it will not only highlight the principal consequences of tourism for the Lake District's environment, economy and local communities, but it will also address the ways in which these impacts are managed both sustainably and also, of course, according to the aims and objectives of a national park. Firstly, however, it briefly suggests a framework for addressing the impacts of tourism, and the management responses, within the Lake District.

Tourism Impacts in the Lake District: a framework for analysis

Not only are the impacts of tourism inevitable, but also they have been in evidence for as long as people have been tourists. As early as 1848, for example, Thomas Cook wrote in his handbook for visitors to Belvoir Castle in Leicestershire that:

> "It is very seldom indeed that the privileges extended to visitors of the mansions of the nobility are abused; but to the shame of some rude folk from Lincolnshire, there have been just causes of complaint at Belvoir Castle: some large parties have behaved indecorously, and they have to some extent prejudiced the visits of other large companies. Conduct of this sort is abominable, and cannot be too strongly reprobated" (Ousby, 1990: 89).

Similarly, some early tourist practices in the Lake District undoubtedly impacted upon the environment. For example, Rollinson (1967:139) describes how, in the early nineteenth century, some hotels and inns were equipped with small cannon; "on the payment of a fee the guns were discharged to produce an echo – the more money paid, the louder the echo". Moreover, much of the present-day built environment of the Lakes is directly related to the early development of tourism. By 1830, inns had been built even in the most remote dales, such as Buttermere, Ennerdale and Mardale (Rollinson, 1967), whilst the tourist centre of Windermere/Bowness is, essentially, a Victorian town that evolved to meet the growing numbers of tourists arriving by train at what was then the village of Birthwaite. Nor were such impacts always welcome. In 1934, for example, Cumberland County Council's plans to improve a number of roads within the central part of the region to provide better access for car-borne visitors were met with significant opposition (Berry and Beard,1980).

However, as observed above, it is only since the 1960s that concern for the impacts of tourism, both generally and in the particular context of the Lake District, have come to the fore. Moreover, it is no coincidence that such concerns have increased as participation in tourism has itself increased. Indeed, it is widely perceived, perhaps erroneously, that a causal relationship exists in any destination between the scale of tourism and its resultant impacts. Certainly, the early literature on tourism impacts, reflecting the prevailing 'Limits to Growth' development ideology, focused on the need to limit the growth and spread of tourism (Young, 1973; Turner and Ash, 1975; Smith, 1977; de Kadt,1979), whilst similar sentiments were frequently expressed in relation to the growth of tourism in the Lake District. For example, Nicholson, writing in 1963, observed that "it is not just that immense numbers of people now come to the Lakes

> ... it is rather that tourism is becoming the dominant industry of the area... Today the visitor is beginning to own the place and, if we are not careful, the whole area will be turned into one vast holiday camp" (Nicholson, 1963: 181).

Interestingly, Nicholson also hinted at the 'solution' that has now been widely adopted in tourism planning. That is, in suggesting that "the only real defence against the erosion of tourism is the survival of the living community, long-rooted in the locality, making its own way and at least partially independent of the visitor" (Nicholson, 1963: 181). He was foreseeing the emergence of sustainable development not only as the dominant tourism development paradigm but also as an implicit objective of national parks in the UK.

The important point here, however, is that although the highly ecocentric perspective of the 1960s and 1970s on the impacts of tourism has been superseded by a more pragmatic, knowledge-based approach (Jafari, 1989), the assessment of tourism's impacts and subsequent management responses – namely, sustainable tourism development – remain problematic. In particular, the study of tourism's impacts is, all too frequently generalised, focusing on specific impacts rather than on the location in which they occur, whilst the concept of sustainable tourism also represents, arguably, a prescriptive, generic and uncontextualised 'blueprint' response to the management of tourism that is unable to embrace heterogeneity of tourism destination environments (Southgate and Sharpley, 2002).

To put it another way, the environment within which tourism occurs and upon which it impacts is complex and dynamic. It may be defined as:

> "that vast array of factors which represent external (dis)-economies of a tourism resort: natural (air, water, soil, wildlife, climate), anthropological, economic, social, cultural, historical, architectural and infrastructural factors which represent a habitat onto which tourism activities are grafted and which is thereby exploited and changed by the exercise of tourism business" (EC,1993: 4).

Moreover, it is infinitely variable; the characteristics of destinations, and their inter-relationships, vary from one place to another to the extent that no two tourism destinations could claim to be identical. Implicitly, therefore, the nature and perceptions of tourism's impacts and appropriate management responses are also highly variable.

Figure 8.0   *A model for the study of the tourism impacts*

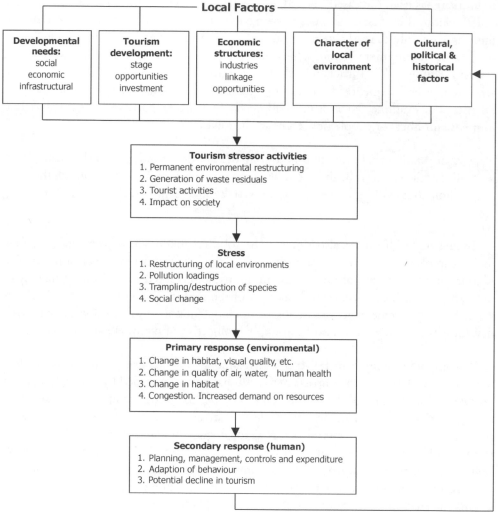

Source: adapted from OECD (1981)

This, in turn, suggests that, rather than assuming a causal relationship between certain forms of tourism development or tourist activity and their inevitable physical, social or economic consequences (and, consequently, proposing a 'one-size-fits-all' solution), there is a need to locate the study of tourism impacts within the particular socio-cultural, political and economic contexts of individual destinations. This would allow, for example, for local communities' environmental attitudes, economic and social needs and perceptions of 'acceptable damage' (Wight, 1998), as well as broader cultural, political and historical factors, to be taken into account. In short, there is a need to establish a framework for the study of tourism's impacts that takes into account the specific characteristics of different destinations.

One such framework is shown in Figure 8.0. Here, following a model proposed by the OECD (1981), the focus is not upon the environmental (physical, social and economic) resources but upon the tourism-related activities that put stress on the environment. The consequences of such stress are referred to as primary responses, whilst secondary responses are the management measures undertaken to limit or control environmental stress. Importantly, however, local factors, such as developmental needs, stage of tourism development, economic structures, political and historical characteristics, environmental values and so on, provide the dynamic context within which the stress-response model is located and, in a continual process, feed into responses to the consequences of tourism development and impacts.

What this framework suggests is that the impacts of tourism, both positive and negative, should not be viewed in isolation but within the dynamic environmental, economic, social and political context of the destination. At the same time, it also proposes that management responses should not be fixed but, rather, should reflect changes within the destination.

For the purposes of this chapter, it also provides the basis for exploring the impacts of tourism and management responses in the Lake District. That is, it highlights the need to consider the impacts of tourism in the area in relation to a variety of characteristics and influences which may determine how such impacts are viewed and what controls might be appropriate. These characteristics and influences include:

➢ The historical and contemporary importance of tourism to the environmental, social and economic development of the Lake District;

➢ Transformations in the area's social and economic structures;

➢ Competing demands, such as farming, forestry, water supply, transport, mineral extraction and military use, on natural and human resources;

➢ Transformations in the demand for and supply of tourism and recreation;

➢ Nature and extent of, and differences in, the physical environment – robust vs. fragile areas; open country vs. settlements, and so on;

➢ Patterns of land ownership and access;

➢ National policies: farming, transport, tourism development, rural development, etc.;

➢ Statutory objectives of national parks;

➢ Changing cultural attitudes towards the rural environment;

➢ Local tourism policy and administrative structures;

> ➤ Local organisational structures, ownership and roles.

This list is by no means exhaustive. However, it serves to indicate the complex political, social and environmental framework within which the impacts of tourism must be considered and, in the following analysis of tourism's impacts in the Lake District, reference will be made where relevant to particular factors or influences.

The Impacts of Tourism

Tourism development is not, of course, an end in itself but, rather, a means to an end. In other words, tourism is not developed and promoted simply to satisfy the needs of tourists, but for the potential benefits that it potentially brings to destination environments and communities. It is not surprising, therefore, that tourism represents an integral element of development policies at the local, national and international level (Jenkins, 1991). The extent to which this developmental contribution of tourism may be realised in practice is discussed widely in the literature (for example, Sharpley and Telfer, 2002). But, in the context of this chapter, tourism development may be considered, albeit simplistically, as a process of balancing the positive and negative impacts of tourism to the overall (sustainable) benefit of the Lake District's environment, communities and visitors.

For convenience, the analysis of the impacts of tourism in the Lake District is structured here under the three broad headings of economic impacts, environmental impacts and socio-cultural impacts. Under each heading, both positive and negative impacts are considered, as are the sustainable tourism management policies and practices related to each. Such an approach is, inevitably, artificial given the inter-relationship between each category of impact and the holistic, integrated approach demanded by sustainable tourism development. For example, the imposition of the Windermere speed limit, referred to in more detail later in the chapter, addresses the perceived negative impacts – in the context of a particular interpretation of the role of the National Park – of one type of tourist activity. Yet arguably it is creating another negative impact, namely, job losses within the local water-sports industry (though these are likely to be significantly fewer than initially anticipated). Nevertheless, the structure here represents the most appropriate and logical approach to assessing the impacts of tourism.

Economic Impacts

Traditionally, the developmental contribution of tourism has been measured in terms of its economic benefits, particularly income generation and employment creation, development (from the modernisation perspective) being considered synonymous with economic growth (see Telfer, 2002). Indeed, despite the broader social and environmental benefits that may accrue from tourism, it is its economic impact that remains the benchmark for the success of tourism development. Moreover, throughout Europe tourism is considered, supported and promoted as, specifically, an effective vehicle for the economic regeneration of peripheral rural areas (Cavaco, 1995; Hoggart *et al.*, 1995).

There can be no doubt that, for many years, tourism has played a vital economic role in the Lake District, a role that has become increasingly significant more recently as other sectors of the local economy, in particular farming, have continued to decline (see Chapter Three). The principal economic benefit, or positive impact of tourism, is usually measured in terms of its contribution to, firstly, local income and, secondly, employment.

Income

The most basic measurement of tourism-related income is tourist expenditure – that is, the total amount that tourists spend in a particular area over a specified period, usually a year. In the case of the Lake District National Park, however, two points must be emphasised. Firstly, tourism expenditure data relating to the National Park have, somewhat surprisingly, been available only recently as most surveys have considered tourism spending in the county of Cumbria as a whole. Therefore, trends in tourist expenditure within the National Park are not available, although it is safe to assume that the growth rate of tourism expenditure in Cumbria as a whole has been reflected, if not exceeded, within the park.

Secondly, a number of discrepancies are evident between the different sources of information; for example, the relative contribution of day visitors as opposed to tourists (those who stay overnight) varies significantly between different surveys. More importantly, perhaps, there are also differences in terminology; whereas the Cumbria Tourist Board's recent figures refer to 'spending', the STEAM (Scarborough Tourism Economic Activity Monitor) survey (Calway, 2001) refers to 'revenue'. The latter includes both direct expenditure (i.e. direct tourist spending on goods and services) and indirect expenditure, or expenditure generated through the so-called multiplier effect. Thus, in a survey undertaken in 1992 (Ecotec, 1993), tourist spending in Cumbria was calculated to be £446 million, but the total revenue generated by tourism was estimated to be £812 million, representing an overall multiplier of about 1.82. The £366 million difference between tourist spending and total revenue was made up of both indirect expenditure – that is, the "purchases of inputs from other local businesses by firms deriving part or all of their direct expenditure from visitors" (Ecotec 1993: 53) – and induced expenditure, representing local expenditure by those whose income is directly or indirectly derived from tourist spending.

Despite these difficulties in obtaining an accurate picture, however, there is no doubt tourism spending in Cumbria as a whole (and, implicitly, within the National Park) is not only of great importance to the local economy, but has also increased significantly over the last decade. Indeed, taking direct tourist expenditure as the basis of measurement, direct tourist spending rose from £446 million in 1992 (Ecotec, 1993) to £918 million in 2001 (see Table 8.1).

Table 8.1   *Tourist spending in Cumbria: 1992 and 2001*

	Day Visitor Spend (£mn)	Overnight Visitor Spend (£mn)	Overnight as a % of Total Spend	Total Spend (£mn)
1992	107.6	338.4	76	446
2001	142	776	84	918

Source: adapted from Ecotec (1993) and CTB (2002a)

It is important to point out, of course, that 2001 was an exceptional year, both in Cumbria and the UK as a whole, as the Foot and Mouth Disease crisis led to a significant drop in tourism in rural areas (see Blake *et al.* 2002). Indeed, Cumbria, along with Devon, was one of the worst affected areas, suffering an overall loss of about £230 million in tourist spending. Therefore, the following discussion of economic impacts is based primarily upon figures for 2000, this being the most recent 'normal' year for which full figures are available at the time of writing.

According to Calway (2001), total tourism revenue in Cumbria in 2000 amounted to £981 million, accounting for 18 per cent of the county's Gross Domestic Product (GDP) of £5,350 million. Interestingly, recent figures indicate that tourism revenue in Cumbria in 2002 amounted to £769 million, or £7 million *below* the 2001 figure (Cumbria 2002) – this does not, however, include figures for day-visits. Moreover, early indications suggest that 2003 will prove to be a record year for the region. Within the Lake District National Park, tourism revenue in 2000 was calculated to be some £551 million, or 56 per cent of countywide tourism revenue and 10 per cent of county GDP. This represents a significant increase over the reported £453.6 million value of tourism in the Lake District in 1999 (see www.thisisthelakedistrict.co.uk). Estimates of the contribution of tourism to the National Park's GDP are not available, although it is likely to be significantly higher than the county figure noted above given the relative lack of other economic or industrial activities within the park's boundaries. Importantly, the 2000 STEAM research indicated that, of the total £981 million tourism revenue, £240 million, or 25 per cent, is indirect expenditure generated through the multiplier effect. This suggests a countywide multiplier of 1.32, significantly lower than the multiplier indicated in the 1992 survey referred to earlier. Table 8.2 shows the expenditure by sector for Cumbria and the National Park.

Table 8.2   *Tourism revenue by sector: Lake District and Cumbria 2000*

	National Park (£m)	National Park (%)	Cumbria (£m)	Cumbria (%)
Accommodation	138.9	25	247.7	25
Food and Drink	93.9	17	168.5	17
Recreation	21.1	4	36.8	4
Shopping	60.4	11	112.2	11
Transport	38.4	7	65.3	7
Indirect	137.1	25	240.0	25
VAT	61.7	11	110.3	11
Total	551.3	100	980.9	100

Source: adapted from Calway (2001)

From the perspective of sustainable development, the most important point is the fact that the Lake District is enormously dependent upon tourism as a source of income and, as discussed shortly, employment is, hence, highly susceptible to changes in what has always been regarded as a volatile tourist market. Indeed, this dependency may be considered one of the principal economic 'costs' of tourism in the area (see below). At the same time, however, it is also important to note the different share of expenditure generated by day visitors and those staying overnight (see Table 8.3).

Table 8.3   *Comparison of size and value of day visitor and overnight tourist markets*

	No. of visits (mn)	% of all visits	Tourist days (mn)	% of total tourist days	Revenue (£mn)	% of total revenue
Day visitors	11.5	84	11.5	58	195.5	35
Overnight tourists	2.2	16	8.4	42	355.8	65
Total	13.7	100	19.9	100	551.3	100

Source: Calway (2001)

As can be seen from Table 8.3, day visitors account for 84 per cent of all visitors to the Lake District but 58 per cent of total tourist days spent in the area. Conversely, just 16 per cent of visitors stay for at least one night, yet overnight tourists account for 42 per cent of total tourist days and, most significantly, 65 per cent of total tourist revenue. Crudely, this suggests that each day visitor spends about £7 per day, whereas an overnight tourist spends about £162 per stay or roughly £42 per day (equivalent figures for 2000 cited by the Cumbria Tourist Board are £192 per stay and £53 per day). Interestingly, the

1992 survey (Ecotec 1993) also found that average day visitor spend was approximately £7 per day, whereas average daily expenditure of overnight tourists was around £24.

Although a direct comparison of these figures is not valid owing to different data collection methods and inevitable changes in the share and costs of different types of accommodation, it is evident that, although day visitors are most numerous and, implicitly, impact most upon the physical and social fabric of the Lake District, on a per capita basis they are worth relatively little to the local economy. Conversely, overnight tourists contribute most to the local economy. Therefore, it would be logical to assume that, in terms of the sustainable optimisation of tourism's contribution to the local economy, policies should focus on increasing the number of overnight tourists, particularly as average room occupancy in Cumbria in 2000 was just 48 per cent.

This is indeed the case, though implicitly rather than explicitly. As discussed in Chapter Five, the principal responsibility for tourism policy in the National Park and Cumbria lies with Cumbria Tourist Board (CTB). In its most recent policy document, *The Regional Tourism Strategy for Cumbria* (CTB 1998), the CTB outlines a number of strategies for sustaining tourism's economic contribution. These include:

> ➢ Increasing the economic benefit of tourism as a whole throughout Cumbria by (a) encouraging development outside the National Park whilst (b) continuing to support the established industry within the park.

> ➢ Improving occupancy levels through a variety of means, including a focus on quality/value for money, marketing the "unique selling points of destinations and individual attractions" (CTB, 1998: 13), and targeting specific holiday markets, especially the 45+ age group short-break sector.

> ➢ Extending the season in order to stabilise the income earned from tourism.

Inevitably, these policies also have an influence on tourism-related employment which, as the following section discusses, is also a principal economic benefit of tourism.

Employment

Whether at the local, national or international scale, tourism is considered a valuable source of employment. Globally, almost 11 per cent of the world's workforce is employed in tourism whilst in the UK, the tourism sector accounts for 7 per cent of employment. Tourism is also regarded as an important source of new or alternative work in areas, both urban and rural, that have suffered economic decline; in rural Britain, for example, the continuing fall in farming related income and employment has underpinned farm diversification and 'pluriactivity', with over 50 per cent of farms operating a non-farming business (see Countryside Agency, 2001). Moreover, in the north-west region, within which Cumbria and the Lake District falls, agriculture and fishing account for just 1.6 per cent of all employment, the lowest proportion of all regions in England and Wales (Countryside Agency, 2002). Interestingly, information provided by the Lake District National Park Authority (LDNPA, 1998a) suggests that, based on the 1991 Census, 9.9

per cent of the workforce within the Lake District are employed in agriculture, forestry and fishing, well above the national average – at the time of writing, equivalent data from the 2001 Census are not available. However, there can be no doubting the importance not only of the contribution to overall employment in the Lake District, but also of sustaining the level, and increasing the 'quality' of, that employment.

In terms of the contribution of tourism to employment in the Lake District, figures are available from a variety of sources and, as with the data relating to tourism expenditure or revenue, some discrepancies are in evidence. The Lake District National Park Authority, for example, indicates that more than 50 per cent of the 'economically active' population of the park, or around 12,000 jobs, is directly dependent upon tourism (LDNPA, 1998a) – this does not include, however, those who work in the park but live beyond its borders. The STEAM model, conversely indicates that, in 2000, tourism supported almost 47,000 jobs across Cumbria as a whole (representing 24 per cent of total county employment), with 55 per cent of these, or 26,034 jobs, being based within the National Park. Of these, 83 per cent are direct tourism jobs and 17 per cent, or 4,401, are indirect (Calway, 2001). A similar figure is proposed by Leslie (2002), who estimates that there are around 15,600 direct tourism jobs, to which about 1,200 owners/managers and some 4,000 indirect jobs can be added. Surprisingly, perhaps, no data are available with respect to the proportion of jobs within the National Park that are directly or indirectly related to tourism but, nevertheless, it is evident that tourism is the major source of employment within the park for those who live both within and outside its borders, potentially accounting for between a half and three-quarters of all jobs in some parts of the park (Bingham ,1988: 93).

Of course, although the overall contribution of tourism to employment is important, it is of equal, if not greater, importance to consider the *nature* of those jobs. That is, criticism is frequently levelled at tourism-related employment creation inasmuch as jobs in the tourism industry tend to be lower-status, lower paid and, as service jobs, perhaps an inappropriate form of work for people more used to other, previous forms of employment. It has been observed, for example, that farmers diversifying into tourism have found it difficult to adapt to the role of service-provider (Hjalager, 1996; Fleischer and Pizam, 1997). At the same time, it is often claimed that tourism jobs are not 'real' jobs (Pearce, 1989: 200), as many are part-time and/or seasonal positions occupied by students or others who are not part of the 'official' labour force. Nevertheless, in peripheral rural areas tourism may, at least in the shorter term, represent the only realistic source of employment and, therefore, the challenge is to improve the nature of the jobs available.

In the Lake District, the seasonality of the tourism industry and, hence, of jobs is less marked than might be imagined. In recent years, the demand for tourism in Cumbria and the Lake District has become more evenly spread throughout the year, although the peak summer season remains the most popular time to visit the region. According to Cumbria Tourist Board (2002a), for example, 31 per cent of visits were made in the July-September period in 2000, 28 per cent in April-June, 24 per cent in October-December and 17 per cent in January-March. Similar figures, though related to revenue as opposed to the number of visits, are provided by Calway (2001) – see Table 8.4.

Table 8.4   *Tourism revenue (%) by quarter, 2000*

	Jan-Mar	**Apr-June**	**July-Sept**	**Oct-Dec**
Lake District National Park	15	28	37	20
Cumbria	16	28	36	20

Source: adapted from Calway (2001)

As a result, recent research into tourism employment in Cumbria found that the majority of tourism businesses in Cumbria operate all year round, with just 36 per cent of hotels and 30 per cent of visitor attractions operating seasonally (Scott, 2002). These 'seasonal' businesses are all open for at least eight months, and some are only closed in January. Thus, although almost half of hotels and up to 80 per cent of attractions do in fact employ seasonal staff, the actual proportion of seasonal staff compared to the number of permanent staff in the tourism sector is relatively low. The most common seasonal jobs are waiting jobs in hotels and restaurants.

Despite this limited influence of seasonality, however, the research referred to above identified a number of factors or characteristics of tourism employment in Cumbria that may be considered more typical of tourism jobs (see Scott, 2002). These include:

➤   The majority of hotels, restaurants and attractions in the region are small businesses employing fewer than 25 staff; one third of hotels and two-thirds of restaurants employ between one and ten staff.

➤   Female employees are predominant within the sector.

➤   There is a significant proportion (approximately 40 per cent) of part-time employment within hotels and attractions. Restaurants are heavily weighted towards part-time staff, with 72 per cent of jobs provided on this basis. This supports the assertion that, between 1981 and 1991, there was a 51 per cent increase in part-time employment in the Lake District (LDNPA, 1998a).

➤   One third of all tourism businesses employ casual staff – many of these tend to be overseas students/travellers who fulfil an important function as it is suggested that there is relatively little local interest in casual work in the tourism sector (Scott, 2002).

In addition, the research identified a number of issues that tend to contribute to the poor reputation of tourism-related employment. Firstly, a small but significant number of businesses were found not to offer contracts of employment, despite a legal requirement to do so. This was particularly prevalent in smaller, family run businesses. Similarly, smaller businesses were less likely to provide their employees with job descriptions. Secondly, in terms of employee benefits, secure benefits such as full sick pay and contributory pension schemes were rarely offered, although many businesses indicated that they provide transport to work for their staff. A large proportion of businesses, other than restaurants, also offer live-in accommodation for their staff. This is seen as a necessity by many businesses because it enables them to attract staff from elsewhere in Cumbria and the UK or from overseas – recruitment of local staff has proved to be difficult and, for potential non-local workers, the cost and availability of alternative accommodation is prohibitive. Thirdly, although all the businesses surveyed pay the minimum wage or above, pay levels remain low for basic jobs.

Collectively, these issues reinforce the notion that, in general, employment in tourism offers poor career prospects and, therefore, undermine the potential contribution of tourism to maintaining a sustainable source of local employment. Moreover, it is unsurprising, perhaps, that many businesses find it difficult to recruit appropriate staff, that turnover is relatively high, and that the staff they do employ lack some necessary skills, pointing to a longer-term challenge to the sustainability of tourism in the Lake District.

However, these problems have not gone unrecognised. Based upon the research described above, Cumbria Tourist Board has proposed a workforce development plan to 'ensure that our workforce contributes to the sustainable nature of tourism in Cumbria' (CTB, 2002b: 2). Its recommendations include:

> ➤ exploring means of creating quality careers in tourism to attract quality, career-oriented entrants into the industry;

> ➤ attracting staff from a wider range of groups;

> ➤ establishing links with local schools and colleges;

> ➤ improving employment practices within the industry;

> ➤ introducing appropriate training programmes for tourism businesses; and

> ➤ identifying career paths and progression for employees.

Evidently, achieving such a fundamental shift in the nature of jobs and employment practices within the tourism industry in an area such as the Lake District represents a long-term challenge and goal – for many businesses, a more pressing need is simply to be able to recruit staff and to remain in business in a volatile market. However, the experience of the Lake District points to the importance of appropriate employment policies as an integral element of sustainable tourism development, something which, interestingly, is also in accordance with one of the main aims of the most recent national policy for rural tourism *Working for the Countryside* (ETC/CA, 2001). This strategy aims to, amongst other things, maintain and increase the availability and quality of employment in rural tourism enterprises. Nevertheless, as the next section suggests, there is also a need to reduce the dependency upon tourism as a source of both income and employment.

Economic costs

Tourism undoubtedly provides significant economic benefits to the Lake District in terms of income and employment. At the same time, however, it also incurs significant economic costs, although these cannot usually be directly 'balanced' against the benefits. In other words, the costs of, for example, refuse collection or the policing of popular areas, particularly at peak periods, are part of the public services provided for, and paid by, the community at large through local taxation. Thus, to separate such costs directly attributable to tourism from those for services provided to the local community would be a difficult task.

A variety of other costs (other than private sector investment in services, facilities and attractions) are also incurred in the provision of tourism services or, more generally, in encouraging and enabling tourists to visit and enjoy the Lakes. For example, road improvements, the provision of car parks and lay-byes, picnic areas, public toilets, information services, waymarked trails, as well as the task of maintaining and repairing footpaths, all require significant investments made by a variety of organisations in the public and voluntary sectors.

In addition to these tangible economic costs of developing and maintaining tourism, other impacts are also often referred to as economic costs. These include issues such as the higher cost of housing within the National Park, the costs associated with road congestion, particularly at peak periods, and the costs of essential goods and services for local people. These and other impacts more logically fall under the heading of environmental and social impacts and are, therefore, considered in more detail later.

In the context of this chapter, however, two specific economic costs demand attention as they potentially limit the sustainable development of the area. These are, firstly, the problem of 'leakages' and, secondly, the issue of dependency on tourism.

(a) Leakages

An economic problem facing all tourism destinations is the 'leakage' of tourism revenue out of the region, either through expenditure on non-local products (i.e. 'imports') to satisfy the needs of tourists or through the indirect expenditure of those who earn an income from tourism. This is commonly thought to be a particular problem for tourism destinations, especially islands, in the developing world. Yet, according to the latest rural tourism strategy for England document referred to above, "in rural areas, the proportion of visitor spending retained locally averages only 30 per cent in accommodation, 20 per cent in catering and attractions and 5 per cent in retail businesses" (ETC/CA, 2001: 10).

One solution – and a key principle for sustainable rural tourism (Countryside Commission, 1995) that is endorsed in the Lake District National Park Authority's Park Management Plan (LDNPA, 1999) – is to encourage forms of tourism that retain visitor spending in local communities. However, this somewhat general principle is difficult to implement in an established destination such as the Lake District and, therefore, it is more feasible to focus on two more specific targets, namely: developing more opportunities for local employment; and encouraging the tourism sector to source its goods and services locally whilst promoting the sale of local goods to visitors. The issue of employment has been addressed above and, given the current difficulties encountered by the tourism industry in recruiting locally (exacerbated by the fact that, according to the 2001 Census, the proportion of 15-40 year olds in the county is below the national average. This points to a continuing challenge – see www.statistics.gov.uk/census2001), it is unlikely that any reduction in earnings-related leakages is achievable in the shorter-term.

More positively, however, recent research suggests that the practice of local sourcing of goods and services by the tourism sector enjoys widespread support within the Lake District. For example, it has been observed that most sectors of the industry 'spend substantial sums of money locally purchasing supplies and maintaining properties' (Friends of the Lake District, 2001: 7), purchases generally being made from suppliers within the National Park. From the opposite perspective, some 80 per cent of the sales of food producers in Cumbria are generated within the park. Similarly, the recent Cumbria Sustainable Tourism Baseline Survey 2000 survey (Enteleca, 2000) found that, of those tourism businesses in the county able to estimate the proportion of goods and services sourced from within the county, almost 27 per cent believed that more than 50 per cent of their goods and services were sourced within the local district, and 47 per cent believed that more then 50 per cent were sourced from within Cumbria as a whole

Nevertheless, it has also been found that there is limited awareness of what products are available locally, and that perceptions of costs, availability and quality tend to deter local purchasing. Indeed, the Baseline survey concluded that more could be done to promote and encourage local supply opportunities, although the Countryside Agency's national 'Eat the View' initiative has gone some way to support this objective. Launched in July 2000, the 'Eat the View' programme aims to increase consumer awareness of, and demand for, locally and regionally distinctive products in order to support rural communities and the sustainable management of the English countryside. In the Lake District, two projects are of note (see Box 8.1)

Box 8.1   'Eat the View' projects in Cumbria

Made in Cumbria

Initiated by Cumbria County Council in 2000, 'Made in Cumbria' is a scheme that supports small-scale food producers in the county. It has some 60 members and has helped 26 new businesses start up from scratch. The scheme's principal marketing effort has been the development of a network of farmers markets around the county, although no such market has yet been established within the National Park. Nevertheless, according to Friends of the Lake District (2001), 'Made in Cumbria' is the most recognised green initiative in Cumbria, known by 68 per cent of businesses.

Cumbrian Fellbred

This scheme is a partnership between local meat businesses and a local supermarket chain. Supported by European funding as a benefit to farmers in the Objective 5b area of Cumbria, the scheme brands selected lamb and beef as 'Cumbrian Fellbred' which is then sold at a premium price in the supermarket, with farmers also receiving a premium price for their products. Public awareness of the scheme has been raised by TV and press advertising throughout the North West of England and, as a result, meat sales in the supermarket chain trebled between 2000 and 2001 and, more importantly, 70 businesses were secured and 20 new jobs created.

Source: www.eat-the-view.org.uk

These projects have also, to an extent, contributed to alleviating another economic cost of tourism, namely an excessive dependence on tourism.

(b) Dependency

Although not a direct economic cost in the strict sense of the word, an over-dependency on a particular sector or industry, such as tourism, represents a potential cost when, as a result of factors beyond its control, that industry loses business or goes into decline. In the case of the Lake District, the tourism sector is, and has long been, a major employer and contributor to the economy of the National Park. Indeed, the area's dependence on tourism was starkly revealed in 2001 when, as a result of the Foot and Mouth Disease (FMD) outbreak, much of the English countryside was, in effect, closed to visitors (see Sharpley and Craven, 2001). The massive losses incurred by the rural tourism industry on the national scale were reflected in Cumbria, where the FMD crisis resulted in a £200 million reduction in direct revenue and a further £60 million loss in the wider economy. Moreover, at the height of the outbreak, tourism business turnover in the worst affected areas was reduced by some two-thirds, causing many businesses to virtually cease trading (Cumbria County Council, 2002). Not surprisingly, therefore, it has been observed that the sustainable, "long term future of the economy would be better based on diversity rather than an over-dependence on one such dominant sector" (Friends of the Lake District, 2001: 9).

In other words, unlike many other peripheral rural areas in Britain that are seeking to diversify *into* tourism, there is a need in the Lake District to diversify *out of* tourism. This is recognised by the Lake District National Park Authority; as part of its statutory duties, it is required by the Environment Act 1995 to 'seek to foster the economic and social well-being of local communities'. This reflects the recognition that "National Parks are a product of the economic and social development of their local communities" (Lake District National Park Authority, 1999: 4). With regard to tourism, the Authority accepts that overdependence on one industry (i.e. tourism) 'may carry significant risks for local communities in the medium to long term' (Lake District National Park Authority, 1999: 69). Therefore, whilst recognising that a buoyant tourism industry is crucial to the future of the area, it argues that efforts should be made to diversify the economy as well as strengthening those traditional industries, in particular farming, that have endowed the Lake District with its environmental and socio-cultural character.

In order to achieve a more diverse economy, the Authority's stated aim (Lake District National Park Authority, 1999: 66) is to:

➢ identify and allocate suitable land for new business or industrial uses;

➢ facilitate the re-use of appropriate traditional buildings; and

➢ protect existing business sites from new uses which would adversely affect the range of job opportunities (see also Lake District National Park Authority, 1998b).

With respect to farming in particular, a thriving industry is considered vital in providing both a secure living and contributing to the environmental and social character of the Lake District. Almost all of the National Park falls within the Lake District Environmentally Sensitive Area (ESA) Scheme which compensates farmers for managing their land in environmentally appropriate ways. However, the Authority also seeks more specific ways of supporting the farming sector, such as a new project, the Fell Farming Futures Experiment (supported by the Lake District Sustainable Development Fund), which aims to provide training to farmers in countryside skills and to add value to local products. The protection of traditional farming in the area is also underpinned by the National Trust's ownership of 91 Lake District farms, whilst the Cumbria Tourist Board sees an important role for tourism in the maintenance of a healthy farming industry:

> "it is anticipated that the additional income generated by farm tourism will offer considerable support to farming businesses and rural communities through the generation of additional income, and by creating and safeguarding new and existing jobs and services" (Cumbria Tourist Board, 1998: 36).

Environmental Impacts

Understanding and managing the environmental impacts of tourism is, in effect, synonymous with sustainable tourism. In other words, tourism is an environmentally dependent industry (Mowl, 2002; Holden,2000); tourists seek out different, distinctive or attractive environments and yet, by their very presence, threaten the physical well-being of those environments. Indeed, the concept of sustainable tourism originally emerged as a result of increasing concerns over the impacts of tourism on the physical environment, from the adverse effects of the development of winter-sports tourism on Alpine ecosystems to the (over) development of the mass tourism resorts along the Spanish 'costas'.

National parks and other protected areas are, of course, particularly susceptible to environmental degradation (FNNPE, 1993; WTO/UNEP, 1992) – they are afforded protection because of their fragile or unique landscapes or ecosystems, but such protection maintains their attraction to ever increasing numbers of visitors. This is certainly so in the case of the Lake District which suffers a variety of negative environmental impacts, from the pollution (physical, noise and visual) of excessive levels of traffic to the serious erosion of footpaths on the fells. At the same time, however, it is important to note that, frequently, tourism also supports the conservation and improvement of the Lakeland environment, whether through the renovation and re-use of traditional buildings or through schemes which directly link tourism with conservation projects. Chapter Five explains the role of the Lake District Tourism and Conservation partnership that is an example of good practice in landscape management.

Thus, tourism has both negative and positive environmental impacts in the Lake District although, in the context of this book, to simply list and discuss them all would serve little purpose. That is, the environmental impacts of tourism in the Lake District are no different to those experienced in other rural areas, although in some instances they maybe more acute or intense. Of greater relevance are the policies and processes designed to facilitate the sustainable management of tourism's environmental impacts and it is on these, therefore, that this section will primarily focus. Firstly, however, it is important to consider the broader context of tourism within the Lake District within which particular environmental impacts should be addressed.

Environmental impacts – the tourism context

As observed at the beginning of this chapter, the Lake District possesses a variety of characteristics and influences that may determine how the environmental impacts of tourism are viewed and what controls might be appropriate. These include, of course, the planning controls and restrictions imposed by the area's overall status as a National Park, which have a significant influence on the nature and scale of tourism developments. At the same time, patterns of land ownership and different degrees of robustness of the physical environment also determine the nature of impacts and potential management policies.

However, by making reference to the 'tourism stressor activities' highlighted in Figure 8.1 above, it is possible to place specific environmental impacts in the broader context of the Lake District, thereby identifying those impacts that are of most significance.

(a) Permanent environmental restructuring

This refers to permanent changes in the physical fabric of an area resulting from the development of tourism facilities, attractions and associated infrastructure, such as roads, car parks and so on. Importantly, much of the Lake District's physical development has occurred over the last two centuries as it has become an increasingly popular tourist destination and some urban centres, such as Windermere and Bowness, effectively owe their existence to tourism. Thus, much of the tourism infrastructure that has developed over time has become part of the area's present attraction. The challenge, therefore, is to ensure that tourism developments should be in keeping with the existing buildings and infrastructure, or of a "character and scale which respects the quality of the environment" (Lake District National Park Authority, 1999: 69) to which previous developments have contributed.

The building or improvement of roads, along with associated facilities such as car parks, lay-byes and road signs, is also an indirect environmental impact of tourism; moreover, it has long been a source of contention within the Lake District. For example, the upgrading of the A66 through the northern Lake District was, at the time, enormously controversial. However, until such time that there is major shift in transport policy (and the behaviour of the travelling public) towards public transport systems, the majority of visitors will continue to arrive by car. Therefore, environmental management policies in this context need to focus on overall effective traffic management rather than simply on road building projects (see Chapter Seven), a fact recognised by Cumbria Tourist Board which proposed a variety of measures to facilitate car-borne visitors (CTB, 1998).

(b) Generation of waste residuals

The generation of waste, resulting in the pollution of air, land and water resources, is a particular problem facing most tourist destinations and the Lake District is no exception. The reduction in air pollution resulting from traffic congestion is, of course, linked to traffic management policies but the pollution of both land and water in the Lake District can mar tourists' experiences as well as posing a health hazard, particularly where people swim in lakes. Some ten years ago, for example, headlines in the national newspapers stated that 'Users turn Windermere into a sewer', with 500 sacks of litter having to be removed from the lake shores. Therefore, there is a need for management policies that both lead to the effective clearance of litter and other physical pollution and minimise the creation of such pollution in the first place.

(c) Tourist activities

The most significant source of environmental stress is the activities of tourists themselves. That is, the physical presence of tourists, often in large numbers, inevitably has an impact on the physical environment. More often than not, such impacts occur as a result of legitimate activities on the part of tourists and the degree to which they become evident depends very much upon the robustness of the environment. Thus, large numbers of visitors in the tourist honeypots, such as Windermere/Bowness or Ambleside, have relatively little physical impact other than crowding and the generation of wastes, whereas the Lakeland fells have proved to be highly susceptible to the most popular physical activity in the area, namely, walking. Indeed, though a seemingly innocuous activity, walking on the fells has created a serious problem of footpath erosion, perhaps the most significant form of environmental impact in the Lake District.

Within the NationPark, there are 3,595 km of rights of way, these being predominantly footpaths, along which people may only walk/run, and bridleways, along which people pass on foot, on horseback or on bicycle. Access is also legally allowed for motor vehicles along unsurfaced unclassified roads, green lanes and other ancient byways across the open fells. The erosion of these rights of way is not, in fact, a recent problem; it has been observed that, 'in 1819, a Lakeland traveller arriving … in Langdale, via Stake Pass from Borrowdale, complained that the route he had just travelled was seriously eroded and in a worse condition than when travelled 10 years previously' (Lake District National Park Authority, 2000). However, since the 1970s, a variety of factors have contributed to erosion becoming a significant environmental problem. These include:

> Increasing popularity of walking on the fells – a 1994 survey revealed that 87 per cent of visitors to the Lake District use footpaths.

> Lengthening of the season – for a number of reasons, including better equipment and changes in demand, many popular routes are walked all year round, not allowing paths to 'recover'.

> New activities – although cycling is actively encouraged as a sustainable form of transport around the Lake District's roads and lanes, the increasing popularity of mountain-biking on bridleways (and illegally on footpaths) is increasing the degree of erosion as well as conflicting with other users. The increasing use of all-terrain four-wheel-drive vehicles on green lanes and other byways is also a serious cause of concern, whilst the greater incidence of events, such as charity walks involving large numbers of walkers, tends to concentrate pressure on paths and trails at the same time as exacerbating traffic/parking problems in the valleys.

Footpath/trail erosion is, perhaps, not only the most visible environmental impact of tourism in the Lake District, but also the most powerful evidence of the conflict between the twin (conservation and recreation provision) aims of national parks. To meet the challenge of managing sustainable access to the fells, the Upland Access Management Group, comprising the National Trust, the Park Authority and English Nature, was established in 1993 to provide a co-ordinated approach to maintaining upland routes. In addition to agreeing a set of guiding principles for footpath maintenance, the Group undertook a survey in 1999 which suggested that some 41,690 man days of work, costing £4,656,512, would be needed to repair the most seriously eroded paths. Such work is on-going, though it is complex, expensive and time consuming; for example, repairing just 450 metres of path off the Buttermere ridge involved six organisations, took three years, and cost £43,000 – one third of which was the cost of airlifting materials by helicopter (Lake District National Park Authority, 2000).

As discussed next, other projects have been implemented which enable tourists themselves to contribute to footpath maintenance and repair, representing a 'true' example of sustainable tourism. However, prevention rather than cure is seen to be the most appropriate solution to the erosion problem and, therefore, a variety of measures are taken, including:

➢ constructing hard-wearing, user-friendly paths;

➢ regular maintenance;

➢ resting routes, by changing the line of paths or re-routing walkers along different paths;

➢ reducing use of the most popular routes by, for example, reducing car parking spaces;

➢ educating users through codes of practice, notices and talks.

In the case of mountain-biking and all-terrain vehicle use on green lanes, attempts have been made to encourage appropriate use through voluntary codes established with bodies such as LARA (Land Access and Recreation Association), an organisation that promotes the responsible use of the countryside by recreation vehicles. However, in the case of all-terrain vehicle use where voluntary schemes have not been successful, the Park Authority has been obliged to impose local Traffic Regulation Orders, though these have proved difficult to police.

In addition to the problem of footpath erosion, environmental stress results from a variety of other legitimate tourist activities. For example, public access is currently allowed (other than along rights of way) over some 25 per cent of the National Park area, a proportion that will increase significantly once the wider access rights to open countryside enshrined in the Countryside and Rights of Way Act 2000 become fully implemented. Thus, activities such as climbing, scree-running, scrambling on crags and gills, camping (legally or otherwise), or simply walking across open land have an inevitable impact on vegetation, wildlife and rocks. At the same time, inappropriate activities (whether through malice or ignorance) also have environmental impacts or cause conflicts with other uses of the land. Illegal car parking, for example, often damages road verges and campfires may destroy vegetation, whilst walkers leaving rubbish or gates open on farmland, or allowing dogs to run off the leash, frequently cause problems for hill farmers. Finally, certain tourist activities have an impact that either conflicts with the enjoyment of other visitors or are deemed to be inappropriate in a national park environment. The most publicised response to such a problem is the recent imposition of the 10mph speed limit on Windermere which has, in effect, banned motorised water sports, such as water-skiing and jet-skiing, from the lake (see Box 8.3 below).

As pointed out above, an extensive description of all the environmental impacts of tourism in the Lake District would serve little purpose. However, as the following section shows, a variety of policies and practices are in place that collectively seek to manage such impacts within the context of the sustainable development of the area.

Tourism: managing its environmental impacts

A list of resource management strategies proposed by the World Tourism Organisation (WTO ,1997) provides a useful framework for considering the management and planning responses to the environmental impacts of tourism in the Lake District (see Table 8.5).

Figure 8.5   *Tourism impacts: planning and management strategies*

Policy/planning	Overall development plans which include tourism.
	Policies and/or regulations to control tourism development.
	Policies for encouraging sustainable tourism resource use.
Development/construction of facilities	Appropriate site choice and site design for development
	Encourage local style, minimal impact construction techniques.
Management of resources	Conduct environmental audits.
	Implement waste minimisation and recycling programmes.
Management of visitors	Systems/processes to control visitor flows.
	Interpretation to encourage sustainable behaviour.
Adapting the environment	Harden sites for protection.
	Facilities to adapt/influence visitor behaviour.
Marketing and promotion	Consider products better suited to the environment.
	Provide information to manage tourist expectations and behaviour.
Education	Develop codes of conduct for staff and visitors.
	Develop education/information services to promote sustainable behaviour.
Research and monitoring	Support research that improves understanding of the tourism-environment relationship.
	Monitor environmental quality/change.

Source: adapted from WTO (1997)

Most, if not all, of these strategies are of relevance to the Lake District context and, as is now summarised, are evident in the policies and work of a number of organisations involved in the planning and management of tourism. Inevitably, however, emphasis is more strongly placed on some strategies than others in order to address specific challenges, whilst there is not always a clear distinction between some strategies.

(a) Policy and planning

Both of the principal organisations concerned with tourism policy at a park-wide level, namely, the Cumbria Tourist Board and the Lake District National Park Authority, embrace the broad policy of sustainable tourism development in general whilst proposing more specific policies and strategies for the sustainable use of environmental resources. The CTB, for example, sought to "ensure that tourism development not only respects environmental limits but also meets the objectives of securing long-term social and economic benefits for the county" (CTB, 1998: 32). Within this broad objective, its policies included:

> ➢ minimising the impacts of tourism by not pursuing developments that will damage the landscape or settlements, cause congestion, lead to conflict between recreational activities or introduce noisy activities;

> ➢ seeking additional resources to maintain and enhance the fabric of the landscape and, in particular, the network of paths and trails;

> ➢ marketing the area in a manner sensitive to conservation interests;

> ➢ promoting green business (see (c) below).

The Lake District National Park Authority, guided by its statutory duty to conserve and enhance the area's natural beauty and cultural heritage whilst promoting the understanding and (implicitly, 'quiet' or appropriate) enjoyment of its special qualities, similarly supports the development and promotion of sustainable rural tourism. It also seeks to promote good environmental practice on the part of tourism businesses, whilst its specific activities with respect to traffic management, footpath maintenance, pollution control and visitor management (see below) attempt to balance the need to conserve the environment with promoting tourism. For example, whilst seeking to promote alternative transport use (in 2001, a donation of £5000 from Railtrack was used to fund public transport displays in Tourist Information Centres), in 2002 it also provided free disabled parking in its car parks at a cost of £40,000.

However, both Cumbria Tourist Board and the Lake District National Park Authority recognised that effective environmental management is dependent upon partnership and co-operation. Thus, in 1993 the Lake District Tourism and Conservation Partnership (LDTCP) (see case study in Chapter Five) was established as a means of linking tourists and tourism businesses with the organisations seeking to protect the Lake District's landscape and manage the impact of visitor pressure on the environment (see Chapter Five). Its founding members were the LDNPA, CTB and the National Trust and, over the last decade, the LDTCP has assumed a leading role in alleviating the environmental impacts of tourism. By 1995, its conservation projects were securing substantial private sector sponsorship and in 1997 the LDTCP became an independent, non-profit company funded by its 114 members (individuals and businesses) who provide 70 per cent of its finance, the remainder provided by the founding partners and other grants from national bodies.

The LDTCP principally operates visitor payback schemes to fund footpath repair, bridge restoration, habitat protection, woodland protection, and so on. These operate in a variety of ways, such as 'donation/voluntary' boxes, percentage-of-sales schemes and special fund-raising events. However, the most widely-used and effective methods are 'opt-in' or 'opt-out' schemes, whereby tourists positively decide whether to opt in or out of paying an extra amount on bills to go towards identified conservation projects. One successful example is the LDTCP's 'Our Man at the Top' scheme, which currently supports the restoration and repair of footpaths in the Langdales, Borrowdale and the Grasmere area – both visitor payback and direct funding from local businesses had raised over £70,000 to date. Overall, the Partnership has raised over £250,000 since 1995, supporting over 80 different projects, whilst it also promotes awareness of sustainable tourism and acts to build a relationship between business, conservation and amenity organisations. It also acts as a focus for other organisations' fundraising activities – recently, for example, the Rheged visitor centre near Penrith donated some £2000 that it had collected in its wishing well to fund resurfacing work and the building of wooden platforms along a popular local riverside walk.

With respect to overall policy and planning, it is important to point out that LDNPA's policies for tourism are guided by the so-called Sandford principle, as enshrined in the 1994 Sandford Review of National parks. This proposes that, where conflict occurs between the purposes of conservation and recreation provision, the former should prevail to maintain the beauty and ecological quality of the area.

(b) Development/construction of facilities/adapting the environment

Overall responsibility for the planning of tourism facilities and attractions within the National Park lies, of course, with the Lake District National Park Authority as the planning authority. Beyond the park's borders, such responsibility returns to the relevant local authority.

The Lake District National Park Authority's policies with respect to the development and construction of tourism facilities and attractions are set out in detail in the National Park Local Plan (LDNPA, 1998b). A full review of these policies is well beyond the scope of this chapter but, in terms of minimising the detrimental impacts of tourism developments on the Lake District's environment, a number of points deserve emphasis. Principally, only developments that would not conflict with the quiet enjoyment of the park and that support the local economy are permitted whilst, based on the understanding that most tourism needs with respect to accommodation, catering and shopping can be met by existing provision within the park (or beyond its borders), "genuine needs for further provision should be met through the development of existing facilities, or through the conversion or re-use of building" (LDNPA, 1998: 41).

More specifically:

> ➤ Development in the open countryside, particularly designated quieter areas, is not permitted where this will cause demonstrable harm through increased traffic, increased recreational use or visual/noise intrusion.

> ➤ Lakeside developments are only permitted where they are associated with appropriate recreational use.

> ➤ New accommodation facilities and large-scale extensions to hotels and guesthouses are generally resisted.

> ➤ The Lake District's "natural beauty and seasonal diversity… continues to be the main visitor attraction" (LDNPA, 1998: 46); only small-scale, appropriate new attractions or facilities are, therefore, permitted.

In short, the National Park context and its associated planning and development regime provides an effective framework for minimising the environmental impacts of tourism developments.

(c) Management of resources

In recent years, two surveys have sought to identify the extent to which sustainable tourism resource management practices have been adopted by the local tourism industry (Enteleca, 2000; FLD, 2001). Though revealing some degree of environmental policy or practice, both concluded that, in general, there is a lack of awareness of the need for and benefits of sustainable resource management. Nevertheless, a recent pilot project, the 'Responsible Tourism Scheme' has been launched in South Lakeland. Funded by the English Tourism Council and co-ordinated by Cumbria Tourist Board and the LDTCP, the scheme aims to encourage local tourism businesses to embrace environmental practices, including an environmental self-assessment of their operations, whilst those participating will be able to highlight their support for sustainable tourism through a 'green label' or logo to be used in promotional material.

(d) Management of visitors/education

It has long been recognised that, in general, effective visitor management is essential for the achievement of sustainable tourism development (Sharpley, 1996), particularly as it is the activities of visitors themselves that, in a rural context, frequently result in environmental impacts. At the same time, it is also accepted that 'regulations are the antithesis of recreation, which connotes the spirit of freedom and spontaneity in the voluntary pursuit of pleasurable and rewarding experience in a preferred setting' (Jim, 1989). Thus, although some form of visitor management is usually necessary, it should, ideally, be unobtrusive and contribute to the overall visitor experience.

Cumbria Tourist Board considered that "to maximise the benefits of tourism and minimise possible pressure on the environment, effective visitor management… is vital" (CTB, 1998: 33). Similarly, visitor management, both to protect the environment and to avoid conflict between different recreational activities and other users of the land, is fundamental to the work and objectives of the Lake District National Park Authority. Such visitor management is manifested in a number of ways, some of which have already been referred to above in the context of footpath management. At the least 'regulatory' level (see Jim,1998), the Lake District National Park Authority produces and publishes a wide range of brochures, leaflets and interpretative panels designed to increase visitors' enjoyment and understanding of the National Park. On the Authority's website, for example, visitor information includes a section entitled: Are You a Good Walker? (see Box 8.2).

Box 8.2   Are You a Good Walker?

Careful walkers protect fragile and vulnerable paths.

Look where you're going

Every footstep causes wear and tear on the environment, and vegetation on the high fells is particularly vulnerable. Place your feet thoughtfully. Your boots are just one pair among many millions that tramp Lakeland paths each year.

Keep away from the edge

Follow the path surface and don't be tempted to walk to one side of it, along the grass and vegetation at the edge of a track. Trampled verges collapse, widening paths into broad, ugly scars.

Don't be led astray

Ignore short cuts and don't make new ones. Water will soon follow fresh tracks, causing damaging erosion. The seconds you save can take years to mend.

Source: www.lake-district.gov.uk

The Lake District National Park Authority also runs the Brockhole Visitor Centre near Windermere which, when it opened in 1969, was Britain's first National Park Visitor Centre. This provides exhibitions, information services and events to increase visitors' understanding of (and, implicitly, behaviour in) the park. Events are also held throughout the park on a regular basis, ranging from guided walks or bicycle rides to craft days.

Signposting or waymarking is also used as an effective form of visitor management employed throughout the area, either at a site level (for example, routing visitors away from sensitive areas) or more widely, as in the case of 'tourist routes' to direct tourists towards, or away from, particular places. Similarly, the provision or reduction of car parking spaces has proved to be an effective means of redistributing visitors, either reducing pressure on sensitive sites or encouraging people to visit more robust areas. At the same time, it is not only natural/landscape attractions that benefit from visitor management – for example, at Dove Cottage, near Grasmere, where William Wordsworth lived from 1799 to 1808, time-ticketing ensures that limited numbers of visitors are in the building at any one time.

In the extreme, however, it is sometimes necessary to impose more regulatory visitor management mechanisms in order to restrict access or particular activities that are deemed inappropriate. Mention has already been made of Traffic Regulation Orders to restrict off-road driving on green lanes but perhaps the most publicised visitor management strategy in recent years has been the imposition of a 10mph speed limit on Windermere (see Box 8.3).

Box 8.3   The Windermere Speed Limit

Despite the number of lakes within the Lake District, few may actually be used for watersports of any kind and, since 1981, when a speed limit of 10mph was imposed on Ullswater, only one lake, Windermere, had been open for motorised activities, such as water-skiing and jet-skiing. However, in 1991, the then Lake District Special Planning Board (now the LDNPA) decided to apply for a 10mph byelaw for Windermere, arguing that water-skiing and other forms of fast power boating were noisy, incompatible with government policies for national parks and conflicted with other quieter and more appropriate uses of the lake. Moreover, the results of a survey at that time suggested that the 'problem' of motorised water sports was increasing – it was found that, on an average day in 1991 there were 812 craft on the water, of which 368 were power boats, representing an increase of 300 per cent in fast boats since 1977.

There followed a protracted public enquiry which eventually found in favour of the byelaw; the outcome was, however, rejected by the then Environment Secretary on the basis of the loss of facilities for power boaters and the potential loss of local income and employment. Nevertheless, an appeal by the LDNPA led to a Judicial Review and, in 2000, subsequent confirmation that the 10mph byelaw will become effective from March 2005. This final decision was based on the belief that not only was there no reason to expect the Lake District to accommodate every kind of recreational activity, but also that the perceived desire of the majority is to enjoy quietly the special qualities of the area. Though not actually banning most motorised water sports from the lake, it is accepted that water-skiing and the use of jet-skis is difficult, if not impossible, at low speeds and, therefore, the speed limit is a form of regulatory visitor management that is being successfully applied to reduce conflicts between different recreational uses of the lake.

(See www.lake-district.gov.uk)

To conclude this section, then, a variety of methods are employed to address the environmental impacts of tourism in the Lake District. The need to protect and enhance the landscape is recognised by all those businesses and organisations involved in tourism in the area. Of particular note is the work of the Lake District Tourism and Conservation Partnership, an organisation which has successfully achieved a sustainable, symbiotic relationship between tourism and the environment.

Socio-cultural Impacts

Much attention is paid in the tourism literature to the social and cultural impacts of tourism (for example, Sharpley, 1999). In the context of the Lake District, however, it can be argued that, with the exception of the village of Grasmere (see case study below), the impacts of tourism, particularly the negative impacts, on local communities and Lakeland culture has been relatively limited. Certainly, at particular times of year the major towns and villages become overcrowded and traffic jams make it difficult for local people to go about their business, but other commonly-cited problems, such as local shops being replaced by souvenir/craft outlets or restaurants, have not occurred to any great extent – Windermere, Ambleside and Keswick remain thriving, diverse centres. Indeed, it is tourism that has underpinned the social and economic development of the Lake District and, thus, tourism has had a positive social impact in contributing to the continuation of local community life.

It is also probably true to say that, since the nineteenth century, tourism and tourists have become part of Lakeland life and, as a result, any social consequences of tourism are likely to be less keenly perceived than elsewhere. In fact, many local residents are former visitors who have retired to the area. However, this points to the one major social issue related to tourism, namely, the impact of second- and retirement-home ownership on housing costs and availability in the Lake District.

The popularity of the area for both holidays and as a retirement area has resulted in between 16 and 20 per cent of all homes in the Lake District being second and holiday homes, whilst in some places the proportion is as high as 40 per cent. Moreover, a recent survey found that, between 1981 and 1991, the number of second homes in Cumbria as a whole increased by 22 per cent (Friends of the Lake District, 2002). Along with the demand for retirement homes, this has led to inflated house prices within the National Park, making it increasingly difficult for local, lower-paid residents to buy homes. In South Lakeland, for example, it is reported that one estate agent estimated that over 60 per cent of houses sold by his company were for second homes, lending credence to the claim by the local authority that 25 per cent of the districts residents will never be able to afford to purchase a home and will have to rely on rented accommodation. However, with over half of all council houses having been sold under the right-to-buy policy, the availability of low cost housing for local people has been further reduced.

The research referred to above also revealed that local communities in the Lake District face potential social problems as a result of the housing issue. In a survey of residents in Windermere, Hawkshead and Langdale, 19 per cent of respondents felt that second homes had no positive impact on the area, whilst 28 per cent noted animosity and segregation within their community. The great majority believed that more housing should be developed for local people whilst almost a quarter believed government intervention is necessary to control second home ownership (Friends of the Lake District, 2002).

These issues have not gone unrecognised by the Lake District National Park Authority, which sees the shortage of affordable housing as a threat to viable rural communities and a diverse economic base already challenged by an ageing population and the in-migration of retired people. Thus, the National Park Local Plan outlines policies to:

➤ ensure that the limited land available for residential development is used to secure housing for local communities;

➤ restrain further housing development unrelated to the needs of local people;

➤ encourage housing associations and other organisations to undertake affordable housing schemes for locals.

Despite these policies, the issue of housing is likely to remain one of the most pressing issues facing the sustainable management and development of tourism in the Lake District in future years.

Tourism Impacts: the future?

The purpose of this chapter has been to outline the impacts of tourism in the Lake District and to highlight the relevant policies and strategies that address such impacts. In so doing, it has emphasised the fact that tourism is, and has long been, inextricably woven into the physical, economic and social fabric of the area; that is, the planning and management of the Lake District, its economic vitality, its socio-cultural structures and the character of its built environment reflect the fact that it has long been, and will continue to be, a major rural tourism destination. Thus, although decreasing the dependence on tourism by encouraging a more diverse economy is a sensible, though perhaps idealistic objective, the sustainable management of tourism's impacts is essential to the longer-term health of the area.

As has been discussed here, sustainable (tourism) development is inherent in most, if not all, development policies and plans and there are a number of examples of effective sustainable tourism policies. In particular, the activities of the Lake District Tourism and Conservation Partnership demonstrate that tourism and its environment can enjoy a symbiotic relationship, with tourists themselves contributing financially to the upkeep of the resource that they come to enjoy. Nevertheless, more could be done to encourage appropriate activities and behaviour, particularly on the part of tourists – indeed, ultimately it may be necessary to create a stronger link between tourists and the Lakeland environment by exploring more explicit means of raising funds to support conservation work. Certainly, the 'polluter pays' principle is fundamental to the concept of sustainable development and, although there are significant challenges inherent in charging for rural recreation (see Sharpley 1993), it may, in the longer term, represent the only effective means of managing tourism's impacts.

Case Study – Tourism in Grasmere

Grasmere is the quintessential Lakeland tourist village lying in a valley near the edge of Grasmere Lake, surrounded by the lower grassy slopes of the nearby hills with views over to some of the more famous fells, including the Langdale Pikes and Helvellyn. Grasmere is a small village where old cottages mingle with Victorian villas, along with a variety of shops, hotels and galleries catering to the needs of tourists. Indeed, it is probably the most famous and popular village in the Lake District, immortalised by the poet Thomas Gray in 1884 and subsequently described in glowing terms by Wordsworth in his *Guide to the Lakes:* '...this circular Vale, in the solemnity of a fine evening, will make, from the bosom of the Lake, an impression that will be scarcely ever effaced'. Paradoxically, it is Wordsworth himself who now draws many tourists to Grasmere, for not only did he live in the Grasmere area (though in a number of different houses, including the famous Dove Cottage) from 1799 until his death in 1850, but also he was buried in the graveyard of Grasmere's 13th century St. Oswald's Church.

It is not surprising, therefore, that Grasmere today is 'totally given over to the tourist industry' (www.visitcumbria.com/amb/grasmere.htm) and that, as a result, its character has come to be defined by the tourism industry upon which it depends. In fact, much of the village has 'grown' with tourism – a number of its larger hotels date from the 19th Century (see Plate 1) – and, thus, it epitomises the challenges of balancing and managing the impacts of tourism. On the one hand, tourism is the principal source of income and local employment whilst, on the other hand, Grasmere (or more precisely, the residents of Grasmere) suffer the impacts typically experienced by local communities in popular tourist destinations.

These impacts can be considered from a number of perspectives. Firstly, and somewhat simplistically, the number of visitors to the village and its surrounding area is completely disproportionate to the size of the local community. In 1981, for example, the village itself had a population of 656 (Northedge ,1991); although not directly comparable, 1539 people, 40 per cent of whom were aged 45 and over, lived in the Lakes Grasmere ward in 1999. This means that the ward has a population density of 0.2 persons per hectare, lower than the county average of 0.7 persons per hectare and placing it in the 'super-sparse' population category (Cumbria County Council, 2003). Thus, the local community is, for much of the year, significantly outnumbered by tourists.

Plate 1 *Grasmere Village*

It would be difficult to estimate accurately the number of tourists who visit the Vale and village of Grasmere. However, as an indication, approximately 135,000 people visit the local Tourist Information Centre each year (LDNPA, 2003), many of whom are interested in Grasmere itself. However, numbers are boosted by the fact that the village acts as a gateway to the northern Lakes, whilst it also lies on the Coast to Coast walking route. Thus, significant numbers of hikers also pass through the village in addition to car-borne visitors, the latter, as discussed shortly, representing one of the major visitor management challenges. Dove Cottage, probably the major attraction in the Vale, attracts around 70,000 visitors a year and, therefore, also acts as a magnet to the village. Of course, not all visitors to Grasmere visit the Information Centre or Dove Cottage and so the actual annual number of tourists is likely to be significantly higher than indicated here. Nevertheless, the figures do demonstrate the scale of tourism that the village supports.

A further indication of the impact of tourism on the village is the supply of accommodation. According to the Cumbria Tourist Board's website (www.golakes.co.uk), there are 13 hotels, five guest-houses, ten bed-and-breakfasts, one inn and two YHA hostels and one independent hostel – that is, a total of 32 establishments offering serviced accommodation. Additionally, seventy self-catering units, such as cottages and houses, are also available. Thus, Grasmere offers a significantly high volume of accommodation that attracts tourists all year round, adding to the pressure of visitor numbers that results from the predominant day-visitor market. The development of accommodation has also, of course, had an impact on the character of the village, as has the number of shops and other facilities catering for the needs of tourists. Indeed, the nature of the majority of shops serve to emphasise the tourism-honeypot character of Grasmere (see Plate 2); it was recently noted by the author that the following tourist shops/facilities are available in the village:

> ➢ 3 art galleries/studios

> ➢ 3 woollen shops

> ➢ 9 craft/gift shops

> ➢ 5 outdoor-wear shops

> ➢ 7 cafés/tea shops

> ➢ 4 specialist shops (gingerbread-shop; ice-cream shop; antique shop; coffee shop).

Plate 2 *A Grasmere gift shop*

In addition, the village boasts a large 'garden' centre which actually devotes most of its retail area to gifts, outdoor wear and a café. Conversely, 'local' shops comprise a small post office, a newsagent, a pharmacy and a limited village store meaning that the local community must travel to Ambleside or even up to Keswick for most goods and services.

As mentioned earlier in this chapter, one of the most evident social impacts of tourism in the Lake District has been the growth in second home/retirement home ownership and the subsequent lack of affordable housing for local people. This is a particular problem in Grasmere. In a recent survey (CRHT, 2002), it was found that not only do houses rarely come up for sale but also when they do so, they are very expensive. For example, in 2002 a three bedroomed semi-detached house was on the market for £160,000 and a two-bedroomed ground floor flat at £94,000. Thus, when houses do become available, local people, most of whom work within the tourism sector on relatively low incomes, cannot afford them. As a result, it was found that one third of all households in Grasmere still have adult children (i.e. over 25 years old) living at home (CRHT, 2002).

The cost of housing is undoubtedly linked to the village's popularity amongst second-home owners and retirees. In the Grasmere, Rydal and Ambleside parish, some 662 properties (roughly 31 per cent of all households) are not permanently occupied, a proportion that suggests 'real issues of sustainability of communities with such high concentrations of second and holiday homes in small settlements' (CRHT, 2002: 2). At the same time, almost 60 per cent of households (though not persons) were found to be elderly or mature, although the number of these that are incoming retirees is not indicated. Nevertheless, it is evident that, overall, tourism-related housing demand has created a significant problem for local people – the survey referred to here suggests that 22 new units of affordable housing are required to meet existing local needs.

Given the scale of tourism in Grasmere, it may be logical to assume that local people would have strong views about tourism and its impacts on their lives. Unfortunately, little recent research has been undertaken in this context although some interesting points emerged from a survey undertaken in 1991 (Northedge, 1991). Firstly, most residents accepted that, over time, the problem of overcrowding has become more acute, with the more elderly residents believing the village has lost its friendly character and atmosphere over the years. Secondly, a degree of resentment was seen to result from the fact that most tourism jobs were held by non-residents; that is, the local community did not feel it was benefiting economically from tourism. Thirdly, and as referred to above, many local people identified the loss of local services, in particular the loss of shops such as the butcher and grocer, as a particular negative outcome of tourism. Additionally, excessive litter and noise were seen as tourism-related problems, but the most significant impact of tourism identified by local people were traffic congestion and careless parking. Indeed, during the peak season, when the village's car parks are often full, many residents regularly experienced the inconvenience of having their driveways blocked by visitors' cars. Certainly, the current supply of car park spaces (a total of approximately 215 in 3 car parks, with a small number of additional spaces elsewhere in the village) would appear to be insufficient given Grasmere's popularity, although increasing the availability of car parking would simply lead to more crowding in the village.

Generally, then, Grasmere appears to suffer the 'typical' impacts of tourism development, though exacerbated by its popularity and fame. It is not surprising, therefore, that an overall finding of the survey mentioned here was that locals believed, for the most part, that their village had become too commercialised and, as a result of tourism, it had lost its traditional character. Nevertheless, many locals also recognised the economic benefits that tourism brings to the local community and hoped for a solution to some of tourism's negative impacts rather than a reduction in its overall volume. However, other than attempts to reduce congestion or improve traffic flow, it would appear that little can be done to alleviate the problems although, in the longer term, pedestrianising the central part of the village as an element of a wider traffic management programme may offer some respite to the local community. At the same time, there is some hope that the acute housing shortage may be addressed by the development of low-cost cottages for local people.

References

Berry, G. and Beard, G. (1980) *The Lake District: A Century of Conservation*. Edinburgh: John Bartholomew & Son.

Bingham, H. (1988) *Learning to Live with Tourism*. GCSE Resource Guide No.2, Kendal: Lake District National Park Authority.

Blake, A., Sinclair, M. T. and Sugiyarto, G. (2002) Quantifying the Impact of Foot and Mouth Disease on Tourism and the UK Economy. www.nottingham.ac.uk/ttri/FMD-paper4.pdf.

Budowski, G. (1976) Tourism and environmental conservation: conflict, coexistence or symbiosis? *Environmental Conservation* 3(1), 27-31.

Burns, P. and Holden, A. (1995) *Tourism: A New Perspective*. Hemel Hempstead: Prentice Hall International.

Calway, D. (2001) *The Economic Impact of Tourism in Cumbria: STEAM 2000*. Windermere: Cumbria Tourist Board.

Cavaco, C. (1995) Rural tourism: the creation of new tourist spaces. In A. Montanari and A. Williams (eds.) *European Tourism: Regions, Spaces and Restructuring*. Chichester: John Wiley & Sons, 129-149.

CCC (2002) *Cumbria Foot and Mouth Disease Inquiry*. Kendal: Cumbria County Council.

CCC (2003) South Lakeland Wards Profiles: Lakes Grasmere. www.cumbria.gov.uk/aboutcumbria/slakeland/default.asp.

Countryside Agency (2001) *The State of The Countryside 2001*. CA 61, Cheltenham: Countryside Agency.

Countryside Agency (2002) *The North West: The State of The Countryside 2002*. Cheltenham: Countryside Agency.

Countryside Commission (1995) *Sustainable Rural Tourism: Opportunities for Local Action*. CCP483, Cheltenham: Countryside Commission.

CRHT (2002) *Grasmere: Housing Needs Survey Report*. Penrith: Cumbria Rural Housing Trust.

CTB (1998) *The Regional Tourism Strategy for Cumbria*. Windermere: Cumbria Tourist Board.

CTB (2002a) *Cumbria: Facts of Tourism*. Windermere: Cumbria Tourist Board.

CTB (2002b) *Tourism Workforce Development Plan for Cumbria*. Windermere: Cumbria Tourist Board.

de Kadt, E. (ed.) (1979) *Tourism: Passport to Development?* Oxford: Oxford University Press.

Dower, M. (1965) *The Challenge of Leisure: The Fourth Wave*. London: The Civic Trust.

Dowling, R. (1992) Tourism and environmental integration: the journey from idealism to realism. In C. Cooper and A. Lockwood (eds.) *Progress in Tourism, Recreation and Hospitality Management, Vol 4*. London: Bellhaven Press, 33-46.

EC (1993) *Taking Account of Environment in Tourism Development*. DG XXIII Tourism Unit, Luxembourg: Commission of European Communities.

Ecotec (1993) *The Impact of Tourism – Cumbria 1992*. Birmingham: Ecotec Research and Consulting Ltd.

Enteleca (2000) *Cumbria Sustainable Tourism Baseline Survey 2000*. Richmond upon Thames: Entelecta Research and Consultancy.

ETC/CA (2001) *Working for the Countryside: a strategy for rural tourism in England 2001-2005*. London: English Tourism Council/Countryside Agency.alphabet.

FLD (2001) *Green Horizons: An Assessment of the Sustainability of the Tourism Industry in the Lake District*. Kendal: Friends of the Lake District.

FLD (2002) *Social impacts of second home ownership in the Lake District*. Friends of the Lake District, Report and Newsletter, Autumn, 48.

Fleischer, A. and Pizam, A. (1997) Rural tourism in Israel. *Tourism Management* 18(6), 367-372.

FNNPE (1993) *Loving Them to Death? Sustainable Tourism in Europe's Nature and National Parks*. Grafenau: Federation of Nature and National Parks of Europe.

Hjalager, A. (1996) Agricultural diversification into tourism: evidence of a European Community development programme. *Tourism Management* 17(2), 103-111.

Hoggart, K., Buller, H. and Black, R. (1995) *Rural Europe: Identity and Change*, London: Arnold.

Holden, A. (2000) *Environment and Tourism*. London: Routledge.

Jafari, J. (1989) Sociocultural dimensions of tourism: an English language literature review. In J. Bystrzanowski (ed.) *Tourism as a Factor of Change: A Sociocultural Study*. Vienna: Vienna Centre, 17-60.

Jenkins, C. (1991) Tourism development strategies. In L. Lickorish (ed.) *Developing Tourism Destinations*. Harlow: Longman: 61-77.

Jim, C. (1989) Visitor management in recreation areas. *Environmental Conservation* 16(1), 19-34.

LDNPA (1998a) *Education Service: Employment Factsheet*. Windermere: Lake District National Park Authority.

LDNPA (1998b) *Lake District National Park Local Plan*. Kendal: Lake District National Park Authority.

LDNPA (1999) *Lake District National Park Management Plan*. Kendal: Lake District National Park Authority.

LDNPA (2000) *Education Service: Footpath Erosion Factsheet*. Windermere: Lake District National Park Authority.

LDNPA (2003) *Personal Communication*.

Leslie, D. (2002) National Parks and the Tourism Sector. *Countryside Recreation* 10(3/4), 5-10.

Mathieson, A. and Wall, G. (1982) *Tourism. Economic, Physical and Social Impacts*. Harlow: Longman.

Mowl, G. (2002) Tourism and the environment. In R. Sharpley (ed.) *The Tourism Business: An Introduction*. Sunderland: Business Education Publishers, 219-242.

Nicholson, N. (1963) *Portrait of the Lakes*. London: Robert Hale Limited.

Northedge, S. (1991) *Grasmere: A Traditional Lakeland Village or Tourist Centre?* Unpublished BA Thesis, University of Lancaster.

Ousby, I. (1990) *The Englishman's England: Taste, Travel and the Rise of Tourism*. Cambridge: Cambridge University Press.

Pearce, D. (1989) *Tourist Development, 2nd Edition*. Harlow: Longman.

Rollinson, W. (1967) *A History of Man in the Lake District*. London: J. M. Dent & Sons.

Scott, P. (2002) *Employment, Skills and Training Issues in Cumbria's Tourism Industry 2000-2001*. Windermere: Cumbria Tourist Board and North West Tourism Skills Network.

Sharpley, R. (1993) Sustainable tourism in the English countryside. *Sustainable Development* 1(3), 49-63.

Sharpley, R. (1996) *Tourism and Leisure in the Countryside, 2nd Edition*. Huntingdon: Elm Publications.

Sharpley, R. (1999) *Tourism, Tourists and Society, 2nd Edition*. Huntingdon: Elm Publications.

Sharpley, R. and Craven, B. (2001) The 2001 Foot and Mouth crisis – rural economy and tourism policy implications: A comment. *Current Issues in Tourism* 4(6), 527-537.

Smith, V. (ed.) (1977) *Hosts and Guests: The Anthropology of Tourism*. Philadelphia: University of Pennsylvania Press.

Southgate, C. and Sharpley, R. (2002) Tourism, development and the environment. In R. Sharpley and D. Telfer (eds.) *Tourism and Development: Concepts and Issues*. Clevedon: Channel View Publications, 231-262.

Telfer, D. (2002) The evolution of tourism and development theory. In R. Sharpley and D. Telfer (eds.) *Tourism and Development: Concepts and Issues*. Clevedon: Channel View Publications, 35-78.

Turner, L. and Ash, J. (1975) *The Golden Hordes: International Tourism and the Pleasure Periphery*. London: Constable.

Wight, P. (1998) Tools for sustainability analysis in planning and managing tourism and recreation in the destination. In C. M. Hall and A. Lew (eds.) *Sustainable Tourism: A Geographical Perspective*. Harlow: Longman, 78-91.

WTO (1997) *International Tourism: A Global Perspective*. Madrid: World Tourism Organisation.

WTO/UNEP (1992) *Development of National Parks and Protected Areas for Tourism*. Madrid: World Tourism Organisation/United Nations Environment Programme.

Young, Sir G. (1973) *Tourism: Blessing or Blight?* Harmondsworth: Penguin.

Chapter Nine

The Future of Tourism in the Lake District

The early years of the 21st century see considerable change in the management and development of tourism in the Lake District. The Foot and Mouth crisis of 2001 has acted as a major catalyst and stimulus for change in the way in which agencies involved in the development of the rural community and tourism are working together, and developing a new vision for tourism in the region. The creation of Regional Development Agencies in the United Kingdom, and their role in developing regional tourism strategies is also contributing to the re-structuring of the administration of tourism within the regions. The North West Development Agency in 2003 published its new strategy for tourism in north west England and this has significant implications for the development of tourism in the Lake District. At the same time there are considerable uncontrollable external forces that will continue to shape and influence the type and form of tourism that develops in the Lake District over the next 20 to 30 years. Thus, at this moment in time, the future of tourism in the Lake District is extremely difficult to predict because of these fundamental influences on the development of tourism in the region. This chapter will, however, identify these key drivers of change for Lake District tourism, before synthesising the different perspectives on the future of sustainable tourism in the region.

The Key Drivers for Change

There are a number of uncontrollable, external forces that are influencing the development of tourism in the Lake District. These forces can be divided into those that will have a positive impact and those that will have a negative impact on the future of tourism.

Factors having a negative impact

The decline of the UK long stay holiday

Since the advent of overseas air-inclusive package tourism in the 1970s, the number of long stay domestic holidays in the UK (typically the traditional two week holiday) has been declining. Tourist destinations such as the Lake District and the seaside resorts around the English coastline received their greatest number of long staying tourists in the 1960s and 1970s. In the mid 1980s, British people took 33 million long holidays in England, and some 16 million holidays abroad. At the end of the 1990s, there had been a 25 per cent decrease in the number of long stay holidays taken in England, and an 80 per cent increase in the number of holidays taken abroad (Locum Destination Consulting, 2003). In 1999 the number of holidays taken overseas exceeded the number of holidays taken in the United Kingdom for the first time. Factors that account for this include the development of modern jet aircraft and the establishment of a wide range of short and long haul overseas tourist destinations where the climate is more favourable than in the UK, and the cost of the holiday package can be relatively inexpensive. This trend will continue in the future to the detriment of traditional UK tourist destinations such as the Lake District.

Turbulence in the short break market

The domestic UK tourism sector was forced to re-structure with the growth of the overseas package holiday. Salvation was initially found in the growth of the domestic short break holiday market (holidays of two or three nights duration). With the growing wealth of the population, in addition to a long stay holiday, households also started to take short break holidays at weekends. These initially were taken in the UK, and the Lake District became a popular short break destination. In the late 1990s and the early years of the new millennium, the growth of the budget airline sector has resulted in more overseas destinations becoming easily accessible for short break holidays, at the expense of UK short break destinations. The growth of airlines such as Easyjet and Ryanair, and the associated provision of accommodation and car hire facilities at the European destinations to which these airlines fly, has created a new short break holiday market. Thus, the short break holiday market is going through a period of change, which may have an adverse impact on the demand for UK short break destinations such as the Lake District.

Intense competition

In the post-Fordist, post-modernist world many localities and regions incorporate tourism development strategies in their local economic development plans. This is partly a result of the development and investment in infrastructure and tourism super-structure that makes previously inaccessible localities more accessible and attractive for tourism. At no time in the history of travel and tourism has competition between tourist destinations been so intense. Urry (1990:7) suggests that a "tourists gaze" can now be socially constructed, that is that a tourist can be directed towards new destinations (perhaps unconventional ones) by "…markers [signposts] which distinguish the things and places worthy of our gaze". The role of advertising and other media images of places are clearly important signposts for directing tourists to new destinations.

These "markers" have resulted in the enhancement of the perceived tourism value of certain regions and localities. In other words, regions and localities that once might not have been thought as being of interest to tourists are now felt to have something to offer. The Lake District competes with other National Parks in the UK, as well as urban and coastal destinations. As more and more local government authorities use tourism as a means of economic development, the range of competing tourist destinations will increase. This will have an impact on the demand for holidays to the Lake District in the years ahead.

The weather

The British weather is notoriously unpredictable, apart from the fact that periods of settled, warm weather are infrequent. This is a major deterrent to domestic tourists considering visiting rural locations. When the British summer is particularly wet, the trend is for the number of domestic holidays taken to fall, which also has an impact the following year as tourists do not want to risk two wet summer holidays in succession. The Lake District experiences some of the wettest weather in the UK, and with few all-weather attractions tourism to the region will continue to be influenced by climatic factors in the years ahead. However, when the British summer is particularly hot there is an increase in the number of tourists visiting the Lake District, as in 2003.

Economic cycles

All tourist destinations and forms of tourism are influenced by the economy of a nation. At times of economic prosperity and growth, demand for tourism increases, and in times of recession and unemployment the tourism sector is one of the first to suffer. Exchange rate fluctuations can also influence flows of international tourism. When sterling is strong compared to other currencies, British tourists find that overseas holidays become less expensive, which has a boost on the demand for holidays abroad.

Labour supply in the Lake District

As indicated in Chapter Three, tourism businesses that operate in the Lake District have difficulty in recruiting employees. This is a result of two main factors. Firstly, tourism is seen as a low income sector of the economy to work in, with unsocial working hours, and with limited career progression opportunities. Young people who have been born and bred in the Lake District do not always see tourism as a sector in which to develop their careers. The lack of other career options within the Lake District, results in an outward migration of young people. The second factor is that the Lake District attracts wealthy retirees who re-locate to the region upon retirement. This elderly population is clearly not economically active. Thus, the out migration of young people, combined with an in migration of retired people reduces the size of the local labour market, which has implications for tourism businesses that might wish to expand.

The stage of the Lake District in the tourist area life cycle

The product life cycle concept (PLC) is a familiar concept to marketers whereby it is felt that a product passes through a number of different stages, as the life of that product evolves, see Adcock *et al.* (1995) and Doyle (1994). The PLC plots sales of the product over time, and at each different stage of the PLC it is felt that a particular marketing emphasis is required in order to assist with the evolution and development of the product.

Butler (1980) adapted the PLC concept for tourism and applied it to the evolution of a tourist destination – the Tourist Area Life Cycle concept (TALC). The concept, like the PLC, suggests that tourist destinations pass through a number of evolutionary stages from the time when they are first discovered as tourist destinations, to the time when they lose their appeal because of over-development, or lack of modernisation. Tourist numbers are plotted over time to arrive at a curve that depicts the destination's life cycle. The TALC suggests different strategies that can be implemented at different stages of the destination's life cycle either to prolong and maintain that destination at it's current stage, or to move the destination into the next stage of its life cycle. Considerable debate has been generated by Butler's concept, with a number of studies being undertaken to demonstrate, or question, its validity (see Brownlie 1985, Haywood 1986, Cooper 1989, Choy 1992, Cooper 1992, and Cooper 1995 for example).

An application of the TALC to the Lake District is slightly problematic in that data are not collected to indicate the number of tourists visiting the National Park annually. Data are available, though, on the number of tourists visiting Cumbria, and given the fact that the Lake District is the main determinant of tourist visits to Cumbria, these data will be used to provide an indication of the stage that the Lake District is at in its life cycle.

The data provided in Table 9.1 refer to all tourists who stay overnight in Cumbria, and include all forms of tourism (holiday, business, visiting friends and relatives for example). The data are considered to be indicative rather than definitive, and have been rounded up to the nearest 100,000. The reliability of the data should also be questioned, given the difficulty of collecting accurate tourism data. The methodology for collecting these data changed in 2000, so although there should be internal consistency in the data up to 1999, the data from 2000 and 2001 cannot be directly compared to the tourist numbers from previous years. Given these caveats a broad picture does emerge of the number of tourist visits to Cumbria over the last 30 years.

Table 9.1   *All tourism trips to Cumbria 1972 – 2001 by UK residents*

Year	Millions of Trips	Year	Millions of Trips
1972	5	1987	3
1973	5	1988	4
1974	3	1989	3
1975	3	1990	2.6
1976	3	1991	2.7
1977	2	1992	2.6
1978	2	1993	2.5
1979	2	1994	2.9
1980	3	1995	3.3
1981	3	1996	3.0
1982	3	1997	3.1
1983	4	1998	3.0
1984	4	1999	3.5
1985	4	2000	3.5
1986	3	2001	4.5

Source: UK Tourism Survey, 1972-2001

The data indicate that on the whole the number of tourists visiting Cumbria over the last 30 years has been relatively stable. Clearly, there are fluctuations on a yearly basis as a result of the economic cycle and climatic influences for example. The overall picture, however, is one of Cumbria being at the mature stage of its tourist destination life cycle. The number of tourist visits to the Lake District has probably reached a peak and the challenge is to prevent a decline in tourist arrivals rather than to increase the number of tourists visiting the Lake District. Locum Destination Consulting (2003) indicate that any growth that might be apparent in the number of tourist visits to Cumbria can be accounted for by a growth in the number of visits to friends and relatives.

In terms of the TALC, the Lake District could be assumed to be at the 'consolidation' stage – the region is clearly a recognised tourist destination for mass tourism, with national companies involved in managing some of the tourism facilities, camping and caravan parks, hotels, and tourist attractions. Butler's (1980) concept suggests that it is at this stage of the life cycle that careful attention has to be given to the management of the destination's tourism activity. The number of tourists visiting the destination may stagnate and decline if some of the problems associated with mass tourism are not addressed – over crowding, pollution, and despoliation of the environment, for example. If these problems (and many others that result from mass tourism) are not tackled then the destination moves into the decline stage. If, however, the destination addresses some of these issues then it may experience rejuvenation as its existing market remains loyal, and as new markets are attracted with investment in improved facilities and resources. The implication of the TALC is that tourism planning and management, with heavy public sector involvement, is critical to ensure the sustainable evolution of the destination. Private/public sector initiatives are required in order to maintain the appeal of the tourist destination.

In reviewing the strategy and policy documents of the public sector agencies responsible for the management and development of tourism in the Lake District (see Chapter Five) it is evident that considerable attention has been given to the future of tourism in the National Park. To some extent there is a degree of contrast in the views of the different agencies, dependent on their role and remit. Those organisations engaged in the conservation of the Lake District see little growth in the number of tourism facilities within the Lake District. Those organisations whose remit it is to develop and promote tourism to the region would wish to encourage investment in tourism facilities to support a growth in the value of tourism in the Lake District National Park (the income generated from tourist expenditure). The different perspectives of these agencies will be presented later in this chapter.

Changes to the farming communities

The Lakeland landscape depends on upland farming for its appearance. Upland farming is not viable without public support (as explained in Chapter Three). At a time when the agricultural industry is under such pressure it is important that European and national politicians do not underestimate the importance of livestock farming to an upland economy. Land management strategies are needed to prevent the landscape from changing and becoming unattractive for tourists. Not all change is bad but the Countryside and Rights of Way Act cannot become a reality without land management (see Chapter Five). Sheep are needed to graze on the land and farmers are needed to manage the sheep and maintain the built features of the Lakeland landscape. Under the present economic conditions, there is a danger that many Lakeland farmers will leave their vocation. If that happens then the relationship between the small farming hamlets and the landscape will be lost. Farmsteads will get a new life as second homes or holiday lets, but what of the outbuildings and walls enclosing the surrounding fields? What of the Lakeland culture? That is what the majority of tourists come to enjoy. There is a fear that central government will fail to see the importance of the small farm in this special landscape.

With incomes from farming collapsing and an over-dependence upon tourism, there is a need to build a new rural infrastructure that will allow the development of new trades and businesses. Design standards for buildings must remain high and the special qualities of the Lake District landscape must be maintained. There is a need to have farmers working the land but there needs to be a 21st century economy; one where the Cumbrian young will prosper. The indigenous young cannot afford local houses and the range of job opportunities in the Lake District is limited. Why should Cumbria continue to export its youth when there is such a desperate need for their energy and innovation? There is a need to create training and development programmes that reflect local needs. Local markets must be created that serve local needs and put wealth back into Lakeland communities.

The Lake District Brand

In 2002, research was commissioned by Cumbria Tourist Board to investigate the brand image and perceptions of Cumbria and the Lake District as tourist destinations. A number of important messages for the Lake District came out of the research. The Lake District is perceived as the pre-eminent holiday destination within Cumbria, but it is seen as being a slightly old fashioned destination, and not 'cool' for teenagers. The research indicated that the Lake District is seen as a 'tourist trap', too commercialised and 'touristy' especially in Windermere. Negative perceptions exist about traffic congestion and poor car parking facilities, (Locum Destination Consulting, 2003a). Clearly these perceptions are significant for the future development of tourism in the Lake District and will have to be addressed if tourist demand for holidays in the region is to be maintained.

Factors having a positive impact

A number of factors can be identified that will have a positive impact on the demand for holidays in the Lake District.

The technology revolution

Developments in communication and information technologies have revolutionised the way in which tourism businesses can communicate with their markets. Small businesses that in the 1980s and 1990s had to rely on expensive printed media to advertise their offerings, can now communicate with global audiences at the touch of a button through the world wide web. Thus, while domestic UK markets are seeking holiday experiences overseas, the opportunity now exists to communicate with a global audience in order to encourage international tourists to visit the Lake District. The technological revolution will continue throughout the early decades of the 21st century, and if the product offering of Lake District tourism businesses is strong and world class, an increasing number of overseas tourists will be attracted to the region.

Cumbria Tourist Board has played a major role in harnessing the benefits that information technology can bring. In 2003, it redesigned its website (www.golakes.co.uk) and introduced a Destination Management System (DMS). The DMS is an electronic database of information about tourism in Cumbria. It enables tourism businesses to provide information and images about their accommodation or tourist attraction, for example, and to update such information at the touch of a button.

Co-ordinated development and marketing of tourism

It has been stated earlier (see Chapter Five) that as a result of the 2001 Foot and Mouth crisis the leading agencies responsible for managing and developing the rural environment in Cumbria have been brought together in order to implement a recovery plan for the local economy. The Cumbria Rural Action Zone (RAZ) strategy embraces tourism as well as agriculture and related industries. Over £250 million is being injected into the rural communities of Cumbria 2003-2008, which undoubtedly will have an impact on the tourism industry in the Lake District. In addition the marketing of the north west of England as a tourist destination in an integrated and co-ordinated way by the North West Development Agency, using the Lake District as an 'attack' brand will undoubtedly increase the number of tourist visits to the region.

Demographic changes to the United Kingdom population

It is forecast that the UK population will become increasingly elderly over the next 30 years. The 45-64 year age group is expected to increase by over 20 per cent by 2011 and "by 2030, the over 60's will outnumber young adults by 20 per cent" (Locum Destination Consulting, 2003:13). These age groups are important for tourism in the Lake District because they have time and money to spend on leisure activities. These members of the population "…have the propensity to take more trips…and are more likely to use serviced accommodation…and are not so concerned about the weather" (ibid:14).

Increasing wealth and mobility of the population

Data from the Office for National Statistics (2002) indicates that the personal disposable income of the United Kingdom population has doubled since 1970 increasing virtually year-on-year. Perhaps as a consequence, the United Kingdom is now more mobile than ever before, with car ownership doubling since 1975. It is felt that these trends will continue in the years ahead as more members of society benefit from inherited wealth. This will be another stimulus for the demand for holidays in the Lake District.

The Lake District is a 'middle class' destination

An analysis of data representing the socio-economic group of tourists to Cumbria and the Lake District indicates that 67 per cent of staying tourists in 2000 were from the ABC1 socio-economic group, the highest percentage of ABC1s in all United Kingdom tourism regions (Locum Destination Consulting, 2003). An analysis of postcodes of members of the public requesting tourist guides from the Cumbria Tourist Board also confirms this 'middle class' profile. The group most likely to request a tourist guide from the Cumbria Tourist Board is 'affluent home owners', who live in wealthy neighbourhoods, most of whom own their own home with little or no mortgage left. Many households benefit from two incomes and enjoy at least two holidays a year (Locum Destination Consulting, 2003). This is beneficial for tourism to the Lake District as the ABC1 members of society are the most frequent holiday takers. The challenge for tourism operators, though, will be providing products that match the quality aspirations and expectations of this middle class market.

Clearly there are a variety of uncontrollable factors that will influence the demand for tourism in the Lake District. In addition the agencies that are specifically responsible for the development and promotion of tourism in the National Park are developing and implementing strategies that will shape and influence the future of tourism in the Lake District.

The Future of the Landscape and Settlements

The Lake District National Park Authority's vision for the future of the Lake District is simple and relevant. It is

> "a place renowned for its outstanding beauty, wildlife and cultural heritage. The National Park will continue to display special qualities that set it apart. It will be an area with vibrant and sustainable communities offering distinctive experiences for its many visitors" (LDNPA, 2003:9). Much needs to be done, however, to ensure that this vision can become a reality.

The National Park Authority accepts that tourism will be one of the main sources of income for Lakeland communities for some time to come (although in some valleys it will still be agriculture). Over time the National Park Authority would like to reduce this dependence, not by reducing the tourism sector but by increasing other sectors of the economy. It will be some years before such a wish can be achieved. In the meantime, tourism must be made sustainable. The tourist is attracted to the Lake District by its outstanding landscape and a number of policies are in place to protect the landscape and its habitats and communities. The revised Lake District National Park Management Plan 2004 has policies for the planning and management of the Lake District under the following headings:

Fostering economic and social well-being

➤   Sustainable Communities.

Enhancing natural beauty, wildlife and cultural heritage

➤   Landscape.

➤   Nature Conservation.

➤   Farming and Land Management.

➤   Built Heritage and Historic Environment.

Promoting understanding and enjoyment

➤   Education, Interpretation and Information.

➤   Access and Recreation.

➤   Tourism.

➤   Traffic and Transport.

The 2004 National Park Management Plan (LDNPA, 2004) includes policy statements directly related to tourism, unlike its predecessor in 1999. The 2004 Plan recognises the importance of encouraging all members of society to visit and enjoy the Lake District. This is important because as stated above the typical tourist visiting the Lake District is from a 'middle class background' and the danger might be that the National Park becomes an elite tourist destination, to the detriment of some of the disadvantaged members of society.

The 2004 Plan also has explicit policy statements relating to sustainable transport and seeks to encourage tourists to travel on foot, by bicycle or public transport, thus alleviating traffic congestion and pollution. Once in the National Park, tourists should be able to enjoy a quiet environment and it will be this that encourages them not only to stay, but also to return in the future. The Management Plan also sees partnership with the tourism industry as being crucial for the continued development of sustainable tourism. The Plan indicates that the National Park Authority wishes to encourage the local tourism industry to contribute more strongly to the development of sustainable tourism by for example, encouraging more tourism businesses to source their inputs locally. In addition, local tourism businesses, and their customers, are also to be encouraged to become involved with projects that protect the natural environment of the region.

The final element of the tourism policy concerns the local labour market – the National Park Authority wants to see young people born and bred in the Lake District staying in the region after leaving school and college, and working within tourism. However, to achieve this, there is a recognition that remuneration levels for tourism jobs need to increase, that the local property market has to be able to provide housing opportunities for young people on the first rung of their career ladder and that the tourism businesses have to invest in training and development programmes to enhance the skills of their workforce. The policies set out in the 2004 Management Plan clearly address a number of the challenges facing the development of sustainable tourism in the Lake District but will require concerted efforts by the National Park Authority and its partners to make significant progress.

The Cumbria and Lake District Joint Structure Plan 1991-2006 (1995) sets out the policy framework for the development and use of land in the Lake District National Park up to 2006. This document is very explicit in terms of the development of land in the National Park:

"The scenic beauty, natural resources and quality of the built environment of the Lake District National Park will be firmly protected and enhanced whilst fostering the quiet enjoyment and understanding of the Park and the social and economic well being of the community in a manner which does not conflict with the conservation objectives" (Policy 5, page 17).

"To protect the intrinsic qualities of the National Park, the growth of tourism should be restrained and future development should not conflict with its quiet enjoyment" (Policy 10, page 18).

"Tourism development within the National Park will only be permitted when it does not conflict with the quiet enjoyment of the area, is of a character and scale which respects the quality of the environment and does not introduce inappropriate activities or significant additional numbers of visitors likely to have an adverse impact on the site or surrounding area. In particular:

(i)   major new proposals for additional holiday accommodation and for tourist attractions unrelated to the purpose for which the Park is designated will not normally be permitted;

(ii)   the quieter areas and particularly sensitive localities of the Park will be protected from developments and increases in use which would be detrimental to their special qualities;

(iii)   development to cater solely for peak recreational demands, or which has a material adverse effect on quieter periods by virtue of its physical impact or the additional use it generates will not normally be permitted" (Policy 50, page 50).

The 1991 – 2006 Cumbria and Lake District Joint Structure Plan is currently being reviewed and updated. The new Joint Structure Plan covering the time period to 2016 will be just as stringent as the existing plan in relation to tourism developments within the Lake District National Park. "The Structure Plan must protect the area from harmful development and recognise the vulnerability of designated sites and features, areas of undeveloped countryside and coast, and particularly sensitive areas such as lake shores and the fells", (Cumbria County Council, 2003:12). This will act as a major restraint to any developer or entrepreneur wishing to invest in new greenfield capital projects within the Lake District in the future.

From the above, and from the perspective of the National Park Authority, the landscapes and settlements of the Lake District, will continue to be conserved and preserved for enjoyment by future generations. This will be further enhanced if World Heritage Status is conveyed on parts of the 'cultural landscape' of the Lake District by UNESCO.

World Heritage Status

The National Park Authority intends to seek World Heritage Site Inscription for the Lake District. By this means, a long-term management plan that truly binds all parties responsible for the management and development of tourism can be developed and implemented. World Heritage Site status in itself will not increase the tourism market for the Lake District but the disciplines associated with Inscription will ensure that a sustainable framework is made available to the industry.

World Heritage Sites are nominated by State Governments and inscribed by the United Nations Education and Science Committee (UNESCO). The Lake District was nominated in 1985 as a Natural Area but that bid was deferred, as it could not pass the test of 'natural integrity'. Learning from the experience of dealing with the bid, UNESCO has developed a new category of World Heritage Site, the cultural landscape, where the test is the 'outstanding universal significance' of the site. The Lake District is thought to be an outstanding example of a landscape which:

1. illustrates significant stages in human history;

2. is an outstanding example of a traditional human settlement and land-use which is representative of early English cultures which are vulnerable under the impact of irreversible change;

3. is directly associated with events, living traditions, ideas and with artistic and literary works of outstanding universal significance.

Given that 2001 was the National Park's 50th anniversary, the application for Inscription was reactivated with support from Central Government (DCMS, 1998). For the bid to be successful, the universal significance(s) of the Lake District must be identified and agreed. An active partnership to protect those significance(s) must be created; and that protection must be demonstrated by presenting the Government with a 30-year Management Plan that binds all the principal players to co-ordinated action.

Some fear that Inscription may create a 'negative halo' around its boundary, with other parts of Cumbria being disadvantaged in order to protect the Lake District. Such fears presume that the buffer zone will fall outside the National Park but it is more likely that the World Heritage Site will lie within the boundary of the National Park. Nations have signed a Convention to protect all World Heritage Sites, which means that adequate resources for their protection must be provided. Designation is a material planning consideration. The Lake District's true worth would be there for all to see – at a time when rural England is under significant pressure. No Government could ignore the call to restore and enhance a World Heritage Site. And what better way to ensure the planned management of sustainable tourism in the Lake District?

But not all stakeholders support unreservedly World Heritage Site classification. Cumbria Tourist Board (CTB), while recognising the benefits that classification will bring also identify the potential disadvantages. The additional policy controls that will inevitably arise through classification will compound the existing stringent planning regulations, making it even more difficult for some planning applications to be approved. CTB argues that the Lake District is already an internationally recognised tourist brand and World Heritage Site classification will not bring additional visitors. CTB asserts the need for the debate and discussion on World Heritage Site classification to continue, and for all stakeholders to be fully involved in the final decision on applying for Inscription.

The National Trust, one of the key landowners in the Lake District, will play a very significant role in the management and development of tourism in the future. Following the outbreak of the Foot and Mouth crisis in 2001, the National Trust published its vision for the future. The vision centres on four areas of wellbeing for the Lake District: social, environmental, economic and cultural elements of development.

Social wellbeing

The National Trust seeks a "thriving and diverse Lake District Community" where due respect is given to the social wellbeing of the resident population who contribute to the sustainable management of the landscape. At the same time, there should be access to the environment for members of the public.

Environmental wellbeing

There should be land use planning based on a sustainable approach, with the tourist industry providing for visitors in a socially and environmentally responsible way.

Economic wellbeing

The vision is for the Lake District to develop a "diverse and competitive economy which engages actively with the rest of the North West area". For business people operating in the Lake District, opportunities should exist for them to supply products that can be sold to tourists.

Cultural wellbeing

There should be respect for the special cultural qualities of the Lake District, and recognition of the aesthetic qualities of the landscape.

Source: The National Trust (undated) *A Vision for the Lake District after Foot and Mouth*.

Clearly, with any vision statement, the approach adopted in writing tends to be broad, rather than detailed in content. But vision statements do help to set the focus for the attainment of future goals. The National Trust's vision of the future also considers how the four aspects of wellbeing are to be achieved. Partnerships are a main feature of the delivery of strategies to attain the goals, with partners being identified both from outside and within Cumbria.

The Friends of the Lake District also has a perspective on the future of sustainable tourism in the Lake District, and made a number of recommendations following its study into sustainable tourism practices being implemented by the tourism sector in 2000 (Friends of the Lake District, 2001). Its recommendations are quite varied, including the adoption of environmental management systems and annual environmental auditing by tourism enterprises, and actively encouraging tourists to adopt alternative means of transport to car use. In addition, in its Green Horizons Report, the Friends of the Lake District also proposed a new lead body being established to "…represent the tourism sector and all organisations involved in tourism, LA21 and the environment" (Friends of the Lake District, 2001:11).

How tourism in the Lake District will be administered in the future was also an area of consideration in the Cumbria Foot and Mouth Disease Inquiry Report (2002). This issue of the governance and administration of tourism in the Lake District will now be explored.

The Governance and Administration of Tourism

The 2001 foot and mouth crisis had a major short term impact on tourism in the Lake District. Whilst it was felt that the national government was relatively slow to acknowledge the full impact on the tourism sector, concerted efforts by regional stakeholders to achieve a medium – long term recovery plan have been significant. The early establishment in the foot and mouth crisis of a Cumbria Foot and Mouth Disease Task Force and its subsequent role in proposing a Rural Action Zone marked a turning point in the development of the rural communities of Cumbria. The findings and recommendations of the Cumbria Foot & Mouth Inquiry (2002) also influenced central government to look anew at supporting the rural communities in their recovery from foot and mouth. This contributed to the Regional Development Agency – the North West Development Agency – taking a clear role in establishing a vision and strategy for the future development of tourism in the north west of England. Perhaps, if it had not been for the foot and mouth crisis, tourism in the north west of England might not have been seen as a priority sector, and the attention that it is currently being given, might not have materialised.

In thinking about the future of tourism in the Lake District, a review will now be made of the key shapers of the future vision and strategy for tourism in the region.

The Rural Action Zone

The Rural Action Zone (RAZ) programme provides a policy and strategy framework to address the challenges that face rural Cumbria in the years ahead. The Cumbria RAZ is the first of its kind to be established in the UK and can be considered to be highly innovative. The vision of the RAZ is "to enable the rebuilding and development of a dynamic rural economy for Cumbria, which is financially, socially and environmentally sustainable" (Cumbria Foot & Mouth Disease Inquiry Report, 2002:84). Five strategic priorities have been set within the vision:

> ➢ to develop a rural economy that is financially, socially and environmentally sustainable;

> ➢ to improve the environmental quality of land and waters;

> ➢ to increase opportunities for all who visit Cumbria to enjoy the countryside, towns and villages through improved access and facilities;

> ➢ to create integrated services for the rural communities of Cumbria;

> ➢ to sustain the cultural landscapes of Cumbria.

Strategic objectives will result in the strategic priorities being attained.

The intention of the RAZ is to deliver its strategies through local partnerships and community involvement with a budget of £275million. In terms of tourism the RAZ recognises the need for tourism in Cumbria to develop through broadening the range and quality of the tourism facilities and resources available. This will primarily occur outside the Lake District National Park, in order to protect the natural and cultural heritage of the Lake District. The intention of the RAZ tourism strategy is to provide Cumbria with a more varied tourism product that will appeal to wider market segments. Nevertheless, the tourism industry of the Lake District will be a key beneficiary of the raising of the profile of tourism in Cumbria arising from the work of the RAZ.

The Cumbria Foot and Mouth Inquiry Report (2002) also makes the case for a new administrative structure to be established to manage the development of tourism in Cumbria in the future. The Inquiry became aware of the multitude of different stakeholder groups involved with the regional tourism industry, ranging from small businesses to the public sector funded regional and national tourism promotion and development agencies. Balancing the interests and needs of different stakeholder groups is complex under the existing structures for the governance and administration of tourism in Cumbria.

At a national level VisitBritain is responsible for marketing the UK and its regions both within the UK and overseas. The North West Development Agency is responsible for the promotion and development of tourism within the region. At a sub-regional level there are marketing strategies for sub-brands, promoting specific localities, for example Keswick. Thus, as can be seen, the promotion and development of tourism in the Lake District is complex and the Inquiry Report states that "…we have reservations about the industry's capacity to articulate shared goals and work in concert to achieve them" (Cumbria Foot and Mouth Inquiry Report, 2002:91). The Report recommends that "…a Cumbria Tourism Forum is established with an independent Chair from the private sector, to facilitate the different sectors of the industry in co-ordinating funding bids related to the RAZ programme" (ibid:93).

Cumbria Market Forecasts

In 2002 Cumbria Tourist Board commissioned Locum Destination Consulting (2003a) to conduct a comprehensive review of tourism in Cumbria with one of the aims being to produce data that could inform the development of a new tourism strategy for Cumbria. One aspect of this research was to produce market forecasts for tourism to Cumbria. The headline market forecasts produced by Locum Destination Consulting are:

Table 9.2   *Market Forecasts 2000 – 2010 for overnight tourists to Cumbria*

2000	Actual	Forecast Annual Growth	2005 Projections	2005 vs 2000	2010 Projections	2010 vs 2000
Domestic						
Holidays	4,100,000	1%	4,309,141	5%	4,528,951	10%
VFR	500,000	7%	701,276	40%	983,576	97%
Business	400,000	5%	510,513	28%	651,558	63%
Other	100,000	2%	110,408	10%	121,899	22%
TOTAL	5,100,000	2%	5,609,197	10%	6,285,984	23%
Overseas						
Holidays	140,000	1%	147,141	5%	154,647	10%
VFR	50,000	3%	57,964	16%	67,196	34%
Business	20,000	5%	25,526	28%	32,578	63%
Other	10,000	2%	11,041	10%	12,190	22%
TOTAL	220,000	2%	241,278	10%	266,611	21%

Visitor Spend Forecasts 2000 – 2010 for overnight tourists to Cumbria

	Actual	Forecast Annual Growth	2005 Projections	2005 vs 2000	2010 Projections	2010 vs 2000
Domestic						
Holidays	£654 mn	4%	£796 mn	22%	£968mn	48%
VFR	£22 mn	11%	£37 mn	69%	£62 mn	184%
Business	£87 mn	9%	£134 mn	54%	£206 mn	137%
Other	£7 mn	6%	£9 mn	34%	£13 mn	79%
TOTAL	£770 mn	5%	£973 mn	26%	£1,249 mn	2%
Overseas						
Holiday	£28 mn	5%	£36 mn	28%	£46 mn	63%
VFR	£18 mn	7%	£25 mn	40%	£35 mn	97%
Business	£5 mn	9%	£8 mn	54%	£12 mn	137%
Other	£1 mn	6%	£1.3 mn	34%	£1.8 mn	79%
TOTAL	£52 mn	6%	£69 mn	34%	£95 mn	82%

Source: (Locum Destination Consulting, 2003a:84)

The data presented in Table 9.2 forecast an increase of 10 per cent in the number of tourists staying overnight in Cumbria 2000 – 2005, an increase of 23 per cent between 2000 – 2010 and an increase in visitor spend of 26 per cent in Cumbria 2000 – 2005, and an increase of 62 per cent between 2000 – 2010. However, Locum Destination Consulting (2003a:8) feel that currently "...tourism in the Lake District is not as healthy as it should be" and achieving such growth forecasts will require a number of the region's problems to be addressed.

A review of hotel occupancy rates indicates that in comparison with other regions of the United Kingdom, accommodation occupancy ratios in the Lake District are low, with "...substantial excess capacity within the National Park" (ibid:20). Levels of investment in the accommodation sector is also of concern with investment primarily being to redecorate, rather than to improve the quality of facilities. Some accommodation providers find themselves in a vicious circle – the inability to improve the quality of their product restricts bookings, which makes it difficult to generate surplus funds to re-invest in the quality of the product. Marginal financial returns also affect retailers and other businesses located in the honeypot resort towns. With the number of tourists visiting the Lake District being static these businesses have difficulty in increasing turnover, and of generating surplus funds for reinvestment in their businesses. This is felt to be contributing to some of the honeypot resort towns looking shabby and in need of investment (ibid:20).

Another challenge facing tourism in the Lake District is the structure of the sector, being dominated by small, independent operators, at a time when the national tourism trend in the United Kingdom is for branded products with clear brand values and attributes. Locum Destination Consulting (2003a:8) also feel that there is a degree of complacency with the tourism operators in the Lake District who do not all see the need to invest regularly to upgrade the quality of the product that is offered to tourists – "a challenge therefore, is to give the Lake District more contemporary appeal". Problems are also felt to exist with the marketing of the Lake District as a tourist destination, with a need to upgrade the brand identity. Currently four sub-brands incorporating the Lake District identity are used in Cumbria:

➢ Central and Southern Lakeland.

➢ Keswick and the Northern Lakes.

➢ The Lake District Peninsulas.

➢ Western Lake District.

This is a result of the work and interests of the different local authorities in Cumbria and the two tourism partnerships – one in West Cumbria and the other in the Furness Peninsulas. Clearly, there will be a major duplication of resources when establishing and promoting these four brands, and some confusion for tourists – which brochure do they need to plan their holiday to the Lake District?

The challenges identified here manifest themselves in the fact that the number of tourists staying overnight in the Lake District is static. Tourism to the Lake District is characterised by a high number of repeat visits, with few first time visitors being attracted to the region.

Recommendations made by Locum Destination Consulting include:

➢ marketing the Lake District as a separate brand with an updated image, based around excellence in "high energy" outdoor activities and "low energy" sedentary activities such as eating out, shopping and visiting cultural attractions. Investing in the quality of the tourist experience and tourist product will be vital for the sustainable development of tourism in the Lake District;

➢ upgrading the honeypot resorts of Ambleside, Bowness, Keswick, and Windermere in terms of their built environment with the possible addition of a new visitor attraction that is capable of achieving national acclaim;

➢ raising awareness of the special qualities of the Lake District National Park, and establishing it more as an internationally acclaimed national park in the same way as Yosemite and Yellowstone National Parks have been developed. Suggestions for achieving this include building more visitor centres, upgrading the main National Park Visitor Centre at Brockhole, Windermere, branding the National Park more heavily, and developing high quality shuttle buses between key sites;

➢ making it easy for tourists to find information, make a booking and travel to the region. Investment needs to be devoted to web-based technologies operational 24 hours per day, and the transport infrastructure needs improving to make the Lake District easily accessible from airports, urban centres, and the coast. Easy to access information needs to be made available to facilitate the visitors' enjoyment of their holiday in the Lake District.

In terms of target markets, Locum Destination Consulting (2003a) identify certain key markets:

➢ overnight tourists rather than day visitors;

➢ couples whose children have left home;

➢ the ABC1 socio-economic groups;

➢ tourists living within 3 hours drive time of the Lake District;

➢ activity and eco-oriented tourists.

Issues affecting the future development of tourism in the Lake District include:

➢ the challenges of recruiting staff to work in the tourism industry;

> poor road signage;

> the administration of tourism in the region. Locum Destination Consulting concur with the views of other agencies in this chapter that there is a need to review the organisation of tourism in Cumbria with a "...profusion of associations, agencies and partnerships and a multiplicity of brochures etc. competing for the same territory" (ibid:28);

> the over supply of small tourist accommodation units, and under supply of residential accommodation; one solution might be to convert small bed and breakfast establishments and small hotels back into residential accommodation.

North West Development Agency

The North West Development Agency (NWDA) has been given responsibility for tourism development in the north west of England. A Tourism Forum for North West England has been established by NWDA in order to develop a tourism strategy for the region (NWDA, 2003). Membership of the Forum comprises representatives from those agencies involved with the development and promotion of tourism in the north west. The first task of the Forum was to publish a vision and strategic framework for the region (NWDA, 2003), from which action plans have been designed to enable the vision to be realised. Elements of the vision that have relevance for tourism in the Lake District are presented below.

Transport infrastructure

The vision recognises the importance of transport infrastructure in facilitating the development of tourism in the region. There is a recognition that the transport infrastructure has to be improved to give tourists better accessibility. The vision questions if there is a role for Carlisle airport (to the north of the Lake District) to be used for incoming flights, as well as acknowledging that the rail system serving the north west needs upgrading. At the same time, the vision indicates that more radical transport management initiatives might need to be implemented in the Lake District to encourage people to use alternative forms of transport to the car.

Tourism workforce development plan

The development of people working, or aspiring to work in tourism, is a priority area identified in the vision. The vision recognises that a well qualified, committed and motivated workforce is essential for the success of the tourism industry, but acknowledges that currently this is a weakness within the region that needs addressing. To improve the skills base of the tourism workforce the North West Development Agency will implement a Tourism Workforce Development Plan.

Brand-oriented approach to tourism

The vision states that "tourism marketing strategy in the UK has been moving from a local, district-oriented approach to one that focuses on regions, themes and brands" (North West Development Agency, 2002:18). The strategy for developing and promoting tourism in the north west will be based around brands that have the greatest potential to attract the desired number of tourists. Brands will either be developed around themes (sport for example) or locations (the Lake District). The Lake District brand will be used as an 'attack' brand not just to attract tourists to the Lake District itself, but to the region in general. Indeed, the Lake District will be promoted as a hallmark brand – recognising its international significance as a world class tourist destination. Once tourists have been attracted to the Lake District, the strategy will be to disperse some of them around the county of Cumbria with brands such as 'Undiscovered Cumbria – Hidden Treasures or Gems' and themes which have potential for growth, for example capitalising on the current interest in 'gardens'. This approach to branding is considered to be one that transcends the political boundaries within the region whilst contributing to the economic sustainability of tourism within Cumbria. If successful these marketing strategies should:

➢ increase the value of tourism expenditure in the Lake District National Park;

➢ improve the seasonal spread of tourism within the National Park;

➢ increase the number of tourist visits outside the National Park; and

➢ increase the value of tourism expenditure outside the National Park.

Organisational structure

Just as the Friends of the Lake District and the Foot and Mouth Inquiry Report identified the need to review the administration and governance of tourism in the region, so too does the North West Development Agency. The NWDA has created five new Destination Management Organisations (DMO) in the region. Cumbria will have its own DMO responsible for "...destination marketing, relations with the industry, research and project delivery" NWDA (2003:10). The Cumbrian DMO will replace Cumbria Tourist Board. The NWDA will be responsible for the "strategic direction of tourism in the region..." (ibid:10) and through its regional tourism executive group will co-ordinate the work and activities of the five DMOs.

Promoting excellence

The Tourism Vision for the region recognises that investment should be made in promoting excellence within the region. The Lake District is identified within the Vision as the region's most recognised brand, but an area which has lacked investment to establish itself as a truly world class, excellent destination. The Vision identifies the need for further investment in the Lake District to improve the quality of the visitor experience, but the source of such investment is not yet clear.

The above are just five elements of the Vision statement for tourism in the North West that relate to the Lake District. It is evident that the Lake District in the future will take a more prominent role in the marketing of the north west with the intention to develop the Lake District as a world class tourist destination. This marketing strategy is needed as the number of tourists staying overnight in the Lake District is static (given the fierce competition in tourism mentioned previously). To prevent a decline in the number of tourists, which might be welcomed by some people, there needs to be investment. Not only in the marketing of the brand, but investment in the product and its features to ensure that the visitor experience matches the images communicated through the brand strategy.

What does the Future hold for Tourism in the Lake District?

It is clear from the issues presented in this chapter that there will be many influences on the future of tourism in the Lake District. Predicting the exact future of the region is extremely difficult because a number of the influences are uncontrollable and by definition cannot be influenced by those agencies charged with the management and development of tourism in the Lake District. There are though policies in place that will have major impacts on the form and scale of tourism in the Lake District. The most appropriate way, therefore, to summarise this chapter is to present a scenario that synthesises the different perspectives.

It is felt that there are two major influences on the future of tourism in the Lake District. Firstly, the outcomes arising from the implementation of the Cumbria Rural Action Zone and secondly, the outcomes arising from the new regional tourism strategy devised by the North West Development Agency. These two major policy interventions will be key drivers of change in the years ahead. On the one hand efforts will be made to ensure the sustainability of rural communities on which tourism in the region is so dependent. And on the other hand considerable investment will be made to promote tourism to the Lake District to ensure the sustainability of the tourism sector. Integrated sustainable rural development when combined with a promotional strategy that is co-ordinated for the north west region as a whole should result in a renaissance of tourism in the Lake District. The planning controls currently in place and administered by the Lake District National Park Authority will ensure that the landscape and settlements of the Lake District will not change in character or appearance in the years ahead. This will be critical for maintaining the appeal of the Lake District as an area of outstanding natural beauty.

Accessibility to the Lake District will be improved, not just in the conventional sense of providing better transport infrastructure, but also in enabling wider participation from members of society who might previously have been unable to travel to and benefit from the natural qualities of the Lake District. Although car and bus park and ride schemes are currently not provided in the region, such a means of transport management cannot be ignored in the future. Policies to make disadvantaged and minority groups within society aware of the attractions of the Lake District will be implemented. This is to ensure that the Lake District is not just a recreational zone for the well off retired members of society, but that it is a National Park for all members of society.

In terms of tourist accommodation there will be structural shifts in this sector. Unless the number of tourists staying overnight increases in the years ahead, there will be an oversupply of serviced accommodation stock. Such surplus accommodation will have to be converted into alternative forms of accommodation, for example hotels being converted into self-catering units, or may be converted into care homes to cater for the needs of an increasingly elderly, and dependent indigenous population resident within the Lake District. Indeed, as the population of the United Kingdom becomes more elderly it may be that some of the Lake Districts' existing large hotels are developed as resort hotels. These will provide all-inclusive short and long stay holidays, meeting the needs of elderly tourists who have time and money to spend on leisure activities. Other tourist accommodation might be converted into residential accommodation for first time buyers who currently have difficulty in buying residential property in the Lake District.

With regard to the recreational use of the landscape, the pressures to conserve and preserve the natural environment for future generations will continue unabated. This will result in the decline of the use of power boats on the lakes, with sailing and more sedentary and ecologically appropriate forms of water transport (electrically powered boats) being the norm. The fells will see a control on recreational uses that erode the footpaths with greater encouragement for tourists to walk rather than to ride.

The number of tourist attractions will increase in the Lake District as a result of the policies to continue developing the tourist product, but clearly the development of new attractions will be subject to the planning regulations in force for that locality. The continued development of tourism, though, will be adversely affected by the labour market problems explained at the beginning of this chapter. As tourism is a labour intensive industry, the reluctance of local people to work in the industry, and the current skills gap will have to be addressed. With the inward migration of wealthy retirees inflating house prices, and few opportunities to build new houses, younger people are unable to find suitable residential accommodation. As a result they leave the region to seek work and housing in other regions of the United Kingdom, with few actually returning to the Lake District. It is these issues of imbalanced communities, and the lack of affordable housing, that probably pose the greatest challenges for those stakeholders involved with the planning, management, and development of the Lake District as a tourist destination.

It is clear that in the early years of the 21st century that tourism in the Lake District is about to undergo a renaissance. For over 200 years the lakes, fells, and valleys have been attracting tourists from all over the world. The chapters of this book have demonstrated that although the behaviour and characteristics of tourists have obviously changed over the last two centuries the essential features of the Lake District tourism product are still the same today, as they were in the 19th century. The Lake District is an example of sustainable tourism in practice, and this book illustrates the many ingredients that are required for the principles of sustainable tourism to be achieved. Probably, at no other time in the history of tourism in the Lake District is there such a shared understanding by all stakeholders as there is today, of the need but also the means by which, to manage tourism sustainably.

References

Adcock, D., Bradfield, R., Halborg, A. and Ross, C. (1995) *Marketing Principles and Practice*. 2nd Ed,London: Pitman.

Brownlie, D. (1985) Strategic marketing concepts and model. *Journal of Marketing Management* 1,157-194.

Butler, R. W. (1980) The concept of the tourist area cycle of evolution; implications for management of resources. *Canadian Geographer* 24,5-12.

Choy, D. J. L. (1992) Life cycle models for Pacific island destinations. *Journal of Travel Research* 30(3), 26-31.

Cooper, C. P. (1989) Tourist product life cycle. In Witt, S. F. and Moutinho, L. (Eds) *Tourism Marketing and Management Handbook* Hemel Hempstead: Prentice Hall.

Cooper, C. P. (1992) The life cycle concept and strategic planning for coastal resorts. *Built Environment* 18(1), 57-66.

Cooper, C. P. (1995) The destination life cycle: an update. In Seaton, A. V. *et al. Tourism the State of the Art conference proceedings*. Scottish Hotel School, Strathclyde University.

Cumbria County Council and the Lake District National Park Authority (1995) *Development for the 1990s, Cumbria and Lake District Joint Structure Plan 1991 – 2006*. Kendal: LDNPA.

Cumbria County Council (2002) *Cumbria Foot & Mouth Disease Inquiry Report*. Carlisle: Cumbria County Council.

Cumbria County Council and the Lake District National Park Authority (2003) *Cumbria and Lake District Joint Structure Plan 2001-2016: Deposit Plan*. Kendal: Cumbria County Council.

Friends of the Lake District (2001) *Green Horizons – An Assessment of the Sustainability of the Tourism Industry in the Lake District*. Kendal: Friends of the Lake District.

Cumbria Tourist Board (2002) *Branding and Perception Study*. Windermere: Cumbria Tourist Board.

Doyle, P. (1994) *Marketing Management and Strategy*. Hemel Hempstead: Prentice Hall.

Haywood, K. M. (1986) Can the tourist area life cycle be made operational? *Tourism Management* 7(2), 154-167.

Lake District National Park Authority (1999) *Lake District National Park Management Plan*. Kendal: LDNPA.

Lake District National Park Authority (2003) *Lake District National Park Management Plan, Part One, Policies, Consultation Draft*. Kendal: LDNPA.

Lake District National Park Authority (2004) *Lake District National Park Management Plan*. Kendal: LDNPA.

Locum Destination Consulting (2003) *Cumbria Strategic Tourism Market and Development Forecasts, Market Trends Report – Final*. Haywards Heath: Locum Destination Consulting.

Locum Destination Consulting (2003a) *Cumbria Tourism Market Forecasts, Final Report*. Haywards Heath: Locum Destination Consulting.

Office for National Statistics, (2002), Social Trends 32.

North West Development Agency (2002) *A Tourism Vision for the Region*. Manchester: NWDA.

North West Development Agency (2003) *The Strategy for Tourism in England's Northwest*. Manchester: NWDA.

The National Trust (undated) *A Vision for the Lake District after Foot and Mouth*. Ambleside: National Trust.

Urry, J. (1990) *The Tourist Gaze: Leisure and Travel in Contemporary Societies*. London: Sage Publications.

Index